new in literary studies
from duquesne

We take pleasure in sending you this review copy.

Reexamining Deconstruction and Determinate Religion: Toward a Religion with Religion

Edited by J. Aaron Simmons and Stephen Minister
$30.00s paper / ISBN: 978-0-8207-0457-9
Publication Date: October 2012

About the Book

Reexamining Deconstruction and Determinate Religion addresses the conventional conflicts between those who desire a more objective, determinate, and quasi-evidentialist perspective on faith and religious truth and those who adopt a more poetic, indeterminate, relativistic, and radical one. Drawing on both continental and analytic philosophy, this unique volume offers a sustained challenge to the prominent paradigm of a "religion without religion," proposed in a deconstructive philosophy of religion.

While especially relevant to anyone interested in an overview of and constructive dialogue with deconstructive philosophy of religion, *Reexamining Deconstruction and Determinate Religion* will be of interest to scholars and students interested in all areas of continental philosophy of religion and its potential benefit to determinate faith practices.

Contributors: Bruce Ellis Benson, John D. Caputo, Drew M. Dalton, Jeffrey Hanson, Stephen Minister, J. Aaron Simmons, Merold Westphal

J. AARON SIMMONS is assistant professor of philosophy at Furman University. **STEPHEN MINISTER** is assistant professor of philosophy at Augustana College.

We will appreciate receiving two copies of the review when it appears.
Contact: Lori Crosby / 412-396-6610

DUQUESNE UNIVERSITY PRESS
600 Forbes Avenue, Pittsburgh, PA 15282
Toll free for orders: (800) 666-2211
www.dupress.duq.edu

REEXAMINING DECONSTRUCTION
AND
DETERMINATE RELIGION

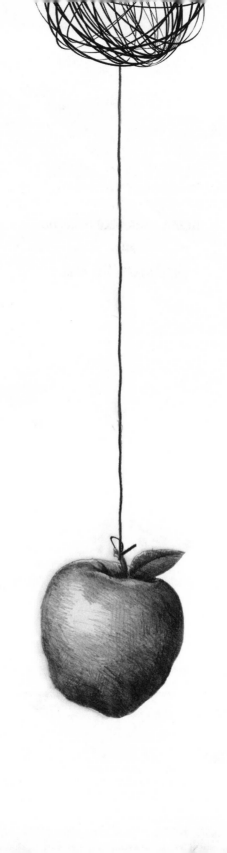

REEXAMINING DECONSTRUCTION
and
DETERMINATE RELIGION

Toward a Religion *with* Religion

edited by
J. AARON SIMMONS *&* STEPHEN MINISTER

DUQUESNE UNIVERSITY PRESS
Pittsburgh, PA

Published in the United States of America by
Duquesne University Press
600 Forbes Avenue
Pittsburgh, Pennsylvania 15282

Library of Congress Cataloging-in-Publication Data

Reexamining deconstruction and determinate religion : toward a religion with religion / edited by J. Aaron Simmons and Stephen Minister.
    p. cm.
    Includes bibliographical references and index.
    Summary: "Draws on both continental and analytic philosophy to challenge the prominent paradigm of a 'religion without religion' proposed in a deconstructive philosophy of religion; the authors offer instead a philosophical basis for practicing determinate religions that rejects binary options between undecidability and safety, or between skepticism and dogmatism"— Provided by publisher.
    ISBN 978-0-8207-0457-9 (pbk. : alk. paper)
    1. Religion—Philosophy. 2. Deconstruction. 3. Postmodernism. I. Simmons, J. Aaron, 1977–II. Minister, Stephen.

    BL51.R329 2012
    210—dc23

                                                              2012032490

∞ Printed on acid-free paper.

To Ernie T. Hitte,
for his example and encouragement

Contents

ACKNOWLEDGMENTS

This book began as a conversation between J. Aaron Simmons and Stephen Minister at lunch in Dallas, Texas, during an American Academy of Religion meeting. That this book is now a reality is due to the generous time, energy, and support of many others. First, we would like to thank the other contributors to this volume: Jeffrey Hanson, Drew M. Dalton, Bruce Ellis Benson, and, especially, Merold Westphal and John D. Caputo. We invited Jeff, Drew, and Bruce to be part of this project because they are some of the most exciting voices in contemporary continental philosophy of religion and they all, in various ways, have made their own significant contributions to the scholarly literature.

Additionally, were it not for the exceptional authorships of Merold and Jack, it is unlikely that either of us (or the other authors) would be engaged with the particular philosophical questions that now occupy our attention and our lives. They have jointly made it respectable for continental philosophers also to be serious philosophers of religion. Their work and, for many of the authors herein, their friendship have been very influential not only on our lives as scholars, but also on our lived engagement with ethics, politics, and religion.

We greatly appreciate the care and rigor with which the manuscript was reviewed by Duquesne University Press and are grateful to Susan Wadsworth-Booth for her support of the project and helpful recommendations along the way.

Stephen would also like to thank the Augustana Research and Artist Fund of Augustana College for providing a grant to assist in the writing and editing of this project.

We both want to express our unending gratitude to our families for their encouragement and love: LeAnn, Scout, and Soren (Minister), and Vanessa and Atticus (Simmons). Finally, Aaron would like to express his debt to his grandfather, Ernie T. Hitte, to whom this book is dedicated. He was the perfect example of someone whose grace, hospitality, and thoughtfulness was a lived apologetic for what could rightly be termed a postmodern Christianity.

On Necessary Interruptions

J. Aaron Simmons

BEGINNING WITH THE OTHER: AN ANECDOTE

A funny thing happened while writing this introduction. I was sitting in a coffee shop with a stack of books on postmodern theology and philosophy of religion on my table, when a gentleman at the next table leaned over and said, "I hate to bother you, but can you tell me what you are working on?" Figuring that his interest was motivated more by the sheer volume of the books than it was by their titles, I simply replied, "I am working on a book dealing with postmodern philosophy of religion." Instead of giving me an odd look and taking his leave with a polite "Oh, well have a good afternoon"—the typical kind of response I elicit when I try to explain what I do—the gentleman took a seat at my table and engaged me in further conversation, explaining that he had just finished his M.A. in religion at a university known for being very theologically and socially conservative. When he told me this, I admit that I found myself with a new set of expectations: namely, that he would begin to tell me about the evils of postmodernism and about the absolute Truth (with a capital *T*) that can be found in Christianity. However, again my expectations were precluded when he said, "Although I have heard a lot about postmodernism and I admit that I have my reservations about it, I would love to hear more about your work because I have not done much reading in that area myself." Rather than coming at me with the walls of dogmatic narrowness and arrogant self-assurance that are often understood to be typical of religious fundamentalism, this man approached me with a genuine interest in dialogue. As a result, we talked for quite a while and before leaving he said "I still have my reservations, but you have changed my view of postmodernism and I would love to meet again to talk about these things further."

Though that gentleman still has reservations about postmodernism and I still have (substantial) reservations about his alma mater (and perhaps both stances are deserved given our own contexts and communities), we both left the conversation with a different sense of the "Other" with whom we had been confronted. *In this encounter, we were both interrupted.* I was interrupted by his intellectual curiosity and dialogical generosity. He was interrupted by my account of postmodernism, which I explained to allow room for determinate religious beliefs, practices, and traditions. As a result of this conversation, I am no longer able to remain comfortable in my assumptions about *all* of the alumni of his institution and he is no longer able to remain comfortable in his assumptions about *all* of postmodernism. In good Levinasian fashion, we allowed ourselves to be surprised by the Other and, in good Derridean fashion, we allowed our conversation to be guided by hospitality and charity rather than dogmatism. Despite our substantial theological, social, political, and philosophical differences, or perhaps because of them, the conversation was productive indeed.

RELIGION *WITHOUT* RELIGION: THE CONTEXT

I chose to begin this book with this story of confronting the Other because it illustrates the tension that motivates this book as well as the persistent risk that accompanies it. The animating tension is between postmodern (specifically deconstructive and phenomenological) philosophy and determinate religion. The risk that attends to thinking about this tension runs in two directions. On the one hand, those who would argue in favor of determinate religion within a deconstructive framework are, in the minds of many deconstructive philosophers, likely to be assumed to be as conservative and reactionary as I assumed that this gentleman would be. On the other hand, those who argue in favor of deconstruction as a productive and promising philosophical framework are, in the minds of philosophers working in other traditions (especially in mainstream analytic philosophy of religion), likely to be assumed to be as nihilistic and incoherent as this gentleman assumed postmodernism to be. It is as though you are damned if you do and damned if you don't (and given some views on the topic, the damnation might be literal!).

It is because the tension is serious and quite understandable (viz., there are good reasons to be suspicious of moves toward religious determinacy within a philosophical perspective that emphasizes the "undecidable" and the "endless translatability" of the name of "God" into other names), that the risk continues to be so pressing. Some philosophers have found this risk to be worth taking in the attempt to better understand deconstruction itself. Perhaps the most influential example of this may be seen in the work of John D. Caputo. In a series of much discussed books and edited volumes, Caputo has persuasively argued that deconstruction is misunderstood when situated as opposed to religion.[1] According to Caputo, deconstruction is inherently religious in that it attends to such structures of relationality as expectation, futurity, alterity, impossibility, hospitality, justice, the gift, secrecy, and gratitude. Like religion, deconstruction is about the priority of faith to knowledge: "The import and the impulse, the drive and the desire of deconstruction is not cognitive or constantive but performative; deconstruction is not a matter of knowing or seeing, but of believing."[2] Yet Derrida's notion of deconstructive faith is not identical to what often passes as religious belief. "For me," Derrida says, "there is no such thing as 'religion.'" He explains that he has "no stable position on . . . the prophets and the Bible," and that he is not interested in religion as such, but rather in what is going on in religion:

> Within what one calls religions—Judaism, Christianity, Islam, or other religions—there are again tensions, heterogeneity, disruptive volcanos, sometimes texts, especially those of the prophets, which cannot be reduced to an institution, to a corpus, to a system. I want to keep the right to read these texts in a way which has to be constantly reinvented. It is something which can be totally new at every moment. . . . If by religion you mean a set of beliefs, dogmas, or institutions—the church, e.g.,—then I would say that religion as such can be deconstructed, and not only can be but should be deconstructed, sometimes in the name of faith.[3]

Within such a Derridean framework, Caputo should not be read as attempting to turn deconstruction toward religion, but instead as turning our attention to the religious dimension that is always already operative in deconstruction. Caputo's argument is that Jacques Derrida is a profoundly religious thinker and that this fact, as Derrida himself notes in *Circumfession*, has not been appreciated or correctly understood.[4] As a way of naming this attentive reading, Caputo and Derrida both suggest that deconstruction can be understood as "religion without religion."[5]

Tarrying with the "without" (*sans*) is dangerous business on many fronts because it is not a simple negation and yet it also resists any simple formulation as a positive alternative to determinate religions. "This *sans*," Caputo writes, "separates Derrida's prayers and tears from, even as it joins them to, the determinable faiths. Derrida's *viens* [come] occupies the unstable space of something that cannot be a pure ahistorical a priori even as it must not sound too Jewish."[6] This immediately raises questions for deconstructive philosophers about how close to determinable religions is too close and yet how far is too far. On Caputo's formulation, the affirmation of propositional beliefs internal to a religious worldview gives way to the welcoming of that which one cannot see, have, or know (*sans voir, sans avoir, sans savoir*).[7] Alternatively, the straightforward modernist critique of religion offered in the name of secular standards of public reason is abandoned because "deconstruction is always more complicated, more plurivocal and heterogeneous than any secularizing, modernist critique of religion."[8] As such, religion without religion is meant to resist the idea that there is a tension *between* determinacy and deconstruction. Deconstruction already contains this tension within itself insofar as it calls all determinate (or determinable) communities of faith to their knees, as it were, in repentance for the idolatry that accompanies faith when it forgets the "without"—that is, when it closes itself off to the coming of the unknown and unforeseen by reducing "God" to the discourse in which "God" is articulated. Recommending, instead, a "faith without faith," Caputo suggests that "over and beyond opening up a certain space for faith, for the determinable faiths, while saving them from their worst, most dogmatic side, deconstruction is *itself* a form of faith."[9]

Not to be confused with the determinate religious traditions that believe in the "possible" (as seen, had, and known), deconstruction "comes down to an affirmation or hope or invocation which is a certain *faith* in *the* impossible, in something that pushes us beyond the sphere of the same, of the believable, to the unbelievable, that which exceeds the horizon of our pedestrian beliefs and probabilities, driving us with the passion of *the* impossible, *the* unbelievable."[10] "Deconstruction," Caputo writes in agreement with Derrida's own claim, "is not the destruction of religion but its reinvention." It reinvents religion, or allows religion to reinvent itself, by constantly haunting it from within by placing a question mark after every period. The upshot of this haunting is that deconstruction helps religion to avoid its most problematic tendencies (which accompany the assumption that faith is actually a knowledge given only to a chosen few), namely, "dangerous and absolutizing triumphalism."[11]

RELIGION *WITH* RELIGION: THE THESIS

Although there are a variety of movements and alternatives in continental philosophy of religion and postmodern theology that are more broadly construed,[12] the specific focus of this book is on the philosophy of religion that draws primarily and explicitly on the phenomenological tradition ranging from Heidegger to Derrida. As such, despite the criticism it has received from many distinguished scholars, religion without religion stands as *one of the dominant paradigms* in deconstructive and phenomenological philosophy of religion. For scholars contributing to the continually expanding field in this area, it is much more common (and respectable) to assume the general framework of religion without religion than it is to resist such a framework. For example, while several edited collections have been devoted to the work of Caputo, none of these is presented as a sustained challenge to the dominance of religion without religion.[13] Rather, all seem limited to showing the variety of responses that Caputo's work has generated. This is not a failing in any of the books, which have goals quite different from the present work. However, we think that more can and should be said to expand the conversation concerning alternatives to religion without religion from within deconstruction and phenomenology.

Given the prominence of continental philosophy of religion that has emerged in relation to the work of such thinkers as Gilles Deleuze, Slavoj Žižek, Alain Badiou, and Giorgio Agamben, one might wonder why this book focuses so exclusively on debates occurring in light of phenomenology and deconstruction. The reason is threefold. First, defending the continued importance of deconstructive phenomenology does not mean rejecting the importance of other approaches within continental philosophy of religion. Indeed, we look forward to the productive dialogue with proponents of these other approaches that will hopefully occur in light of this book. Second, there are important differences of philosophical focus between those who are primarily working in light of deconstructive phenomenology and those who are primarily working in light of neo-Nietzschean philosophy, psychoanalysis, and critical-theory (for example, deconstruction and phenomenology are more open to considering transcendence and ethical life in ways that contrast with the primarily materialistic account of immanence and political subjectivity found in the latter approaches). Third, there continues to be a significant amount of scholarly interest in the relation of deconstruction and phenomenology to contemporary philosophy of religion.[14] These three reasons are offered not in the spirit of critical assessment, but simply to show that although continental philosophy of religion is not reducible to deconstructive philosophy of religion, deconstructive phenomenology remains important for the contemporary debates in philosophy of religion. Indeed, the authors of this book were selected because of the previous work they have all done to sustain this continued importance.[15]

This book is as a dialogue among a group of scholars who all are in agreement that the dominance of the paradigm needs to be challenged, but not *from outside*, as it were, but *from inside*. In this way, the authors of this book understand their viewpoints not to represent a break with deconstruction, but a turning of the deconstructive gaze back upon itself. As such, we take this book to be a significant step forward in the contemporary literature in that it *challenges the without from within* its own philosophical framework. Taking as a starting point Caputo's basic contention that deconstruction is not only relevant to religion, but is essentially religious in some of its most basic moves, this book offers a coherent and sustained resistance to religion without religion as exhaustive of what this deconstructive religiosity entails. Accordingly, the basic thesis of this book, and a thesis that is defended in every essay in one way or another, is that *a postmodern, and specifically deconstructive, philosophical framework does not entail the indeterminacy of "religion without religion."* Importantly, this is a claim that Caputo himself countenances when he locates messianicity internal to concrete messianisms. Unfortunately, Caputo's often dismissive and derisive rhetoric regarding "strong theology" and "positive religion" can understandably lead to confusion on this point.[16] As James H. Olthuis conveys in the title of his excellent edited collection on Caputo's *Prayers and Tears*, the "without" itself is unstable: "with/out."[17] While we appreciate the slash as a performative way of stressing the undecidability of deconstruction, the goal of the present book is not simply to tweak religion without religion or to stress something already expressed within it, but to offer a deconstructive alternative to it. So, we propose that while deconstruction can certainly be read as *religion with/out religion*, it can also be understood as *religion with religion* without the slash. "Religion *with* religion"—this phrase names a challenge to take up, an invitation to receive, and a path to pursue; not as a rejection of the deconstructive hesitancy to determinate religions, but as a particular way of inhabiting that very hesitancy internal to a historical and religious location. Accordingly, the guiding question is whether or not postmodernism excludes determinate religious content in favor of only structural accounts of a "postmodern God" that always remains in scare quotes.

Although we take "religion *with* religion" to be an alternative to "religion *without* religion," we want to resist the impression that it is, therefore, prescriptive of the contours that such determinacy ought to take when put in practice within one's religious life. The authors of this book all come from different religious backgrounds and draw upon different philosophical resources, differences that animate their agreement and make it all the more productive. Nonetheless, this book should be read as drawing deeply upon the work of those thinkers who have already pressed Caputo regarding the possible room for more determinate religion within deconstruction. It is the exceptional work of such thinkers as Richard Kearney, Kevin Hart, B. Keith Putt, James K. A. Smith, and especially Merold Westphal that has made this book possible. Moreover, like Caputo's attempt to turn our attention to the religious dimensions in deconstruction, we are not trying to read something into the phenomenological tradition, but to draw deeply on the work of the New Phenomologists, who have already opened spaces for thinking about religion *with* religion.

Jean-Louis Chrétien's sophisticated analyses of the call and response structure, Michel Henry's considerations of the "Truth" of "Life," Jean-Luc Marion's notion of revelation and givenness, Jean-Yves Lacoste's account of "Liturgy," Emmanuel Levinas's appreciation of the intersection of alterity and obligation, and even the "Prayers and Tears" of Jacques Derrida all serve as the context in which this book occurs.

Yet, and this is decisive for all of the authors of the present book, we do not understand New Phenomenology to amount to a "theological turn" in phenomenology as Dominique Janicaud has famously suggested.[18] Instead, more akin to Hent de Vries's contention that philosophers can productively draw upon theological archives without becoming theologians,[19] we largely agree with Jean-Luc Marion's contention that *as phenomenologists* these thinkers are concerned about the possibility, rather than the actuality, of religious life and the phenomena internal to it. For our part, we do not assume the truth of Christianity and then begin to do philosophy in this book. Rather, we are content to remain agnostic about whether Alvin Plantinga is right to call for specifically "Christian Philosophy."[20] Our goal, as phenomenologically inspired philosophers of religion, is to offer an account that is phenomenologically adequate to, and existentially aware of, the diverse forms of life and practice that constitute this thing called "religion." Doing so, we believe, requires us to push back against religion without religion. Accordingly, *religion with religion does not assume that something like a fairly orthodox Christianity, or any other determinate religion, is true, but instead contends that postmodernism (understood in line with deconstruction and phenomenology) does not close down the possibility that it might be.*

In the remainder of this introduction, I will give an overview of how this book stands in relation to the current debates regarding religion without religion by looking at critics of Caputo who have offered objections similar to those offered here. Then, I will consider the structure and substance of Caputo's responses to such critics and suggest that they do not undercut the project of religion with religion, but instead make such a project necessary. Finally, I will provide an outline of the present book by summarizing the specific arguments set forth in the chapters that follow.

CAPUTO AND HIS CRITICS: THE BACKGROUND DEBATE

Attesting to the two-pronged risk articulated above about likely perceptions of those who work at these dangerous intersections, Caputo claims that he realized the risk he was taking with *The Prayers and Tears of Jacques Derrida* (1997) before he even began to write it:

> On the one hand, the secularizing deconstructors will not want to hear a word about it. The pious, on the other hand, will say—as a distinguished philosopher of religion indignantly protested to me in a session on *Prayers and Tears*—"I have nothing to learn about religion from Derrida and I will thank him not to expose his circumcision!" They will all cup their ears and cover their eyes. Still, if any one reads it, this book will set the record straight about Derrida, exposing the heart of a supposedly heartless deconstruction. It will also give me still another chance to scandalize the pious, another chance to prove my impious piety, another opportunity to needle the orthodox and to sound an alarm about fideistic violence.[21]

Caputo's expectations were certainly not wide of the mark. His work since 1997 has been met with protestations from both sides of the theological and philosophical aisles.[22] However, it has also met with significant praise and appreciation from both the philosophical and theological communities. Crucially, and Caputo knows this quite well, praise by one's colleagues is usually offered not as a blanket endorsement, but instead as a measured expression of thoughtful consideration and criticism. Indeed, even those largely sympathetic to Caputo's reading of deconstruction as displaying a fundamental religious sensibility have expressed concern with the specifics of his reading (and the entailments of it).

A general line of critique that has emerged over the past decade or so, and one that resonates nicely with our project here, is that religion without religion overstates the indeterminacy (or indeterminableness) of deconstruction at the expense of historical religious communities. In other words, the "without" might end up leading to tildes rather than question-marks such that deconstructive "reinvention" can appear to slide toward what can seem to be outright rejection.[23] Let's look at just a few such critical replies in order to set the stage for the dialogue that will unfold in the present book.

For Kevin Hart, religion without religion potentially misses the phenomenological depth of religious practice as historically undertaken: "I am worried by something in the philosophy of religion, even as revamped by Caputo: the lack of engagement with the particularity of revelation and the actual practices of the faithful. A description of Christianity that is not centered on prayer and the sacraments is insufficient as phenomenology. Oddly enough for someone who has rendered the philosophy of religion impure, Caputo has a way of making his philosophy of religion a little too pure."[24] In response to Caputo's claim that deconstruction is always more complicated and plural than the modernist critique of religion, Hart suggests that religion without religion should be read as a continuation of the old liberal move of affirming a general structure while denying a specific content: "The only religion one can plausibly endorse is one that is not committed to an exclusive religion. Once again, we see the Enlightenment model: religion is a genus of which the positive religions are the species. And once again we can see how 'religion without religion' follows the Enlightenment program of passing from the positive religions to a universal religiosity that has remained pure because it has always abided in the realm of possibility."[25] As such, Derrida and Caputo might be understood as continental versions of Ludwig Feuerbach, John Hick, or Gordon Kaufman.[26]

From a more ethico-political direction, Ronald Kuipers claims that religion without religion misses the practical promise of determinate religious communities by overstating the necessity of their violence. "I suspect," Kuipers writes, "that the determinable faiths are not as determinate as deconstruction often holds them to be. They are frail human institutions, to be sure, and they too often mistake dogmatic certitude for faith. Yet they are also composed of singular individuals who are separate and face each other. This saves them from being monolithic.... That is, these communities, while often operating like totalities, can also be "infinities," and when they are, we should celebrate them more than deconstructionists seem willing or able to do."[27]

Further, Merold Westphal and Richard Kearney both (in slightly different ways) suggest that Derrida and Caputo explicitly advocate undecidability between *Khôra* and God, while seemingly tipping the scales toward *Khôra*. While for Westphal this amounts to a forgetfulness in Derrida about the "hypothetical" status of some of his own proclamations that can lead to a possible non sequitur,[28] Kearney goes further and claims that Caputo borders on inconsistency due to a pronounced indecisiveness:

> I am suggesting, in short, that Caputo cannot have it both ways. He cannot claim on the one hand that Derrida takes the path of a-theological desertification and then reclaim him as a saintly anchorite father. Nor will it do to refuse the two alternatives altogether and declare the issue undecidable — God and/or/neither/nor *Khora?* That too is having it both ways. Not an option, I would submit, for the believer. (Though a perfectly consistent one for the deconstructionist). By believer I mean, incidentally, not just a believer in God but also — why not? — a believer in *khora*. Perhaps *khora* is no less an interpretative leap in the dark than religious faith is? God and *khora* are conceivably two different names for the same thing — the same nameless, indescribable experience of the abyss. But the choice between names is not insignificant. Which direction you leap surely matters.... There is a genuine difference between anchorite fathers and deconstructive sons. A healthy difference to be sure; but one that can't be magicked away or turned into a soft-shoe-shuffle of undecidability. One cannot sit on double-edged fences forever.[29]

In light of such objections, it is clear that Caputo has been hit from all sides, and we might even say *especially* from those scholars generally sympathetic to the religious dimensions of deconstruction.[30] For these critics, rather than maintaining the "spooky" (as Caputo would say) aspect of deconstruction internal to determinable faith communities, religion without religion comes close to abandoning the lived realities of religious communities in the name of a technical deconstructive discourse about "God," which no longer seems to need God at all. As Derrida even says in an interview:

> I have the feeling that no name, as such, is indispensable, and especially not in my texts. That would be true for the name of God also. I could have written almost everything I wrote without the name of God, and even without the name, *différence*. Yes, I could do without it. This would not change the stakes and the content of what I am saying essentially. Of course, it would change both the strategy and economy.... Each time I write "absolute," I could, of course, replace this common attribute with "God." So, I can imagine a transformation of my texts in which the words "God" and "*différence*" would simply

disappear without causing any damage. This may mean either that the name of "God" is useless, or because it is so powerful it can be replaced by any other. It is everywhere. It is a useless, indispensable name.[31]

While Derrida's point is surely missed if understood as simply a recommendation to stop using the word "God" (indeed, he suggests that we might not be able to stop using it even if we wanted to), for many religious persons, the name of God is certainly not so structurally indispensable. And, for the critics considered above and for the authors of this book, there might be better ways to be appropriately deconstructive in relation to religion than to seem to abandon so much of the traditions in which individuals find themselves (and internal to which they work for social justice, care for the widow, the orphan, and the stranger, and live humble lives of hospitality and gratitude).

TAKING RISKS AND GIVING RESPONSES

In light of the objections considered above, it might seem odd that something like the sustained challenge offered in the present book has not previously appeared in the literature. Yet reasons for the hesitancy to move further in the direction of religion with religion can surely be offered, even if only speculatively: if one is convinced that deconstruction is relevant to religion, it is Caputo who is largely responsible for having provided arguments supporting that conviction. But if one wants to challenge Caputo's formulations, it comes at the risk of rejecting deconstruction itself (which has now been understood by many *as* religion without religion). Offering a serious challenge to religion without religion can be quickly viewed as a wholesale abandonment of the deconstructive turn in favor of the safety and security that come with determinate (in this case, religious) community identity.

It is here that the twofold risk of likely perceptions comes back to bite again in the opposite direction. Caputo walked a fine line between what he termed the "secularizing deconstructors" and the "pious," but in so doing, he can be interpreted as having closed down the possibility of a "pious deconstructor" being anything other than someone who "rightly passes for an atheist," as Derrida characterized himself. But, what about someone who identifies as a theist, a

Christian, or, dare I even say, a Pentecostal?[32] Or, to draw on another tradition, what about someone who identifies with Reform Judaism, or even with a more Orthodox version of Judaism?

Caputo's responses to such questions, as sometimes asked in various ways by Kearney, Hart, and Westphal, tend to emphasize the undecidability of these matters and to warn against thinking that deconstruction can be helpful in making decisions internal to positive religious traditions. In so doing, Caputo raises the specter that if one wants more than the basic undecidable structures of religion without religion, then one abandons deconstruction. Here, one might rightly worry that the "spookiness" championed by Caputo can slide, even if quite unintentionally, into a ghost that makes it "scary" for continental philosophers of religion to live in haunted houses and, instead, encourages them to abandon their lodging. As such, Caputo may inadvertently introduce a ghost that keeps in place the new orthodoxy of professional continental discourse about a postmodern "God."

Importantly, Caputo's own, quite sensible, worry that deconstruction can, if we are not careful, be confused with another determinate messianism, can be read as anticipating the worry being raised here. His basic strategy in response is to point out that (1) religion without religion is a second-order move and not a competing first-order religion in its own right , that is, it is about "faith" (*foi*) and not about "belief" (*croyance*); and (2) though it is impossible to have faith outside of a specific belief context, the point of deconstruction is never to decide in favor of one set of beliefs or another, but to trouble all such beliefs by reminding them of their contingency and frailty. Remember that Derrida does not say that he has decided against the prophets and the Bible, but that he has "no stable position" on them.[33] Caputo's double-gesture can be seen in the following response that he offers to Kevin Hart's charge of being "too pure" and merely a continuation of the Enlightenment legacy:

> I do not think of this "pure" faith or "religion without religion" as a faith that somebody believes, or a religion that somebody can inhabit, or a position that somebody takes, or as a proposition that somebody can propose. I am not an advocate of religious abstractionism or an abstractionist religion. I take this pure *foi* as a ghost, a specter, that haunts us in the sorts of concrete positions—philosophical, political, and religious—that we do take, the displacing place (*khôra*) in which

they are situated. A religion without religion is not an abstract religion that anyone actually holds—you can't report it on the next census or expect to get a tax break by making a charitable contribution to its cause—but a specter that disturbs the hold our various faiths have on us....That I recommend we not "leave" the love of God to the theologians and religions now means—here is its spooky sense—do not leave them alone (the theologians and religions), do not let up on them, give them no rest, no leave.[34]

For Caputo, those critics that desire more room for determinacy have missed the point about the distinction between messianicity and messianism:

> The messianic is always the messianicity of some concrete messianism. It is the messianic impulse in the concrete messianisms, and the point of making this distinction is to remind us that the messianic can always take another form....I do not think that the messianic can exist as such, that it can assume a real form as such, that it can define the lives of real people, of socially, historically, political situated communities, not as such. That is why I argued...that even deconstruction is itself one more messianism, of a late modern democratic sort.[35]

To those who would respond that this radical substitutability yields merely an epistemic constraint on *how* one holds beliefs and not on *what* beliefs one holds, which is a position put forth by Westphal and one that I also defend, Caputo replies that they fail to appreciate the riskiness demanded by the deconstructive critique of onto-theology. Consider, for example, Caputo's response to Westphal on precisely this point:

> In sum, my concern is that in Merold's version of overcoming ontotheology, this critique has been cut down to size, that the openness it demands has been contracted to, assimilated into, or appropriated by the most classical Christian conception of the mystery or incomprehensibility of God, with the result that this critique is stripped of its most novel and disturbing features. Merold wants to enlist the help of the critique of ontotheology within the context of his Christian faith, which puts a limit on the critique of ontotheology. What would it look like to situate his Christian faith in the context of the critique of ontotheology, taken in all of its "aphoristic energy," as Derrida puts it?[36]

With Caputo's response in view, we should realize that it is entirely possible to appreciate the importance of Caputo's question above while rejecting the claim that asking serious questions about how to be determinate within a deconstructive philosophical framework (or how to be deconstructive without abandoning religious beliefs and practices) is to desire nothing but safety. Religion *with* religion demonstrates that, like the forced option of being either pious or a secular deconstructionist, the dichotomy between *either* undecidability *or* safety is entirely too stark.[37]

AN OUTLINE OF THE BOOK

In order to lay out the philosophical framework for religion with religion as an alternative worth taking seriously, in part 1 of this book, "The Philosophical Basis for Religion with Religion," Stephen Minister and I both engage Caputo directly in the attempt to offer reasons to think a bit further about the entailments of deconstruction when it comes to religious belief and social practice. However, and this is crucial, unlike several other excellent edited volumes, though this book is decidedly motivated by Caputo's deconstructive philosophy of religion, its goal is not primarily critical. While Caputo's work serves as an important and influential point of departure, all of the essays offer positive contributions to specific debates in continental philosophy of religion.

The essays in part 1 are meant to set the stage for the more positive work in part 2. In my own essay, I wrestle with the possible inconsistencies between postmodernism and Pentecostalism. Distinguishing between "metaphysical" and "epistemological" postmodernism, I argue that the metaphysical variety (represented by Caputo) faces possible incoherence because it appears to stipulate "what" beliefs can be affirmed rather than focusing only on "how" beliefs are held.[38] Drawing upon Justin Martyr, I contend that despite the significant (and very reasonable) protests against what has passed under the heading "apologetics,"[39] there remains room for a distinctively postmodern apologetic enterprise. Moving from the philosophy of religion to postmodern ethics and politics, Stephen Minister offers a reading of Caputo's work that presses upon possible confusions and misunderstandings that can occur in light of some of Caputo's formulations. For Minister, Caputo need not be so resistant to positive theology and determinant ethics as he seems. Moreover, the account of religion and social justice offered by Caputo is well worth considering

quite seriously. In Minister's view, this requires a willingness to entertain the notion of religion *with* religion rather than merely coming
down so solidly on the side of the without. And, although we might
stand "against" ethics as classically formulated, this does not mean
that we are really "against" ethics when properly revised (and Minister
suggests that Emmanuel Levinas, Alain Badiou, and Chantal Mouffe
are all resources for Caputo on this front).[40]

In part 2, "Religion with Religion in Practice," which features chapters by Jeffrey Hanson, Drew M. Dalton, and Bruce Ellis Benson, the
positive possibilities of religion with religion are explored. Providing
a rigorous re-reading of Derrida and Kierkegaard, Hanson considers the role of secrecy in the life of faith. For Hanson, secrecy need
not evacuate determinate content, though it might indeed affect
how one holds such content. What is crucial is the openness to alterity, to being surprised, to being interrupted. However, one is open
only while standing somewhere quite specific and this affects how
we appreciate and appropriate determinate religious traditions (and
the beliefs and practices that go along with them). Expanding on
some of his own previous work[41] while drawing on Anders Nygren,
Gene Outka, Augustine, Levinas, Derrida, and Plato, Drew Dalton
takes a close look at the notion of agapic love in the attempt to show
that the account of love offered in the Christian Scriptures is phenomenologically robust and well worth defending as part of a postmodern religion *with* religion. Bruce Ellis Benson continues Dalton's
focus on the Christian Scriptures by offering a deconstructive reading of the soteriological formulations and recommendations offered
by Jesus in the Gospels. Agreeing with Caputo that the temptations
toward absolutism and arrogance are persistent in determinate religions, Benson shows that, at least as they concern salvation, claims
to algorithmic certainty are entirely out of place. Though something
like confidence might be possible internal to the personal relation
with God, the received words of Jesus go a long way to themselves
interrupt any slide toward clear demarcations of who is "in" and who
is "out."[42]

All three chapters in part 2 operate in light of the philosophical
framework laid out in part 1, but they all demonstrate the ways in
which religion with religion opens up spaces for further thinking

rather than closing down such spaces in the name of some new (whether radical or not) Orthodoxy. In particular, Hanson's account of silence ought to be read as a companion to my argument regarding the possibility of "apologetic" speech; Dalton's considerations of love exemplify both the dialogical model of apologetics that I advocate and also the deliberative democratic intuitions that underlie much of Minister's notion of a productive postmodern political project; and Benson's notion of what might be termed the interruptive soteriology found in the Gospels echoes much of what Minister says about the complicated logic of inclusion/exclusion in deconstructive ethics, as well as the inherent revisability and humility that animate my account of postmodern apologetics.

So that the book may enact a dialogue, each of the chapters in parts 1 and 2 is followed by two short responses by other authors. Then, in part 3, "Responses to Religion with Religion," essays by Merold Westphal and John D. Caputo consider the conversation of the book as a whole and the very idea of *religion with religion*. As will become clear, the authors of this book are more interested in dialogue than in refutation and more concerned about internal criticism than about throwing stones from outside. It is because of these commitments that we conclude the book with these responses from Westphal and Caputo. Westphal's chapter displays the argumentative rigor, charitable readings, and unflinchingly critical engagements for which his prolific authorship has become so well known and respected. Though he is certainly more sympathetic with the project of religion with religion than is Caputo, he is hesitant to accept some of the specific claims made by the authors in this book.

Caputo's chapter is one of the most succinct and accessible accounts of his own philosophical (and theological, or theopoetic) project to date. For readers not familiar with Caputo, his essay gives an excellent introduction to his thought and it puts on display the wit, playfulness, and yet profound seriousness with which he writes. As will be clear, Caputo is unconvinced by the arguments presented in this book, but showing his characteristic dialogical generosity, his response clarifies points of possible confusion and misunderstandings. In the end, disagreements remain, but we are confident that the conversation will continue to move forward in productive directions.

CLARIFICATIONS AND CONCLUSIONS

To clarify some of what has already been said, three stipulative points are necessary here:

(1) The coherence of religion *with* religion is primarily *philosophical*, not theological, and it is doctrinally minimalist. The unifying claim is simply that working in light of New Phenomenology and deconstruction need not entail affirmation of religion without religion as the only viable option. The authors of this book have significant disagreements about the best ways in which to understand the specific positive visions that remain viable in this book. We see this divergence as a strength of the dialogue and understand it to leave significant room for continued conversation in the scholarly literature. Hence, "religion with religion" is, at least in this structural way, more like "Reformed Epistemology" than it is like "Radical Orthodoxy," say, in that it is a coherent challenge to a dominant paradigm in philosophy and not a decidedly unified perspective that tends to recommend a very specific theological outlook.[43]

(2) Because of the positive spaces opened by religion with religion, it allows for a more substantive engagement between so-called "analytic" philosophy and "continental" philosophy. Accordingly, the authors of this book have intentionally striven to write in a way that bridges these discursive communities that are all-too-often seen as at odds with each other.[44]

(3) Talking about content is difficult without reference to a particular tradition. In this book, we focus on what the "with" might look like internal to Christianity. This focus should not be understood to imply that one could operate only within such a framework. We hope that this book will invite essays exploring religion with religion by other philosophers situated in relation to other religious traditions.

As Socrates so aptly demonstrates time and again, it is only when we are honest about where we stand that we are able to engage each other humbly about whether there are better places toward which we should move. Problems occur both when we fail to stand for anything and when we stand too rigidly for something. On the one hand, one is in danger of being taken for a skeptic or sophist, and on the other hand, of walking too close to the edge of a problematic dogmatism. Therefore, the twofold risk articulated at the beginning of this introduction continues to press upon this book as well. For some, religion with religion may seem to be just one more conservative reaction to the radical dimensions of postmodernism in general and deconstruction in particular. For such readers, it will likely be seen solely as an attempt to make deconstruction just a bit safer for those of us who are not willing to own up to the riskiness of welcoming *the* impossible. For others, religion with religion may continue to seem all too deconstructive, squishy, and hesitant.

Between the spectral "God" of religion without religion on the one hand, and the "God" called upon to justify a particular vision of (usually) conservative politics and fundamentalist exclusivism on the other hand, lies a wide middle-ground that should be explored not only by theologians and sociologists, but also (and perhaps primarily) by philosophers. The "middle" between skepticism and dogmatism does not have to be a mushy compromise, but could potentially present a vigorous and compelling invitation to gracious dialogue. Our hope is that this book not only offers this invitation, but also embodies it. Richard Kearney is right to say that it surely matters in which direction one leaps and what names one uses in the process. Continental philosophers of religion have a responsibility to provide well-reasoned and clearly presented arguments regarding what is at stake in the difference between the various alternatives.

As with my surprising encounter with the gentleman at the coffee shop, revisiting our assumptions is often a step toward opening productive futures with new conversation partners. This book operates unapologetically within a deconstructive frame, but also unapologetically draws upon analytic philosophy of religion, epistemology, and political theory as critical resources for thinking well. Hopefully, this book will invite responses from those not otherwise disposed to take Derrida seriously while also encouraging replies from Derrideans who are skeptical of getting too close to determinate religious belief and practice. Risks abound when conversations occur across communities (whether scholarly, social, or religious), but they are risks worth taking. And, in accordance with Derrida's own vision of the democracy to come as guided by constant questioning and charitable listening, we think that such risks *must* be taken.

Let me close by saying that our proposal of the idea of religion *with* religion is not an attempt to make either deconstruction or Christianity safe. Religious safety, like absolute guarantees, epistemic certainty, and strong foundations, is something we would all do well to regard with suspicion. However, one need not turn to deconstruction, in particular, to realize this; Christianity, like most of the world's religions, itself challenges absolutism and certainty as products of misguided human arrogance. Rigorously interrogating the "without" does not entail running to solid ground that would now be insulated against all critique, but opens spaces in which to allow the critical conversation to continue even regarding what might be considered emerging "dogmas" of postmodernism. In a decidedly deconstructive fashion, the *with* can, and should, interrupt the *without*...even as the *without* continues to haunt the *with*.

Part One

THE PHILOSOPHICAL BASIS FOR RELIGION WITH RELIGION

ONE

Apologetics after Objectivity

J. Aaron Simmons

"My atheism gets on in the churches, all the churches, do you understand that?"

— Jacques Derrida

"For some reason or another, I get invited to Christian colleges with evangelical cultures to talk about deconstruction and religion. I don't know why they do this."

— John Caputo

"Come now, let us reason together, says the Lord."

— Isaiah 1:18

INTRODUCTION

The question of this chapter is whether or not a "rational defense" can be given for the determinate truth-claims of Christianity within the context of continental philosophy of religion (CPR).[1] Simply put, is a postmodern (specifically Christian) apologetics possible? Let me unambiguously make clear that I am wary of "classical" apologetics as traditionally found in the history of philosophy, and especially as displayed sometimes in contemporary philosophy of religion and popular Christian writing, which I find to be all too often defined by epistemic arrogance and theological triumphalism.[2] Accordingly, I am not concerned, here, with whether or not such an apologetics will be successful in the sense of being "convincing" to non-Christians. My goal is simply to inquire into whether an apologetic task is coherent within postmodernism and, if so, what such a practice might look like. Now, if apologetics requires objectivity, universality, and neutrality, then the postmodern critique of reason and the emphases on subjectivity, singularity, and existential situatedness that accompany such a critique would appear to make apologetics impossible (and rightfully so). In other words, if the practice of apologetics is "after" objectivity in the sense of seeking to achieve or obtain such an objective perspective, then attempting to articulate a postmodern apologetics is a task that is best abandoned. However, if one attempts to formulate an apologetics "after" objectivity in the sense of following on and appropriating the postmodern critique of Enlightenment notions of objectivity, then the proposal of a postmodern apologetics need not seem quite so odd.

Being careful about which notion of "after" one is deploying is crucial for understanding the difference between attempting a simplistic rejection of "Religion *without* Religion" for specifically Christian reasons on the one hand, and attempting to think about the possibilities of "Religion *with* Religion" in the very context of the *without,* as it were, on the other hand. While the former tries to make faith safe, the latter tries honestly to own up to the risk of faith without abandoning the content of that faith. Depending on what one means by "postmodernism" and what one understands "continental philosophy of religion" to entail as a philosophical practice, I propose that engaging in apologetics is not something that postmodernists must necessarily abandon. In order to defend this claim I will proceed as follows.

In part 1, I will, first, explicitly formulate a possible dilemma between postmodernism and Pentecostalism (a dilemma that is both existential and logical) that illuminates the need for a postmodern apologia for Christianity. Second, I will consider what I take to be the two main varieties of continental philosophy of religion occurring in the deconstructive or phenomenological tradition—which I will term *metaphysical postmodernism* and *epistemological postmodernism*.[3] I will look in detail at the work of John Caputo and Merold Westphal as examples of the two views, respectively, and suggest that while Caputo's account potentially leads to incoherence, Westphal's does not. Accordingly, when I speak of postmodern apologetics, I understand postmodernism to be defined according to an epistemological conception.

In part 2, I turn my attention to the possibility of a positive post-modern apologetics and give some suggestions as to what such a project might involve. Specifically, I will consider the work of Justin Martyr as an example of how apologetics was originally characterized by an existential relevance that has been lacking in much of contemporary professional philosophical discourse. Then, drawing upon John G. Stackhouse Jr. and David K. Clark, I will sketch some characteristics that any postmodern apologetics will need to possess if it is to remain legitimately postmodern and yet legitimately apologetic. In my conclusion, I will raise and respond to a Kierkegaardian objection.

It is my hope that this chapter will demonstrate that one can affirm and defend determinate Christian belief while still affirming and defending a critical postmodern perspective (that is, religion with religion continues to appropriate and take very seriously the "*without*"). Said slightly more poetically, it is my contention that one can be "after" objectivity without being "after" objectivity.

PART 1

FORMULATING THE PROBLEM: POSTMODERN RELIGIOUS IDENTITY AND THE NEED FOR APOLOGETICS

As a Pentecostal Christian and a postmodern philosopher of religion, I am faced with the following disjunction regarding my philosophical perspective and my church affiliation:

(1) Either I believe the Christian beliefs that are constitutive of my religious community are true or I do not believe that they are true.

As expressed, this might merely seem like an expression of the law of the excluded middle. However, the situation is not quite so simple. The complication is due to my plural identity. On the one hand, part of my identity is as a Pentecostal Christian and, as such, more than a few truth-claims serve as the backdrop for my tradition's practices. I offer the following as a few definitive truth-claims of my particular religious community:[4]

(2) God is personal and characterized by certain traits of personhood: desire, hope, risk, etc.
(3) God continues to manifest Godself in the world through the action of the Holy Spirit.
(4) Salvation is obtained through a relation to this personal God, as made possible through the life, death, and resurrection of Jesus, and by the work of the Holy Spirit.[5]

Since I take these to be beliefs central to my own Christian tradition, let us term these *C-beliefs*. Let me emphatically note that *Christianity is not reducible to a set of propositions*. Similarly, I do not want to suggest that Christian salvation is only a matter of intellectual assent to such propositions. Yet, Christianity does *involve* affirming some things as true even if such affirmation is not the most important part of Christianity (which I take to be more a matter of a transformed life in relation to human and nonhuman others).[6] The first point to make here is that *part* of my religious identity includes the affirmation of certain propositions (C-beliefs) as true.

On the other hand, I am also a postmodernist and specialize in continental philosophy of religion. As such, another part of my identity involves this perspective. In other words, I am not, personally, a Pentecostal on Sundays and a postmodernist from Monday through Saturday. I am a Pentecostal Postmodernist, or a Postmodern Pentecostal, in *every* moment.[7] Yet, even a cursory glance at some of the key texts in the field of continental philosophy of religion make it seem difficult to understand religious existence/identity as at all being a matter of truth-claims and belief affirmation concerning the person of God (which the C-beliefs seem to require at least in part). It is more often presented as a certain sort of receptivity to an "impossible event" that requires a radical critique of Christian "orthodoxy." Consider just a few representative passages from two leading postmodern philosophers of religion:

- Jacques Derrida:
  We should stop thinking about God as someone, over there, way up there, transcendent, and, what is more—into the bargain, precisely—capable, more than any satellite orbiting in space, of seeing into the most secret of the most interior places. It is necessary...to think of God and of the name of God without such idolatrous stereotyping or representation.

Then we might say: God is the name of the possibility I have of keeping a secret that is visible from the interior but not from the exterior.[8]

- John Caputo:
  The idea behind a postmodern theology is to release the event that stirs in the famous covenantal scenes and not allow it to be contracted to any present form or constricted by its local conditions. The event is the unconditional that is astir in these local conditions, what is undeconstructible in any historical construction or discursive practice.... The name of God is very simply the most famous and richest name we have to signify both an open-ended excess and an inaccessible mystery.[9]

- John Caputo:
  My idea is to stop thinking about God as a massive onto-logical power line that provides power to the world, instead thinking of something that short-circuits such power and provides a provocation to the world that is otherwise than power.[10]

From these passages, I contend that we can extrapolate a different set of beliefs that generally reflect some of the key ideas of postmodern philosophy of religion (let us term these *P-beliefs*):[11]

(5) God is not best thought of as a transcendent person, but rather as the possibility of radical secrecy in relation to the Other.

(6) Postmodern religion is not about a set of propositional claims concerning God's existence and attributes, but is instead primarily concerned with fostering an openness to the excessiveness of the event of "the impossible."

(7) God should not be understood according to a discourse of power, but a discourse of love, hospitality, and humility.

(8) God is not adequately articulated in the vocabulary of a determinate religious tradition, but better (though still inadequately) considered in a vocabulary of expecting the unforeseen.

To summarize these P-beliefs, then, we might say that they de-empha-size the sovereignty, knowledge, and being of God, and emphasize

the importance of hermeneutical, ethical, and eschatological paradoxes that accompany the name "God."

With a very loose sketch of C-beliefs and P-beliefs in front of us,
we are now better able to see the beginnings of the possible dilemma
for a Postmodern Pentecostal. For many, these two sets of beliefs are
in tension with each other. For example, (2) and (5) seem to indicate
that God is a person and that God is not a person. Similarly, (3) and (4)
both are decidedly linked to specifics of Christian theology—namely,
a Trinitarian conception of God and the uniqueness of the historical
kenotic message of God in Christ—and yet (8) resists determinate
religious truth-claims such as these. While C-beliefs are necessarily
committed to claims that are certainly located within the particular
history of a determinate religious tradition, these beliefs are not only
historical (as Kierkegaard's Johannes Climacus has reminded us).[12]
As evidence, consider Caputo's extension of P-beliefs as follows:
"Deconstruction regularly, rhythmically repeats this religiousness,
sans the concrete, historical religions; it repeats nondogmatically the
religious structure of experience, the category of the religious."[13] So,
while C-beliefs are intentionally offered as "dogmas" of a particular
understanding of the Christian faith,[14] P-beliefs, according to Caputo,
are "nondogmatic" as such. So, it seems that I can continue to inhabit
my identity as a Pentecostal by resisting my identity as someone who
advocates the postmodern turn, or I can embrace my identity as a
continental philosopher of religion by abandoning my identity as a
Pentecostal Christian. Now, as Stephen Minister rightly points out in
his reply to this chapter, one's identity is never entirely stable since it
is always a complicated negotiation of influences, overlapping communities, and power structures. Nonetheless, affirming a postmodern
decentered self does not mean that one has to affirm contradictions.
One's identity does not have to be entirely understood in order to
realize that one should avoid incoherence and inconsistency as much
as possible.

Crucially, since I take postmodernism to be the very space in which
I affirm my C-beliefs, something like P-beliefs are just as much a
part of what it is for me to be a Christian as C-beliefs are. While the
C-beliefs express aspects of my theology, pneumatology, and soteriology, postmodernism helps me articulate aspects of my hamartiology
(viz., the noetic effects of sin), Christology (viz., the way in which
incarnation is phenomenologically ([im]possible), and religious

hermeneutics (viz., the sociohistorical context of all discourse and textuality).

It seems that, at least for some persons committed to a postmodern framework and to the determinate content of Christianity (within a particular tradition), *to abandon C-beliefs is to abandon Christianity, and yet to abandon postmodernism is also to abandon Christianity.*[15] Accordingly,

> (9) If I am a postmodernist, then I do not affirm that C-beliefs are true.

And,

> (10) If I affirm that C-beliefs are true, then I am not a postmodernist.[16]

Thus, we can now see that:

> (11) Because of my Christian identity, I am a postmodernist.
> (12) Accordingly, because of my Christian identity, I do not affirm that C-beliefs are true (from 9 and 11).
> (13) If I do not affirm that C-beliefs are true, then I must abandon my Christian identity.
> (14) Therefore, because of my Christian identity, I must abandon my Christian identity (from 11–13).

It seems that we have, indeed, run into a problem. The apparent tension between postmodernism and Pentecostalism illuminates the need for postmodern apologetics in two ways.[17]

First, the Postmodern Pentecostal should be able to give some sort of "rational defense"[18] of how it is that the specific claims of Pentecostalism and the claims of postmodernism are not necessarily incompatible with each other. Yet this is a task undertaken internal to quite specific communities of discourse. Thus it is, again, important to differentiate between "classical" apologetics, which tends to operate according to universal and objective criteria, and "postmodern" apologetics, which does not. Hence, *I take it as a postmodern apologetic task to demonstrate how the dilemma possibly faced by the Postmodern Pentecostal need not obtain.* There are several options for how to proceed here. The dilemma would be avoided by rejecting (11), as I take many Christians critical of postmodernism to do, or by rejecting (13) as Caputo and other postmodernists seem to do, but given my specific religious identity, neither of these options are available to me (and others who share my general perspective). Instead, I contend that the premise that needs to be contested is (9) and that doing so will require revisions to (5)–(8) such that postmodernism is understood as an epistemic proposal and not a metaphysical one.

Second, for anyone who affirms C-beliefs and also considers herself a postmodernist, it should be possible to argue that C-beliefs are worthy of intellectual assent for other postmodernists as well. In the first case, the task is to show that being a postmodernist need not exclude holding C-beliefs. In the second case, the task is to show that holding C-beliefs (in the context of postmodernism) is a worthwhile thing to do.[19] In this way, we might say that postmodern apologetics can have both negative and positive dimensions. The levels of epistemic success are going to be different in the two cases. For example, regarding the possible compatibility of P-beliefs and C-beliefs, it is either the case that they can be simultaneously affirmed without yielding a contradiction or it is not. Regarding whether or not someone should affirm C-beliefs at all, however, we should not expect the same scope for assent (and, I contend, *we should no longer even desire it*). Nonetheless, successfully demonstrating the compatibility of the two sets of beliefs and then simply leaving room open for a *possible* defense of C-beliefs themselves as true is sufficient for our purposes here.

Varieties of Continental Philosophy of Religion

CPR occurring in the deconstructive/phenomenological tradition can be loosely divided into two general camps. On the one side there are those who contend that postmodernism is primarily an *epistemological* (or methodological, or hermeneutic) gesture that can be summarized by the claim that "we cannot even peek over God's shoulder."[20] On the other side, there are those who understand postmodernism to provide a more "radical" claim about the very content of our God-talk itself. At the risk of inviting what I am sure will be robust protestations, I propose that this second account of postmodernism is rightly described as *metaphysical* (as opposed to epistemological). Whereas epistemological postmodernism stresses the limitations of human knowing and contends that beliefs are only held in specific contexts (whether those contexts be cultural, religious, or linguistic), metaphysical postmodernism stresses that particular sorts of claims are fundamentally off-limits to postmodern God-talk. This version of postmodernism remains "metaphysical" insofar as it *prima facie* rejects some determinate accounts of the divine, transcendence, and religious belief. In order to consider these two versions in more detail, I will associate the epistemological approach with the work of Merold Westphal and the metaphysical approach with the work of John Caputo.

Westphal's Epistemological Postmodernism

Caputo himself affirms a distinction between two types of postmodernism in his review essay of Westphal's *Overcoming Onto-Theology:*

> Postmodernism is not simply an epistemological way to delimit human knowledge here in time in order to make room for the world as it is eternally known by God; it shows us more mercilessly how exposed we are to the possibility that the world is not known comprehensively by anyone and that no one knows [that][21] we are here. It does not dogmatically proclaim that, but it exposes us to that. Deconstruction is not only the continuous reminder that we are not God but it is the claim that the name of God is endlessly translatable into other names, like justice, and that we are in no position to stop this fluctuation.[22]

Caputo does not describe his own perspective as "metaphysical," but instead as a "more radical" postmodernism than Westphal's postmodernism, which is due to Caputo's seeing himself as practicing a more radical hermeneutics than does Westphal. I contend, however, that epistemological postmodernism is already *sufficiently* radical. Westphal explains his position as follows:

> As the desire and demand to see things *sub specie aeternitatis,* metaphysics is the not terribly subtle desire and demand to be God: and *deconstruction is the continuous reminder that we are not God.* In fact, it claims, we cannot even peek over God's shoulder.
>
> Derrida's arguments are quasi-transcendental arguments about the conditions of the possibility of human meaning. They are Kantian arguments in the sense that they show, when they are successful...that we cannot have Absolute Knowledge, cannot stand at the Alpha or Omega points that look in on time from the security of a *pou sto* outside of it. Properly construed, they have Kantian limits. (*Overcoming Onto-Theology,* 189)

Westphal follows this articulation of the deconstructive limits on human knowing by claiming, "They show us something about human thought and language, but nothing about what else, if anything, there may be" (189). The most important part of this sentence is the "if anything." Here we see Westphal being *as radical as one needs to be* in light of the Derridean (or Kantian, or Kierkegaardian) insights into the noetic realities of embodied and finite human existence. This is not to say that Westphal is somehow problematically conservative, however. When he stresses the inescapable need for epistemic humility, Westphal challenges the arrogance that would threaten to accompany belief affirmation.[23] Similarly, as displayed in *Whose Community? Which Interpretation?: Philosophical Hermeneutics for the Church*,[24] Westphal makes clear that the interpretive task does not disappear because of one's religious identity. Indeed, religious identity heightens hermeneutic requirements. Nowhere is making Christianity "safe" the goal for the epistemological postmodernist. Yet Westphal does leave in place the possibility of religious belief as part of what it means to be an historically existing individual. As such, he sees no need for a conflict between deconstruction and determinate religion. For Westphal, the basic deconstructive gesture can be summarized in the words of Johannes Climacus: existence might be a system for God, but it cannot be a system for "any existing [*existerende*] spirit" (*Overcoming Onto-Theology*, 190).[25] Accordingly, Westphal suggests that Derrida "ought to speak like Kierkegaard's Johannes Climacus" (189). However, as Westphal quickly points out: "Derrida does not speak this way. He does not so much argue for the unreality of God as assume it, so when he shows that we are not the Alpha and Omega he talks as if he has shown that there is no Alpha and Omega. This is a non sequitur, and my primary criticism of Derrida is that he regularly falls into it" (190).

Westphal continues, "My complaint is not that he assumes atheism, but that he forgets that he has done so. He has the same right to assume that no one inhabits the Eternal Now as Kierkegaard has to assume that someone does. That either must first prove theism or atheism before thinking within that framework is a prejudice of Enlightenment evidentialism. But then they need to remember that conclusions into which their assumption essentially enters remain hypothetical" (*Overcoming Onto-Theology*, 190).

Two points are worth noting here. First, Westphal locates himself (as a postmodernist) alongside such contemporary analytic philosophers of religion as Alvin Plantinga and Nicholas Wolterstorff, who reject the strong evidentialist criterion that is operative in much of Modern philosophy and is so closely aligned with strong foundationalism. This is important because Westphal refuses to be caught in the trap of self-referential inconsistency by affirming Kierkegaard's starting point while rejecting the structurally similar one found in Derrida. Second, he stresses the epistemic humility that must accompany perspectives freed of such Enlightenment "prejudices." As he puts it, the assumption of theism or atheism requires that conclusions drawn on the basis of such an assumption "remain hypothetical." Though Westphal eventually concludes that Derrida remains of significant importance to the philosophy of religion in general and Christian thought in particular—as he puts it, "There just may be some gold to be mined in them thar hills" (*Overcoming Onto-Theology*, 196)—he does note that it is Derrida's frequent forgetfulness of his own atheistic assumptions that leads many to "reject deconstruction as bad philosophy" (190). Such a kneejerk rejection, Westphal notes, "would be to throw out the baby with the bathwater" (190). By recognizing this misstep in Derrida's argumentation, we are able to become ever more vigilant in recognizing those places where Derrida offers profound insights that Christians, as well as members of other religious traditions, would do well to consider.

Caputo's Metaphysical Postmodernism

Responding to Westphal's reading of Derrida, Caputo suggests that "deconstruction is not only the denial that we are God; it is also the denial that we would ever have the authority to deny that there is a God."[26] Importantly, Caputo's claim implies that deconstruction denies our ever having the authority *to affirm* that there is a God. If this were all Caputo claimed, I think Westphal would not have much of a problem with it. One's having "authority" can plausibly be read as a stand-in for one's affirming a claim that demands universal assent. Once the strong evidentialist criterion is rejected, which both Westphal and Caputo do, it becomes plausible to assert that no one could claim "with authority" that there is or is not a God. Westphal's point was *not* that Climacus was correct to say that *there is* a God for whom existence is a system, but correct *to leave open the possibility* that such a claim might be true. Hence, we can say that for both Caputo and Westphal:

> (15) As finite, embodied, existing individuals, we lack the ability to claim *with authority* that there is a God and we lack the ability to claim *with authority* that there is not a God.[27]

So, if the resistance to one's having such authority is not really what distinguishes Caputo from Westphal, then what is the difference? I propose that the difference concerns what each thinker considers to be legitimate possibilities for religious belief in the context of postmodernism. Caputo suggests something similar in the following passage: "The upshot of Merold Westphal's postmodern delimitation of onto-theology is that, when all is said and done, we are free to believe everything that onto-theological arguments, in all their clumsy woodenness and misplaced absoluteness, were getting at. We are perfectly free to believe in the God of metaphysical theology: that God is an infinite eternal omnipotent omniscient creator of heaven and earth."[28] Though couching his account in a notion of "radical translatability"[29] and positioning it as a gesture of hospitality to other religious traditions and beliefs, Caputo's critique of Westphal is difficult to interpret as indicating anything except that when all is said and done, we are *not free* to believe such things about God. When interpreted in this way, Caputo's "metaphysical" inclinations begin to show. For Caputo, a belief such as "God exists as a personal being with certain superlative attributes" seems to be a nonstarter for a postmodernist. In *The Weakness of God*, Caputo makes clear just what he thinks of such notions:

> Jesus does not merely tell parables; he *is* a parable. . . . The kingdom of God releases us from evil the way Jesus releases paralyzed limbs, the way he released his executioners on the cross. Dead bodies rise, substances are transmuted, impermeable walls are permeated. But none of this is to be confused with a strong force, with the power of a super-being or a super-hero to bend natural forces to his almighty will with a display of awe-inspiring power. In such deadening literalism, God becomes the ultimate laser show at Disneyworld, an exercise in world-weary fantasizing that, when we awake from our reveries, leaves us face

to face with the grim visage of ineluctable reality, with the dead bodies of the tsunami or the victims of ethnic cleansing. The kingdom narratives are meant to hold up to us the possibility of the impossible, the possibility to be otherwise than being.[30]

For clarity's sake, let us simply term the claims that are characteristic of what Caputo names "metaphysical theology"as *MT-beliefs*. From the above passage, we can see that MT-beliefs would include such claims as "God is a personal being who was incarnate in history," and "God can unilaterally intervene in the world." It seems to follow, then, that Caputo understands postmodernism to exclude MT-beliefs from the outset. So, for Caputo,

(16) Some beliefs about God (MT-beliefs in particular) are *prima facie* excluded by postmodernism.

Now, Caputo does not say this explicitly. However, it is fairly clear that he hopes his readers will come to find MT-beliefs silly and childish—how else are we to understand the rhetoric of "Disneyworld"? As such, Caputo comes dangerously close to falling into the same trap of forgetfulness that Westphal finds so problematic in Derrida. Importantly, the problem of forgetfulness does not accompany Caputo's own "more radical" understanding of God and religion, *as such*, but emerges when he seems to suggest that being "more radical" continues to leave open all possibilities regarding who or what God is, or what religion is. For example, Caputo might be right to suggest that believing in a personal God is tantamount to believing in "magic" and that religion is not about representational truth-claims (as he frequently does in *The Weakness of God*), but then he should be more willing to admit both the *exclusivity* (i.e., if he is right, then it is false that a personal God continues to be plausible and that religion is a matter of accurately describing reality) and the *hypothetical* status of such claims (i.e., postmodernists also lack an external and neutral *pou sto* from which to speak and, accordingly, MT-beliefs *might* be true).

Significantly, Caputo sometimes explicitly recognizes the hypothetical status of his own claims. For example, in *The Weakness of God,* he claims that his suggestions are "heterodox hypotheses,"[31] and in the section "God without Sovereignty," Caputo offers his series of theses all beginning with the word "suppose."[32] While I applaud this rhetorical strategy (as opposed to the use of "magic" and "Disneyland")

and I think that it does, to some degree, guard against the forgetfulness about which Westphal worries, it does not operate consistently throughout Caputo's work.[33] This is especially the case in Caputo's distinction between "strong theology" and "weak theology." He offers the following account of the two notions:

> In a strong theology, the name of God has historical determinacy and specificity—it is Christian or Jewish or Islamic, for example—whereas a weak theology, weakened by the flux of undecidability and translatability, is more open-ended. A theology of the event is in part a second-order act that maintains a certain ironic distance from strong theologies, which in a certain sense are the only theologies that "exist," that are found in concrete historical communities. I love the strong theologies that I know the way I love great novels, but I maintain an ironic distance from them occasioned not only by the fact that they are invariably in league with power but also by my conviction that the *event* that is astir in the name of God cannot be contained by the historical contingency of the names I have inherited in my tradition. There are many traditions, many forms of life, and on Pauline grounds I hold that God is not partial. On this point, I dare to expand the teachings of Johannes Climacus on the question of the historical point of departure for eternal happiness: not only is it possible, but there may be several such points.[34]

In this passage, Caputo begins with the hypothetical dimension decidedly in play—hence the importance of the reference to a "second-order act" (I will return to the idea of a second-order discourse below)—but he ends the passage by affirming a straightforward first-order claim about a particular understanding of religious pluralism. While I grant that Caputo is probably right to say "there may be several such points," the second-order act undertaken from an "ironic distance" is not innocuously related to the determinate first-order claims affirmed internal to the traditions themselves.

Let me push a bit further here. Throughout *The Weakness of God*, Caputo is unambiguously opposed to "strong theology" because he claims that it misunderstands what religion is about and how the name "God" functions in human discourse. That said, it becomes difficult to hear the "hypothetical" status of Caputo's critique of strong theology and the claims offered therein. Ultimately, Caputo affirms *normative* religious pluralism (which might be a very sensible thing to do), but that requires him also to affirm an *exclusivist notion of truth* according to which *religious exclusivism* is false.[35] Caputo's account of what goes on in religion requires him to reject the accounts offered of the same thing by those strong theologians who affirm MT-beliefs. As long as Caputo claims that religion is simply not a matter of representational truth-claims, he is committed to rejecting the view that religion *is* about representational truth-claims. Again, there is no problem with Caputo's denying the truth of MT-beliefs; perhaps he is right to do so, but there is a problem when he seems to indicate that all options are nonetheless still on the table.

In order to give this problem a bit more specificity, let's look at Caputo's particular version of pluralism, which he presents in the following passage: "Faith itself takes many forms, Christian and non-Christian, religious and non-religious, with or without Christianity or biblical religion, with or without religion, so that one finds oneself radically non-privileged.... To fess up to the radical hermeneutical situation is to fess up to the radical translatability of what one cannot simply call 'divine revelation.' For there [are] many such revelations."[36] Reminiscent of Meister Eckhart, Caputo rightly contends that all discourse about God threatens to become what Jean-Luc Marion would term an "idol" that reflects our own perspectives and prejudices rather than "iconically" opening us up to the radicality of God's otherness. For Caputo, this radicality is best captured in the phrase "the impossible."[37] Indeed, despite his general resistance to apologetics, elsewhere Caputo even suggests that we should give an "apology for the impossible."[38]

This is where the normative weight of Caputo's religious pluralism requires him to do some bullet biting, however. The very claim that "there [are] many such revelations" entails the falsity of the claim that "there are *not* many revelations." As such, normative pluralism requires being exclusivist at least when it comes to religious exclusivism. Following this line of reasoning, we might encapsulate Caputo's claims in "Methodological Postmodernism" and *The Weakness of God* by saying that,

> (17) There are many "revelations" expressed in many forms of faith.

And:

> (18) Postmodernism precludes affirming the truth of any single revelation while denying the truth of others.

While I share Caputo's frustration with the arrogance that so often characterizes God-talk in both political and philosophical conversation, there continues to exist a troubling tension in his thought that is not a productive paradox.

Assessing the Two Varieties of Postmodernism

In the above passages we have seen Caputo make the following claims:

> (15) As finite, embodied, existing individuals, we lack the ability to claim *with authority* that there is a God and we lack the ability to claim *with authority* that there is not a God.
>
> (16) Some beliefs about God (MT-beliefs in particular) are *prima facie* excluded by postmodernism.
>
> (17) There are many "revelations" expressed in many forms of faith.
>
> (18) Postmodernism precludes affirming the truth of any single revelation while denying the truth of others.

I have suggested that Westphal could readily grant (15), and it seems clear that he would also be able to grant (17). So, I find the real difference between epistemological and metaphysical postmodernism to reside somewhere in (16) and/or (18). Can (16) and (17) be affirmed together without problems arising? If (17) is understood to simply claim that there are more than a few legitimate expressions of faith and more than a few accounts of revelation, then (16) and (17) are not incompatible. It could be the case that (16) is simply saying that every form of faith and every revelation *other than* MT-beliefs are legitimate in postmodernism. So, although Westphal would not affirm (16), it does not seem that (16) *by itself* poses a problem.

However, when (16), (17), and (18) are taken together then problems arise. When we add (15)–(18) to (5)–(8) as all being part of the set of P-beliefs (let us call this larger set P-beliefs*), we see that Caputo's affirmation of the set of P-beliefs* requires him to grant as legitimate possibilities whatever "revelation(s)" as expressed in the form(s) of faith he understands to be compatible with P-beliefs* (unless there are other subsequent reasons for rejecting them). Yet if we understand "revelation" simply to be something like "religious interpretation" then according to (18) it seems that we have a potential inconsistency internal to P-beliefs*, which do affirm a specific "revelation"—namely, the original set of P-beliefs, which are now included in P-beliefs*. In other words, the Derridean-Caputoian notion of "religion without religion" expressed, at least in part, in P-beliefs, would seem to count as one of these "revelations" that, by (18), now cannot be affirmed with any consistency.

Further, if one affirms (17)—that there are many revelations—and also affirms (16)—that at least one revelation will not be legitimate (namely, that revelation that contains MT-beliefs)—it becomes impossible to simultaneously affirm (18)—that there is any single revelation that is better (or truer) than another (hence Caputo's particular brand of religious pluralism). To affirm a particular postmodern revelation according to which MT-beliefs would be excluded, say, while rejecting a different revelation, for example, that MT-beliefs are true (as (16) requires), would itself require rejecting (18). So, again, affirming the truth of P-beliefs* potentially requires denying P-beliefs*.

This possible problem is avoided altogether if (16) and (18) are rejected—so now we would be left with a set of postmodern beliefs that include (5)–(8), (15), and (17). This set of beliefs looks very similar to epistemological postmodernism. Expressing the fundamental limits of human epistemic capacities, but without then going on to exclude particular religious beliefs within a postmodern context, escapes the possible incoherence of metaphysical postmodernism because (following the Climacian distinction between objective and subjective truth) it understands P-beliefs, throughout, to be a matter of *how* whatever beliefs one holds are held rather than *what* beliefs can be held in the first place. As such, I suggest that we should revise (5)–(8) to eliminate the problematic metaphysical baggage that might attend them as follows (I refer to each with an "e" to distinguish it as a revision internal to the "epistemological" notion of postmodernism):

> (5e) *Whether or not God is thought of as a transcendent person,* we should remember that the relation to this God is one that requires sensitivity to a radical secrecy in relation to the Other.

(6e) *Postmodern religion should not be reduced to* a set of propositional claims concerning God's existence and attributes, but, because of the epistemic limitations of human perspective, the religious person should be concerned with fostering an openness to the excessiveness of the event of "the impossible."

(7e) *The discourse on/about God* should be guided by dialogical hospitality and ethical humility. Further, such a discourse is plausibly fostered by resisting *the primacy of* metaphors of power in our God-talk and instead deploying metaphors of love.

(8e) *Though it is possible that* God might be more adequately articulated in the vocabulary of one determinate religious tradition than in another, such a claim is beyond human knowledge (i.e., we might indeed have knowledge of God, but it is unlikely that we could know that we have such knowledge) and so a better (though likely still inadequate) way to inhabit religious traditions is as a fallible attempt to relate to what cannot be entirely circumscribed.

So, the set of beliefs that are generally characteristic of epistemological postmodernism include (5e)–(8e), (15), and (17): let's term this set *EP-beliefs*.

Now, one might respond that surely Westphal's perspective also excludes some beliefs such as:

(19) All EP-beliefs are false.

It does seem that (19) is excluded by Westphal's perspective just as MT-beliefs were excluded by Caputo's. While affirming any claim will always necessitate rejecting some other claim, EP-beliefs are statements about the limitations of human knowing and reminders about the importance of epistemic (and theological) humility (regardless of what particular religious tradition one follows). Accordingly, epistemological postmodernism excludes beliefs about *how* beliefs should be held rather than about *what* beliefs should be held. So, we might expand (19) such that it can be seen to involve claims of the following sort:

(20) Humans can know that they have absolutely certain knowledge of God.

(21) Epistemic humility should be avoided and epistemic arrogance celebrated.

As such, the epistemological postmodernist would be right to reject (19), (20), and (21) because of the general framework EP-beliefs require. Yet, the key difference between EP-beliefs and P-beliefs* is that EP-beliefs do not exclude any particular religious tradition. Instead, they simply require that *if* a religious tradition affirms (20) and (21) *then* it will be problematic when affirmed alongside EP-beliefs because of *how* that religious tradition holds its beliefs and not because of the specific claims the tradition holds about God or religious life.[39]

To summarize the argument to this point, we might simply say that if one is an epistemological postmodernist (following Westphal), then the possible incoherence that accompanies metaphysical postmodernism (following Caputo) is avoided. Accordingly, in the attempt to articulate a postmodern, Christian apologetics, of the two options considered here only epistemological postmodernism is compatible with such a project.[40] Such a perspective does not require postmodernism to be affirmed as a set of beliefs about reality (as P-beliefs* do), but instead merely as a set of beliefs about how one ought to hold one's beliefs about reality. As such, epistemological postmodernism is more methodologically pluralist (both philosophically and theologically) than metaphysical postmodernism because it does not exclude or affirm any single metaphysical perspective, which, despite (18), P-beliefs* require (due to [17]). Accordingly, even on its own terms, metaphysical postmodernism is a rather unpromising prospect.

THE POSSIBILITY OF POSTMODERN APOLOGETICS

With this distinction in place between two different varieties of postmodernism, we can return to the possible dilemma of the Postmodern Pentecostal. Immediately we see that there is no contradiction in being an epistemological postmodernist (now understood as someone who holds EP-beliefs) and being a Pentecostal (understood as someone who holds C-beliefs). As such, (9) "If I am a postmodernist, then I do not affirm that C-beliefs are true" along with (10) do not obtain and, accordingly, the original dilemma I articulated is overcome. This result follows because EP-beliefs are not metaphysical theses (e.g., God is not personal, religion is not about propositional claims, God is not omnipotent, etc.), but are more properly considered as hermeneutic recommendations in order that philosophers better heed Merold Westphal's two "warnings": the "Warning against Philosophical Arrogance" and the "Warning against Theological Arrogance."[41]

For example, (5e) resists allowing God to become a philosophical postulate instead of transcendence encountered in intimacy; (6e) does not say that we are not to affirm any propositional claims about God, but instead says that we should not get seduced into thinking that our propositions are affirmed without risk; (7e) is a reminder that philosophy of religion and theology can very quickly degenerate into shouting down those who disagree rather than function as an invitation to "come now, and let us reason together" (Isa. 1:18); and (8e) stresses the importance of dialogical engagement with other traditions. Thus, my earlier claim that postmodernism contributes to my understanding of hamartiology and Christology, etc., remains true, but not exhaustive. Postmodernism cannot, by itself, provide a doctrine of sin or a doctrine of incarnation, but it can help to locate such doctrines within the confines of human social existence, which is crucial to religious belief as functional in the lives of existing individuals, as Kierkegaard would say.

Ultimately, I find Westphal's philosophy to itself serve as a postmodern, Christian apologetics. He consistently demonstrates that being a postmodernist does not require abandoning the specific claims of one's historical religious tradition (whether they are MT-beliefs, C-beliefs, or the beliefs of different versions of Christianity, or other frameworks such as Islam, Hinduism, and even Atheism, etc., which, again, can't be reduced to propositional content, but do involve such content), even though it might cause us to rethink how those claims are affirmed and appropriated.

A POSSIBLE OBJECTION

Before concluding part 1, I want to raise and respond to one possible objection to my characterization of Caputo's project. It might be suggested that "religion without religion," although certainly depending (parasitically we might say) upon the existence of determinate religious traditions, is best thought of a second-order discourse about those traditions rather than another first-order alternative to them. In this way, as Caputo frequently suggests, deconstruction "spooks" these traditions and calls them to self-critical reflection. Support for such a proposal could be provided by Caputo's own suggestion that the inability for any "name" to be adequate to the "event" is due to the fact that the event is not "what happens," but what is "going on in what happens." As he explains, "an event is not an ontico-ontological episode on the plane of being but a disturbance within the heart of being, within the names for being, that makes being restless."[42]

As Caputo himself suggests in his chapter in the present volume, claiming that the notion of "religion without religion" is, in many respects, a particular "revelation" that competes with other revelations around which determinate religious traditions have been organized, is to confuse a second-order claim with a first-order claim. Namely, he suggests that it confuses deconstructive "faith" (*foi*), which is a certain way of being in the world as opened to "the impossible" (which is a second-order act), with "belief" (*croyance*), which is a matter of propositional claims made about what is the case (which is a first-order affirmation). According to such an objection, suggesting that Caputo affirms P-beliefs* as claims about reality internal to the perspective of "metaphysical postmodernism" is simply to misunderstand his work.

While I think that this objection is serious and offers a helpful distinction between faith and belief that is worth taking seriously, I do not think that it successfully overcomes the problem that I have presented above. The worry I have about the possible incoherence of Caputo's account is not due to the specifics with which he does or does not define "God," "religion," "belief," or "faith." I am sympathetic with Caputo's attempt to resist the finality and limitation that can so often accompany determinate religious traditions when they suppose that we can have knowledge of the adequacy of a name to the event. And, to this extent at least, I agree with him when it comes to a possible rationale for religious pluralism. The problem is that metaphysical postmodernism appears to undercut itself *on its own terms.*

When Caputo suggests that this "more radical" notion cannot be "metaphysical" because it is about "faith" rather than "belief," he does not sufficiently consider that even the claim that "'faith' is not to be equated with 'belief,'" is itself a belief. Again, normative religious pluralism remains exclusivist (at the level of truth) in order to even make sense as an alternative to religious exclusivism (at the level of practice). That said, I take this critique of Caputo's project to be a small matter of dispute occurring within a much larger agreement with his deconstructive approach. It is because I find both Caputo and Derrida to be so important for contemporary philosophy of religion and postmodern religious thought in general (i.e., I think that there is *quite a bit* of gold in "them thar hills"!) that it is essential to get clear on where there might be places in their thought worth pushing back against, namely, places where it gives in to its own variety of problematic excess. While Caputo is right to say that analytic philosophy of religion and strong theology can tend toward kataphatic excess, I add that continental philosophy of religion and weak theology can tend toward apophatic excess.[43] Epistemic postmodernism is worth defending because it can help us to live and think between such extremes while drawing upon the important philosophical and theological resources offered by both traditions. As such, it opens space for a *postmodern kataphaticism*.

Having outlined the sort of postmodern perspective that leaves room for apologetics, in part 2 I will consider Caputo's suggestion that apologetics is concerned only with "explicating a philosopher's faith" rather than with the God that resides "in the hearts of believers."[44] Looking to a very early example of Christian apologetics, I will show that apologetics need not be seen as simply a game for professional philosophers, but instead can (and, I believe, should) always be characterized by its existential traction in the lives of religious believers. In this way, I think the stress that Caputo places on *faith* regardless of one's *beliefs*, although extremely important, can be interpreted as a false dichotomy. Defenses of one's beliefs themselves are at stake in the risky existential investment that one makes in the attempt to be "faithful."

Part 2
Justin Martyr on the Existential Traction of Apologetics

Concerns about the lack of existential traction in contemporary philosophy of religion (and apologetics, specifically) are not found only in continental philosophy. In the process of offering the Free Will Defense as a response to the logical problem of evil, Alvin Plantinga writes the following:

Confronted with evil in [one's] own life or suddenly coming to realize more clearly than before the *extent* and *magnitude* of evil, a believer in God may undergo a crisis of faith. He may be tempted to follow the advice of Job's "friends"; he may be tempted to "curse God and die." Neither a Free Will Defense nor a Free Will Theodicy is designed to be of much help or comfort to one suffering from such a storm in the soul...Neither is to be thought of first of all as a means of pastoral counseling. Probably neither will enable someone to find peace with himself and with God in the face of the evil the world contains. But then, of course, neither is intended for that purpose.[45]

In light of Plantinga's admission of the seeming existential irrelevance of some apologetic gestures in the philosophy of religion, I want to turn to one of the earliest "apologists" in the Christian tradition, Justin Martyr. I will look to his *First and Second Apologies* in order to show how apologetics need not to be considered as merely a matter of concern for a "philosopher's faith," as Caputo suggests. Justin is worth looking at in this regard because, as one scholar notes, though "the Apostolic Fathers had dealt with the practical day-to-day problems of the Church[,] speculative thought and Christian philosophy begin with Justin."[46] For Justin, the practice of apologetics was originally designed and deployed as a response to real existential threats faced by Christian believers (regardless of their philosophical aptitude). Justin Martyr offers a profound example of how apologetics, though often formulated according to technical philosophical vocabulary, should be *at least initially* characterized by existential traction rather than detachment and abstraction.

L. W. Barnard offers the following summary of Justin's apologetic goals as they occurred in the philosophical context of his time:

> Justin's philosophical background is predominantly that of eclectic Middle Platonism, although it is well to remember that this was not a philosophical system, as such, but rather a philosophical transition stage. In many respects Justin is a better mirror to the intellectual forces to which he was exposed than any other Christian writer of the second century. He was not an original genius who wished to construct a logical, unifying, philosophic system of his own. But he was a genuine seeker after the truth who brought into the Church the intellectual strivings of his age. And in his search Platonism, as understood by the contemporary Middle Platonist schools, was a predominating influence.

Yet to isolate Justin's philosophical background could do him a disservice and merely perpetuate his memory as a second-century eclectic. It was above all his acceptance of the Christian Faith which proved to be the goal of his philosophical journey. Now he knew that he had found the one "true" philosophy.

Justin's reverence for philosophy, as finding its consummation in Christ, was of great importance for the Church, for it meant that educated pagan converts were no longer obliged to deny the insights of their philosophical backgrounds. Platonism was now seen to be as valid a preparation for the Gospel as Judaism had been. The Church, at least in its more sensitive minds, came to see that all apprehensions of truth in Greek philosophy and in the intellectual searchings of men were due to the power of the same logos who had become incarnate in Jesus Christ. Justin faithfully reflects the eclectic Platonism of his age. What is remarkable is his clear grasp of Christianity as the one, true philosophy.[47]

There are three points that I want to highlight here. First, Justin reflects the philosophical perspective of his time. Second, Justin understands this perspective to be compatible with the truth of Christianity. Third, Justin's philosophical work yields important consequences for the Church. All three of these points are just as viable when describing the apologetic task in the context of continental philosophy of religion (CPR). Like Justin, the continental philosopher of religion who attempts to defend Christian faith will do so in the context of the postmodern philosophy characterizing CPR itself. Whereas Justin's main influence was Middle Platonism, CPR's might be phenomenology, deconstruction, feminism, critical theory, etc. Also, whereas Justin argued that Platonism and Christianity were not opposed to each other, many (such as the authors of the present volume) have found postmodernism to offer profound resources for Christian thought. Finally, deconstruction and phenomenology are not philosophical movements isolated within the walls of academe and the halls of Society of Existential and Phenomenological Philosophy conferences. Instead, as reflected in the epigraphs to this chapter, postmodernism has also had a substantial impact on the Church.[48]

Despite these possible points of similarity, one might suggest that these intersections have no bearing on the fate of apologetics, but instead only attest to the long relationship that Christianity and philosophy have had with each other. In order to show that Justin's apologetic task itself remains viable (though the specifics of his perspective might not), I will offer four themes characteristic of Justin's apologies that bear upon postmodern apologetics as well.

First, *apologetics is to be conducted because of real (or at least perceived) existential threat and not merely to further intellectual banter.* In §1 of Justin's First Apology, he begins: "To the Emperor Titus Aelius Hadrianus Antoninus Pius Augustus Caesar, and to his philosopher son Verissimus, and to Lucius the philosopher/ Caesar's natural son and Pius's adopted son, a lover of culture, and to the Sacred Senate and all the Roman people—on behalf of people of every nation who are unjustly hated and grossly abused, I, Justin, son of Priscus and grandson of Bacchius, from Flavia Neapolis in Syria-Palestine, myself being one of them, have drawn up this address and petition."[49] Notice here that Justin locates himself within a familial heritage and historical community. Moreover, his work is addressed to a very specific set of people in a very specific set of circumstances. Crucially, those circumstances are the continued persecution of Christians. Just as I have claimed that my own concern is with the possibility of a postmodern *Christian* apologetics, I take this to be a defense of the possibility of a postmodern *Islamic,* or *Jewish,* or *Atheist* apologetics. While Justin's own concern is for Christians, his appeal here is made not only on their behalf, but "on behalf of people of every nation who are unjustly hated and grossly abused." Justin begins his philosophical reflections and apologetic arguments in the name of eliminating injustice and violence.[50] This dedication is similar to that offered by Emmanuel Levinas at the beginning of *Otherwise than Being.* There Levinas writes, "To the memory of those who were closest among the six million assassinated by the National Socialists, and of the millions on millions of all confessions and all nations, victims of the same hatred of the other man, the same anti-Semitism."[51] For both Justin and Levinas, doing philosophy was meant to change the situation for people who were being victimized. Ideas have consequences. Justin's apologetic strategy was to use ideas to make tomorrow better than today for those facing persecution simply because of the truth-claims that they affirmed and the religious tradition to which they belonged.

Second, *one of the tasks of apologetics is to get clear on what a particular religious tradition believes.* Justin recognized that given the sociopolitical context in which he lived, the mere affiliation with

Christianity was enough to get an individual condemned. As he notes:

> For from a name neither approval nor punishment could fairly come, unless something excellent or evil in action could be shown about it. For you do not punish the accused among yourselves before they are convicted; but in our case you take the name as proof against us, and this although, as far as the name goes, you ought to punish our accusers. For we are accused of being Christians, and to hate what is favorable is unjust. Again if one of the accused deny the name, saying that he is not [a Christian], you acquit him, as having no proof that he is an evildoer; but if any one acknowledges that he is one, you punish him on account of this acknowledgement. You ought also to enquire into the life both of the confessor and the denier, that by his deeds it would appear what kind of person each is. For as some who have been taught by the Teacher, Christ, not to deny him encourage others when they are put to the test, so similarly do those who lead evil lives give some excuse to those who, without consideration, like to accuse all the Christians of impiety and wickedness. And this also is improper. For in philosophy, too, some assume the name and the dress who do nothing worthy of their profession. (I, §4, pp. 24–25)

Justin shows that praise and blame are only legitimate if they reflect the truth of a person's identity rather than simply the group with whom the person is said to affiliate. This point is relevant to postmodern apologetics for two reasons. First, though my evidence is only anecdotal, I have found that being understood to affiliate with Christianity (or even the philosophy of religion in general) is often sufficient to exclude one from academic opportunities in continental philosophy.[52] The same is true in the opposite direction concerning positions in philosophy of religion or positions at "Christian" institutions. For anyone attempting to compete for such positions, being a postmodernist is far too often viewed as reason to be suspect (not only of one's theological inclinations, but also of one's philosophical ability).[53] Getting clear on exactly what it is that Christians (of a particular tradition) actually believe is crucial if the affiliation with Christianity is not to be immediately equated with one's being a "fundamentalist."[54]

Second, getting clear on exactly what it is that CPR affirms as a general philosophical trajectory is crucial if we are to avoid the misconceptions that so often characterize critical accounts of postmodernism.

In this way, I consider Caputo's own "defense of the impossible" to be a fundamentally apologetic strategy that attempts to clear away reasons for rejecting postmodernism.

Third, *apologetics should be characterized by clear and lucid argumentation that is rigorous and relevant.* Though this might seem like it is more of a concern for professional decorum and best practices, I propose that we understand this theme as a concern for impacting one's given audience. The commitment to clear and lucid argumentation should not be read (either in Justin's context or in our own) as something singularly characteristic of professional philosophy, but instead as a recognition of how important it is to be understood by one's conversation-partners.[55]

For Justin, the persecution of Christians was something based on error and, hence, the need for an "apologia" of Christian belief. Though he contends that Christianity was the complete and final truth of philosophy and believed that all rational persons should recognize this fact (a claim with which I expect postmoderns rightly to take issue), far more prominent is his attempt to lay out exactly what it is that Christians believe in order that they might be fairly judged: "We ask that the charges against us be investigated, and that, if they are substantiated let us be punished as is fitting. But if nobody can prove anything against us, true reason forbids you, because of an evil rumor, to wrong innocent people, and indeed rather [to wrong] yourselves, who think fit to instigate action, not by judgment, but by passion" (I, §3, p. 24). When it comes to being persecuted, evidence of wrongdoing on one side or the other is necessary. In such a context, Justin's task is to express, in terms understandable to those outside his own community, why he believes what he does, and why such beliefs are not morally reprobate. His apologetic enterprise would be entirely misconceived if it were characterized as only a matter of supplying argumentative support to what would otherwise collapse (as Caputo suggests of traditional philosophy of religion).[56] Justin's apologetic goals are to show others why Christianity does not make a person irrational, morally bankrupt, and a bad citizen.

Once his case has been presented, Justin expects his audience to weigh and consider it. Yet he offers a warning: "If you also, like thoughtless people, prefer the custom to truth, do what you have power to do. But just so much power have rulers who respect reputation rather than truth, as brigands have in a desert" (I, §12, p. 30).

Justin's point here is that once he has shifted the burden of proof to his accusers, they then become morally blameworthy for not responding according to the reasonable standards of the community. "If our account seems to you reasonable and true," Justin claims, then "respect it; but if it seems foolish to you, despise it as nonsense, and do not decree death against those who have done no wrong, as against enemies" (I, §68, p. 72). If CPR denies the possibility of apologetics because of a resistance to the supremacy of transcendent rationality, then fine; but Justin shows that apologetics does not begin with an appeal to such rationality, but merely to the reasonable judgment of people with whom one shares a community. *While it is surely a straw man of Derrida to claim that he never offers arguments (as some in analytic philosophy claim), it is also a straw man of apologetics to claim that it can only function internal to an Enlightenment conception of strong foundationalism and uncompromising evidentialism.*[57]

Fourth, *apologetics should be aimed at truth and not simply persuasion.* Following on the last point, for Justin, apologetics is not just a game of "when they say this, you say this back." Justin attempts to bring the life of the mind to bear on the life of faith. Anselm and Augustine both remind us that it might indeed be faith that opens the space for genuine truth-seeking. But they also remind us that being a Christian does not mean that one has checked one's mind at the door of the Church. I believe that much of the resistance to apologetics within CPR comes from a frustration with the perceived arrogance and lack of charity found in the work of some popular apologists. Often it can seem that apologetics is done in order to avoid listening to objections. As someone who has been raised in the evangelical Christian subculture, I can attest to the fact that very often this is how apologetics is deployed within the churches: as a tool for protecting one's Christian mind (understood in a very narrow way) rather than as a means of opening oneself to truth-seeking. This leads to closed-minded sophistry instead of genuine engagement with one's neighbor. Justin anticipates this worry and in a statement that could be as appropriately directed to contemporary evangelical Christianity as to the Roman leadership, he claims, "But lest we should seem to deceive, we consider it right, before embarking on our promised demonstration, to cite a few of the precepts given by Christ Himself. It is for you then, as powerful rulers, to find out whether we have been taught and do teach these things truly. Short and concise utterances come from Him, for He was no sophist, but His word was the power of God" (I, §14, p. 32). Simply put, Jesus was no sophist and so his followers should not be. Here Justin demonstrates how apologetics can also be used as a critique of misrepresentations of Christianity and as an encouragement for Christians to return to the humble and invitational example of Jesus' own charitable engagement with others.[58]

POSITIVE APOLOGETICS IN CONTINENTAL PHILOSOPHY OF RELIGION

Apologetics is often understood to reflect theological and philosophical (not to mention political) arrogance. If a positive *postmodern* apologetics is to occur, then this perceived arrogance needs to be overcome. Two thinkers (not themselves affiliated with postmodernism or CPR) offer models that are helpful for beginning to envision how such a positive postmodern apologetics might proceed. John G. Stackhouse Jr.'s "humble apologetics" and David K. Clark's "dialogical apologetics" are both examples of how apologetics need not presume a "view from nowhere" (Nagel) or occupy a position from which we can "peek over God's shoulder" (Westphal). They both emphasize the importance of being open to difference, humble about one's own claims to knowledge, cognizant of one's dialogical context, and genuinely receptive to criticism. As Clark points out: "Traditionally, apologetics has been defined as the *art of the reasoned defense of the Christian faith.* This is the rational side of apologetics. To this rational dimension, dialogical apologetics adds the personal: apologetics is the art of the reasoned defense of the Christian faith *in the context of personal dialogue.*"[59] And, as Stackhouse notes, we need apologetic conversation "without perverting it into a destructive exercise in triumphalism."[60] Though no strong proponent of postmodernism himself, Stackhouse admits that his conception of apologetics can find some fertile soil in certain varieties of postmodernism: "It is not clear whether postmodernism is a new, coherent paradigm that replaces the modern, or simply the rubble from the collapse of the old. But various forms of postmodernism aim to construct more than a hodgepodge of old and new simply to entertain, or turn a profit, or win a battle. They sincerely aim to liberate the mind and improve the human lot while recognizing how little we actually do know with no certainty that we are heading in the right direction."[61] I believe that Westphal and Caputo would both agree with Stackhouse here.

Additionally, however, if a legitimately *Christian* postmodern apologetics is to occur then we must also go beyond the "non-dogmatic" religion *without* religion and begin to think about what religion *with* religion might entail in a postmodern world. In other words, we must think about the *with* after having appropriated and affirmed the *without*. Religion *with* religion is not a rejection of the *without*, but merely a resistance to the interpretations of it that give into the apophatic excesses I mentioned earlier. Though Justin exemplifies working within the philosophical context of one's own time, he also holds fast to what he takes to be central tenets of Christianity (his own version of C-beliefs). Expressing a worry about the potential cultural captivity of the Church, in his *Unapologetic Theology*, William Placher notes that apologetics can quickly slide from an important aspect of Christian existence into a regrettable legacy of theological compromise: "'Apologetics' traditionally constitutes the part of Christian theology devoted to defending Christian faith to a non-Christian audience. It can be an honorable enterprise, but it always risks becoming 'apologetic' in a bad sense: defensive, halfhearted. Christian apologists can adopt the language and assumptions of their audience so thoroughly that they no longer speak with a distinctively Christian voice. As a result, they not only cease to give a faithful account of the Christian tradition, they cease to be interesting to their non-Christian listeners because they do not seem to have anything new or different to say."[62] While Placher's worry is sensible, he overlooks the resources that postmodernism offers for being able to defend Christian belief while avoiding arrogance and compromise. It is possible to coherently be a Christian postmodernist without, thereby, having made Christianity "safe" and postmodernism "nonradical."

The main characteristics of the "humble" or "dialogical" apologetics[63] that I want to appropriate and advocate can be articulated as follows (all of the following are drawn from either Stackhouse or Clark but are explained in relation to CPR).

- *Apologetics is not primarily a results-based enterprise, but a "service-oriented" one.*[64] As Stackhouse says, "apologetics is about winning the friend, not the argument."[65] A postmodern apologetics operating in this dialogical/humble way will never see the goal of such engagement to be mere conversion but genuine conversation. However, within the relationship of trust that accompanies such conversational contexts, a reevaluation of one's own perspective while seriously considering the perspective of one's conversation partner does often follow.

- *Apologetics is not primarily "content-oriented" but "person-oriented."*[66] As Justin modeled centuries ago, the "content" of Christianity must be expressed and articulated in terms that other persons can understand. If a defense of Christianity is to retain the existential traction that it had for Justin, then the practice should first and foremost be seen as a way of better encountering others.

- *Offering "proofs" for God is not a zero-sum game.*[67] The apologetic conversation itself is not *merely* to be viewed as an attempt to convey the truth of a particular set of propositions (though this might be *part of* the conversation). Instead, dialogical/humble apologetics recognizes that reason operates in contexts and arguments only work when considered and accepted by other persons (who are themselves contextually located). A proof for God might be something that works in some contexts and with some people and not in others with different people. Hence, I would suggest that so-called "cumulative case" arguments are likely to be much more prominent in postmodern apologetic discourse than any affirmation of one single proof.[68]

- *Apologetics must be sensitive to the differences of cultural location and discursive practices.*[69] Philip Goodchild suggests that there is a "self-inoculation against difference" that has for too long characterized philosophy of religion. Goodchild contends that a suspicion might develop that: "Arguments in the philosophy of religion are 'justifications' of highly localized and particular religious opinions—'justifications' which masquerade as public and universal judgments of what is the case, and thus attempt to entrap the interlocutors into abandoning their own local and different perspectives, so as to accede to the judgments of the master thinker."[70] Though

I worry about Goodchild's often less than charitable reading of analytic philosophy of religion, he is correct to worry about how philosophical argumentation can often seem to fall back into the objectivist discourse of modernity. Postmodern apologetics should take seriously what Jean-François Lyotard might call the "local narratives" that operate internal to a specific cultural heritage. Religious belief is not something outside culture, but internal to it. However, this does not cede the day to Placher's worry about the cultural captivity of Christian theology. Instead, we must remember that one only believes the tenets of a particular religion from within a historico-cultural space.

Moreover, the tenets themselves can only be expressed in the language of one's historico-cultural context. This does not mean that one has to grant all perspectives as equally valid, though. Further, it does not mean that it is impossible to critique one's context in the name of one's religious perspective (e.g., consider Kierkegaard's critique of the Hegelianism of his "age," which he took to be incompatible with authentic Christianity). It simply means that, as Caputo and Plantinga would both point out, there is no neutral place from which to consider which perspectives are worth taking seriously and which are not. This difficulty is not a slippery slope toward vulgar relativism, but merely the reason why a multicultural sensibility is so important if we are going to be oriented toward serving people while still standing within the narrative of a particular religious tradition.

- *Apologetics will never totally eliminate the riskiness of religious belief (which is best understood as a relation of trust).*[71] One need not operate within postmodernism to realize that rationality need not entail universality, objectivity, or certainty.[72] All apologetics might be able to do is to break down barriers to belief by inviting others to take seriously that the claims of Christianity. However, this invitation is never offered as a guarantee. Apologetics ought never to be understood as eliminating all mystery from the life of faith.[73]
- *Though offering "rational defenses," apologetics should operate according to a healthy fallibilism.*[74] This final characteristic is not primarily derived from a philosophical perspective, but

from a theological realization that the "noetic effects of sin" are going to make such claims to certainty hard to come by. The persistent role of critique in Derrida's philosophy (especially in his notion of the "democracy to come") is something that can quite nicely be understood as a nontheological way of conveying these epistemic limitations. Again, when working internal to an epistemological postmodernist framework, epistemic limitation need not, thereby, exclude affirming religious beliefs.

Before concluding, I want to propose two more characteristics that are likely to be crucial for a postmodern apologetics that is dialogically and humbly oriented. The first characteristic I will term *Charitable Exclusivism*. Simply put, we must not abandon a concern for rational discourse even though granting the critique of Enlightenment reason that is offered by the postmodern turn. Even within postmodernism, contradictions are to be avoided and represent some sort of epistemic or logical failure. When applied to religious belief, a postmodern appreciation of cultural difference and perspectival location does not erase the law of noncontradiction. In response to Caputo's claim that there are many revelations found in many faiths (see [17] above), I suggested that Westphal could also grant this claim as long as it is understood to mean that it is likely no single religious tradition is *entirely* correct while every other religious tradition *entirely* incorrect. However, if what Caputo means to say is that Hinduism and Christianity, say, are *identically* true, then I suggest we should part company at that point. If Hinduism is understood to claim that "Jesus is not uniquely God incarnate" and if Christianity is understood to claim "Jesus is uniquely God incarnate," then it is logically impossible for both Christianity and Hinduism to be right (at least regarding this particular claim). As I have already indicated, in order for religious pluralism to even make any sense, it requires that *if* it is true *then* religious exclusivism must be false. Attempting to resist theological triumphalism by denying the law of noncontradiction is simply patronizing—viz., it requires no difference between a religion being true and its being false.

The key here is to realize that often what is taken to be a contradiction on the order of $(X \wedge \sim X)$ is really (after much consideration) better understood as not really being contradictory at all, e.g.,

(X ^ Y). Charitable Exclusivism helps us to realize that the process of attempting to wrestle with the various truth claims of different traditions enacts the hospitality and generosity of conversational engagement that we were seeking to foster. The belief that incompatible truth-claims cannot be simultaneously held need not lead to marginalization in philosophical practice or political life.[75] Real disagreement should not trouble us, for it requires real engagement in order to be articulated. The danger lies in covering over disagreement in the name of openness. Unless we see the other person with her actual beliefs and expect her to see us with ours, then this openness is just a mask for continued dismissiveness.[76]

The final characteristic of positive postmodern apologetics is what I will term an *Apologetics of Exemplars*. I draw this idea from Edith Wyschogrod's conception of "postmodern saints."[77] For Wyschogrod, we can no longer appeal to a universal criterion for moral behavior, but instead need to look to the narrative lives of individuals devoted to serving other people. Drawing upon Wyschogrod, when it comes to "rational defenses," one of the most substantive ways to offer such a defense is to provide testimonies of transformed lives.[78] While this is certainly only an inductive sort of argument, it nonetheless shows examples of individuals who have lived *Imitatio Christi* and stand as models of human behavior, and action goes a long way toward making Christianity itself more plausible as a way of life (and even, to some extent, as a set of truth-claims).[79]

CONCLUSION: ON POSTMODERN RELIGIOUS IDENTITY

I began this chapter by considering my seemingly problematic, and maybe even incoherent, identity as a Postmodern Pentecostal. I suggested that addressing this problem illuminated the need for a postmodern apologetics. We have seen that if postmodernism is taken to be an epistemological expression of the limitation and finitude of human knowing rather than a metaphysical account of what beliefs remain legitimate options, then apologetics is possible in the sense of showing that a determinate religious tradition (in my case Pentecostal Christianity) is compatible with postmodernism. By then looking at the way in which apologetics was originally understood as existentially relevant in the work of Justin Martyr, we saw how a postmodern apologetics need not operate merely in the pages of philosophy journals, but can gain traction in the hearts of postmodern religious believers. Finally, I suggested that a postmodern apologetics can go beyond the negative gesture of simply showing the compatibility of determinate religion and postmodernism, by positively contending for the truth of a particular religious tradition. This second aspect of postmodern apologetics, I claimed, will essentially operate according to a dialogical and humble model in which reason is not taken as a universal, objective, and neutral, but instead as local, contextual, and invitational.[80]

I will conclude by considering a Kierkegaardian objection to apologetics, namely, the charge that even attempting a rational defense of Christianity is to misunderstand Christianity itself. Kierkegaard articulates this objection in his *Journals:*

> It is easy enough to show how false and basically traitorous, even though unconscious, all this defense of Christianity is—yes, even the very form which discourse about Christianity ordinarily takes. The fact of the matter is that pastors and scholars, etc., do not believe in Christianity at all. If a person himself firmly believes that the good he is discoursing about is the highest good, if he almost sags under the impression of its exceedingly abundant blessedness—how in all the world could he ever come to defend it, to conduct a defense of its really being a good, or even to talk in the following manner: This is a great good for three reasons—this supreme good, this good which makes the wisest of men's understanding dizzy and reduces it to tiny sparrow-like understanding, this is a great good—for three reasons. What an anticlimax! Imagine a lover. Yes, he can keep on talking day in and day out about the gloriousness of his beloved. But if anyone demands him to prove it with three reasons, or even defend it—I wonder if he would not regard this as a demented proposal; or if he were a bit more sagacious, he no doubt would say to the person who suggested this to him: Oho, you do not know what it is to be in love, and you half believe that I am not either.[81]

In this passage, and in plenty of others,[82] Kierkegaard rejects rational defenses of Christianity because he thinks that such attempts force the essentially intimate (and paradoxical) personal relation with God into the speculative vocabulary of philosophy. Such a reduction of the Christian message is to make it no longer Christian. In light of Kierkegaard, must we conclude that postmodern apologetics really is a bankrupt project, after all, but for theological reasons rather than for philosophical ones? I do not believe so. Kierkegaard offers a reminder that what has too often passed as authentic Christianity is really nothing more than the entrenchment of political and philosophical structures. For Kierkegaard, as for Marion, the religious establishment can quickly become idolatrous if it forgets its own fallibility and finitude. Christianity itself resists the complacency of Christendom. As Caputo argues so convincingly, Jesus can be seen as a radical deconstructionist.[83] Ironically, I contend that Caputo (despite operating according to a problematic postmodern framework) and Kierkegaard (despite explicitly rejecting rational defenses of Christianity) are two of the best examples of how postmodern apologetics can function in the mode of getting clear on what it is that Christianity might be about.[84] Like love, Kierkegaard suggests, faith is risky and does not admit of a traditional conception of "defense." And yet, in arguing for such a claim, Kierkegaard himself makes Christianity something worth taking seriously. Hence, in at least the postmodern sense I have described here, Kierkegaard rationally "defends" Christianity.[85]

Having started this chapter on a personal note, I will end it on one as well. In my own life, it has been Kierkegaard's work that has primarily showed me how to be a Christian "after" objectivity and it has been Caputo's work that has significantly showed me how to take religion seriously as a postmodern philosopher. Engaging in postmodern apologetics is risky business. There are dangers and temptations lurking on all sides: philosophical arrogance, theological vacuity, patronizing behavior, etc. Yet, as Levinas (himself, I would argue, a postmodern Jewish apologist) so aptly notes: "To hear a God not contaminated by Being is a human possibility no less important and no less precarious than to bring Being out of the oblivion in which it is said to have fallen in metaphysics and in onto-theology."[86] Attempting to develop the ears to "hear" such a God is not something we should abandon just because we have overcome onto-theology and moved past presumptions of objectivity and universality. I admit that apologetics may not be a practice in which all continental philosophers of religion will want to engage. However, I have shown that being a continental philosopher of religion need not place such a practice off-limits.

In the end, it is not Derrida's "atheism" that "gets on in the churches," but rather his very sensible resistance to a particular way of being a theist. Similarly, it is not Caputo's rejection of evangelicalism that evangelicals are so eager to welcome, but rather his understandable opposition to the arrogance that is so often found among evangelicals. A postmodern apologetics helps us to see just that.

Chapter 1, Reply 1
"As Radical as One Needs to Be"
— A Response to J. Aaron Simmons

Bruce Ellis Benson

I n "Apologetics after Objectivity," J. Aaron Simmons remarks
that Merold Westphal (rather than John D. Caputo) is "as
radical as one needs to be." This way of putting it really does
seem to get at the heart of the matter. In effect, Caputo sees Westphal's radical postmodernism and raises it. And so it goes. Yet just
how radical does one need to be to do whatever it is that is truly
post-modern and get over exactly whatever it is that needs to be overcome? I use the term "whatever" precisely because I am—all the
more so *now*—uncertain as to exactly what it is we need to overcome
and why it is so bad that it needs overcoming. Although my remarks
will weave in and out of Simmons's text, let me be clear up front that
I fundamentally agree with him. However, what I will be questioning is the very assumptions that frame this game. For, as far as I can
see, the exact terms and ideas that we are debating in this book are
far from obvious, however obvious they might be assumed to be.
Thus, with Friedrich Nietzsche, I intend to step back and consider
this entire debate and *squint*. Nietzsche speaks of the philosopher's
"*duty* to be suspicious these days, to squint as maliciously as possible
out of every abyss of mistrust."[1] In short, I intend to be suspicious of
being suspicious of religion.

Simmons starts with the obvious question given the postmodern situation: can we give a rational defense for whatever it is that Christianity claims to be true? Of course, it is worth mentioning that this has *always* been a question, going back to whenever we can say there was such a *thing* as Christianity. Even though it is Justin Martyr who gives us some early examples of detailed apologetics, one finds hints at apologetics in Paul, when he speaks of the risen Christ having been seen by Cephas, the 12, and then more than 500 people (1 Cor. 15:5). Another early version of "evidentialist apologetics" is to be found at the end of John's Gospel, where he writes of "testifying to these things" and says that "his testimony is true" (John 21:24). Whatever exactly Paul or the writer of John had in mind in mentioning these points, it is probably safe to say that they were not thinking of their apologetic comments as needing what Simmons mentions: "objectivity, universality, and neutrality." Perhaps they were thinking in terms of "universality," though I doubt it. So those criteria obviously had to be imported somewhere along the way. Even Jesus' own statement, "I am the way, and the truth, and the life" (John 14:6) can only be read in terms of scientific objectivity and neutrality *by scientific moderns*. And what *exactly* Jesus meant by this is certainly up for debate (even if Christian orthodoxy is quite clear regarding the centrality of Jesus to Christianity and salvation).

But let us turn to Simmons's own way of laying out the dilemma. On the one hand, he either believes or does not believe basic truth-claims like "God is personal," "God continues to manifest Godself in the world," and "Salvation is obtained through a relation to this personal God" (2–4). Simmons rightly insists that Christianity is not reducible to a set of truth-claims, but being a Christian certainly entails some kind of belief in such claims, which Simmons terms "C-beliefs." On the other hand, postmoderns like Caputo and Jacques Derrida (a rather nontraditional believer and one who "rightly passes for an atheist")[2] tell us to "stop thinking about God as someone, over there, way up there, transcendent" and instead to think of God as "the most famous and richest name we have to signify both an open-ended excess and an inaccessible mystery."[3] Put into "P[ostmodern]-belief" terms, instead of God as "transcendent person" we have God as "radical secrecy in relation to the Other," "openness to the excessiveness of the event of the 'impossible,'" "hospitality and humility," and the "unforeseen" (5–8). Not surprisingly, Simmons doesn't find "P-beliefs" popping up in many sermons at his Pentecostal Church, and "C-beliefs" are pretty well absent from postmodern philosophy. As an Episcopalian, I could quite easily respond that something along the lines of "P-beliefs" might well be found in *my* church, which is why some conservative Episcopalians are leaving it.

However, let us tend to each side of the dilemma. While there is no doubt that certain Christian claims are put forth by some Christians with a high degree of robustness, it is far from clear that they necessarily consider those claims to be "ontotheological" in the sense of claiming a view that is *sub specie aeternitatis*. One could at this point appeal to Alvin Plantinga's rejection of classical foundationalism and absolute certainty, as well as the recognition on his part that one's views are often clouded by self-interest. Or one could turn to the observation by C. Stephen Evans and Westphal that both analytic and continental philosophy have recently turned away from an Enlightenment idea that reason is either "pure" or certain.[4] Yet Plantinga reminds us that such a move is not "new": theologians such as Augustine, Aquinas, John Calvin, and Jonathan Edwards were never in the thrall of "classical foundationalism" and never saw what they were putting forth regarding God and Christianity as something like "the absolute truth" or "the final word." I suspect that we could considerably expand this list, and that gets us to a point that I find generally overlooked in this debate. That point could be put as follows: simply because one states various things about God and salvation with some degree of clarity and certainty does not *necessarily* mean that one is therefore in the business of ontotheology. Although we would need to take up each case one by one, Christian theologians have, I think, generally been all too aware of the complexities of speaking about God in anything like an "adequate" way. Starting with Saint Paul, we get this: "O the depth of the riches and wisdom and knowledge of God! How unsearchable are his judgments and how inscrutable his ways! 'For who has known the mind of the Lord'" (Rom. 11:33–34). Whatever else Paul may have said, this is hardly the voice of someone making any claims to see things *sub specie aeternitatis*. Rather, this is the wholesale denial of any perspective that makes any claims to know "the mind of the Lord." Or consider what John Calvin claims about God's revelation of Godself to us: "For who even of slight intelligence does not understand that, as nurses commonly do with infants, God is wont in a measure to 'lisp' in speaking to us? Thus such forms of speaking do not so much express clearly what God is like as accommodate the knowledge of him to our slight capacity. To do this he must descend far beneath his loftiness."[5] Here Calvin is merely referring to how God speaks about Godself. But this recognition on the part of Calvin is quite startling. For, if *God* has to speak in baby talk to communicate to us truths about Godself, imagine how limited *we* must be in speaking about God. But if Calvin, one of the theologians most thought of as having a kind of "system" and ability to answer all theological questions, goes so far as to cut off at the knees any talk or expectations of "Absolute Knowledge," then it may not be too much to infer that other theologians have likely followed suit. Indeed, the usual criticism of the neo-scholastics who followed Calvin is that they were not circumspect enough in their theological claims. Yet we are left with the following question: Are Saint Paul and Calvin strange exceptions to the rule or are they actually typical? Again, anything remotely resembling a comprehensive answer to this question goes far beyond the scope of this short response. Yet the problem here is that, given the terms of the ontotheology debate, it would seem that theologians are normally considered guilty until proven innocent. But this is an assumption that has no real basis, except for a pervasive underlying suspicion of theologians and Christians in general. However, I am suspicious of this suspicion, and most particularly suspicious of its tendency to consider itself the default position. Instead, I see it as an ungrounded prejudice. In response, I would suggest that not merely charity but also verity should lead us to think that theologians and others who make religious claims are innocent until proven guilty. Yes, I am quite sure that there really are theologians guilty of ontotheology. Yet I contend that, by and large, the Christian tradition has encouraged a healthy appreciation that only God is God and that our abilities to understand God are quite limited. It may be a kind of mantra among some conservative Christians that they have the "absolute truth," yet it does not take all that much inspection to see that such claims are simply unwarranted, nor does it take much inspection to see that such claims are normally made to counter those who have Enlightenment-like pretensions in their denial of Christian truth. Thus, this seems to be a particularly "modern" sort of tendency that particularly (though in no way exclusively) arises when modern pretensions to absolute scientific truth arise. As yet one more coun-terexample, Caputo is fond of quoting Augustine asking "what do I love when I love my God?" That question arises in the following con-text. Augustine first says: "My love for you, Lord, is not an uncertain feeling." Yet then he goes on to say: "But when I love you, what do I love?"[6] Augustine goes on to speak of God in terms of light, sound, fragrance, taste, and an embrace (in short, covering the five senses), affirming these as what he loves but making it clear that these hardly exhaust what it is that he loves. One hardly needs to be a negative theologian to realize that one cannot speak adequately of God.

In sum, having looked at the first side of this dilemma, I have attempted to argue that, when Christians put forth truth-claims about God, they need not *necessarily* be seen as putting them forth as *sub specie aeternitatis* claims. Like anyone, Christians run the risk of seeing their claims as being the "absolute truth." But I am not sure that this is any more a problem for Christians than for, say, the New Atheists, who seem as convinced of the "absoluteness" of their claims as do any conservative Christians. The result is that Simmons's "dilemma" is considerably less problematic than it might at first seem. Yet let us now tend to the other side of the dilemma and see just how seriously it should be taken. Here the problem is one of P-beliefs threatening or disallowing C-beliefs. For instance, if we are to follow Derrida, we should give up ideas of God as "someone" who is "up there." Derrida considers this "idolatrous stereotyping." In response, I have to say that I (almost) completely agree. To think of God as the big grandfather in the sky is to think in a truly idolatrous fashion. Of course, it does not take postmodern analysis to arrive at that conclu-sion: Christian theology has generally been nuanced enough to avoid such simplistic conceptions of God, even if not all believers have had such sophistication. If we follow Caputo, we must think of God as "an open-ended excess and an inaccessible mystery." I do not have any problem with this either, in one sense. Indeed, I am even ready to go so far as to think about God as short-circuiting power. God as hospitality, God as the unforeseen—both of these are fine with me. In effect, I am quite willing to have my thinking about God both challenged and broadened: challenged, because I know that I am an idolater, and broadened, because I am sure that, in whatever way I think of God, it ultimately fails to do justice to who God is. As far as I can see, there is virtually no end to helpful ways of thinking about

God, and thus expanding our notion of God is only appropriate. As helpful as it has been to think of the Trinity in terms of one essence and three persons, I am at least open to the possibility that some future way of talking about the Trinity might emerge as somehow "better."

Yet let me be clear as to exactly where my problem lies. First, as willing as I am to have my thinking about God challenged and broadened, I am equally *unwilling* to give up traditional notions of God.[7] Indeed, my worry here is that, far from being *expanding* images for God, if we are limited to what Derrida and Caputo have prescribed, then we will have a woefully *deficient* conception of God. In other words, I think biblical orthodoxy has considerable room for expanding its images of God, but I see no reason to get rid of all other images. "The grandfather in the sky" needs to go, yet "father images" in general are quite helpful ways of thinking about God. Of course, we have to recognize that these analogies only go so far. Yet that is equally true for God as "mystery" or "the secret" or any other ways of thinking about God. They *too* only go so far. Or, to make this point even more pointedly, let me turn to one of Emmanuel Levinas's well-known passages on God: "God is not simply the 'first other' [*autrui*], the other [*autrui*] par excellence, or the 'absolutely other [*autrui*],' but other than the other [*autre qu-autrui*], other otherwise, other with an alterity prior to the alterity of the other [*autrui*], prior to the ethical bond with the other and different from every neighbor, transcendent to the point of absence, to a point of a possible confusion with the stirring of the *there is* [*il y a*]."[8] It would be ungenerous of me not to recognize the spirit in which this passage is offered. Levinas is to be thanked for working hard to remind us that God is really and truly *other*. Yet I am troubled with this notion of God that is so "other" that God might end up being confused with the *il y a*. This is not because I am so wedded to Christian ways of talking about God. Rather, it is because I find this absolutely other God *simply not enough*. Or, to put this another way: Caputo, Derrida, and Levinas (at least in this passage) all have one thing in common—they give us a God that has, in at least one important sense, the same problem as the God of ontotheology. As Heidegger memorably put it: "Man may never pray to this God, nor may he sacrifice to him. Confronted by the *causa sui*, man may neither sink onto his knees nor could he sing and dance."[9] We Episcopalians are not famous for our dancing (and here Simmons's Pentecostal church might help us out), though bending the knee in prayer and singing are two things for which we are well known. But I do not see myself as praying or singing to the secret or the inaccessible mystery or that which might be mistaken for the *il y a*. That is something we leave to the Unitarians. Instead, even we Episcopalians have a considerably more robust conception of God, though I think it is safe to say that we are a rather circumspective lot and realize that our ways of thinking of God are far from representing anything remotely like "absolute knowledge." Frankly, I think we are as radical as we need to be and, speaking for myself, that's (with apologies to Dennis Rodman) as radical as I *wanna* be.

Yet I wonder if, when all is said and done (as Caputo likes to put it), *any of us* have truly "overcome" ontotheology. To be sure, we can probably overcome the sort of ontotheology that makes *sub specie aeternitatis* claims or makes God out to be the *ens realissimum* or the *causa sui*. Yet now the matter really becomes one of semantics, that is, whether we say we have overcome ontotheology in this strict sense. For the problem remains as follows: if I say *anything* about God, I am certainly claiming that my assertions about God do in *some* way correspond to who God really is. And I suspect that Caputo is doing the same thing, for it is hard to imagine his God-talk as *in no way* reflecting who God is—or else what sense could it possibly have? However much one "allows" the deity to enter into theology or philosophy (and indeed we must admit that we are always in the business of "allowing," to whatever extent—benign or less benign), then it would seem that something like "ontotheology" must come into play to some degree. So we are left with a situation in which, much like Derrida's comment on narcissism,[10] there is no "ontotheology" and "nonontology" (or whatever one wants to call it). To whatever extent God is discussed *in human terms*, I do not see how something like ontotheology can be avoided. At this point, Caputo might suggest that his level of radicality is really what we "need" to achieve some sort of overcoming. However, the difference between his radicality and mine is ultimately the level of specificity of language that can or should be used regarding God. And I do not see that more specificity necessarily equates with more ontotheology.

So where do we go from here? Perhaps we need to work at cultivating a different way of speaking about God, one that has significant precedents in both Jewish and Christian traditions. Westphal is fond of saying that the question is not so much "what" we say about God but "how." I find that distinction helpful. Elsewhere, I have suggested the "how" of *bearing witness*.[11] In the same way that signs point to that which they are not, so we can "testify" to that which we do not control and to the One whom we are not. That does not mean that our ways of talking about God are not going to be colored by our ways of thinking. There is no "pure" theology. But, of course, longing after some kind of pure theology is longing after that which we neither could understand nor would truly want. We simply are not beings who relate to the truth in unmediated terms. Yet we *are* beings who have the possibility to envision what we are doing in different terms. The Hebrew prophets saw themselves as bearing witness or testifying to a word that they had been *given*, not something of which they were the authors or could master. Thus, rather than claiming anything like scientific objectivity, we recognize our proclamation as only imperfectly pointing to the God who is absolute truth. And our speech or *logos* is directed toward the *Logos* in such a way that, much like John the Baptist, we are lowered precisely in the moment of lifting up the One to whom we bear witness.

Chapter 1, Reply 2
Apologetics after Identity?
— A Response to J. Aaron Simmons

Stephen Minister

In his "Apologetics after Objectivity," J. Aaron Simmons makes a compelling case for the legitimacy and necessity of a rational defense of Christianity in continental philosophy of religion and, more broadly, in the lives of Christian believers in a postmodern era. I find little to criticize in this conclusion, and were I Pentecostal, I would probably have exclaimed "Amen!" many times as I was reading the essay. One such place would have been Simmons's insightful and appropriate contrast between Caputo's and Westphal's characterizations of postmodernity's implications for the philosophy of religion. However, though like Simmons I generally side with Westphal in this debate, I would like to push on Simmons's and Westphal's position a bit by challenging the notion of "identity" that Simmons deploys throughout his essay.

Importantly, Simmons sees the tension between Christian faith and postmodern philosophy as rooted on the existential level. His concern is not merely about the logical consistency of certain claims, but about the consistency or integrity of a practical, lived identity. This is not to oppose theoretical belief-claims to a practical, lived identity, but instead to acknowledge that belief-claims play a role in clarifying and constituting our practical, lived identities. So, consistency of our lived identities requires some consistency among the belief-claims related to those identities. But, we can ask, how much consistency or integrity ought we to expect or even desire in our practical, lived identities?

Caputo, in a direct response to Westphal, suggests an answer to this question. He writes: "'I' am a multiplicity of voices competing within me so that what I call the 'I' is at best a shorthand for the one who does the talking.... Being at odds with ourselves is not so much part of being a self, or something we just have to put up with; it is pretty much what we mean by a 'self,' whereas a dull mono-vocal settled self-identity is pretty much what we mean by a post."[1] Caputo thinks that this view of the self is implied by postmodern philosophy and is thus one of the ways in which postmodern philosophy goes beyond merely epistemological or methodological reminders. My purpose here is not to consider whether and how this view of the self is implied by postmodern philosophy; rather, I am interested in the way in which it challenges Simmons's project of reconciling his Christian faith with his postmodern philosophy. Caputo raises this point as a challenge to Westphal's reconciliation of his Christian faith with his postmodern philosophy, but Westphal, perhaps too easily, swats it away.

In a reply to Caputo's criticism, Westphal states simply that he agrees with Caputo's point and goes on to provide biblical backing for this position, citing the confession made by the father of a boy possessed by an evil spirit: "I believe; help my unbelief!" (Mark 9:24).[2] While this confession gives evidence for the possibility of a divided self, a self that both believes and does not believe, the confession does not concede the necessity of a divided self, since it is aimed precisely at overcoming this division. More than that, priority is given to one voice (the believing voice), while the very presence of the second voice is seen as a personal failing that ideally could be overcome. Far from agreeing with Caputo that a multiplicity of voices is "pretty much what we mean by a 'self,'" Westphal's use of this biblical quote seems to suggest that a multiplicity of voices is pretty much what we mean by "lack of faith," maybe even "sin." Be that as it may, in the present context what interests me is not the metaphysics of the self, but the relation between belief-commitments. As noted, the father's confession gives priority to the believing voice over the voice that troubles this belief. Perhaps it is precisely this prioritization that Caputo means to question. The father has his doubts, but he does not really seem to be haunted by the undecidability of the situation. He knows what he ought to believe, even if he cannot bring himself to fully believe it.

For Caputo, the multiplicity of voices undermines this prioritization by denying privilege to any particular voice. The voice of postmodern philosophy is not merely the nephew of Kant's tribunal of reason, patrolling our belief-claims to make sure that they stay within their appropriate limits (fallible, humble, open), but is instead a specter haunting even fallible claims. Caputo suggests this through what he calls the "hauntological" principle, namely, that "we should all be a little spooked by [the thought of our contingency], a little haunted that there are no hooks to lift us above that 'situatedness' or 'contextuality.'"[3] The key point here is that postmodern philosophy for Caputo is not just about acknowledging the contingency of our beliefs, but about *being-haunted* by this contingency. Postmodern philosophy does not merely offer a set of propositions (P-beliefs or EP-beliefs) for our consideration, but attempts to slip one more voice (a still, small voice?) into our internal dialogue, a voice of dissent and questioning, a voice that raises a suspicion of our own religious views sufficient to keep us open to listening to the criticisms and insights of others. The openness to others made possible by the multiplicity of voices within the self and endorsed by the voice of postmodern philosophy indicates the reason that such a multiplicity of voices is, whether or not necessary, ethically desirable. When we do not have voices of uncertainty and suspicion within ourselves, it is hard for us to hear voices of dissent and criticism from outside ourselves. Closing off the voices of dissent within the self runs the risk of closing oneself to the voices of those who disagree with us. Given the contingency of our own beliefs, such a closing of oneself cannot be finally justified.

The upshot of this is that for Caputo postmodernity does not simply remind us how we ought to go about doing Christian theology (fallibly, humbly, openly), but raises the question of whether we ought to be doing *Christian* theology at all. Westphal declines to engage this question when, in his response to Caputo's concern that he too easily takes up traditional metaphysical language to talk about God, he writes, "the goal is not to create an ideal metaphysical system but to be faithful to biblical revelation so far as is humanly possible."[4] But why is this the goal? Does postmodern philosophy's recognition of our contingency not call into question taking this as a goal? Simmons's project similarly seems to assume the priority of his Christian commitments relative to his postmodern commitments. But why doesn't postmodernity question this deeper identity? Is Simmons's identity sufficiently haunted?

For both Westphal and Simmons, their postmodernity seems to be rooted in *and so delimited by* their Christianity. One wonders whether postmodern philosophy simply gives them a vocabulary in which to articulate certain Christian beliefs, beliefs that they were already inclined to endorse anyway, such as, for example, a belief in the noetic effects of sin. It seems to me that the same cannot be said for Caputo (and it certainly cannot be said of Derrida). For Caputo, Christianity and postmodern philosophy are independent voices, which means at the very least that some of the lessons postmodern philosophy has to teach are not already present within Christianity. The presence of two independent voices might leave us with tension, confusion, inconsistency, and paradox at times, but as Johannes Climacus, a shared hero of Simmons, Caputo, and Westphal, puts it, "one must not think ill of the paradox, for the paradox is the passion of thought and a thinker without the paradox is like the lover without passion."[5] A religion *with* religion need not be a religion with everything figured out.

But this is not quite to concede the point to Caputo. Simmons's concern for integrity is not completely frivolous or wrongheaded. Indeed, Caputo's description of the self steers perilously close to an account of certain psychological disorders. Even if we should not expect and ethically dare not try to enforce full consistency within the self, is not some semblance of integrity necessary to distinguish "normal" self-separation from dissociative identity disorder? Moreover, while one can hold inconsistent beliefs or have mixed feelings, actions do not admit of this sort of inconsistency. One either helps the stranger or one does not; one cannot do both. So even if a multiplicity of voices is possible, or even necessary or desirable, one must still act. This returns us directly to Simmons's original concerns: either he participates in his church's worship service or he does not, either he writes in defense of postmodern philosophy or he does not. If he is to both participate in his church's worship service and write in defense of postmodern philosophy, there must be "enough" consistency to allow him to maintain a normal semblance of integrity. This is why Simmons's argument for consistency matters, even if it tends to make the situation of postmodern Christians a bit too neat, a bit too univocal, not quite haunted enough.

To my mind, the above considerations do nothing to undermine the possibility of, but actually intensify the need for, the postmodern Christian apologetics that Simmons's envisions. Why do *Christian* theology? Why attend *Pentecostal* worship services? The haunting voice that wonders whether these beliefs and practices are simply the result of one's particular upbringing calls for a response. But it is not clear to me that this response presupposes a fully consistent belief-set. Can one not explain one's reasons for holding certain beliefs and partaking in certain practices, including reasons rooted in testimonial experience, while also holding other beliefs that would call into question or suggest reinterpretations of those beliefs and practices? I need not foundationally prove beliefs before bringing them into public debate, and similarly I need not prove their consistency with my other beliefs before exposing them to the light of day. Even, and perhaps especially, when we are doing apologetics, philosophical reasoning is not simply a matter of reporting our fully justified and consistent conclusions to others, with argumentative or testimonial evidence as necessary, but is rather the ongoing task of thinking through our experience together.

Two

Faith Seeking Understanding

Stephen Minister

onstruct a theology, and you will have a theology. Deconstruct a theology, and you will also have a theology. Whether you construct a theology or deconstruct a theology, you will have a theology either way. Construct an ethics, and you will have an ethics. Deconstruct an ethics, and you will also have an ethics. Whether you construct an ethics or deconstruct an ethics, you will have an ethics either way. This is the quintessence of all John Caputo's religious writings.

Though Kierkegaard's young aesthete may have been overly cynical about the significance of our choices in life, I would like to suggest that Caputo is overly optimistic in thinking that his deconstructive approach to religion, his theology without theology and an-ethics without ethics, offers us a genuine either/or with the strong theologies and ethical theories he criticizes. To be sure, Caputo's theology and religious ethics differ from orthodox theologies and ethics, but I think these differences are simply theological and ethical differences and not a matter of departing from theology or ethics as such. My goal herein is not to refute or reject Caputo's religious work. In fact, I like his account of religion very much. As I read his work, I find myself saying, "Oui, oui! Amen!" precisely because I agree with most of his theology and his religious ethics. My point is to confess that this is what his work is. Not "almost" a theology, not a "theology without theology," but theology straight up.[1] Such an admission need not be bad news, since this admission frees us to theologize and theorize about ethics, articulating our views on God and justice, without the encumbrance of having to take back in one breath, what we uttered in the previous one. This need not lead to the demise of critical thought and conversation, but simply seeks to find a balance between the need for deconstruction and the need for determinate belief, a need that Caputo undoubtedly recognizes.

When it comes to religion, none of us knows *for sure* what we are talking about. I happily concur with Caputo on this point. Religion is a faith-based enterprise and so the theologizing and ethical theorizing that come out of it cannot claim to be indubitable knowledge. To my mind, this calls us not only to a Derridean deconstruction of religion, but also to theological and ethical argumentation, stating our positions and giving reasons for them, which Derrida himself confesses is absent from his work.[2] After all, we all have theological and ethical positions, which is to say that our lives and actions express beliefs about God and ethical values. Since ours is always a life lived with others, we ought to be honest about these beliefs and values, be willing to articulate them to others, and be open to others' responses, both critical and constructive. This is not a strategy for going beyond faith, but simply a return to Anselm's task, the task (as Johannes Climacus would say) for a whole lifetime: *faith seeking understanding*.

This essay will consider some of the contours of this task. I begin with Caputo's writings on religion, which I think are at work on this task, though I am unsure whether Caputo would put it that way himself. In the first two sections, I suggest that Caputo's theology without theology and an-ethics without ethics comprise theological and ethical positions of the same sort that he wants to distance himself from. I also suggest that his reluctance to clearly, rigorously lay out his positions and the arguments for them, renders his deep insights less helpful than they could be. My goal here is simply to indicate some points where I see tension or ambiguity that seems to me to be unnecessary. In response to these criticisms, the third and final section of the paper reconsiders the relationship between reason and revelation, arguing that revelation (the event) calls us to reason, albeit a sort of reason different from what modern philosophy or even premoderns like Anselm had in mind. Here certain themes from the work of Alain Badiou, Emmanuel Levinas, and Chantal Mouffe are introduced to help us think through this relationship. My goal in bringing in these thinkers is not to reject Caputo's project, since his project is one I largely endorse, but instead to clarify and so strengthen certain points within that project that I find ambiguous or unconvincing.

My primary concern is not that "religion without religion" is a bad idea, but that Caputo's "religion without religion" seems to emphasize the "without" more than the "religion." Perhaps this is necessary given the fact that religions generally have neglected the "without," but I worry that an overemphasis on the "without" makes the pendulum swing too far in the opposite direction. My goal is to think about whether a better balance can be struck between the "religion" and the "without religion."[3] As Aristotle reminds us, finding the balance is very difficult, so I do not presume that this essay has it all figured out, nor that we will ever have it all figured out, nor that having it all figured out is even really the point in life. Nonetheless, I do think religion needs the search for understanding, which is to say that it needs theology and ethics. Rather than trying to distance ourselves from these fields, we should, as responsible faith (and deconstruction itself?) demands, embrace them.

CAPUTO'S THEOLOGY

Caputo's advocacy of a religion without religion indicates that there is an aspect of religion that he approves of while there are other aspects about which he worries. What he approves of is the way in which religions call us to the love of God, that is, to commit ourselves unconditionally to something beyond our self-interest and understanding. What is it that we are committed to when we love God? This Caputo thinks is the critical question of religion, to which no decisive, fully justified answer can ever be given. Caputo points out that if we are honest with ourselves, none of us has certain insight into who or what God is and thus the descriptions of God proliferate: God is love, truth, beauty, justice, and so on. Consistent with this view, Caputo's own descriptions of the good part of religion proliferate as well. So he talks about "the event," the transformational moment in which we are overtaken by that which is beyond being and beyond our horizon of expectations, but which cannot be adequately contained or uniquely described in human language. As he puts it repeatedly, the event is not *what happens,* but what is *going on in* what happens. This helps bring out the point that religious commitment, the love of God, is rooted not in the autonomous decision of a rational subject, but in something that happens to us, in unexpected moments of passivity. Caputo also uses the notion of the "kingdom of God," drawn from the New Testament, as one possible name for the event. This indicates the unexpected and anarchic character of the justice that calls us to action. These characterizations reinforce Caputo's view of religious faith as an ongoing journey of openness to the unpredictability and goodness, that is, the transcendence, of what we name "God."

Caputo is rightly concerned that religious institutions all too often try to cover over this uncertainty and indeterminacy by defining specifically what or who God is, how we as humans can know God, and how we ought to live. This is the part of religion about which Caputo worries. The event demands nomination, that is, descriptions that allow us to communicate about, remember, and consider the event. Yet these names never fully capture the event, which, after all, is not something to be captured but something that captures us. Moreover, the names given to the event are not themselves given by the event, but are *our* responses to the event. Not only are the tools we have for describing the event inadequate, but they are also *our* tools, humanly constructed languages and meanings. Upon these meanings we have built determinate traditions with ceremonies, literatures, theologies, moral systems, and administrative hierarchies to oversee all these constructions. As Caputo rightly points out, were an individual born into a different time or a different context, these determinacies would likely be very different. However, being rooted in the event, religion is not merely a human construct, but it is in part a human construct. Even when it is based on sacred texts, we must take responsibility both for the choice of sacred texts and the interpretations we make of those texts.

At their best, determinate religious traditions remind us of the love of God and help us hear the call of the kingdom of God, but at their worst they become ends-in-themselves, replacing God as the object of our love. When this happens we fall into idolatry, clinging to and worshiping our own human constructions, whether institutional, theological, or ethical. In addition to the violence this does to genuine faith, Caputo is rightly concerned that it all too easily turns into violence toward others. When one clings to and worships a religious tradition, it is all too easy to elevate that tradition's claims to the status of incontrovertible knowledge so as to justify one's unquestioned commitment. When these historically contingent, humanly constructed claims are regarded as obvious and provable to any honest, rational person, those who go on denying these claims can only be regarded as irrational, immoral, or otherwise recalcitrant to God's truth and the true way of life. The potential for violence this stirs up is particularly worrisome for Caputo as he thinks that the call to love God is intimately connected with the call to justice and to the love of others.

As a response to this danger Caputo suggests, "We must keep a hammer handy for these idols and be ready to theologize with a hammer—in the name of God. The idea is not to level these structures to the ground, because we need them, the way we need other structures made with human hands, but to keep them open-ended, revisable, honest."[4] The hammer Caputo likes to keep handy is deconstruction. Caputo describes deconstruction as "a theory of *truth,* in which truth spells *trouble.*...[It is] meant to expose the contingency of what we like to call the 'Truth,' with a capital T," while calling attention to "the truth of the event" (*WWJD* 30). Deconstruction reminds us of the historical contingency of determinate religious traditions, of the role of humanly constructed meanings and human decisions in the construction of "orthodoxy." The goal here is not destructive or nihilistic, to reduce all structures of meaning to nothingness, but to refocus us on the event rather than on the names we give it. Thus Caputo says that though the church is deconstructible, the kingdom of God is not. Clearly then, Caputo is not out to get rid of religion, but to combat the idolatry of religion. Deconstruction reminds us that our religious beliefs and practices are not a matter of knowledge or objective certainty, but of faith, a faith rooted in the event of being grasped by that which is beyond us, not taking charge over those around us. Hence, Caputo writes that, "Deconstruction...is not a determinate position, a definite 'what' or worldview with a manifesto, or a platform or a set of positions....It provides an unsettling reminder about how to hold any given position, about how not to hold any given position, about not holding it in too settled a way with too much complacency and self-assurance, and about allowing ourselves to be held" (55).

So far, so good. Caputo makes these points brilliantly and compellingly. I can only echo, "Oui, oui! Amen!"

So far we have seen that Caputo raises two problems for religious traditions, namely, that they are always inadequate representatives of the event they harbor and that their believers tend to forget this, thinking they possess knowledge rather than faith. Caputo tells us that because of these problems, because "the *event* that is astir in the name of God cannot be contained by the historical contingency of the names I have inherited in my tradition," he "maintains a certain ironic distance from strong theologies, which in a certain sense are the only theologies that 'exist,' that are found in concrete historical communities" (*WG* 9). Given the argument thus far, this seems like a curious leap. After all, plenty of traditional religious thinkers argue that our historically contingent names for God are inadequate and a matter of faith, while engaging directly in theology and concrete historical communities. Ibn Sina (Avicenna), Thomas Aquinas, and Moshe ben Maimon (Moses Maimonides) are only the most obvious names to come to mind. Ben Maimon goes so far as to claim that he who ascribes positive attributes to God "has abolished his belief in the existence of the deity without being aware of it," and yet he did not maintain a certain ironic distance from the Jewish tradition.[5] Sensitivity to these two problems is not limited to the Medieval period or academic theologians. Indeed I was first taught to be on guard against these problems in the youth group of the conservative, evangelical church I grew up in (though without all the language of deconstruction of course).

Perhaps I have missed the reasoning that justifies Caputo's move, but I wonder if this move is rooted in the modernist suspicion toward particularity. Here I have in mind Descartes's conviction that getting at the truth requires going beyond the particularity of one's culture since the particular amounts to the parochial. To be sure, Caputo undeniably has broken with Descartes's project and argues explicitly that the event shows up and in a certain sense is maintained by the particular religious traditions. Caputo is definitely not a Cartesian. And yet, I am not sure how else to make sense of maintaining a "certain ironic distance" from determinate religious traditions, if not because of a suspicion of particularity itself. If this is right (and I am open to the possibility that it might not be), then the problem of violence is rooted in not just *how* we believe (i.e., that determinate religions are dangerous because we tend to forget they are based in faith), but in *what* we believe itself, or more to the point, *that* we believe one thing rather than another. The root of the problem would then be the very determinateness of religious traditions, a determinateness that not only puts limits on that which is uncontainable (the event), but that is exclusionary and so violent as such. All determination is negation, so the claim that God is something in particular is meaningful only because it simultaneously asserts that God is *not* something else. The determinate affirmations of religious traditions render them essentially exclusionary, since their affirmations amount to negations of other religious traditions. If this is right, then for Caputo, genuine faith would seem to require not only recognizing the limits of our knowledge, but also eschewing or at least regarding with suspicion *any* determinate theological beliefs. Hence "a certain ironic distance." Hence, "theology without theology."

Perhaps this is an expansion of Rousseau's view of theological exclusivity. As Rousseau wrote, "Those who distinguish between civil and theological intolerance are mistaken, in my opinion. Those two types of intolerance are inseparable. It is impossible to live in peace with those one believes to be damned."[6] The religious claim to exclusivity, that is, the claim that one's religion is the only true religion, damages the social unity necessary for a cohesive, functioning body politic. Rousseau thought that people committed to religions that claimed exclusivity would inevitably turn to violent and discriminatory means when efforts at converting the uninitiated fail, thereby undermining peaceable social existence. Because Rousseau recognized the irreversible fact of religious pluralism, he argues that "tolerance should be shown to all those that tolerate others.... But whoever dares to say 'outside [this] church there is no salvation' ought to be expelled from the state."[7] Hence, a just, peaceful society requires the rejection of theological exclusivity. Caputo seems to reprise Rousseau's position, reiterating his logic while greatly generalizing the scope of theological censure. Theological exclusivity is to be avoided since it leads to violence, but, Caputo seems to add, *every* meaningful, determinate theological claim constitutes an exclusion.

Despite this necessary violence, Caputo is not prepared to give up on determinate religious traditions. However, he does suggest that we need to reconsider how we think about them. Caputo claims that all religious traditions are inspired by and attempt to express the love of God or the event, though none of them are able to do this adequately. Because of this inadequacy, he urges us to abandon questions about which religion is the true or right one, a question he regards as "not only wrong-headed and non-sensical...[but] also impious, irreligious, and insolent" (*OR* 131). All religions are "true" insofar as they point to the event, but "false" insofar as they get us focused on rituals, theologies, moral systems, church politics, etc. Rather than thinking of religious truth on the model of scientific or mathematical truth where only one theory can be right, we should think of it on the model of literary truth where many works of literature, despite telling different fabricated stories, can all contain elements of truth (110; *WG* 118). What matters most is not which religious narrative is right, since that requires us to understand religion at the level of representational truth, but these narratives' capacity to point us beyond themselves to the kingdom of God. This is also, Caputo tells us, how we should understand his religious writings. His theology without theology is a theology without logos, what he calls a "theopoetics." Whereas a logic is "a normative discourse governing entities (real or possible)," a poetics is "an evocative discourse that articulates the event" (*WG* 103). Thus Caputo takes his work as a theopoetics to be an evocative discourse aimed at pointing us toward the event that is harbored in the name of God. However, I would suggest that even as a theopoetics, Caputo's work invites us, exhorts us, calls on us to adopt certain determinate theological principles and to exclude other principles. If correct, this suggestion would complicate the distinction Caputo makes between his "weak theology," his theology without theology, and the "strong theologies" he criticizes.

To begin with, his view of truth seems to require a rejection of any claim to special revelation. Caputo acknowledges as much, arguing that special revelation "sounds much more like our ways, not God's, our own very unmysterious and human all too human ethnocentrism and egocentrism, our own nationalism and narcissism, our own sexism, racism, and self-love writ large, in short, a gross human weakness that is being passed off as a Great Divine Attribute. The *nerve* of some people!" (*OR* 114). While I readily concur that special revelation smacks of ethnocentrism—as Richard Rorty puts it, "the postulation of deities who turn out, by a happy coincidence, to have chosen *us* as their people"[8]—how does Caputo know that making a universal appeal through a historically singular event is "not God's" way? Given his emphasis on divine inscrutability, it is difficult for me to see how we could know this. Moreover, Johannes Climacus gives an extended argument for the exact opposite case, that a God revealing God-self in a particular time and place is a great offense to our human ways and a mystery—Climacus's word is paradox—to human reason.[9] Caputo counsels openness toward God but does not seem open to the possibility of special revelation. This also makes me wonder whether there is any significance to the choice of Jesus in Caputo's question "what would Jesus deconstruct?" If Jesus does not constitute a unique moment or special revelation, does it matter that it is Jesus deconstructing? Would the Buddha deconstruct different things, perhaps the individuated self? Do we need a particular religious reference at all, since such references only tend to obscure the event and, as we are told, deconstruction happens and is not something one does, presumably not even Jesus (*WWJD* 29)? Should the question simply be, "What would deconstruct?" My point here is not to defend the idea of special revelation, nor to defend any particular claims to revelation, but simply to point out that to deny special revelation is to assert a determinate theological claim, and more specifically, a claim about God.

Though Caputo makes clear that the second-order "theology" he endorses makes no sense without the first-order determinate faith traditions, he here seems to be very close to an error common among those who attempt to articulate a religious pluralism. In an effort to regard all religions as legitimate, one can so significantly reinterpret religion that few religious believers would recognize the religion they practice. For most Jews, Christians, and Muslims, the uniqueness of Moses, Jesus, or the Prophet are not obscure bits of theology, but beliefs that are central to their religious faith. So instead of legitimating their religion, Caputo's apparent suggestion that the religious abandon these beliefs cannot help but be received by many as an existential threat to their faith. In the end, Caputo's view seems closer to a religious inclusivism, the theory that there is only one true religion, for Caputo the religion of the event or of the love of God, but that this one true religion can be accessed and lived out through a variety of religious traditions. However, on this reading, Caputo would be attempting to articulate the one true theology, however minimal, or at least some fundamental theological points (e.g., the love of God is about doing justice), which determinate religious traditions embody

more or less well. What is crucial is not the representational particu-
larities of these traditions, but the general nonrepresentational truths
that underlie them. These general truths can then be used to criticize
the particular traditions, pointing out the places where the particular
traditions are unfaithful to the general truths. This can quickly begin
to sound like a reduction of the other, the diversity of practices and
beliefs, to the same, the one fundamental truth that underlies and in
some cases overrules the diversity.

As an example of such criticism of a particular religious tradition,
we could consider Caputo's treatment of fundamentalism, a religious perspective that Caputo thinks has disastrously lost sight of the
event.[10] Though Caputo argues that all religious traditions contain
truth and is very critical of institutional religion for attempting to
manage faith by discriminating between the orthodox and the heterodox, thereby standing as judge over whose faith counts as legitimate,
Caputo himself seems to repudiate the faith of persons he regards
as fundamentalists. Such people, Caputo claims, have replaced the
love of God with the love of their own "determinate set of beliefs
and practices" (*OR* 107). Caputo rejects fundamentalism for both
its lack of fallibilism and its specific theological and ethical positions
(102–04). Fundamentalism, according to Caputo, is "a failure to see
that the love of God is uncontainable and can assume uncountable
and unaccountably different forms" (107), though apparently not the
form assumed by fundamentalism.

While I completely agree with Caputo's condemnation of fundamentalism as dangerous to its practitioners and everyone else, what
is significant is the fact that even Caputo's attempt at religious inclusivity cannot help but define itself through the exclusion of certain
theological positions. This exclusion is assured when Caputo admits
even that he *loves* certain determinate beliefs and practices. Referring
to "the defining idea of modernity," the idea that we have the rights
to freedom of thought and speech, Caputo says, "I love that idea
very much" (*OR* 62). As for the "postmodern idea," that there is no
pure reason, "that idea I *also* love" (62). My point is not to criticize
Caputo for being committed to certain determinate ideas—indeed
I share Caputo's dedication to these ideas—but rather to encourage
us not to be squeamish about such commitments, attempting to hide
them behind repeated claims of epistemic limitation. These points of

tension in Caputo's theology indicate that even the attempt to articulate a religion without religion must be committed to determinate, exclusive beliefs about God, sacred texts, and religious practices. So much the better.[11]

As I see it, Caputo's work may be a theopoetics, but it is a theopoetics *with* theology. Short of abandoning religion, there is no escaping theology. Because of this, I think we should stop talking about theology without theology, a theology that pretends to take away with one hand what the other has given, that tries to carve out an (a)logical space in which we can maintain a "certain ironic distance" from theology. Caputo presents us with a powerful and compelling theology. I do not think there is really anything detrimental about recognizing it as such. I do not think we postmoderns need to feel guilty about having theological positions, as if they were akin to "a weakness for sex or money" (*WG* 1). Instead, a better response to the contingent, exclusive, and potentially violent nature of our theological commitments is to bring them out in the open and expose them to the responses and criticisms of others, especially those with whom we disagree. More on this in the final section of the essay.

Caputo's Religious Ethics

For a long time now, Caputo has been against ethics. Caputo thinks ethics suffers from the same sorts of defects as theology since it reduces the uncontainable event (obligation or responsibility to others) to a few snappy principles or virtues or commandments. These guidelines make us feel like we have things all figured out and *know* how we ought to live, but in reality amount to humanly constructed generalizations that neglect the particularity of lived situations. Instead of ethics, Caputo favors a "poetics of obligation," which he has since supplemented with an anarchic an-ethics of the kingdom.[12] In this section, I will suggest that Caputo's an-ethics of the kingdom, his attempt at a sort of ethics without ethics, is in fact an ethics with ethics. As above, my concern is not to criticize his ethics, which again I find quite compelling, but simply to try to recognize it as such.

Caputo claims that if there were an "ethics" of the kingdom of God, it would be an an-ethics since it would not be based on a universal, fixed principle (an *arche*), but on an-archy (*WG* 133–46).

Drawing on Jesus' claim that "the last will be first, and the first will be last" (Matt. 20:16) and Paul's assertion that "God chose what is low and despised in the world, things that are not [*ta me onta*], to reduce to nothing things that are [*ta onta*]" (1 Cor. 1:28), Caputo argues that the kingdom of God revolves around reversals of the prevailing order. Thus he writes: "The kingdom of God obeys the law of reversals in virtue of which *whatever* is first is last, *whatever* is out is in, *whatever* is lost is saved" (*WG* 14). Later he remarks, "One of the most interesting events, or laws of the event, in the New Testament is that the out are in and the in are out" (133). Of course Caputo is not recommending that we constantly switch sides to support whatever happens to be the underdog at the moment; rather, he clarifies that these reversals are not literal, rigid principles, but strategic exhortations that "are meant to counterbalance an effect that is currently tilted in the opposite direction, because in the kingdom God is not against anyone" (134). Being out is not a good in itself (for surely that would not make any sense according to the deconstructive prohibition against such notions), but is rather a succinct poetic way to indicate the irrelevance of the humanly constructed social order while reminding us to attend to those this order neglects. But then, on the next page, Caputo claims that "In the kingdom of God, one valorizes difference, alterity, being out, being nothing in the eyes of the world; the most account is taken of those who are of no account whatsoever" (135). There seems to be a tension here, with Caputo at times emphasizing that God is not against anyone and at other times emphasizing the priority of those who are out, that God is for some more than others. Caputo repeats this tension throughout his work, at times privileging the outsiders (or those who attend to the needs of the outsiders) and at other times emphasizing the equality of the kingdom, which is, ostensibly, given to us by grace. Taking this tension as a clue, I would like to consider three ambiguities that confront Caputo's use of strategic reversals. Perhaps these ambiguities do nothing to diminish the poetic value of his strategic reversals, but I think they raise problems for connecting the poetic evocations to practical action. Given Caputo's overriding concern for *facere veritatem*, doing the truth, I would think this might be of some concern for him.

What or Who

The first has to do with distinguishing *what* is out and *who* is out. As the quotations in the previous paragraph indicate, Caputo sometimes claims that in the kingdom of God *whatever* is out is in, while at other times, the reversal is formulated as *whoever* is out is in. Though Caputo more often seems to have the latter formulation in mind, he employs the former when considering the question of gay rights. Caputo suggests that if Jesus were around today, he would support gay rights. Part of Caputo's argument for this is that "Jesus systematically took the side of the outsider, of those who are excluded and marginalized" (*WWJD* 109). I strongly support gay rights, but I do not think this is a helpful argument for gay rights since this claim trades on the ambiguity between the what and the who. Though Jesus certainly associates with and cares for outsiders, the *who*s, it is not at all clear that he takes "the side of the outsider," in the sense of supporting *what* the outsider has done, what it is that makes the outsider an outsider. So, Jesus shows care toward women who are prostitutes, but obviously no one, and certainly not Caputo, is claiming that this is an endorsement of prostitution. Jesus looks forward to being in paradise with one of the criminals being crucified next to him, but he does not make a case for this man's innocence. Even when Jesus saves the woman caught in adultery from being stoned, it is not on account of his support for open marriages, but an account of the guilt of all. These cases can be used to support the claim that in the kingdom of God, *whoever* is out is in, but not the claim that *whatever* is out is in. At best, they remind us *who* we ought to be standing with, but not *what* we ought to be standing for. Perhaps this, and no more, is what Caputo's reversals are meant to indicate, but I worry that the use of "whatever" instead of "whoever" introduces an unhelpful ambiguity. Rather than appealing to this strategic reversal, why not go straight to the good arguments that exist for gay rights, which Caputo, apparently leaving the poetics behind, also sometimes does (109–12). Once we've done this, it becomes clear that we should stand for gay rights, not simply because gays are out, "excluded and marginalized," but because there is nothing wrong with being gay. Being gay is not a *what* that should be out.

Out or In

The first ambiguity plunges us straightaway into the second problem with this strategic reversal. Who exactly is out anyway? At present, the difficulty that can accompany this determination is again evidenced in the debate over gay rights. Are gays and lesbians currently in or out? For the social liberal, it is obvious that they are out given the numerous state laws banning same-sex marriage, the lack of civil rights protections, and the stereotyping, harassment, and even violence which gays and lesbians suffer. Meanwhile, social conservatives complain that the problem is precisely that homosexuality is in, pointing to the growing social acceptance of gays, lesbians, and same-sex relationships, the favorable portrayal of gays and lesbians in the media, the "activist" judges who have legalized same-sex marriage, and the presence of openly gay pastors, priests, and bishops. In the debate over gay rights, both sides think that they are swimming against the tide, pushing back against the strong cultural forces arrayed against them. The irony is that Caputo's strategy of reversal is quite happily at home within fundamentalism. As Caputo acknowledges elsewhere, "The 'world,' the present age, the *saeculum*, seems quite mad to the fundamentalist mind" (*OR* 101). "Sodomy" and abortion are protected by law, while prayer in school is illegal. Divorce and drugs have become commonplace and AIDS continues to spread. Yet when the fundamentalist fights for what is out, for the criminalization of homosexuality, for the "rights of the unborn," for prayer in school, or at least abstinence-only sexual education, Caputo calls this reactionary religious imperialism from people who are unwilling to accept the contemporary pluralistic and high-tech world, that is, unwilling to accept the way things are (105–06; cf. *WWJD* 116). While I certainly agree that we ought to condemn fundamentalism, I am not convinced that strategic reversals help here. Though fundamentalists are much-maligned at present, they apparently do not count as outsiders who are in. Fundamentalists, it seems, cannot even win for losing.

   Instead, Caputo's list of outsiders seems to be populated by precisely those groups liberal intellectuals (myself included) love to love: "gays and lesbians, illegal immigrants, unwed mothers, the HIV-positive, drug addicts, prisoners, and, after 9/11, Arabs" (*WG* 133). Elsewhere Caputo includes the poor, blacks, and women, though he specifically excludes "ruthless billionaires, pederasts, and homicidal rapists," despite the very bad opinion most of us have of such persons (*WG* 137). It is not that we do not have a responsibility to these persons, we do, but, Caputo adds, "this responsibility does not consist in accommodating and affirming their actions but in restraining their violence and changing their hearts. The kingdom is for sinners, the lost sheep, but that does not mean affirming and encouraging sin" (137). Fair enough, but I am not sure how this distinguishes these persons from drug addicts and prisoners. Surely our responsibility to them does not consist in accommodating and affirming their actions. The exclusion of pederasts seems particularly puzzling as it is difficult to imagine a group that is at present more socially hated or legally discriminated against than those who commit sexual crimes against children. In addition to the shame and incarceration that come with a conviction for such crimes, the use of life-long public registries after incarceration permanently brands a person as a child sexual offender, making it more difficult to find and keep a job and often leading to harassment or violence. Jean Genet's branding as a "thief" seems tame by comparison.[13] This is not to deny the severe damage caused by pederasty, but simply to sharpen the question to Caputo of how we distinguish between who is out and who is in. As I think Caputo would agree, this poetic phrase only has practical significance when it is concretized, when we start making judgments about who is out and who is not. If this distinction is not to be arbitrary, then there must be some general reasons for making it in one way rather than another. Caputo seems to concede such a basis for this distinction in the form of a peculiar understanding of alterity.

The kingdom of God, Caputo claims, is organized around alterity, difference or singularity, rather than universality, at least a certain sense of universality. Caputo retains the claim that the kingdom of God has universal scope or appeal, it is open to everyone, but denies that it has any universal content. Instead, the kingdom of God is universal in scope precisely because it appeals to individuals in their singularity. "The event itself that was being universally preached was the sacredness of each singular one, each one in his or her an-archic singularity, precisely insofar as they tend to drop out from universal schemata" (*WG* 134). It is not clear to me how this squares with Paul's claim, which Caputo associates with kingdom universality, that "there is no longer Jew or Greek, there is no longer slave or free, there is no longer male or female; for all of you are one in Christ Jesus"

(Gal. 3:28). This statement affirms a universal identity abstracted from difference, rather than affirming differences, which would require the claim that in the kingdom there is both Jew and Greek (and Muslim, Hindu, African, Latino, etc.), both male and female (and intersex, transgendered, etc.), both slave and free (though this is one difference we are hoping to eradicate).

This concern notwithstanding, Caputo takes the kingdom of God to be organized around alterity. He goes on to clarify this concept, writing that, "the biblical and the deconstructionist notion of 'alterity' is focused on the *qualitatively* other, which is not the same as the *quantitatively* other. It picks out the out-of-power and dispossessed . . . the *me onta* who suffer from their otherness . . . alterity refers to the victims not the victimizers. . . . It refers to those who are ground under by the system, crushed by their alterity" (*WG* 137). The kingdom of God is focused on victims, victims of "the system." It is on this basis that Caputo purports to exclude ruthless billionaires, pederasts, and homicidal rapists, that is, the victimizers, while including drug addicts and prisoners, that is, the victims. But one could ask whether this distinction holds in a way that is really helpful for social action. After all, drug addicts victimize their families by their unreliability, absenteeism, wasteful spending, and potential incarceration. Given the high percentage of pederasts who were themselves sexually abused, are not most pederasts also victims? It is not at all clear to me that we can neatly separate the victims from the victimizers, those who are out-of-power from those with power. While granting that some types of victimization are much more damaging than others, is it not part of Paul's message that all have been victimizers and fallen short of the glory of God (Rom. 3:23)? While some of the people Jesus reached out to were undoubtedly the victims of unjust social systems, such as the women forced into prostitution or lepers whose physical illness was compounded by social ostracization and religious condemnation, it is difficult to make that case for Zacchaeus, the Roman Centurion, or the prodigal son. It is hard to feel much sympathy for a rich kid with loving parents who blows his trust fund through wild parties and stupendous mismanagement. Yet the fatted calf is slaughtered even for these. My point here is not to deny the very difficult situations some people find themselves in, nor to justify the callousness that many "religious" people show toward those in need, but simply to try to get to the bottom of Caputo's talk about alterity, difference, and being out.

This attempt at understanding runs into a further snag when we consider Caputo's claims about what constitutes membership in the kingdom of God.[14] Sometimes Caputo appears to favor universal inclusivity, as when he writes, "whether one is a Jew or a non-Jew, master or slave, male or female, none of that makes any difference. The kingdom is everybody's" (*WG* 261). But in the very next paragraph, it seems like some of these distinctions do make a difference: "when it comes to getting into the kingdom, there is actually a certain privileging of the outsider, a strategic reversal meant to make a point about the kingdom. The conditions of admission to the kingdom are quite unaccountable: the ones who get *in* are the ones who are *out*" (261–62). Elsewhere Caputo sharpens this distinction, suggesting not just a privileging of the outsider, but an exclusion of the insider: "The kingdom belongs to the unwashed, not to aristocratic Greeks or to the healthy, well-fed bourgeoisie of modern Christianity" (133). What happened to Jews *and* Greeks, slaves *and* free? Complicating the situation further, it sometimes seems that kingdom membership is not a matter of being an insider or an outsider at all, but about helping outsiders. In this vein Caputo claims, "My hypothesis is that making the truth happen, *doing* hospitality, is what *constitutes* membership in the kingdom" (268), and "the kingdom is filled with people who never heard of the kingdom or do not want to hear about it, but who forswear power and swing wide the doors of hospitality" (277). So then it would seem that the kingdom is populated by the hospitable. But again, Caputo immediately makes such a conclusion difficult to maintain. "Who then is *in?* According to the beautiful poetics of the impossible, the outsiders are in, the ones who have no papers to present . . . [ones who are] gay and not so gay, black and not so black, repentant and not so repentant, male and female, orthodox and heterodox, constructionists and deconstructionists, theists and atheists, religionists and religion-without-religionists" (278). Now we seem to be back to the universalist view that the kingdom includes everyone.

What accounts for this ambiguity? I can't help but wonder if in the absence of an ethical account of justice, Caputo gets caught between three plausible commitments: (1) a commitment to be faithful to the kingdom of God parables that give preference to outsiders, "both good and bad" (Matt. 22:10); (2) a commitment to encourage hospitality, especially toward outsiders; and, (3) a commitment to be inclusive, to avoid the violence and exclusivity that normally come with determinate religion. Though all three commitments are worth taking seriously, it is unclear how Caputo's attempt to hold all three together can work in the way he suggests. What we end up with is a theopoetics where at best ambiguities, and at worst inconsistencies, proliferate. I am not convinced that these ambiguities can be defended by pointing to the madness of the kingdom of God, a madness as mad as any party Lewis Carroll's hatter ever threw, as Caputo likes to remind us. Instead, what we need is a straightforward account of justice that is attentive to all, but also demanded of all. I think this will require withdrawing ethical significance from the distinctions between outsiders and insiders and between outsiders and those who offer them hospitality.

Possibilities for Power

The final ambiguity that arises from Caputo's strategic reversal is the reluctance to defend some things that are in. As I have already mentioned, Caputo's denouncement of power, the powers-that-be, what is, seems to commit him to a critical stance toward whatever is in. However, while acknowledging the harmful inequalities that persist between men and women, we must also celebrate the achievements of the women's rights movements in the twentieth century, such as securing for women the right to vote, legal protections against spousal abuse and marital rape, and the legal requirement of equality in education. These changes are achievements precisely because they were codified in law, accepted by the powers-that-be, even if enforcement of some of them remains problematic. These are laws that I am in no hurry to deconstruct. Or consider the notion of "equal protection under the law," a universalizing formula that abstracts from the singularity of persons. While this notion may be directly contrary to the view of justice as attentive to singularity, its value in fighting the injustice of discrimination is undeniable. While Caputo at times recognizes that there can be no justice without law, I worry that his seemingly disproportionate focus on the fact that law can never achieve justice discourages us from recognizing the ways in which the powers-that-be may already be serving justice.

Caputo's critique of being and presence leads him to a deep pessimism about what is, what's in, the powers-that-be, what Paul calls *ta onta*. Caputo seems so committed to pointing out that no concrete, determinate institution is completely just that all existing institutions, both the better and worse, get tarred with the same brush. As existing institutions they all share in "the disastrous concept of power" (*WWJD* 88). But why think power is disastrous? This ethical judgment seems to derive from the view of justice and violence that Caputo picks up from Derrida. Referring to Derrida's work on religion, Caputo writes that justice is only accomplished in "a relation without relation, punctuated by distance and respect.... Violence always crosses the distance of the other who commands a halt, violates the space of the other."[15] This view of violence seems to curiously retain the modernist conception of autonomous agency. While antihumanism and poststructuralism precipitate the death of the autonomous subject, the discourse of alterity resurrects the notion of autonomy in the bodies of others.[16] Thus violence seems to be the result of any infringement on the autonomy of others, the space in which the other is sovereign. Hence power, which is necessarily power over, power to which someone is subject, is disastrous.

This condemnation of power leads Caputo to rhetoric that seems to portray human life as a battle between the evil, heavy, self-interested power of "the world" and the good, light, other-centered weak force of "the kingdom of God." But of course, the strong distinction between "the world" and "the kingdom" comes undone, is deconstructed, by the aforementioned social progress and legal protections that increase justice. Instead of defining the kingdom of God in opposition to the powers of the world, I think we would be better off recognizing that the kingdom of God is incarnate in precisely those moments when our powers, individual and collective, are bent to the good, to the service of others, rather than to our own narrow self-interest. This view would imply that power itself is not "disastrous," but can be used in better or worse ways. Rather than blanket denunciations of what is, we need an account of justice that allows us to distinguish between the just and the unjust in the present order.

These three ambiguities in the kingdom's formula for reversal problematize Caputo's use of it to describe practical ethical and political positions. When it comes to making the kingdom of God happen, Caputo suggests that rather than being a matter of knowing what to do or putting a conception of the good into practice, an-ethics is a matter of the heart (*kardia*). Given his belief that justice is about being attentive to differences and singularity and that universal principles fail to do this, it is no surprise that Caputo has no taste for the decision-making strategies of Kantian or utilitarian ethics. He finds more to like in Aristotle's notion of *phronesis*, though he argues that this too has its shortcomings (*WWJD* 67; *WG* 142–43).[17] Through the notion of *phronesis*, Aristotle rightly emphasizes the importance of attending to the particulars of a situation as he recognizes that general rules can apply differently to different situations. Because of this, *phronesis* cannot be learned through abstract reflection, the way mathematics can, but requires real life experience. While Caputo likes this attention to difference and experience, he is concerned that *phronesis* remains too cognitive, too tied to universals. *Phronesis*, as Aristotle says, is "a state of grasping the truth," an attempt to "see" how universals apply to a particular situation.[18] As Caputo puts it, "*phronesis* is not *kardia*. *Phronesis* is a kind of *nous*, a practical *nous*, to be sure, but always a matter of insight and seeing. . . . [In an-ethics] the rule of a strictly cognitive *nous* is broken and replaced by a heart-based *nous*" (*WG* 142–43). While the characterization of Aristotle's view of ethical decision making as "strictly cognitive" seems a bit too strong, Caputo's subsequent explanation indicates his apprehension toward any ethical system based on applying rules to particular cases.

Caputo points to the example of Jesus healing a man's withered hand on the Sabbath, suggesting that in this case Jesus "does not bring the universal schema to bear upon the particular situation, but he lifts or suspends the universal in the face of the demands of the singularity before him. The weight, the demand, the claim, the call of the singular one outweighs and trumps the requirements of the law. This is suspension, not application, choosing in the face of conflicting demands, not a smooth implementation" (*WG* 143). Caputo may be right to point to this as an example of Jesus contravening the law in response to the needs of the singular other before him, but does this mean that Jesus has not brought an ethical schema to bear on this situation, that this situation amounts to the suspension of ethical schema? Caputo's conclusion that it does seems to conflate an ethical schema with the requirements of the law, thereby allowing him to contrast the demands of the singular individual and ethical universals.

But this is to conflate Aristotle and Kant. For Aristotle, ethical principles are not the rigid, inflexible universal laws of Kant's pure reason, but instead fallible, revisable generalities drawn from experience.[19] The point of *phronesis* is that in many cases smooth implementation of ethical principles is not possible.

Rather than suspending ethical principles and application, could it not be argued that Jesus' action expresses the ethical generality that we ought to help people in need, as well as the ethical judgment, indeed the *phronesis,* that in this case this man's need outweighs whatever obligation he has toward religious law? As I understand it, Caputo's point in this example is that our responsibility to help needy others always outweighs the demands of religious law, which sounds a lot like an ethical generality, if not a universal principle. Rather than embracing this as a general ethical principle, Caputo tends toward the strictly noncognitive. "*Kardia* is precisely *pathos* and sensibility, a communication of flesh with flesh; it is a sensibility that triumphs over the universalizing impulses of reason, a matter of sensibility in the Levinasian sense, which is a deep and sensitive pathos that suffers with the suffering of the other" (*WG* 144). Ironically, for Levinas, this sensibility precisely calls forth universalizing reason, making it less of a triumph and more of a reorientation, or dare I say, reversal. For Levinas, responsibility may be a matter of sensibility, but response is a matter of rationality—thematizing, comparing, weighing, judging, even universalizing.

In the chapter titled "What Would Jesus Deconstruct?" in the book of the same name, Caputo considers what practical political positions might result from the kingdom of God. What is striking about this chapter is that, despite its title, it almost completely lacks deconstructive techniques and terminology. Undecidability, rejection of binary oppositions, and the use of historical counterexamples to upset contemporary common sense have been replaced by arguments for public policy positions based on liberal, humanistic values.[20] Far from showing deconstruction's value in addressing contemporary ethical and social questions, this chapter tends to underline its dispensability. This point is driven home by Caputo's admission that Derrida's arguments in "Force of Law" could be used in defense of antiabortionists' views as easily as it can be used to defend his own (*WWJD* 113). Now, I am not arguing that we should dispense with deconstruction. I think deconstruction is valuable in criticizing and loosening up traditional categories and the positions and policies constructed on their basis. However, deconstruction is not as valuable when it comes to thinking through what ethical and political positions one ought to support. Caputo seems to acknowledge this, admitting that there is "no 'derivation,' no straight line, from the poetics or theopoetics of the kingdom to any concrete political structure or public policy" (87), but later on the same page he claims that the kingdom of God is clearly opposed to the policies of the Christian Right. Though I tend to agree with Caputo's political positions, I am concerned by the hastiness with which some of these judgments seem to be made. Caputo's slide from the kingdom of God to a liberal political agenda, bringing in without justification loaded notions like the dignity of choice, the blanket call to respect freedom, and accusations of religious imperialism (112, 116), can lead to dismissing conservatives without actually arguing against their positions. What does love really look like? When should we respect freedom and when is coercion appropriate? If we are to actually engage the Christian Right on these issues, we need cogent, honest, ethical argumentation.

When we consider Caputo's ethical and political positions, what I find worrisome is that his views, far from overturning binary oppositions, tend to harden oppositions between rich/poor, white/black, men/women, and Right/Left. Caputo seems to need these oppositions in order to give concrete expression to his abstract poetics of reversal that gives preference to whoever is out. Thus Caputo argues that economic justice demands priority for poor, black children and suggests that the practical help given by nuns in North Philadelphia humbles the male-dominated hierarchy of the Catholic Church. While I agree with the impetus for both of these claims, I worry that rather than affecting a reversal, this concretization (quite contrary to Caputo's intentions) seems to reiterate the equation of women and blacks with powerlessness that the feminist and civil rights movements have been working to overcome. This is not to deny that in America on average whites are much better off than blacks on a range of metrics, nor that the political and economic positions of power in the world are still heavily dominated by men. It is instead to suggest that ethical views, such as Caputo's, that take powerlessness or alterity to be their central term of approbation will tend to be intellectually conservative since concretizing ethical claims will require designating historically marginalized persons or groups as powerless, rather than emphasizing their potential for empowerment. I also worry that this tendency shows up in Caputo's consistent depiction of the pursuit of justice as occurring when "we" give up lives of ease, of mutual funds and cigar smoking, to go to the worst streets in the most dangerous inner-city neighborhoods to help all the needy people there (*OR* 114, 123, 133, 135; *WWJD* 28, 118). Though it may be entirely contrary to Caputo's intended views and practices, justice begins to sound like an exotic adventure for bored suburbanites. In order to avoid this pitfall, I think what we need is not an ethics built around the concept of powerlessness or alterity, but one inspired by humanity's positive potentials.

To my mind, the root of the ambiguities in Caputo's ethics is found in his attempt to be faithful to both deconstruction and justice. But no one can serve two masters, even if the former can sometimes be put at the service of the latter. Deconstruction engenders a strong sense of fallibilism, whereby we not only recognize that we do not know if our beliefs are true, but also suspect that they always falsify something since they are historically rooted generalizations based on contingently constructed categories and as such invariably cover over differences. It is the injustice of this falsification that motivates the practice of deconstruction. Because of the inevitability of such falsification, Caputo replaces epistemological conceptions of truth with an existential one. What matters is not *knowing* the truth, cognitively contemplating necessary and universal principles, but *doing* the truth, *facere veritatem*, making the kingdom of God happen in the world. Actively working for the kingdom, for justice, is more important than doctrinal rectitude. We can call Caputo's subordination of theological beliefs to the task of doing the truth "religious pragmatism." However, I think Caputo's religious pragmatism not only grows out of deconstruction, but also outgrows it. Whereas deconstruction can help us remember "how" to believe "what" we believe, keeping our beliefs flexible, open-ended, and revisable, actions do not admit of these qualities. Once an action is done, it is done and one cannot take it back, no matter how much one regrets it. We can ask for forgiveness, but this does not change what has happened, Peter Damian notwithstanding (*WG* 182–207). It would be a category mistake to apply fallibilism to doing the truth. When it comes to acting for the sake of justice, what we need is not the reminder that our beliefs are beliefs and not knowledge, but some idea about what we ought to be doing, even if this idea is itself fallible, revisable, and negotiable.

What we believe, and not simply how we believe, is crucially important to our relations with others and our attempts to make justice happen. For this we need the sort of ethical argumentation that Caputo seems to eschew in his move toward a theopoetics. The point of argumentation in ethics, as I will suggest in the next section, is not to prove with certainty—Caputo's right that we should give up that goal—but to dig deeper, to think through, and above all to expose ourselves to the understanding and criticism of others.

REASON AND REVELATION

In order to develop and defend a positive notion of theological and ethical argumentation, I would like to supplement Caputo's view of religion with a better account of the relationship between reason and revelation (i.e., the event). So far I have suggested that Caputo's attempt to distance religion from theology and ethics, to describe a religious stance unencumbered by the theological and ethical commitments of determinate religious traditions, has led to ambiguity and possible problems at the level of both theory and action. For better or for worse, religion has a theology and an ethics. But rather than thinking these in accordance with either modernist rationality or Caputo's poetics, my constructive, supplementary proposal is that we need a revised conception of reason, one that is not opposed to revelation but can be its servant, one that, as Levinas puts it, can be "the wisdom of love at the service of love."[21] This is a tall order, perhaps too tall, but I think we can get some pointers to what it might look like from Badiou's notion of a truth process, Levinas's ethical recontextualization of reason, and Mouffe's theory of agonism. These thinkers help us give a broad sketch of a contemporary interpretation of faith seeking understanding, one that to my mind does not refute Caputo's project but provides some additional resources for responding to the aforementioned ambiguities.

Truth Processes and the Good

Badiou and Levinas are natural interlocutors for Caputo. All three agree that our ultimate commitments are rooted in a passive experience of a transcendent event that both upsets the current order and calls us to a good that is beyond self-interest and social norms. Beyond that very significant agreement, there are of course some disagreements. For Levinas, the event always refers us to our ethical responsibility to other persons, an interpretation of the event that Caputo finds overly narrow (*WG* 271). For Badiou, events can be artistic, scientific, political, or amorous, but not religious. Though Badiou thinks that Paul's writings help illustrate the universal structure inherent in events, he discounts the possibility of religious events since he regards religious stories as fables that fail to touch the Real.[22] Despite these differences, Badiou and Levinas give insight into the relation between reason and the event that can be usefully brought to bear on Caputo's account of religion.

Badiou defines ethics as "a part of philosophy, that part which organizes practical existence around a *representation* of the Good."[23] For the considerations at hand, the important word here is "representation." Ethics requires a representation of the Good, a determinate articulation of something worth working for and committing to, something worth organizing our practical existence around. Being determinate need not imply that this representation is static, but as we will see shortly, it is part of an ongoing truth-process. Before we get to that, though, Badiou specifically criticizes some of Caputo's ethical categories, arguing that a meaningful representation of the Good cannot be based on either qualitative alterity or the concept of victim.

Badiou suggests that the proponents of qualitative alterity manifestly respect only those differences which, like them, respect differences, that is, which share in their *identity* as respecters of difference. Such persons have no respect for others who do not share their ideal of tolerance or whose cultural background includes ideals at odds with their own. This self-contradiction is so blatant that Badiou thinks the only surprising thing is how widely it is ignored. While the discourse of alterity appears to make difference sacred, the tolerance and multiculturalism it recommends respect only certain differences, all the while failing to produce arguments justifying the legitimation of those differences but not others. Since even the attempt to respect differences cannot help but lapse into identitarian thought, Badiou argues that ethics ought to focus, not on the alterity of the Other, but on the establishment of identities of the Same. Such a task is much more difficult than the attempt to acknowledge otherness since every situation contains numerous differences. Alterity cannot be the basis for ethics, not because it is a figment of our imagination, but because it is the "banal reality of every situation."[24] What we need is not an affirmation of difference, nor the exaltation of one type of difference, but the formation of identities that are more significant than the differences. For Paul, this is the *one*ness of Christ that transcends ethnic, socioeconomic, and gender differences. Only in this way can we establish a positive conception of the Good worthy of commitment, or in Badiou's preferred terminology, *fidelity*.

Badiou is also critical of basing ethics on the concept of victimization, which he thinks is at the root of the contemporary human rights discourse. The conception of humanity in terms of victimization presupposes the equation of the subject with humanity's animal nature, the biology of needs, pain, and mortality. Yet, as Badiou argues, sometimes experiences of extreme victimization, such as prison camp torture, reveal the capacity to remain resilient amidst victimization. Such experiences point to the possibility of a subjectivity that is more than just the passive recipient of beatings, more than just biological needs and mortality, but instead is an "immortal," that is, an agent capable of distinguishing himself from his existence as a mortal being in his resistance to his torturers despite the submission of his body, and perhaps even his mortality. While I am not as eager to dismiss the human rights discourse as Badiou is, I think he is rightly concerned that a narrow focus on human beings in their capacity for victimization neglects our highest possibilities and potential for flourishing. Secondly, Badiou points out that the ethics of victimization begins by defining evil and only subsequently defines the good. This pattern is a repetition of Nietzschean slave-morality insofar as it is rooted in rejection, designating certain actions or powers as evil and then deriving the good from that. As with slave-morality, the ethics rooted in victimization tends to define the good in terms of passivity; having defined violence in terms of interference with others, the ideal of justice becomes simple noninterference. Power and active projects are henceforth regarded with suspicion, so that any attempt to define and work for determinate, positive good is dismissed as inevitably violent, a step down the path toward a "totalitarian nightmare."[25]

Rather than conceiving of ethics in terms of abstract categories like "alterity" and "victim," Badiou suggests that ethics happens as a lived truth-process arising from a concrete event. As with Caputo's account of the event, for Badiou, an event is that which breaks with "what is," with the ruling ideology and social organization. Because of this, the event calls us to invent a new way of being, to reformulate the practical and theoretical habits we have inherited from our societies on the basis of the event. Badiou designates this reformulation as "truth," which he defines as "the real process of a fidelity to an event: that which this fidelity *produces* in the situation."[26] Like Caputo, for Badiou truth is something one does, *facere veritatem,* and specifically something one does out of faithfulness to the event. Like Caputo, Badiou sees the task of doing the truth, being truthful to the event, as an ongoing process by which we never reach the final, right answers. Indeed, acting as if one has reached the final, right answers is what Badiou calls a "disaster," which is one of his major categories of evil and neatly parallels Caputo's notion of the idolatry of the truth.

The difference between Caputo and Badiou arises in the mechanics of making the truth happen. Whereas Caputo prefers to view *kardia* as the key to faithful action, Badiou praises the power of thought. For Badiou, "thought" signifies the human capacity to go beyond our biological drives, conventional morality, and socialized responses, including our emotional responses. It is through thought that we are able to transcend "what is," to consider what could be and how we can go about making that happen. It is through thought that we are able to construct determinate articulations of the good, which I think is precisely what Caputo is doing when he writes about the kingdom of God. It is through thought that we must work to distinguish genuine events from the seductions of biology and sociology, especially when they are dressed up as pseudo-events, what Badiou calls simulacra. Doing the truth happens then when "the subject maintains thought in the power of doing," that is, when we put the power of action in the service of thought, that is, our representations of the good.[27] While Badiou recognizes that the event is not a matter of thought, nor can it be rationally proved, the practice of thought is

vital to our faithfulness to the event. Faith without seeking thoughtful, lived understanding is dead.

Badiou regards truth as universal in the sense that events make
appeal to all persons and so all persons can participate in a truth process. Badiou distinguishes this kind of universality from the conceptual universality that dominates the Western philosophical tradition.
Badiou argues that because of the diversity of linguistic and conceptual systems, "the conditions for the universal cannot be conceptual,
either in origin, or in destination."[28] Though determinate articulations employing historically contingent concepts may be a necessary
part of the truth process, the universality of the truth is not to be
found in universal concepts, a priori or otherwise. This allows Badiou
to avoid a direct confrontation between universal truths and particular cultures. Whereas cultures are constituted by what Badiou calls
"opinions," the "cement of sociality" that gives people within a culture a common basis for communication, truth processes transcend
cultural differences. Thus Badiou writes that truth is "an indifference [to cultures] that tolerates differences."[29] Note that this is not
the tolerance recommended by multiculturalism or the discourse of
alterity, which valorizes difference itself, but a tolerance for cultural
difference based on the recognition of a universal truth that admits of
a variety of cultural embodiments. Universality lies not in concepts or
customs, but in the universal address of the event, the openness of the
truth process to anyone. Thus universality is conceived as a concrete
potentiality rather than an actuality, either abstract or concrete. The
event is for all, even if not everyone is willing to recognize it or be
faithful to it. The event does not address us in our alterity or singularity, as Caputo has it, but rather in our shared capacity to recognize
the event and work for the embodiment of the good. Universality
is found in our capacity to be partners and helpmates for each other
rather than in our isolated individuality. To underscore this point,
Badiou states that to be an "I," that is, a subject constituted by fidelity to an event, is to be "for all."[30] This notion fits well with Caputo's
concern for hospitality and helps us to clarify the notion of membership in the kingdom of God. Whereas the kingdom of God is
addressed to all in the event, and so universal, only some people are
engaged in the truth process it opens up, that is, are pursuing justice
and hospitality. The kingdom has an open membership policy, but
that does not necessarily mean that everyone is already in.

Reason and Responsibility

Whereas Caputo's qualitative conception of alterity comes (allegedly) from the Bible and deconstruction, Levinas's conception of alterity is rooted in phenomenology. He picks up the term from Husserl's later work, where "the Other" is used to refer to other subjects, regardless of their qualitative similarities or differences. Because Husserl's concerns are primarily epistemological, he tends to think of others simply as fellow inquirers or co-constitutors of the world. Levinas surpasses Husserl by arguing that others have a fundamental ethical significance prior to any epistemological concerns, though he repeatedly states that this ethical significance is not based on any qualitative characteristics of other persons. Levinas sometimes seems to treat "the widow, the orphan, and the stranger" as privileged others, but this simply reflects the fact that we are more likely to be aware of our responsibility to others when confronted by those clearly in need. Despite this, responsibility extends to all, which may be why Levinas replaces "the widow, the orphan, and the stranger" with "the neighbor" in *Otherwise than Being*. Thus justice is not simply about attending to "victims," but responsibility toward all. As Levinas puts it, quoting Isaiah, "peace to the neighbor and the one far-off."[31] For Levinas the ethical task consists not in switching our concern from our family and friends (those that are in) to the victims of the system (those that are out), but extending our concern from those close to us to those whom we, both individually and socially, do not normally consider or even those whom we positively neglect. As Levinas's account demands justice for all, it also demands justice from all. Since responsibility is the structure of subjectivity, ethical living is a task for everyone.

For Levinas the term "epiphany" parallels Caputo's notion of the event. An epiphany occurs in those moments when the recognition of our responsibility to others interrupts our normal, daily routine, which, in Levinas's terminology, we live in accordance with our "economy," that is, the practical and theoretical structures we employ in order to be at home in the world. An epiphany calls our economy into question, judging it as unjust for neglecting our responsibilities to certain others. Given the call to justice revealed in such an epiphany, how should we respond? For Levinas, before we can begin to think through that question (and we do need to *think* through it), it is necessary to recognize the context of the call to justice. Though persons have significance independent of their contexts, or precisely because of this, justice requires that we exercise responsibility toward all others. What then does justice look like? For Levinas this is a difficult question that requires the hard work of rational thought. Rather than giving into whichever direction our *kardia* pulls us, we must think through how best to respond to others. We must, Levinas says, compare "incomparables," which means, ceasing to think of other persons as alterities, as infinitely other. Levinas goes so far as to say, "We must . . . *de-face* humans, sternly reducing each one's uniqueness to his individuality in the unity of the genus, and let universality rule."[32] Comparison is only possible for items sharing some common ground. As with Badiou, for Levinas ethical action and justice take us beyond difference and alterity to commonality. In order for this comparison to be helpful in discerning to whom we should respond, we must also have some ideas about what it means to be human and which features of humanity are relevant to ethics. Thus, in one place Levinas equates "comparing what is incomparable" with "knowing men."[33] I suspect that Caputo would be reluctant to endorse this talk of "universality" and "commonality," though to my mind he implicitly deploys such notions when he praises freedom and the dignity of choice, since these seem to have a general scope.

For Levinas, this work of comparison is part of the task of philosophical reasoning. Levinas regards such reasoning as not merely propaedeutic to just actions, but as itself an integral part of "the work of justice."[34] This claim may seem surprising given Levinas's sharp criticisms of reason and philosophy. However, it is important to recognize that these criticisms aim not at the "end of philosophy," but at the reconceptualization of reason as called forth by our ethical responsibility to others and so as essentially intersubjective. This reconceptualization offers an alternative to the internal monologue conception of reason, conceived along the lines of Socratic recollection or Cartesian rationalism, of which Levinas is so critical. Instead of thinking of reason as a dialogue the soul has with itself in order to achieve harmony with itself, Levinas recommends that it be thought of as the dialogue an ethically responsible subject has with others. This way of conceiving of reason is rooted in Levinas's claim that the concern for truth, that is, for objectivity and universality, arises only in a subject who is already concerned with others and their perspectives, who recognizes beyond his or her own limited perspective, the validity of others' perspectives. Pluralism does not threaten the legitimacy of reason, but precisely founds it. It is when we expect to overcome this pluralism, to attain "rational consensus," that disagreement can easily turn into violence. Rather than seeing reason as a tool to puff up our own positions, Levinas encourages us to see reasoning as an ongoing, honest, open, reason-giving dialogue an ethical subject has with others. In this dialogue, the goal of rational argumentation is not to "win," but to expose ourselves to others, sharing our world and running the risk of being understood, questioned, and criticized. Alongside our practical acts of hospitality, we should also say to others, "Come, let us reason together." This is what ethical argumentation, in both senses of the phrase, would look like.

If it is possible to draft the power of reason into the service of justice, then it is also possible, Levinas thinks, to put the power of one's economy and one's state to work for justice. Levinas writes that the self must respond to the other "with all the resources of its egoism: economically.... [The ethical relation] is not instituted in a homogeneous or abstract medium, but in a world where it is necessary to aid and to give. It presupposes an I, an existence separated in its enjoyment, which does not welcome empty-handed the face and its voice coming from another shore."[35] Though economy is not self-justifying or essentially ethical, it is not, for all that, antithetical to responsibility. Instead, when put to the service of ethical responsibility, economy has a positive value. Rather than regarding economy and even enjoyment as distractions from the ethical relationship, these are essential to the life of responsibility. Responsibility is not enacted in an unseen or mystical spiritual realm, but in the concrete, material world. In this world, responsible action requires giving of our time and resources to help others, having some understanding of what is helpful for another, and even the possibility of enjoyment. If enjoyment, a good life or human flourishing, is not possible, then why bother helping others to live?

When it comes to the state, Levinas is not naïve enough to harbor utopian aspirations as he recognizes that the generality of law will always neglect particular cases and that the temptation to bend the power of the state to serve self-interest is ineradicable. Nonetheless, he is not willing to give up on the power of the state, that is, our capacity for collective action, as a means to work for justice. As mentioned above, in the last 100 years, women's movements and the civil rights movement have clearly shown how the powers of the state can be used to bring about a more just society. Power need not be opposed to the kingdom of God, even if the task of bending it to the service of justice is a difficult and never-ending challenge. Ethical argumentation is a key component of taking up this challenge.

Agonism and Religion

Unlike Badiou and Levinas, Mouffe is not a natural or obvious interlocutor for Caputo, but I think her conception of political identity and the agonism that arises from it is instructive for thinking through religious identities based in faith and the competing theological claims that arise from them. Mouffe's theory recognizes that passionate commitment to an identity requires determinate content and exclusivity, but seeks to avoid violence through modifying how we understand our commitments, the commitments of others, and the lived relationship between these. I would like to suggest that the main themes in Mouffe's theory can be extended to faith, that is, religious commitment, so that we can accept the inevitability of theological exclusivity while discouraging civil intolerance on its account.

Mouffe's conception of political identity is rooted in a criticism of the prevailing theories of liberalism, theories that trace their roots in modernity to the same movements to which Caputo's conception of religious tolerance seems to be heir. According to Mouffe, liberalism's primary error with regard to the political is to dismiss affective identification with collective, political causes as a result of archaic passions that inevitably lead to violence.[36] Such affective identification, so their thinking goes, needs to be overcome by appeals to universal reason, or as some contemporary liberal thinkers argue, rational procedures. Examples of this thinking stretch from Rousseau's conception of the general will to John Rawls's "principles of justice." Even when liberalism is tempered by what Caputo calls the "post-modern idea," the ideal remains a consensus that is as universal as possible about the value of individuals that are as autonomous as possible.

However, given the failure of universal reason and the necessity of exclusion for the creation of identity, it is more consistent, as Mouffe argues, to reject the ideal of universal consensus as unfounded and instead recognize that the diversity and conflict we experience is an essential aspect of social existence. Mouffe calls this aspect the political, though for our purposes it is crucial to understand this in a very broad sense of the term. Mouffe critically appropriates some of Carl Schmitt's work to argue that the political sphere inherently employs we/they oppositions.[37] Hence, even liberalism's attempts to achieve universal consensus on the basis of reason makes sense only on the basis of the distinction between "us" rational people and "those" irrational people. Mouffe thinks that these attempts to overcome we/they oppositions in the name of some alleged universal standard, by denying the necessity of a we/they distinction, demonizes those who are against us. "They" can only be regarded as irrational, immoral, or in some other way subhuman. The ideal of universal consensus, far from overcoming antagonism and violence, actually encourages it.

Rather than embrace the ideal of liberalism, we should allow the partisan character of the political sphere and recognize the depth of political identity in both its intellectual and affective dimensions. The goal then becomes not finding a common standard that we can all agree on, but creating the space in which opposing political commitments can compete and confront each other without resorting to violence. Mouffe calls this possibility agonism without antagonism. A key to achieving this is to recognize that because one identifies with a political cause on the basis of intellectual and emotional responses to certain lived experiences, political identities may not be fully rationally justifiable or reconcilable with opposing identities. This recognition leaves open the possibility of giving reasons for one's position while giving up the assumption that the continued disagreement with one's political opponents is due to *their* irrationality or immorality. Because political identification involves extrarational aspects, we cannot expect others to share our commitments simply on the basis of reasoned argumentation. This allows us to consider the political views of our opponents as, in Mouffe's terminology, "legitimate."[38] It is crucial to recognize here that "legitimate" does not mean equally true or good, since commitment to particular political views expresses the fact that one regards those views as truer or better than the alternatives. Thus, within Mouffe's terminology it is completely compatible, and actually the form of agonistics, for political participants to say that their opponents' views are wrong and yet legitimate, that is, that they disagree with their opponents' views, but since those views are not necessarily the results of irrationality or immorality they can-not rightly say that their opponents *ought* to abandon them, that they have a responsibility as humans to repudiate them, that they are unnatural. Recognizing the lived, nonrational elements of political identity undermines our typical avenues for normative claims, mean-ing that our opponent's views can be regarded as legitimate, even as we passionately believe they are wrong.

Mouffe points to functioning parliamentary democracies as places where this sort of agonistics can occur. Here we can have opposing political visions competing with each other, arguing for the right-ness of their positions, trying to draw support and yet not reverting to physical violence to achieve their ends. This is most dramatically on display when a political group loses an election. The loss need not and usually does not lead the members of the losing group to conclude that they were wrong. Instead they can peacefully accept the rule of the opposing party while continuing to work for their own political agenda. This commonplace example illustrates that pas-sionate, enduring commitments need not lead to violence even when those with contrary commitments are in the positions of power in a society. Here we have an example of contrary identities constituted by exclusive commitments coexisting without violence.

I think we would do well to consider the ways in which religious identity parallels Mouffe's description of political identity in the hopes that such a conception of religion would retain deep personal commitments to beliefs, practices, and institutions while encourag-ing religious devotees to see the adherents of other religions not as enemies deserving of antagonistic violence, but as offering a differ-ent and competing way of life which they can nonetheless regard as legitimate and with which they can peacefully coexist. Though reli-gious identity differs in important ways from political identity and while the comparison should not be taken as implying a specific role for religious commitment in political practice, I think political com-mitment is a better model for religious commitment than are the models suggested by Caputo. Religious commitments, like political commitments, are rooted in lived experience and involve an affective and intellectual identification with certain determinate beliefs, prac-tices, and institutions. The idea of conversion as a way into religious commitment indicates the extrarational nature of religious identity.

Rather than attempting to weaken commitment to determinate beliefs as Caputo seems to suggest, we should rethink religious truth and tolerance by taking such commitments as essential to religion.

Claims to religious truth, being rooted in the religious commitments that arise out of one's particular lived experiences, cannot achieve rational and objective justification. This does not mean that one cannot give reasoned explanations for why one came to hold the religious commitments one does or why such commitments are beneficial. Nor does it mean that one cannot learn by listening to others describe their religious commitments. It simply suggests that no universally recognizable rational argument can be given to engender religious commitment. One can accept this and still regard the beliefs one has come to through the course of one's life as valuable, helpful, and right, that is, as true. We must simply give up the expectation that others will agree with us once we explain ourselves and the assumption that their failure to do so is a mark of irrationality or immorality. This view thus agrees with Caputo that we should not conceive of religious truth on the model of mathematical or scientific truth, but finds his analogy with literary truth wanting. The way in which commitment to certain religious beliefs can constitute one's identity is more akin to political commitment than to having a favorite novel. Such commitment is incompatible with the claim that all religious traditions are equally true and none has unique truths. To be a Muslim rather than a Christian or a Buddhist rather than a Jew is to be committed to certain theological and ethical views, certain determinate beliefs and practices, and not others.

Obviously this understanding of the notion of religious truth requires a different conception of tolerance than that suggested by Rousseau's or Caputo's rejection of religious exclusivism. Here Mouffe's notion of "legitimacy" is instructive. Since we cannot claim that our own religious commitments are fully rational, we cannot demonize religious commitments that differ from ours as the results of irrationality or immorality. This is completely consistent with holding that one's own theology is right and that the theologies of others insofar as they are at odds with one's own are wrong. Thus we can retain passionate commitment to determinate religious beliefs while tolerating others' religious commitments as legitimate. This takes us beyond Caputo, whose religion without religion seems to be constructed by contrast with fundamentalism, making fundamentalism the excluded outside essential to the constitution of his religious identity. Rather than regarding fundamentalist religion as legitimate (in Mouffe's sense of the term), Caputo seems to depict fundamentalism as the result of a moral defect or vice, of personal weakness, insecurity, and an inability to handle change (*OR* 91–108). The view of religious commitment I have sketched here avoids the demeaning of fundamentalists while nonetheless allowing those of us (Caputo included) whose theological and ethical positions are at odds with fundamentalism to unequivocally claim that fundamentalism is wrong and bad. To be clear, I have no desire to defend fundamentalism. Instead, it is precisely because I think fundamentalists are harmful to themselves and others that we must find nondismissive ways to engage them.

While I find this account of religion more logically consistent, descriptively accurate, and practically helpful, it also indicates the potential difficulties and enduring fragility of a peaceful religious pluralism. Just as conflicting political identities always harbor within them the possibility of violence, so too do contrary religious commitments. Rather than trying to put an end to this potential once and for all by postulating a religion that rejects determinate religious commitment, we should recognize the nature of that commitment and the legitimacy of the commitments of others.

CONCLUSION

I like Caputo's theology and ethics, but I think we should recognize that this is exactly what he offers us. Ironically, Caputo once criticized Derrida for a similar pretension when he rejected Derrida's distinction between the messianic and messianisms. For Derrida, messianisms are the determinate religious traditions and the messianic is the call to justice that he claims is at the heart of these traditions. Caputo rejects Derrida's attempt to escape determinate religion suggesting that "rather than taking Derrida's messianic as in anyway overarching the three historical messianisms of the religions of the Book, or the three plus one, if you include Marx's messianism, I would say that Derrida's is a fifth... that is to say, *one more* messianism... every messianic structure takes the form of some sort of messianism... [with] *certain* determinable features" (*PT* 142). Far from giving us a religion *without* religion, a theology *without* theology, an ethics *without* ethics, Caputo too has given us one more messianism, one more theology, one more ethics, one more religion. Caputo's interpretation of religion does not get us at the secret, hidden truth of all religions, but is an interpretation competing with other interpretations, many of which it necessarily excludes. This exclusion does not in itself constitute violence; it is simply the structure of religious commitment, that is, of faith. The most responsible response to this situation is neither pretending that we *know* what we are talking about, nor replacing reasoning with poetics, but faithfully seeking understanding together.

Thinking More Positively...
and Indeed Why Not?
— A Response to Stephen Minister

Jeffrey Hanson

S tephen Minister's incisive engagement exposes with devastating force the weaknesses of John Caputo's weak theology and ethics. My response to his critique will largely echo the fundamentals of his concerns while offering complementary considerations.

First I take it that Minister is incontestably correct to regard Caputo's project as just another form of theological and ethical reasoning, not a true alternative to the necessity of theological and ethical reasoning, which in turn entail difficulties that can neither be foregone nor consigned to die the death of a thousand qualifications. Equally indisputable is the concession that no one knows for sure what we are talking about when we talk about religion—though I prefer to limit this concession to talk about God more than talk about religion, and in either event, this concession can be cheerfully made without elevating it to the level of constitutive principle, as Caputo and his mentor Derrida do. Minister is right, too, to point out that "we all have theological and ethical positions, which is to say that our lives and actions express beliefs about God and ethical values," though he does not spell out the important point that undergirds this assertion: such issues cannot be a matter of indifference; we can make all the hesitations and qualifications we like, but at some point we have to live out and live with our choice.

Similarly I echo the recognition that our religious conceptuality and vocabulary are inevitably human products and thus have to be susceptible to revision. But I find it odd that Minister, echoing Caputo, argues of determinate religious traditions that "at their worst they become ends-in-themselves, replacing God as the object of our love." I do not know that this ever actually happens, and I certainly find it strange to claim that anybody "worships a religious tradition." What believer of even the most pious orthodox conformity would countenance being told that they worship not God but Judaism? Or Lutheranism? The problem Minister and Caputo have in mind is imprecisely formulated. Furthermore, while I acknowledge the danger of idolatry, I question the one-sided presumption that historic tradition is susceptible only to such decline. As we learn from Marion, a concept can of course operate idolatrously, but our concepts can also be iconic.[1] The fact is, we cannot eschew such traditions and linguistic structures, and indeed they are often enough the iconic means of grasping, to whatever extent we can, the ungraspable. Failing to admit this fact does not do justice to the experience of religious believers or to the power of human creativity and expressiveness.

Another deep reservation I have about the material that Minister endorses in Caputo is the presumptive association between determinate religious tradition and violence. This cliché is surprising only for its durability. I fail utterly to understand how it is that sincerity of belief is meant to be linked to disposition to violence. If we were to adapt Slavoj Žižek's distinction between the inauthentic and authentic fundamentalist, we could consider the Taliban government in Afghanistan's decision to dynamite the Buddhas of Bamiyan in 2001 as an example of how less-than-firm conviction leads to violent aggression. The Taliban's action was motivated not by firm belief in Allah as the one true God but by secretly self-suspect commitment to monotheism. If Allah really is the one true God, how could the impassioned adherent to Islam regard the statues of the Buddha with any attitude more malign than bemusement? They need to be destroyed only if their mere existence represents a genuine threat to the shaky faith of the extremist Muslim. The authentic fundamentalist as Žižek calls him, by contrast, is convinced of his own belief so much so that the unbelief of others does not drive him to a frenzied envy of the jouissance of the nonbeliever, which is for him the object of cool indifference.[2]

Furthermore, it seems to me underlying the alleged association of religious belief and violence is a suppressed premise, one that is never made explicit. The belief that "I am right about my religious views" does not in any way entail the belief that "I can do violence on you because you do not share my religious views." Somewhere between these propositions has to be inserted a copula to the effect that "Anyone who is right about his views on a matter of substantive importance is thereby entitled to do violence on those who must by necessity be incorrect about their view on the same matter." I would be the last to deny that this argument has been made in completed form in the distant historical past and is made today. But in Caputo and in many others the argument seems still to hold force despite being emptied in the vast majority of believing circles of its key premise, such that the assumption remains that all religious commitment entails a propensity to violence, which it seems to me cannot be true unless the perpetrators of such violence cling to the suppressed premise that has been largely jettisoned.[3] It is of the utmost necessity when making such generalizations to keep them rooted in concrete and contemporary facts. It is one thing to complain in the abstract about religiously motivated violence, another to seriously engage the complex historical, political, economic, and social circumstance of any particular manifestation of religious violence. This is especially the case when, as Caputo and Derrida frequently acknowledge, the religious can never be fully disentangled from the social, political, economic, and so forth; if we take that claim seriously, we cannot disingenuously flog the same refrain about the long and bloody history of religion as Caputo does. Why not lament instead the long and bloody history of economics?

In the same vein, Minister does well to cast some doubt on Caputo's wholesale subscription to a metaphysics of transcendental violence. When Caputo writes that he cannot "see how any religious tradition or theological language can take shape without violence" he may as well assert the same of any language (perhaps he would do so cheerfully), but the price to be paid for such hysteria is the refusal of discourse itself. Meaningful commitments are indeed formed by negation of some other position from which one withholds one's commitment. This state of affairs is hardly a matter for vigorous hand-wringing. It is what is asked of anyone who is to make mature and thoughtful judgments; the only way we could possibly aspire to an intelligible conversation that somehow did *not* involve asserting that God is one way and therefore not another is if we tacitly agree in advance that God means nothing whatsoever and certainly not anything of personal import to the conversation's participants; that such consensus is possible has been demonstrated by the most vapid forms of ecumenism, which become pallid, not to mention mirthless, to the degree that those involved think they have nothing to disagree about. I can only add to Minister to point out that there is here and elsewhere in Caputo's thinking an elision from the platitudinous to the hyperbolic. That discriminations can and must be made as a function of any significant conversation does not warrant the conclusion that discourse (or religious discourse uniquely?) is always an act of morally blameworthy violence. The situation could just as easily be encoded more positively, and indeed why not? Why not argue that the work of discrimination and judgment contributes to an endless and endlessly open-ended process of creative supplementation?[4] With such a view, ongoing conversation about God would not merely be commendable but mandatory, for there would forever be more to be said. I think of the end of John's Gospel, when the evangelist writes, "And there are also many other things which Jesus did, the which, if they should be written every one, I suppose that even the world itself could not contain the books that should be written" (John 21:25). I would emphasize this plenitude rather than fret overly about any tradition's attempt to corner the truth market.

Minister is entirely justified in pointing out that the iron fist has been in the velvet glove of tolerance from the beginning: Everyone is right and should be welcome except those who do not think everyone is right — those people should be flung out. Again I would point out Žižek's work as doing much to refute this inconsistency and its correlate, neutered multiculturalism, according to the tenets of which the Other is always welcome as long as we mean the Other's quaint tribal customs. If we mean their actual Otherness (read: fundamentalism), well then there we draw the line; there are no fundamentalists allowed in the food court.[5]

Minister's diagnosis of the instabilities in Caputo's ethics is likewise wholly on target. The last-shall-be-first-and-first-shall-be-last formulation is one that never fails to appeal, since it never cuts against the one who is wielding it. No sooner is it proclaimed (though not for the first time) in Matthew 20 than an enterprising mother who wants only the best for her boys tries to ensure their success in the kingdom. If the last shall be first, she (and we) figure there surely must be some way to capitalize on the reversal. But Matthew 20 among other passages suggests that the point of the principle is not reversal at all, which might account for Caputo's inability to apply a logic of reversal consistently and his theory's collapse into what I can only assume Minister intentionally characterizes as an Orwellian position: "God is not against anyone, but God might be for some people more than others."

After Jesus is asked to guarantee a position of "first-ness" for the sons of Zebedee, he makes it clear that while being first among the Gentiles means exercising dominion over others, to be first in the kingdom will mean being the servant of all. Those who see in this a simple exchange between insider and outsider status do well to attend closely to the parable in the same chapter of the landlord who hires workers for the vineyard. He contracts with them all for a penny, though he hires some early in the day, who do a full day's work in the sun, and some later, who work much less for the same wage. When the early group complains against the later groups the landlord protests that he has done no wrong: "didst not thou agree with me for a penny? Take that thine is, and go thy way: I will give unto this last, even as unto thee. Is it not lawful for me to do what I will with mine own? Is thine eye evil, because I am good?" Jesus glosses this parable by saying "So the last shall be first, and the first last: for many be called, but few chosen" (Matt. 20:13–16). This parable, like the episode with the mother of James and John, implies that eligibility for the kingdom is not to do with social status but with readiness for service without complaining about another's reward or grubbing for our own reward when that has already been promised. It is precisely resentment against the perceived privileges of the Other, however privilege is perceived, that is condemned as incompatible with the king's will for his kingdom and an offense against his largesse. That the first shall be last then means not that there will be a reversal to the disadvantage of "them" but that one way or another all shall have their reward, some or even many apparently out of keeping with their just deserts. Those who are not content with that state of affairs are invited to go their way.[6] So membership in the kingdom has little to do with outsider status or how successfully you have been able to fetishize yourself as a victim, but with your willingness to be a servant and your contentment with the generosity of God toward all.[7] Such a picture is certainly more compatible with the theoretical framework that Minister explores with the help of Badiou, Levinas, and Mouffe than with the one advanced by Caputo.

Religion in the Postmodern Public Square

— Thinking after Stephen Minister

J. Aaron Simmons

O stensibly presented as a critique of John Caputo's denial to be engaged in the practice of doing theology and ethics, Stephen Minister's chapter is certainly not limited to a negative philosophical gesture. Although Minister offers a robust set of objections to Caputo, far more importantly, he also considers how continental philosophy of religion stands in relation to matters of contemporary ethical and political existence. Minister basically proposes the following three theses:

(1) Deconstructive theology and ethics are still rightly considered theology and ethics.
(2) Deconstructive political theory tends to be rather conservative in its liberalism.
(3) Postmodernism offers profound resources for rethinking religion in the public square.

In this brief consideration of Minister's chapter, I want to explore the rationale behind, and implications of, these three claims.

In recent decades, it has become a common practice within continental philosophy to talk quite a bit about what one cannot talk about. Now, it is certainly true that this paradox is not something new to philosophy. As Minister points out, such thinkers as Maimonides, Avicenna, and Aquinas all, in various ways, anticipate the postmodern recognition of the contextual obstacles to God-talk. However, what these thinkers seem to avoid, and what some of deconstructive philosophy of religion does not, are the claims that (1) human language is inadequate, *as such*, regarding all religious matters, and that (2) knowledge of God is *impossible*. Though Maimonides, Avicenna, and Aquinas (among many others) affirm the centrality of faith to knowledge of God, which should invite substantial epistemic and theological humility, they do not deny that determinate religious traditions still might be viable options for relating to the divine. Accordingly, they leave open the possibility that the various traditions in which they locate themselves might get *some* things right (if not about God, as such, then at least about religious experience, the limits of language, human anthropology, etc.). Even if only regarding the claim that propositional expression is largely inadequate in relation to God, such thinkers still might have reasons to continue to locate themselves in a particular religious tradition minimally because it does a better job than others at recognizing this very linguistic inadequacy. As Minister notes, Maimonides' general apophatic inclinations did not lead him to hold an "ironic distance from the Jewish tradition."

It is in this context that Minister engages Caputo's philosophy of religion. Although drawing primarily on Derrida, Caputo's deconstructive perspective also finds significant resources in the history of negative theology. However, Caputo's a-theology seems to rest on a stronger claim of absolute linguistic and conceptual inadequacy than does the thought of these historical predecessors. In particular, it occasionally seems that Caputo moves from the historical claim that

> All particular discourses about God *are probably, at least in part, inadequate* to "the event."

to the claim that

> All discourse about God *is entirely inadequate* to "the event."

As Minister rightly points out, Caputo's basic apophatic move is certainly understandable given the gross abuses that often accompany claims to theological absolutism and epistemic certainty. The violence that Caputo worries about in the name of determinate religion is not merely a speculative possibility, but is a historical reality and, consequentially, does invite the temptation to reject all claims to knowledge about the divine. Like Minister, I too have been raised in the evangelical Christian subculture and I am quite sympathetic with Caputo's resistance to the arrogance with which religious belief is often held (at least within American evangelicalism). However, precisely in the name of what Caputo is *trying to do*—viz., emphasize the need for epistemological humility and ethical openness—I think that we should be hesitant fully to embrace what Caputo so often *seems to do*—viz., deny the truth of historical religious affirmations (at least as first-order claims about reality).

Consider Caputo's claim that "the *event* that is astir in the name of God cannot be contained by the historical contingency of the names I have inherited in my tradition."[1] There is quite a difference between Caputo's strong claim that "the name of God *cannot be* contained" (emphasis added) and the weaker (and I would suggest more historically prominent) claim that we should be suspicious about the adequacy of historically contingent names. If Caputo means to suggest that, due to the inescapability of using historically contingent names, human language *cannot say anything whatsoever* about God, then deconstructive language would be in the same boat as everything else. But, then, the language of "the impossible," and "the event," etc., would be just as inadequate as the language of ontotheology or conservative biblical liberalism. I think that Caputo's deconstructive vocabulary is, in many ways, a better way to approach the divine than are the overly literalist ontotheological accounts found in much of American Christianity. Accordingly, I think that we should be able to give good reasons for why this discourse is better than others; but if Caputo is right about the absolute linguistic inadequacy of God-talk, then such reason giving is problematic. Caputo, thus, appears to face what we might term a *motivational obstacle:* namely, internal to the framework of "religion without religion," he seems philosophically unable to advocate for the deconstructive discourse as a better model of God-talk than the views that he so stringently opposes—such as "fundamentalism" or "strong theology."

Further, Caputo faces an even more troubling challenge, which we might term the *problem of perspectivalism:* namely, if Caputo is right about the inescapability of human socio-historico-cultural location and the epistemological and theological limits that such a location would imply, then the very claim that "the *event*...cannot be contained" is something that should cause us to ask where Caputo is able to stand in order to know such a thing? Caputo comes quite close to assuming an epistemic perspective that deconstruction rightly problematizes, that is, the "view from nowhere." Moreover, where would one have to be in order to have knowledge of the uncontainability of the event? If Caputo simply means to suggest the general idea (which would seem to draw somewhat upon a quasi-externalist semantic theory) that we should be wary of proclamations of *knowing that we know* our "names" are adequate to the "event," then I agree with him. But, then, the most that could be claimed is that "the event that is astir in the name of God cannot be contained by the historical contingency of the names I have inherited in my tradition, *or so it seems to me as located internal to this historical tradition.*" Or as Merold Westphal might put it, "the truth is that there is Truth." This might be all Caputo intends to say, but the rhetorical strategies deployed in different texts regarding "fundamentalism" and "strong theology" raise some doubt about this reading. Alternatively, maybe Caputo is simply claiming that it is possible to have knowledge that "the name of God cannot be contained" *if* we assume the existence of a truth-maker that would make such knowledge possible, and yet this existence is itself uncertain. However, given Caputo's resistance to ontological discourse that understands God as a being (as opposed to an event, though I would point out that this strict dichotomy between being and event is surely contestable), even the framework whereby such a truth-maker would be a "thing" that "exists" such that truth could be secured seems problematic. But without a more substantive account of the epistemology and semantics underlying Caputo's account, it is difficult to be sure if these weaker interpretations of his claims are plausible.

In the quite sensible attempt to stress the humility and fallibility of human accounts of God, it is easy to slide to an extreme position and affirm that humans cannot know anything about God. This is a temptation that is not limited to deconstruction, but accompanies all apophatically sensitive theological and philosophical discourse. But, again, the irony is clear: given such radical humility and fallibilism, how would someone operating internal to such a framework "know" that she cannot know anything?

The key to Minister's link between deconstructive philosophy of religion and political theory is his assertion that Caputo's a-theology and an-ethics are still rightly considered theology and ethics. Paraphrasing Minister's first paragraph, deconstructive theology is still theology; deconstructive ethics is still ethics. As such, deconstructive theology is not necessarily outside the tradition of determinate religion, but, as Caputo himself sometimes admits, might turn out to be a particular form that such religion can take. Similarly, deconstructive ethics is not necessarily beyond moral philosophy, but might merely be a particular way of doing moral philosophy. Minister's point is worth considering because deconstructive philosophy of religion occasionally appears to be quite dismissive of determinate religion and traditional ethical discourse. The problem with such apparent dismissiveness, as Minister makes quite clear, is that it can begin to be patronizing to actual religious believers who defend a specific account of moral action in light of their religious beliefs. For all its rhetoric about being open to hearing the call of the Other, when all is said and done, deconstruction can sometimes seem quite resistant to listening to *some* others—namely, social and theological conservatives, strong theologians, etc. But notice the problem here: in the attempt to avoid the violence of theological arrogance, deconstructive philosophy itself walks a fine line relative to the violence of discursive exclusion. In its attempt to be inclusive, deconstruction can end up excluding those who hold their religious beliefs as exclusive truth-claims (as do most religious believers around the world). Now, as I point out in my own chapter, there is nothing wrong with being exclusivist in this way, *as such,* but there is a problem *if* one claims to be radically inclusive while doing so.

It is in this respect that deconstruction can itself be very conservative in its liberalism. That is, when one takes infinite obligation (e.g., as advocated by Levinas and Derrida, among others) together with the radical contingency and perspectivalism of postmodernism (e.g., as proposed by Foucault and Lyotard, among others), then it seems that one becomes unable to *prima facie* reject the views of a social conservative, say, without either contesting that one is so deeply obligated or so deeply located internal to one's context. Now, this is not to say that one cannot reject such views (perhaps we should), but simply that doing so is itself a *political decision* and not something that gets outside of the contingency of one's political existence. If deconstruction is on the side of the marginalized, then it is necessary to explain how this radical claim is *not so radical* as to require that one must stand with the marginal *even when* they are those people with whom one deeply disagrees. Indeed, some deconstructionists appear to suggest that some particular social groups and beliefs could *never* be marginalized (which is quite historically contestable). While I grant that the obligation to defend a racist who feels marginalized because of the increasing prominence of civil rights is troubling, it can sometimes be unclear how the very radicality of the "liberal" deconstructive project would not require such a thing. This does not mean that deconstruction cannot critique stupid ideas and violent people. Indeed, it must do so. Some marginalization is necessary, as Derrida himself frequently admits, even if it is done without *final* justification. Yet getting clear on how to operate in light of these various infinite obligations while enmeshed in particular political contexts is difficult work indeed. Importantly, Caputo and Derrida have both attempted to work though these difficulties. As I read Minister, he is simply pushing at some of those points where questions remain.

Considering Caputo, in particular, there are two ways that one might suggest he can account for infinite obligation, on the one hand, and radical contextualism, on the other hand. First, he could admit that the seeming exclusion of some views is really nothing other than a political gesture reflecting his own perspectives and interests. This model allows Caputo to retain his radically inclusive articulation of a-theology and an-ethics, but requires him to bracket such a notion when it comes to the determinacy of political life. Namely, his theoretical perspective is not what motivates such exclusion, but merely what underlies his own political views. Similar to Richard Rorty's reading of Derrida, one might suggest that when it comes to a guide for living and making sense of why and when exclusion might be necessary, Caputo's philosophy would be of poetic or aesthetic interest, perhaps, but of only limited theological, ethical, or political value. Let us term this the *inclusivist alternative*. Second, Caputo could admit that what he is doing is really theology and ethics and then bite some rather hard bullets—namely, that any account of theology and ethics will necessarily require some other accounts to be rejected as false. On this model, there is still no *final* justification for exclusion, but *there are certainly reasons that one can provide*, albeit from within one's own theological account or ethical position, *for why exclusion was necessary in a particular case.* Let us term this the *exclusivist alternative.*

With these two possible alternative strategies in place, we can now make sense of Minister's appropriation of Alain Badiou, Emmanuel Levinas, and Chantal Mouffe as critical interlocutors for Caputo's project as it relates to the question of religion in the postmodern public square (or the relation of faith to reason within postmodernism). All three, in different ways, provide reasons for preferring the exclusivist alternative. Badiou and Levinas demonstrate that just because one is committed to the necessity of exclusion, one does not have to deny the perspectivalism of postmodernity. Badiou's notion of fidelity and Levinas's account of exposure are meant to stress the fact that really seeking understanding requires a certain amount of *faith* (which, as in the case of Badiou, would certainly be a "religious" gesture even if made in the name of a "secular" event). In more concrete terms, Badiou and Levinas emphasize that doing theology and ethics does not require that one be infallible and that one's basic commitments be nonrevisable. On this front, Caputo's deep appreciation of Kierkegaard should allow him to recognize that even though faith requires risk, faith is never empty—*if it were, it would not require risk!* Caputo's work is extremely valuable as an example of how deconstructive philosophy of religion challenges the theological and ethical arrogance displayed so often in religious communities, and as an example of how postmodern ethics requires a different approach to moral decision making than that found in the prominent alternatives in the history of philosophy. In the very attempt to defend what is right about Caputo's work, however, we seem to need to go beyond the "religion *without* religion" framework in which it is articulated in order to allow the exclusivist alternative to be plausible.

Since faith is always already implicated in knowledge claims, and since even a-theology is still *a* theology, arguments for excluding religious belief, *prima facie,* from the postmodern public square are unsustainable. For example, consider Mouffe's agonistic model of a radical and plural democracy, which draws upon Derrida's notion of the "constitutive outsider." Minister's extension of Mouffe's account to the issue of religious belief and civil intolerance is something that should cause all liberal postmoderns to become uncomfortable about the way in which they are so often quick to defend the plight of the Other, but just as often refuse to consider the voice of their conservative neighbors. As a side note, though Minister does not go in this direction, the same could be said about the ease with which some continental philosophers ignore voices within analytic philosophy (and vice versa). To marginalize within one's own discourse those who have traditionally marginalized you from theirs, is not to be virtuous, but to display the very vice that one originally opposed.

For Mouffe, there is rarely a justified need entirely to exclude those with whom one disagrees (regardless of whether such exclusion is from the political square, philosophy conferences, or academic positions). Conversely, it is precisely the give and take between interlocutors (or citizens) holding quite different positions that strengthens the democratic society in which we all live. As Minister points out, this does not mean that disagreement will eventually be overcome, however. Following Derrida, Mouffe identifies this agonistic space as *productively perpetual*. To say that the fundamentalist is wrong (which I think is something that *should* be said) should be proposed while admitting that the fundamentalist is still rightly a participant in the political discourse in which one finds oneself.

Political exclusion might, indeed, ultimately be necessary if particular voices threaten the very democratic society itself. Yet such exclusion requires that we do three things. First, *we must be honest* that such exclusion is what we are advocating rather than continuing to act as if we are radically inclusive. Second, *we must give reasons* why such exclusion is required rather than acting as if it is simply obvious. And third, in light of the radical obligation that is rightly affirmed by deconstruction, we ought to work to move forward in such a way that such exclusion becomes less frequent in the communities in which we find ourselves. Such honesty may not be appreciated and such reasons might not be granted by all, but this dialogical openness helps to protect against any suspicion that things could not be otherwise. Critique must continue regarding the actions that one takes and the reasons that one offers for taking such actions. Mouffe will say that some sorts of political exclusion are justified, but only for the sake of the democratic conversation itself (i.e., a society in which we can continue to challenge such exclusion after the fact by perpetually being open to contrasting opinions and perspectives; I take Levinas's defense of "the liberal state" due to its being open to "charity after justice" to express the same sentiment). The complicated task is how to appropriate this Mouffian realization such that (self-)critique can continue without sliding into a Schmittian notion of the "state of exception" such that critique is closed off in the name of power. Further, the Mouffian account of democratic ideals should be understood in a Derridean way: namely, they are not offered in the name of a particular historical democracy, but in the name of the democracy *to come*.

Ultimately, I take Minister's essay to stand as an important contribution to continental philosophy of religion concerned about ethical and political existence because it demands that such philosophy be self-reflective about its own entailments and honest about its own *necessary* epistemic exclusion and *potential* political exclusion even in the name of continuing to try to be ever more epistemically humble and politically hospitable.

Part Two

RELIGION WITH RELIGION IN PRACTICE

The Phenomenon of the Good
Reconstructing Religion
in the Wake of Deconstruction

Jeffrey Hanson

"I shall not die, but live, and declare the works of the Lord."
— Psalm 118:17

KIERKEGAARD AFTER DERRIDA

In his essay "Literature in Secret: An Impossible Filiation," Derrida continues his remarks on the silence of Abraham, the silence in which is born Abraham's faith and the faith of his many descendants. Echoing his argument in the previous sections of *The Gift of Death*, he reverts to Kierkegaard's *Fear and Trembling* pointing out that Kierkegaard could not stop talking about Abraham's silence: "His insistence in *Fear and Trembling* is a response to a strategy that deserves a long and detailed analysis all by itself; concerning notably the powerful conceptual and lexical inventions of the 'poetic' and the 'philosophical,' of the 'aesthetic,' the 'ethical,' the 'teleological,' and the 'religious.'"[1] This is surely true, as Kierkegaard's strategy in his most potent text is more involved and the structure of the work that implements his strategy more labyrinthine than Derrida himself even knows or that his reading—and he calls it a "reading" here, not an "interpretation" on purpose (*GD* 121)—reflects. Derrida calls it a reading rather than an interpretation because his effort is certainly not directed to reconstructing Kierkegaard's intended message but to isolate the secret at the heart of *any* message.

According to Derrida's reading of Kierkegaard, "It is a secret without content, without any sense to be hidden, any secret other than the very request for secrecy, that is to say the absolute exclusivity of the relation between the one who calls and the one who responds 'Here I am:' the condition of appeal and response, if there ever is such a thing, and presuming it can be conceived of in all purity" (*GD* 154). This reference to a secret without content reproduces rather faithfully not only a typically deconstructive gesture but a popular device in post-Heideggerian phenomenology. It is also a device whose usefulness is now to my mind very much in question, and dependence upon it for a meticulous study of Kierkegaard may be, as I will argue, more a hazard than a help. For from the beginning of *Fear and Trembling* the strategy deployed by Kierkegaard is one that unifies the form and content of communication to a degree and in a manner that cannot be ignored. Communication to Kierkegaard is not merely a matter of a secret at the heart of meaning but is the bringing about of transformation in relationship, which is a process that is both content-rich and also formally distinct from both simple transmission of information and Socratic maieutics.

The larger issue that is at stake is nothing less than the nature of the Good. The closest Derrida comes to identifying the Good in his engagements with Kierkegaard is to say that responsibility is possible when the Good is taken to be a movement of intention toward the Other (*GD* 51) and not a (presumably classically understood) transcendental objective. Yet I will argue that *Fear and Trembling* seeks to understand these together, in such a way that the intention toward the Other expands upon, supports, and validates the Good. In what follows, I do not propose to defend Kierkegaard from Derrida (a vain thing, fondly imagined) but to retread yet again the path to Mount Moriah (a test that cannot be foregone) with these two thinkers in an effort to reimagine the ground of contemporary philosophy of religion in the wake of, while often against, the legacy of deconstruction. Following a brief exposition of Derrida's interpretation of silence in connection with the Attunement of *Fear and Trembling*, this chapter will offer an alternative understanding of silence that takes into account Kierkegaard's elaborate development of the theme in Problema III. The fourth section presents an account of faith as it is born out of divine silence. The fifth section rereads the Attunement counter to Derrida's interpretation and in light of what has been clarified from Problema III, and the sixth and final section reinterprets *Fear and Trembling* as a whole.

Tuning-Up

Kierkegaard is often more scandalous than Derrida expects. The crucial point about secrecy is not simply that it is a content-free constitutive element of communication, but more so that while secrecy or silence is at the core of communication, communication of content takes place anyway in a way that deranges language itself. For Kierkegaard, communication is transformation of relationship. This is the goal of his authorship, and in large part it is his theme in *Fear and Trembling*.[2] In a sense his goal is impossible, akin to but not exactly the same as the way Derrida perennially speaks of the "impossible." For Kierkegaard the impossible is precisely that which happens in a way that cannot be comprehended but only lived.

Derrida is pleased to call the four versions of the story of Abraham that appear in the Attunement "*movements*...in the musical sense" (*GD* 123), which is quite right, as the title itself suggests the metaphor. But as the title further suggests, these movements are by no means finished scores (as Derrida reads them) but only the musician's attempt to find the right key, to hit the right note, for telling Abraham's story. We are only tuning up at this early stage, and the curtain has not even risen on the drama.

There is much reason to believe that one must read every one of these four movements far more tentatively than does Derrida. "Such fables belong to what one would no doubt have the right to call literature. They recount or invent the biblical story in their own way" (*GD* 123). The way they relate or interpret the biblical account is indirectly, by way of showing precisely the *failure* of these movements to convey the essential about Abraham. After these four movements are rehearsed, the unnamed "man"[3] who is invoked at the opening of the Attunement—the man who heard in his childhood the story of Abraham and unlike his peers never felt the need to go further than this story, never outgrew this story but instead was consumed by a desire to tarry with it, to not go further than Abraham but to linger with him on his way—collapses in recognition of his inability to understand Abraham even after pondering the events at Mount Moriah "Thus [in these four] and in many similar ways" (*FT* 14).[4]

So with Derrida, "Let us underline the words that give rhythm to the resounding echo of these silences" (*GD* 123), but before we do so, let us recall that as we are told in Problema III, there is silence and *then there is silence,* and only the one who is silent can tell the difference, or perhaps John the Silent, with his outsider's perspective, can. I will contend that Derrida's reading of the Attunement passages fails insofar as he is apparently committed to a univocal notion of silence. Wherever silence appears in the text he reads it as unproblematically identifiable with silence and secrecy as he construes them. But Silentio is at pains to distinguish between demonic and divine silence, which bear an undeniable outward resemblance to each other but which also stand at dialectical opposites from each other. Silence can take either form, and it is critically important to appreciate the distinction. Only a careful study of the least-understood section of the text, devoted to silence explicitly, can elucidate the multivalent character of silence and stage a conversation with Derrida on the subject. For a full understanding of this key theme we must turn to the least-discussed portion of *Fear and Trembling,* Problema III.

REREADING SILENCE IN PROBLEMA III

Silence reemerges as a theme in this final major portion of the text, and it does so in the context of not the ethical but the aesthetic. The ethical is the terrain of publicity, openness, as Derrida recognizes, and as such it presents no puzzle on the issue of silence. Silence is not tolerated in the ethical. Silentio focuses in the first two problems on a dimension of the common understanding of ethical obligation and the way in which that ordinary understanding endangers the exemplary nature of Abraham's faith. In the common understanding of ethical commitment, what is right is what is out in the open, so to speak, that is, it is public. The tragic heroes make a difficult choice to sacrifice a private attachment for the sake of a higher ethical good. In so doing they are able to articulate their choice in publicly available, transparent ethical categories. They justify themselves by appealing to concepts we all understand and appreciate. And this is an obligation expected of each of us. Ethically speaking, our job is to make an account of ourselves and our behavior. To stay silent is to evade public responsibility, accountability, the explanation we could and should offer for what it is we are doing. We take it that moral community is only possible if people are willing and able to represent publicly their actions and the motivations for their actions. On this understanding, Abraham is again in trouble, because he does not speak about what he intends; he doesn't give away his plan. The only way Abraham can be regarded as heroic is if there is a defensible form of silence, a way to stay in secret that is not merely evasion of the ethical or avoidance of responsibility but a manifestation of the religious task beyond both the ethical and the aesthetic.

But often silence is not tolerated by the aesthetic, either, for the aesthetic responds to our demand for the artistically or narratively satisfying. "A few examples" (*FT* 85) will be permitted to Silentio. "The road I must take is dialectically to pursue hiddenness through esthetics and ethics, for the point is to have esthetic hiddenness and the paradox appear in their absolute dissimilarity" (85). As Silentio suggests, when a young girl is in love but keeps her secret to herself out of duty to her family, who wish her to marry another, she freely chooses to keep quiet. Or a young man could have his beloved at the price of ruining an entire family, but he freely chooses to stay silent. "Their hiddenness is a free act, for which they are responsible also to esthetics. But esthetics is a courteous and sentimental branch of knowledge that knows more ways out than any pawnshop manager. What does it do? It makes everything possible for the lovers. By a coincidence, the respective partners in the prospective marriage get a hint of the other party's magnanimous decision. There is an explanation, the lovers get each other and also a place among authentic heroes" (85).

Aesthetics comes to the rescue because as observers of this story we are unlikely to be content with the outcome if it rests tragically with mutual concealment. Aesthetics is a resourceful and sentimental discipline as well as being the most faithless, and so it resorts to coincidence to bring about an ending whereby everyone literally lives happily ever after. Yet this sort of story is really only appropriate to light comedy or a Hollywood tearjerker and hardly ever happens in real life. "The esthetic idea," he writes, "contradicts itself as soon as it is to be implemented in actuality" (*FT* 87).

But ethics contradicts itself when applied to reality, too. Ethics has no patience for the aesthetic's lack of seriousness nor for its *deus ex machina* resolutions. "Ethics does not lend itself to debate, for it has pure categories" (*FT* 86), says Silentio.[5] Accordingly, ethics is shipwrecked on the concept of sin and repentance (98n).[6] The moment the ethical is violated it proves its own limits. It is unable to cope with the fact of sin, that sin is brought into the world each time the sinner sins, a happening that is always unique and peculiar to the individual. The ethical's demands are the same even when those demands are flaunted. If I go further than the ethical, Silentio writes, "I always run up against the paradox, the divine and the demonic, for silence is both. Silence is the demon's trap, and the more that is silenced, the more terrible the demon, but silence is also divinity's mutual understanding with the single individual" (88). I will term this dynamic *the breakdown of the Good*. The ethical, which presents us with a picture of the Good as well as we can appreciate it without further illumination—which represents the zenith of the Socratic project—collapses under the weight of its own impracticability.

But aesthetics, too, is powerless against the reality of human affairs. Often enough in life there is no happy coincidence, no comedic resolution. By themselves neither the aesthetic nor the ethical can discriminate between the silence of the divine and the silence of the demonic, which I will argue we can catch a glimpse of in the imperfect tellings of the Abraham story from the Attunement. I will term this hard fact of life *the breakdown of the Beautiful*. The aesthetic ideal, the voluptuary's desire for tranquil repose in the garden of earthly delights, collapses under the despairing realization that reality does not afford an unmarred panorama of pleasure.

Only faith can harmonize the Good and the Beautiful, justice and grace. The aesthetic heroes, like the Delphic bridegroom for example, who jilts his bride to avert a foretold catastrophe if he goes through with the wedding, can speak (and ethically speaking probably should) but freely choose not to (*FT* 89). The same could be said of the merman, who if he admits his sin to Agnes, his desire to possess her as the prize of his predatory lust, may transform his relationship to her as a truly beloved human being and not as a victim.[7] To do so, however, he cannot merely aesthetically renounce his role as seducer. That "aesthetic" outcome, according to Silentio, is a given.

He is saved by Agnes; the seducer is crushed, he has submitted to the power of innocence, he can never seduce again. But immediately two forces struggle over him: repentance, Agnes and repentance. If repentance alone gets him, then he is hidden; if Agnes and repentance get him, then he is disclosed.

But now if the merman is seized by repentance and he remains hidden, he certainly will make Agnes unhappy, for Agnes loved him in all her innocence; even when he seemed to her to be changed, however well he concealed it, she still thought it was true that he merely wished to show her the beautiful stillness of the sea. Meanwhile, in his passion the merman himself becomes even more unhappy, for he loved Agnes with a complexity of passions and in addition had a new guilt to bear. Now the demonic in repentance probably will explain that this is indeed his punishment, and the more it torments him the better. (96)

The merman cannot merely resort to the ethical, to the Good, to repair himself and his situation, for ethics cannot cope with his willingness to have seduced Agnes. A new category of possibility is introduced here, and that is the "demonic." The merman and Agnes collide in such a way that innocence meets evil intent, and one way for that collision to end up introduces a new possibility for human life, one that illustrates its difference from faith by being its exact opposite. If the merman remains alone in concealed repentance only, then he and Agnes both are unhappy. She is unhappy because she loves him innocently and entrusts herself to him only to be told that he is merely demonstrating the calm of the sea. He is unhappy because he feels guilty over his willingness to have seduced her and carried her off. This becomes the occasion for him to engage in demonic self-torment. The merman cannot be reconciled to Agnes if he wallows in self-flagellation, which reveals not true spiritual depth but only prideful refusal to actually be healed by meaningful relationship with another.[8] This, too, would be silence, though silence of the demonic and not the divine type. "With the assistance of the demonic, therefore, the merman would be the single individual who as the single individual was higher than the universal. The demonic has the same quality as the divine, namely, that the single individual is able to enter into an absolute relation to it. This is the analogy, the counterpart to that paradox of which we speak. It has, therefore, a certain similarity that can be misleading.... The merman stands at a dialectical apex" (97, 98). It is because the merman could take this demonic path that he stands at a kind of opposed pole or "dialectical apex." This is one extreme option. In that sense it is analogous to the silence of Abraham, though again in a way that is potentially misleading. Superficially it is the same kind of silence, but the silence of the merman would be the silence of determined self-enclosure, a refusal to make contact with others or to enter into relationship with God but instead a turning-in that obsessively cultivates resentment toward others and hatred of self.

That the merman must break this form of silence and reconcile himself to Agnes means that in faith he must also reconcile himself to himself, his former self that was willing to make of the beloved nothing more than the object of sexual conquest. That degenerate vision of the other must be sacrificed for the hope of getting the beloved back as a partner and equal, the beloved who will complete the lover's life in a substantive way.

> Or he can be saved by Agnes. This must not be interpreted to mean that by Agnes's love he would be saved from becoming a seducer in the future (this is an esthetic rescue attempt that always evades the main point, the continuity in the merman's life), for in that respect he is saved—he is saved insofar as he becomes disclosed. Then he marries Agnes. He must, however, take refuge in the paradox. In other words, when the single individual by his guilt has come outside the universal, he can return only by virtue of having come as the single individual into an absolute relation to the absolute. (*FT* 98)

Repentance alone drives the merman to the demonic extremity; at the opposite extremity is the possibility that he will repent with Agnes and be married to her. In this sense he is "disclosed," but his disclosure comes via the paradox, through the silence that is divine. This recapitulation of himself and his relationship can be won only through faith because the ethical or the Good alone cannot save the merman; he has gone *too far* for that. The demonic person is someone who in a way has gone beyond the ethical by recognizing what it requires and realizing that he has failed and further that he is perversely attached to the idea of himself as a perpetual failure.

The Good cannot secure the continuity necessary for living through or understanding our lives as a coherent whole simply because the

Good is not achievable. But neither can aesthetics provide a coherent account of human life fully lived. It can only give us the highlights of such a life. In a footnote to this portion of the text Silentio remarks, "Esthetics throws the cloak of love over the merman, and everything is forgotten. It is also superficial to believe that marriage is like an auction, where everything is sold in whatever condition it is when the auctioneer's hammer falls. Esthetics just sees to it that the lovers find each other and does not concern itself about the rest. If only it would see what happens afterwards, but it has no time for that" (*FT*97n). Bored with trivialities like the "dull bits"[9] of life, coquettish and faithless, aesthetics savors the heady thrill of the wedding day but rushes past the daily difficulties of mutual heartbreak, annoyance, and the trials of actually loving another human being and being loved in return. It is this reality that the merman must embrace as he wins back his beloved in a transformed manner, for if he repents with Agnes he cannot repent with her as she was to him (merely an object of sexual desire) any more than he can remain exactly who he was. The question of the continuity in the merman's life touches upon the drama of Moriah, long forgotten by this point in the text. Abraham and Isaac must remain who they are, but they cannot be unchanged by the events on the mountain. Their lives are continuities, transformations in relationship that occur in the crucible of anxiety and faith.

FAITH AND SILENCE

For continuity in the merman's life or in Abraham's and Isaac's lives, the limits of the Good must be both trespassed and expanded by the encounter with the Other. Faith can deliver this transformation. Ethics can only insist on the inflexibility of its demands: "Thou shalt not seduce innocent girls" and "Thou shalt not kill thine only son." But what if we prove ourselves to be the sort of people who are willing and ready to break these rules? What then do we do? How do we respond to ourselves and the reality of our condition? We can close ourselves off in demonic silence or we can become new creations by the strength of faith, a faith that does not and cannot wholly leave behind who we were, like the alcoholic who after years of sobriety insists on calling herself a "recovering alcoholic" and never "a former alcoholic," but nevertheless inaugurates a new sort of life lived in the shadow of a transformed and expanded sense of responsibility and the beauty thereof. The very term "recovering alcoholic" combines the old, the person I once was, with the new, the person not that I am but that I am forever becoming in an ever-renewed act of faith "one day at a time," an act that is always the same but of necessity always different at the same time.

Such continuity can be established by faith, which is realized in a kind of imaginative analogy.[10] If Abraham's trial could communicate nothing to us at all of what faith means, it would not be worth discussing. It does communicate, indirectly of course, and by appeal to the faculty of faith, which sees the likeness and unlikeness of his situation and ours. It is essential to the individuality of faith that no person's trial will be *exactly like* Abraham's, but it must be enough alike to be at least equally unprecedented.[11]

This possible way of reading Kierkegaard along the lines of imaginative analogy is opened up most completely by the story of Sarah and Tobias. Sarah is under a curse to have her husband killed by a jealous demon on her wedding night, and Tobias is prepared to love Sarah, though he knows his love for her will mean the sacrifice of his own life, and their mutual faith in God delivers them from the demon's hand. And while none of us is likely to be subject to a demonic curse as Tobias and Sarah are, it is true that if any of us will wholeheartedly love another, that love will in an important sense kill us; it will be the death of ourselves as the selves we are. But love will not only ask of us a gift of death; it will promise us a resurrection too. For while in love we cannot remain the people we are, we will become new people. This is why Silentio argues it is harder to be loved than to love. "Tobias behaves gallantly and resolutely and chivalrously, but any man who does not have the courage for that is a milksop who does not know what love is or what it is to be a man or what is worth living for; he has not even grasped the little mystery that it is better to give than to receive and has no intimation of the great mystery that it is far more difficult to receive than to give" (*FT* 103–04). Sarah, then, the one willing to accept another's love at the potential price of the beloved's death, is the genuine heroine of the story. Silentio brings up this story precisely because here sin and repentance do not figure in as they do in the story of Agnes and the merman (102). Tobias's heroism and his willingness to confront danger obviously appeal to our aesthetic sensibilities, and the figure of marriage is paradigmatically ethical. But again it is faith that makes the relationship whole in a truly divine comedy that consummates the ethical figure of marriage and the aesthetic figure of the happy romantic conclusion. Through no fault of her own, Sarah is crippled, but her faith means her own healing. The Good alone cannot save her. As Silentio says, "Ethics actually only makes sport of them, just as it would be a taunting of Sarah for ethics to say to her: Why do you not express the universal and get married? Natures such as those are basically in the paradox, and they are by no means more imperfect than other people, except that they are either lost in the demonic paradox or saved in the divine paradox" (106).

Here once more we can appreciate the harmonization of the Good and the Beautiful. Tobias and Sarah's story has a happy ending. It is aesthetically pleasing in a way few events in real life are. Yet it also meets the ethical demand. Duty is fulfilled, and the obligation of one to another is satisfied. And from this tale we learn something of what Abraham accomplishes as well. He is neither an ethical hero (as should be clear without further ado) nor an aesthetic hero. "Esthetics allowed, indeed demanded, silence of the single individual if he knew that by remaining silent he could save another. This alone adequately shows that Abraham is not within the scope of esthetics. His silence is certainly not in order to save Isaac; in fact, his whole task of sacrificing Isaac for his own and for God's sake is an offense to esthetics, because it is able to understand that I sacrifice myself but not that I sacrifice someone else for my own sake" (*FT* 112). Sarah could keep the curse against her silent, but ethics would regard that as a dirty trick played on Tobias. Ethically speaking she probably should make Tobias aware of the extraordinary burden she carries *before* she marries him. He has a right to be fully informed about the danger he is getting himself into.

Similarly it would seem Isaac has a right to be apprised of the situation, but Abraham's silence on this score is not freely chosen but compelled. Of course Abraham is not literally mute, but the final paradox of his position consists in the fact that he can speak but cannot make himself understood. In fact he does speak. In fact Silentio says if he did not speak "the whole event would lack something"

(*FT* 116). One wonders what. Perhaps it would lack something aesthetic? Something of importance to the tale as a tale? "I cannot form in advance any idea of what he is going to say; after he has said it, I presumably can understand it, perhaps in a certain sense understand Abraham in what was said without thereby coming any closer to him than in the preceding exposition" (117–18). Here Silentio lets a little something slip. We cannot know what the other will say. We will necessarily find the outcome surprising, as Silentio says of Abraham's surprise that he will not have to sacrifice Isaac after all (36). But once it is said, we can understand it retrospectively, as life itself can be "understood" in reverse but only lived forward. Not that this "understanding" brings us substantively closer to the act of faith in a way that Silentio has consistently denied is possible. And yet something of Abraham's presence in his word can be discerned. Isaac asks where the sacrifice is, and Abraham's answer is no answer at all. "And Abraham said: God himself will provide the lamb for the burnt offering, my son" (115–16).

> Now, if Abraham had replied: I know nothing—he would have spoken an untruth. He cannot say anything, for what he knows he cannot say. Therefore he answers: God himself will provide the lamb for the burnt offering, my son! From this we see, as described previously, the double-movement in Abraham's soul. If Abraham in resignation had merely relinquished Isaac and done no more, he would have spoken an untruth, for he does indeed know that God demands Isaac as a sacrifice, and he knows that he himself in this very moment is willing to sacrifice him. After having made this movement, he has at every moment made the next movement, has made the movement of faith by virtue of the absurd. Thus he is not speaking an untruth, because by virtue of the absurd it is indeed possible that God could do something entirely different. So he does not speak an untruth, but neither does he say anything, for he is speaking in a strange tongue. (119)

To speak in a strange or foreign tongue, or in perhaps even more appropriate words that Silentio uses in a different passage, to speak "in a divine language" or "in tongues"[12] (114), is the only way to communicate the content of faith. One has to speak without knowing what she is talking about.[13]

Abraham does not say anything, which is precisely his way of saying what he needs to say. Though this might seem to some as just a clear example of a contradiction—Abraham does not say that X, and yet Abraham says that X—it is better understood as an example of what Silentio will term "irony." The remark both does and does not say what is meant. In some sense, Abraham means what he says—he does believe that God will provide a sacrifice. That is his faith speaking. But in another very real sense he does not mean what he says—he thinks Isaac is himself the sacrifice, something that he dare not and cannot say. That is his resignation speaking. So his remark is a paradoxical one. Notice also that Silentio seems to take it for granted that Abraham must give a truthful response. If he says, "I know nothing," then this is not true. But nor can he forthrightly disclose the truth as he understands it, albeit in a limited way. So Abraham cannot say "I know nothing," nor can he say, "You are the lamb to be sacrificed." That too would prove to be untruthful inasmuch as it turns out *not* to be the case that Isaac is the lamb to be sacrificed. Insofar as his answer is an ironic one, which is a kind of paradox, so too does it perfectly express the structure of faith. On the one hand, the remark expresses resignation, in that it holds out the possibility that Abraham really will have to give up Isaac. On the other hand, it expresses faith in the return of Isaac, in that it holds out the possibility that Abraham will get Isaac back and that God will indeed provide a sacrifice that is not Abraham's son or at least not finally so. Abraham utters words, but he speaks in a language that no one can understand, not even himself. And this is the model for all communication about faith, even *Fear and Trembling* itself.[14]

DERRIDA'S SILENCE

Let us return to Derrida and his reading of the Attunement narratives, keeping in mind all that has been said about the working of silence in the text as a whole, not merely in the Attunement narratives themselves. My contention is that in each movement the purpose is to show indirectly how the story must be told by way of showing how it ought *not* to be told.[15] This indirect message is reinforced by the weaning narratives, to which Derrida does not refer, but which are nevertheless essential to full understanding of the text. While each Abraham story depicts a fractured paternal relationship that damages father-and-son rapport, the weaning tales depict a maternal relationship that successfully transforms the relationship of mother to child. The first paternal moments narrate an absence of communication and thus of failed transformation of relationship, while the maternal meditations[16] narrate a successful communication or transformation of relationship that paradoxically establishes greater independence for the participants but at the same time greater intimacy between them.

In the first movement, as Derrida tells it, "They rode *in silence* for three days. On the morning of the fourth day Abraham *said not a word....* But Abraham said to himself, 'I will not hide from Isaac where this walk is taking him.' But he doesn't say anything to him, so that at the end of this *first movement,* one hears an Abraham who understands he is speaking only to himself or to God, within himself to God: 'But Abraham *said softly to himself,* "Lord God in heaven, I thank you; it is better that he believes me a monster than that he should lose faith in you"'" (*GD* 123–24). Indeed, the reader is told that the three days to Moriah pass in silence as does the morning of the fourth day. But the first movement is remarkable in part because in this version of the story Abraham does *not* stay silent. Immediately upon saying to himself that he will not conceal from Isaac where their path is taking him, the overwhelming implication is that Abraham has in fact violated the injunction to secrecy and told Isaac what God has charged him to do. Why else would it be the case that Isaac "could not understand him," that he "pleaded at his feet," that "he begged for his young life, for his beautiful hopes" (*FT* 10)? In this first version, then, one of the most persuasive reasons to think that this version of the story is intentionally misleading is that in it Abraham's vow of silence is not at all maintained but broken. Abraham's second speech, then, is meant only to undo the damage of the first. Having taken matters into his own hands by spelling out Isaac's fate to him, Abraham has to take matters into his own hands again,[17] by diverting the blame from God onto himself. Reluctant to have the boy's faith in God irreparably damaged, he claims at the last moment (again not silently but to his son) that it is not the desire of God that he die after all but his own father's monstrous intent.

The purpose of this movement, then, as is the purpose of all the movements, is indirect and its manner of approach is negative. In this case specifically, the story must be told with the silence of Abraham as an essential component. Contrary to Derrida's reading, silence is *not* here preserved and respected. Furthermore, the suggestion of the first movement is that Abraham cannot undertake the sacrifice on his own terms, assuming the unassigned responsibility of protecting

God's image, so to speak, shielding his son from the perception that God is a monster. Abraham's communication is not truthful, in contrast to his communication discussed above when he tells his son that God will provide the sacrifice. And once again this indirect message is reinforced by the weaning narrative.

What happens when a mother weans her child? She alters the character of their relationship in a way that is ultimately necessary—the child must grow up and take solid food—but that preserves and even strengthens the love between them. The mother's message to the child is "I still love you, and love you more now than ever before, but because of that love I must do something that you will not understand." Thus in the appendix to the first movement of the Attunement we read: "When the child is to be weaned, the mother blackens her breast. It would be hard to have the breast look inviting when the child must not have it. So the child believes that the breast has changed, but the mother—she is still the same, her gaze is tender and loving as ever. How fortunate the one who did not need more terrible means to wean the child!" (*FT* 11). So if we take it that this is a commentary on the defective version of the story of Abraham to which it is affixed, a number of possible readings present themselves,[18] but the most obvious might be that in this version of the story Abraham resorts to more "terrible means" to separate himself from his son, measures of his own devising and that institute not a continuation and deepening of their relationship but its destruction. For in this first version Isaac's attitude toward his father and his betrayed secrecy has changed utterly; Abraham is indeed lost to his son, who does what no child should ever have to do: to call upon God for defense against his own parent. The maternal anecdote offers the requisite corrective: However the story is to be told it must preserve the relationship among the parties. The mother's message is "I have not changed toward you myself, but I must play at deceiving you to transform the love we share in a way that is difficult but important nonetheless if we are to know one another better." Her communication is indeed silent and secret, a secret that she must keep from her beloved child, but a content-rich message is conveyed nonetheless.

Second movement: "They rode along the road *in silence.... Silently* he arranged the firewood and bound Isaac; *silently* he drew the knife" (*GD* 124). Derrida rightly notices the silence that pervades the second movement. Indeed, the silence here is not broken by Abraham as in the first movement, but it is robotic, mechanical, pro forma, and ultimately demonic. It merely anticipates the final grim silence of Abraham when the encounter on Moriah robs him of all his joy. While silence is here respected, again the tale goes awry, proving that it is not silence alone that matters but the style or attitude of silence that Abraham adopts, whether demonic or divine. While in the first version silence is broken, here it is preserved, but in an attitude of bitterness and resentment toward God, which ultimately again poisons the relationship of father and son. "Silently he arranged the firewood and bound Isaac; silently he drew the knife—then he saw the ram that God had selected. This he sacrificed and went home.—From that day henceforth, Abraham was old; he could not forget that God had ordered him to do this. Isaac flourished as before, but Abraham's eyes were darkened, and he saw joy no more" (*FT* 12). The silence here is oppressive and self-enclosed, the secrecy suffocating. The schematic recitation of the events indicates that Abraham's joy is not lost after the events of Moriah but even before them, and the conclusion of the tale only ratifies in fact what has already been inwardly resigned. Where is the joy at the substitution of the ram? Why is the relief of Abraham's burden not hailed with enthusiasm? And what kind of parent is unable to find joy in the flourishing of his or her own child?

Something is assuredly amiss in this version as in the others, and again the weaning narrative puts a finer point on this deficiency. "When the child has grown big and is to be weaned, the mother virginally conceals her breast, and then the child no longer has a mother. How fortunate the child who has not lost his mother in some other way!" (*FT* 12). When the child is weaned it seems indeed that he has no mother, but of course this is not true; he still has a mother, but their relationship is altered.[19] Isaac, on the other hand, in the second movement has indeed lost his parent. Any child unable to stir joy in his father's heart would surely and rightly wonder whether that father loved him at all. The indirect message is thus that however the story is to be told, whatever vocabulary we use, it must include the imperative that the events of Moriah, no matter how much of a strain they provide on the relationships among the parties, must result in their mutual happiness and joy. Secrecy is required, but in a register different from the oppressive secrecy of self-enclosure.

Skipping ahead then to the fourth movement, as Derrida does:

> In the *fourth movement* the secret of silence is indeed shared by Isaac, but neither one nor the other ruptures the secret of what has happened; moreover, they have well and truly decided not to speak of it at all: "*Not a word is ever said of this in the world*, and *Isaac never talked to anyone* about what he had seen, and Abraham did not suspect that anyone had seen it." The same secret, the same silence, therefore separates Abraham and Isaac. For what Abraham has not seen, or so the fable makes clear, is the fact that Isaac saw him, saw him draw his knife, saw his face wracked with despair. Abraham therefore doesn't know that he has been seen. He sees without seeing himself seen. In this regard he is in nonknowledge. He doesn't know that his son will have been his witness, even if a witness henceforth held to the same secret, the secret that binds him to God. (*GD* 124–25)

Silence is not univocal. Here again the tone is unmistakably elegiac, and it shows that something is amiss in this version of events. The crisis at Moriah cannot have instituted an abyss between father and son if Moriah is the place where Abraham and Isaac both kept their faith as opposed to losing it. The implication of the fourth episode is this: what Isaac sees that plunges his relationship with his father into silence, not the structural silence of the decisive moment but the silence of recrimination and blame, is his father's *wavering* before the summons. Derrida minimizes a key textual detail: "Isaac saw that Abraham's left hand was clenched in despair, that a shudder went through his whole body" (*FT* 14).

This shudder of despair is enough to cast Isaac, too, into doubt, doubt over the goodness of God, doubt over the benevolence of Abraham. If this silence that portends absence of communication and relationship between father and son is to be dispelled, then faith must absolve the participants in the drama of Moriah. Again the weaning narrative provides a clue: "When the child is to be weaned, the mother has stronger sustenance at hand so that the child does not perish. How fortunate the one who has this stronger sustenance at hand" (*FT* 14). Are we to take it, then, that in this final episode Abraham has failed to provide "stronger sustenance?" The relationship has not been altered, as in a successful weaning; it has been broken. The child is left without provision, exposed on the rock of Moriah with no sustenance, a fate not even suffered by Ishmael.

Similarly Abraham cannot be allowed to recriminate against himself, the theme of the third movement. Derrida is right that in this version of the story Abraham "implores God. He throws himself on the ground and asks for God's forgiveness: not for having disobeyed him, but on the contrary for having obeyed him" (*GD* 125). But again there is no reason to think that Silentio is telling the story as it must be told to communicate the mystery of faith; on the contrary, there is every reason to think he is deliberately telling it in such a way as to illustrate how *not* to narrate Moriah. In this version Silentio specifies, "It was a quiet evening when Abraham rode out alone, and he rode to Mount Moriah; he threw himself down on his face, he prayed God to forgive him his sin, that he had been willing to sacrifice Isaac, that the father had forgotten his duty to his son" (*FT* 13). This is not the journey to Moriah but a later one, a return to the scene of the crime, so to speak. Abraham is alone, riding out at night. His plea for forgiveness is not a component of faith properly understood but a sign that faith has not taken hold of him.[20] Instead guilt and self-obsession rule his life, to the point that apparently he is unable to enjoy the presence of his son or the company of his family. What kind of father after all leaves his family at night to be alone with the unhealed trauma of his past?

"When the child is to be weaned," Silentio observes, "the mother, too, is not without sorrow, because she and the child are more and more to be separated, because the child who first lay under her heart and later rested upon her breast will never again be so close. So they grieve together the brief sorrow. How fortunate the one who kept the child so close and did not need to grieve any more!" (*FT* 13). Of course there is sorrow when the child is weaned. The mother inevitably must wean the child from his immediate dependence upon her. Her son is growing up to be a man, and a man does not need his mother's constant consolation, her first gift to him. But this sorrow is "brief" and meant to be mourned together. If the child is kept close there is no call for ongoing sorrowing, but in this third episode Abraham is not keeping Isaac close, and his sorrow haunts him well after the events of Moriah have played out.

What is at stake in this altered reading? My claim is that crucial to the notion of faith is the capacity to affirm the goodness of God and by extension the goodness of all things. Derrida continually reads

Fear and Trembling as a meditation on the conflict of the good and the holy, but this conflict is only apparent. It is faith that allows their apparent contradiction to be reconciled. What Abraham bargains is that God is good, despite the fact that he appears to be commanding what is not good. But in his faithful obedience he affirms the impossible, that God remains good and is true to the promise of His covenant. I say faithful obedience purposely. Mere obedience does not constitute faith (*FT* 28–29). The episodes of the Attunement do not present a single scenario in which Abraham is disobedient. On the contrary, in every one he is prepared to make the sacrifice. The question is not whether Abraham will go through with it, but what attitude must he have to go through with it in order to maintain and even enrich the relationships he has with God and with his family. The weaning narratives in particular illustrate the possibility that a content-rich communication can take place in silence. The mother in private terms only expresses her love for her child and provides a pledge of continued nurturing, something that cannot be accounted for merely in formal or empty gestures. Her communication is silent in the divine form, and this is a message that establishes the continuity of her life with the life of her beloved.

Reappraising *Fear and Trembling*

Fear and Trembling is largely about how we respond to reality, to the inevitable heartbreak, separation, and loss symbolized by the weaning narratives in the Attunement.[21] Silentio says as much when he writes, "I shall describe the movements [of resignation and faith] in a specific case that can illuminate their relation to actuality, for this is the central issue" (*FT* 41). Everything turns on the relationship to reality, the relationship to God and to loved ones. The case he has in mind is the lad's impossible love for the princess, a fairy tale love that has a certain aesthetic appeal, but like all fairy tales and all tragedies that have an aesthetically satisfying component, such love "cannot possibly be translated from ideality into reality" (41).

Surely this is the most common experience. What do we do when confronted with the disappointment of our hopes and dreams? When the child of promise is taken away, when the ones we love most of all die in our arms? When the little one to whom we have devoted our lives grows up to stand independently on her own? We can resign ourselves to our fate, trudge up the mountain in a grim silence to do what must be done. The lad can renounce his beloved, but in so doing he does not remain with her but turns her into an ideal. No longer in love with a real human being, we love an idea of her, someone who cannot be and has never been, the child who did not have to be sacrificed, the beloved who never grew old and died, the boy who never grew up to defy us. It is easy to substitute a fantasy for the reality. The young lad is "too proud" (*FT* 44), Silentio says, to let the whole content of his life and love be but a passing fancy. So he never forgets his love but removes it from the flux of the real, keeping it safe and forever "young" (44). Outside of time and petty concern, the love of the resigned hero for his princess becomes an abstraction that the world cannot touch. Invulnerable and pure, this love is no longer subject to risk or transformation; what the princess does can no longer affect the lad in love, for he is no longer in love with the princess but with an idea of her. And again, what could be more familiar? Who among us does not carry an idealized vision of what could have been? And do we not truly know that this vision is idealized?

The harder path is not the silence of self-enclosure and inward brooding over our cherished imaginings, but of faith, the faith that affirms that though love is impossible it will nevertheless come to the lover. The lad believes he will get his princess, not in an imagined future but today, here and now. But of course he cannot imagine he will get the princess just as he loves her.[22] The lad will get his princess, not this particular princess in all likelihood, but the one who for him *is* the princess. And the same is true for Abraham as well. He will get the child of promise, as promised, but the child cannot be the one he has in mind. Does not Abraham get back Isaac, the very one he is prepared to sacrifice? Yes and no, and this is the point of the dialectical imagination as Kierkegaard understands it. The son he takes to the mountain is the same son who comes home with him again, but obviously Isaac is not the same son. How could he be? How could Abraham be the same father? How could the lad be unchanged by his love for another? How could the princess be the same beloved, even if she is the same?

In this sense the "content" of the belief that each has does not matter. Which woman will be the lad's princess does not matter.[23]

In this respect Derrida is right when he argues, "in the end, God's response does not count as much as we might think; it does not affect Abraham's infinitely guilty conscience or abyssal repentance in its essence" (*GD* 127). He argues this way because for him (and for Levinas) there is a terrible purity to the call of responsibility, a call without content but distinguished only by the empty formalism of the response, the "Here I am," the *me voici*, the *hineni*.[24] Again to quote from Derrida, "It is a secret without content, without any sense to be hidden, any secret other than the very request for secrecy, that is to say the absolute exclusivity of the relation between the one who calls and the one who responds 'Here I am:' the condition of appeal and response, if there ever is such a thing, and presuming it can be conceived of in all purity. From that moment on there is nothing more sacred in the world for Abraham, for he is ready to sacrifice everything" (154).

But in another sense it does matter, and in this respect Derrida misses the point entirely. It is precisely not the case that for Abraham there is "nothing more sacred in the world." On the contrary, for Abraham *all* is sacred. Abraham's faith is as Silentio is at pains to emphasize, not *of* but *for* this world. He believes (as Silentio does not [*FT* 34]) that God really does care about his petty concerns, and he expects the reward of his faith not in a far-off future realm but right here and right now.[25] "It is great to lay hold of the eternal, but it is greater to hold fast to the temporal after having given it up" (18). Abraham is "young enough to wish to be a father" (18), and he expects to grow old in the land, surrounded by his loving family. *This is not a promise without content.*[26] Abraham will not be rewarded with a son he does not recognize but with a man who is still his own offspring though decisively changed.

If the response of God is wholly immaterial, why does Abraham not have to go through with it in the end? The tragic heroes have to go through with it. The lad in the attitude of resignation really has to give up the one he loves. Merely formally speaking, the calls upon Abraham are the same; he responds the same way to the command to sacrifice his son as he does to spare his life. What the second moment of response teaches us is not that this is the true high point of the drama as Levinas would have it,[27] but the horrible truth that these two commands are spoken by the *same voice*.

Of Abraham's trial Derrida claims, "This test would thus be a sort of absolute *desacralization* of the world. Besides, since there is no content to the secret itself, one cannot even say that the secret to be kept is sacred, that it is the only remaining sacredness" (*GD* 154). But the world cannot be desacralized by the commands. The commands invest the world with sacramental significance.[28] That Derrida fails to see this is crucial. According to his analysis, the good is fundamentally fractured. On the one hand there is the hopelessly conflictual realm of the real, where irresponsibility is inevitable, where violence reigns unchallenged, where perjury is the norm (126). On the other hand is "the absolute exclusivity of the relation between the one who calls and the one who responds 'Here I am:'" (154). In a different essay in *The Gift of Death* Derrida asks, "On what condition is responsibility possible? On the condition that the Good no longer be a transcendental objective, a relation between objective things, but the relation to the other, a response to the other; an experience of personal goodness, and a movement of intention" (51). I read *Fear and Trembling* as an effort to reject these false dilemmas between an empty formal response on the one hand and a violent conflict on the other; and between the Good as an unstable transcendental object on the one hand and as the appeal of the Other on the other. I have tried to show that these latter two in particular are placed into a more complex relationship by *Fear and Trembling*.[29]

I have argued elsewhere[30] that Derrida cannot be content to leave unresolved the issue of whether the specific content of revelations is prior to the empty formal structures of revealability; I contend that this lack of resolution is not endemic to the problematic that he so often explored between analogues to revelation and revealability, like law and justice, traditional interpretation and deconstruction, economy and the gift. Significantly, it is not the case that Derrida leaves us wholly stranded without practical guidance on how to bring law into conversation with violence, or to vivify the economy with the impossible possibility of the gift, but that his commitments insofar as they are indeed made plain by him—to democracy, to hospitality, to justice—if they are to have any effect must be admitted to be informed by the faith traditions that invest them with content and communicate something of the Good. Instead Derrida sunders these poles in a fashion that is actually consistent with much of twentieth century French thinking.[31]

My effort, then, is to read with Kierkegaard a more synthetic or *sacramental* understanding of the privileged revelation in its relation with the real. When God commands Abraham to stay his hand we learn that God is not a god who desires human sacrifice. This counts as an enrichment of our understanding not just of God but of the Good itself, an enrichment brought about by the relation to the Other, to be sure, but a relation that alters its participants and enhances their appreciation for the Good as well.[32] Here there is no question of choosing between form and content, between the Good as objective correlate and relation with the Other. The revelation of God contributes a positive and creative alteration in the Good, effectively communicates this new truth, and alters the relationships among the involved parties. That this alteration takes place silently is certain, though again I have tried to argue that silence is not univocal.

Perhaps the whole substance of *Fear and Trembling* itself amounts to the effort of Silentio, who tells us time and again that he does not have faith, to speak about what he himself does not understand. The true paradox of divine silence is not that Abraham is wholly incommunicable but that despite the fact that his situation is incommunicable he is able to speak about it in a way that is partially and retrospectively comprehensible. If this were not the case, then *Fear and Trembling* ought not to have been written at all.

Keep in mind that the text's author is named "Silence." And despite the fact that he is of silence he speaks all the time. Does he speak in the way Abraham speaks, ironically, paradoxically, or in words that both do and do not say what he means? Silentio often says he cannot understand Abraham, but perhaps he is at no greater or lesser advantage than anyone else in this respect. If indeed the life of faith is one that is private, if everyone has a silent relationship to God that is not transparent to others, then we are all like Silentio. We are all outsiders; no one can claim absolutely to have Abraham's faith, and we all must be content to speak of it as best we can or to appropriate it into our own lives in a process of endless becoming: Kierkegaard never speaks of *being* a Christian, only of *becoming* one. And despite being outsiders it seems like at the end of the book we realize that Abraham must speak. Johannes must speak. We must speak.

Recall also the very first words of the book, taken from Hamann. "What Tarquinius Superbus said in the garden by means of the poppies, the son understood but the messenger did not" (*FT* 3).[33] The point of this anecdote is that though silence reigns, communication happens nonetheless. Of course Tarquinius's son could just as easily have misunderstood the message. This is a risk that is implicated in every communicative act. We might misunderstand Abraham's words. Perhaps even Isaac misunderstood them. We may misunderstand Silentio's words in this very book. But there is still hope that ultimately our lives can be changed if we are willing to expose ourselves to the message that is being passed in secret. What Abraham is doing, what Silentio is doing, what often enough we are doing when we communicate, is speaking beautiful and true words about what we do not understand ourselves. And perhaps the paradigmatically beautiful and true words that faith allows us to echo are the sanctifying words of Creation: "it is good."[34]

My Lies Are Always Wishes

Reflections on the Fictional
Structure of the Statement of Faith
— A Response to Jeffrey Hanson

Drew M. Dalton

t is difficult to know how to respond to Jeff Hanson's thoughtful exploration of the curious interplay between silence and speech, secret and revelation, presented in the act of faith as probed by Kierkegaard. How are we to discuss that curious and paradoxical transcendence that is the language of faith and the tongue of angels without reducing it to the restless chatter of the ethical ego or the silent complacency of an aesthetic drive? There is, after all, as Kierkegaard asserts and Hanson affirms, a temptation in the face of the seemingly impossible task of straddling this difference to resign ourselves entirely to one side, either to the ineffable silence of secrecy that attempts to endure the encounter with the divine through stolid resignation, as Hanson might hold Derrida does, or to tend to a kind of totalizing neurotic logomania that attempts to evade or gain control of the divine by harnessing it through language, a tendency that, one could argue, might be found in someone like Hegel. But, argues Hanson, neither of these options presents the true position of faith, a position that binds together, paradoxically, silence and speech, secret

155

and revelation, and redeems, as Hanson puts it, the inevitable collapse of the Good and the Beautiful that await those who remain bound to the ethical or the aesthetic, respectively. Ill-content to the aesthetic beauty of stoic silence, faith must speak, it must respond to the call placed upon it, but not in the language of ethical self-accusation or justification.

Instead faith must speak some determinate content about the Other to whom it testifies. The speech of faith, then, is not the empty blather of ethical debate, what oftentimes approaches a mere sound and fury signifying nothing. It is instead a power and potency—one that announces the approach of the divine. In the iteration of faith, as Hanson shows, the daemonic temptation toward either muteness or *furor loquendi* is transformed into a consecrated singular expression, a creative act that does not de-sacralize the world, but affirms its holiness.

The language of faith is a transformative speech act, one that has the power of carrying the orator from one position to another, from here to there. It thus belongs to a movement much larger than itself, the movement of becoming, conversion and metamorphosis. After all, as Hanson points out, the act of faith is, for the majority of us, not about *being* a certain way (i.e., being a Christian), but *becoming* a certain way (i.e., becoming a Christian). As a movement, the declaration of faith must be defined and understood in relation to its *telos*, in relation to the directionality and end of its transcendence. This *telos* operates as a kind of fixed point by which to measure any momentary position, action, or utterance. Given this conception, acts of faith can be understood neither solely within their immediate context (indeed, therein they may appear mad or foolish), nor solely by what precedes or anticipates them. Acts of faith are not oriented toward the past and do not belong to any stable present. Instead, they are inexorably wrapped up in the perpetual coming of the future, a future from which the faith receives its meaning. It is thus only in the context of the eternally future that the speech of faith can be understood properly.

But, we must ask, what is the content of such a sacred speech? What does it speak and what is the value or truth of such an expression? Of course, at first glance such questions strike the reader as very strange, if not entirely redundant. But it is precisely in these questions that, at least to me, one of the most profound mysteries of the language of faith is revealed, one that sheds, I think, significant light on the curious interplay of secrecy and revelation. Now, at least superficially, the answer to such questions should be easy. Truth, the believer might say, is what is spoken in the language of faith; after all, what does the Christian message pretend to if not the truth. Indeed, there are fewer more succinct self-declarative statements made by the one who is called the Christ in the Scriptures than his claim to be "the way, the truth, and the life" (John 14:6). The speech act of faith is nothing, we thus think, if it is not true. This much should be clear: the confession of faith should proclaim and testify to the truth.

And yet in the Abrahamic speech act, the very narrative in which we find the foundation of faith according to Kierkegaard, the statement under question is most definitely *not* the truth, at least not immediately. At least from the perspective of the first-time reader or hearer of these texts, or from the perspective of one who approaches the text from the past or the present (from what has led up to them), Abraham's response to Isaac's concern over the source of their sacrifice that "God will see to the sheep for His burnt offering, my son," (Gen. 22:8) is *not* immediately true. It is an invention, a fiction. In a word, it is a lie. The truth of the moment is that Abraham believes he has been sent to Mount Moriah to sacrifice his son. Thus though his lie may be "white," as it were, intended to conceal, hide, or keep *secret* his intentions from his son to protect him from the trauma of the situation; it is a lie nonetheless. But, of course, this is not the final word on the matter. For as we know, read in its entirety, that is, interpreted not in light of what precedes the action but by what follows it, Abraham's statement is not a lie, but is most decidedly the truth. After all, in the final analysis God *does* provide a sheep for the burnt offering, preserving Abraham from his horrible task and Isaac from his fate. So it is, we assume, that Abraham's statement, though not immediately true, is made *in faith,* and thus must be interpreted not in terms of its immediate truth value but in light of what follows. Thus, though Abraham's statement is proximally and immediately a lie, conceived in the perspective of the future it is true. Still, this truth value, it must be said, though eventually *revealed,* remains a *secret,* concealed to the speaker himself at the moment of the declaration.

Of course the immediate fictionality of the statement of faith is not exclusive to the Abrahamic speech act; it is repeated in any meaningful statement of faith. Take, for example, the statement of the Christian who declares him or herself to be a "new creation," "born again" or "washed clean" and "made blameless," through the baptismal waters. Of course, any honest, self-critical speaker at this moment will be able to admit that such statements, though proclaimed as true in the present, are patently false. Just because one has been baptized does not make them an entirely new person. Quite to the contrary, upon emerging from the baptismal waters one must take up anew the same burdens, concerns, and proclivities that pushed them toward those waters in the first place. Indeed, the real struggle with such tendencies has only just begun at the point of conversion; and conversion, no matter how transformative it may be, does not alleviate the burden of having to be oneself nor the difficulties that are singularly one's own. One is, at the moment of conversion, the same being he or she was before conversion, just as full of fault and dereliction as before. And yet, in *faith* these statements are made. They are thus made not with the expectation that they are true *now*, but, as Hanson puts it so wonderfully, they are spoken with the faith and hope that they will *become* true. These statements, thus fictional in their temporal setting, are made true, it is believed, in eternity, in the approach of the future. In this regard they resemble the evocative lyric "All my lies are always wishes" (from the song "Ashes of American Flags," sung by Wilco frontman Jeff Tweedy in the band's 2002 album *Yankee Hotel Foxtrot*).

In faith, all our lies are wishes, ways of casting ourselves beyond the present into a possible future that we welcome as a messianic promised land in which all our wishes will be granted and all our lies made true. What is more, it is only through such temporal lies, revealed in the end to be eternal truths, that we leap into this future—that we begin our process of becoming. For without this anticipation of the future in which our lies will be made true, our desires fulfilled, and all our tears wiped away, we have not yet begun the journey of faith. Without this fictional leap into the future we remain riveted to a past that condemns us and a present that demands the impossible of us. Put another way, without resorting to the immediately fictional statement of faith, without making such statements that in their very nature stretch beyond themselves, beyond what is immediately true or present, we must remain either silently enraptured in a nostalgic and aesthetic worship of our past or burdened by the impossibility of ethically justifying ourselves to the now, both of which are doomed, as Hanson points out, to failure and collapse.

So it seems that in order to begin the journey of faith we must cast ourselves beyond the aesthetic and the ethical, beyond silence and idle talk, and enter into the play of secret and revelation testified to in the immediately fictional statement of faith. That is, we must tell extravagant lies and dream boldly, to play on Luther's injunction, and make impossible wishes all in faith and hope that in the approach of a messianic future, that which we "bind on earth," in the temporal immediacy of the now, will in the fullness of the eternal future be "bound in heaven" as well (Matt. 16:19). This, it seems to me, is the paradoxical and seemingly impossible mystery of the statement of faith that Hanson in his rereading of Kierkegaard after Derrida invites us to recognize.

Silence, Faith, and (the Call to) Goodness

— A Response to Jeffrey Hanson

Stephen Minister

"Never shall I forget the little faces of the children, whose bodies I saw turned into wreaths of smoke beneath a *silent* blue sky.... Never shall I forget that nocturnal *silence* which deprived me, for all eternity, of the desire to live. Never shall I forget those moments which murdered my God and my soul and turned my dreams to dust."

— Elie Wiesel, *Night*

J effrey Hanson's "The Phenomenon of the Good" offers an insightful reading of the depiction of faith in *Fear and Trembling* by investigating the theme of silence as it appears in the oft-neglected Problema III and the Attunement. Hanson argues, convincingly in my view, that silence need not signify the absence of content, but can actually represent an effective and specific communication. Contrary to Derrida's work, which takes silence and secrecy as signs of the inaccessibility that sets off a perpetual deconstruction, Hanson suggests that silence in fact plays a crucial role in the

construction of positive religious faith, of faith in a religion with religion. While I appreciate the overall direction of Hanson's essay, I have
two concerns that are relevant to the issues this volume addresses.

My first concern centers on the apparent mysteriousness of the
content of faith. Hanson writes, "To speak in a strange or foreign
tongue...is the only way to communicate the content of faith. One
has to speak without knowing what she is talking about." Applying
this to Abraham, Hanson concludes, "Abraham utters words, but
he speaks in a language that no one can understand, not even himself. And this is the model for all communication about faith." If
this simply means that the claims we make in attempting to articulate our faith cannot achieve the status of knowledge according to
modern evidentialist, foundationalist, or Hegelian standards or that
full knowledge and understanding on matters of faith can never be
achieved in this finite human life, then this is a correct and helpful
reminder. However, I think part of the value of postmodern philosophy lies in its rejection of the modern conception of knowledge and
its standards as normative. In light of these rejections, can we not say
that when I talk about the content of my faith, I can know (to some
degree) what I am talking about and other people can understand
(to some degree) what I am saying? Do communities of faith and
interfaith dialogue not presuppose that others can, even if only in a
limited way, understand us? My point here might not be contrary to
Hanson's intention in these claims and might be "merely" semantic,
but I think that if we are to get onto the work of thinking through
faith and religion together we should stop making claims that, even if
only apparently, undermine this possibility.

My second concern is more substantial and centers on the very
content that Hanson ascribes to faith. According to Hanson's reading
of *Fear and Trembling,* faith is called for or becomes necessary when,
in Silentio's words, "life [has] fractured what had been united in the
pious simplicity of the child" (*FT* 9).[1] Our faith or lack thereof is
demonstrated by "how we respond to reality, to the inevitable heartbreak, separation, and loss, symbolized by the weaning narratives
in the Attunement." Abraham's faith is evinced not by his willingness to commit a reckless act of religious violence, as some detrac-
tors have claimed, but by his commitment, amidst his heartbreak at
the course of action laid out before him, to "affirm the goodness

of God and by extension the goodness of all things.... What Abraham bargains is that God is good, despite the fact that he appears to be commanding what is not good." God is like the loving mother of the weaning narratives who remains good, whose act of weaning is good, despite the child's perception of a silence, the absence of the good gifts the child desires and expects. Faith is found in those who continue to affirm the goodness of God and God's creation despite the perception of a silence or an absence of the goodness we desire and expect. As Hanson puts it, "the paradigmatically beautiful and true words that faith allows us to echo are the sanctifying words of Creation: 'it is good.' "

In reading this I could not help but think of Elie Wiesel's use of silence in *Night,* his account of his experience in Nazi concentration camps, and the not unrelated attempts of Emmanuel Levinas to articulate a "religion for adults," a religion for those for whom life, including the reality of the Holocaust, "had fractured what had been united in the pious simplicity of the child." Given the horror of this event, for Wiesel and Levinas, a religion for adults cannot be based on a faith in "the goodness of all things."[2] Instead, Levinas argues, if God is to remain essentially linked with goodness, we will have to conceive of God and the Good not on the basis of being, of "all things," but on the basis of the ethical, the call to ethical responsibility. Thus Levinas writes that "God commands only through the [people] for whom one must act," and that "To go toward God is...to go toward the others who stand in the trace of illeity."[3] Rather than the horrors of the world indicating simply the absence of God, God cries out in the face of every vulnerable and suffering person, issuing a silent, inaudible call to responsibility. As with Hanson's silence, this silence is, I would argue, a "content-rich communication." From a Levinasian perspective, a religion with religion is not a religion that holds fast to the belief in the goodness of all things, but rather a religion called to the ongoing task of working for goodness in a world fraught with violence and suffering.

This interpretation of faith shows up in Levinas's response to *Fear and Trembling,* a response which it must be admitted does more to illuminate Levinas's views than Kierkegaard's.[4] Surely Levinas reveals his own misunderstanding of *Fear and Trembling* when he claims that "Kierkegaard's" interpretation of the Akedah "shocks" him because it seems to justify religiously motivated violence.[5] Nonetheless, it is consistent with Levinas's philosophy for him to claim, *pace* Silentio, that Abraham's decision not to go through with the sacrifice is the "highest point in the drama."[6] It is this moment that demonstrates "Abraham's attentiveness to the voice that led him back to the ethical order," that is, the voice of God calling to him from the face of Isaac.[7] For Levinas, Abraham's faith is found, not in his willingness to follow a senseless command or supposed religious duty, but in his ability to recognize his responsibility to Isaac and refuse to kill him in spite of this command. Abraham's faith is credited to him as righteousness because he was able to hear the "Thou shall not kill," his true religious calling, over the ruckus of his supposed religious duty.

From a Levinasian perspective, Hanson's account of faith invites the moral hazard of theodicy. Levinas regards theodicy as a justifying or rationalizing maneuver designed to give us comfort in the face of the evil and suffering we see and inflict. As such, theodicy is a temptation, the indulgence in which risks betraying our responsibility to others. At best it is an errant casuistry and at worst it contributes to complacency in the face of evil. Levinas proposes that recent history—which in his time included "two world wars, the totalitarianisms of the right and left, Hitlerism and Stalinism, Hiroshima, the Gulag, and the genocides of Auschwitz and Cambodia"[8]—expresses sufficient evil to bring a *de facto* end to theodicy. Though the suffering of others can awaken in us a sense of our responsibility, Levinas does not regard suffering as justified because of this possible outcome. In fact, as one commentator puts it, the whole point for Levinas is that "we cannot justify the suffering that exists," which is precisely why we must do something to alleviate it.[9] It is precisely because everything is not good that we are called to responsibility. I am sure it was not Hanson's intention to diminish our ethical responsibility, and it certainly was not Kierkegaard's as he himself sets a high bar for responsibility toward others in *Works of Love,* but I think Levinas is right to be concerned that a faith committed to the belief in the goodness of all things can allow a complacency toward the suffering of others around us, including the suffering to which we contribute.

What Levinas leaves out, and what Hanson's essay insightfully recognizes, is the problem that results when I recognize not simply that I have failed to be fully responsible, but that, like Agnes's merman,

I have positively and actively trespassed against another. How do I honestly reconcile the trespassing self that I am with the responsible self that I desire to be? What can effect this transformation? As Hanson points out, ethics cannot help us here as it "can only insist on the inflexibility of its demands." Perhaps Levinas's religion for adults fails to account for this transformation precisely because for Levinas religion, so far as I can tell, simply *is* the call to ethical responsibility. More than this, we need a faith that, as Hanson writes, "inaugurates a new sort of life lived in the shadow of a transformed and expanded sense of responsibility...[a faith that] combines the old, the person I once was, with the new, the person not that I am but that I am forever becoming." For this faith we need a God who is more than simply the call to justice issuing from the faces of others, but a God who can create anew, a God who opens up new possibilities. Perhaps Kierkegaard was on to something when he suggested that "the being of God means that everything is possible, or that everything is possible means the being of God."[10]

The Greatest of These
Toward a Phenomenology of Agapic Love

Drew M. Dalton

AGAPE: THE FUNDAMENTAL MOTIF

In the course of forging what might be called a postdeconstructive faith, it is essential that we return to that formative content which serves as the bedrock of religion. But this return should neither be merely a kind of fundamentalist nostalgia nor an inauthentic revival of "that old time religion." Instead, it must be a creative act, one which in its return introduces something new such that the core concepts of faith are not merely preserved, but transformed. Faith is, after all, not to be hidden under a bushel nor protected under a bell jar, and religion is no museum. Faith is a living thing. It is dynamic and fluid and religion must move with it if it is to remain true to the phenomena it serves. It is in part this recognition that fueled the deconstructive turn within religion in the first place and gave rise to the concept of a "religion without religion," a faith, as it were, without content. In our attempt to ask anew the question of religion in light of this critique and investigate, in turn, the possibility of a "postmodern" religion *with* religion, a religion that remains true to the dynamic nature of faith without being stripped of any formal content, it is incumbent that we creatively reexamine the core tenants of faith.

There are few Christian concepts more ubiquitous or popular than its understanding of love. From John's declaration that "God is love," (1 John 4:8) to Paul's evocative poetizations of the virtues of love in 1 Corinthians 13, the New Testament's presentations of love have made it onto the front of greeting cards and into the titles of bestsellers and the liturgy of countless weddings, both religious and secular, and have even been marketed on T-shirts and bracelets. This popularity should come as no surprise, however. After all, love has been called the "fundamental motif of Christianity,"[1] and has been claimed to occupy "a central place in Christianity."[2] Furthermore, the love of the New Testament is, some theologians have argued, "Christianity's own original basic concept," which constitutes its core insight and fundamental difference from other religious traditions.[3] It makes sense then that Jesus' command to "love one another" should be one of the most widely disseminated claims in the West, where Christianity's influence on the shape of society is virtually unparalleled.

But despite this wide acceptance and mass interest, the Christian understanding of love remains one of the most obscure and least understood of its central tenets, resulting in countless theological treatises and debates. Certainly, what the Scriptures mean by "love" and what "love" means in the popular imagination are two fundamentally different things. Indeed, the first thing most biblical scholars will point out about the nature of this love is that it cannot be conflated with our popular understanding of romantic or erotic love. Christian love, they will quickly declare, is *agape,* which stands in contradistinction from our everyday use of the term "love." If this is truly the case, how are we to understand the New Testament's comments concerning love given our own assumptions that serve to preclude real comprehension? What is the nature of this agapic love? Is it truly distinct from erotic love? Exactly how is it different from our quotidian understanding? And, perhaps most importantly, is agapic love an actual existent love available for phenomenological consideration, or a kind of prescriptive ideal love available only for theological or moral speculation? That is, is it something that can be observed operating in the world, or does it remain merely a kind of ideal object, something perceived only through the eyes of faith?

In this chapter I will ask these questions anew by approaching the concept of agapic love phenomenologically in an attempt to creatively return to what is perhaps one of the most essential elements of the Christian faith. It is my hope to, in this way, open yet another way into the kind of postdeconstructive religion aimed at by this volume. There are a few preliminary steps, however. First, we must clear a space for our investigation by setting some parameters of the object of our study. That is, we must attune ourselves to what is claimed concerning the nature of agapic love in the Scriptures and by a few central theologians in order to isolate the object of our inquiry and distinguish it from other similar phenomena. Having done this, we can then compare what is claimed about agapic love to our understanding and experience of erotic love, which we will do by way of an extended investigation of the treatment of erotic love in the Platonic texts. Finally, with this footing beneath us, we will venture a phenomenology of agapic love, which I will argue has in many ways already been accomplished by Emmanuel Levinas. As will become clear over the course of the investigation, it is my belief that agapic love is neither an abstract nor an ideal invention of faith, but an all-too-real phenomenon always already at work in the social realm. It is a phenomenon, furthermore, that has by and large gone on unrecognized as love and that can only really be reclaimed through a phenomenological "return." Finally, it is my belief that the core content of any postdeconstructive Christian faith must be expressed more through recognition of and commitment to this phenomenologically apparent love than through the declaration of any determinate ontological claims.

It would be a nearly impossible task to provide an exhaustive survey of the theological literature on the concept of *agape*. It is undoubtedly one of the most commented-upon Christian concepts in the secondary literature, occupying a central place in the work of both the earliest thinkers, like Clement, Origen, and Augustine, and the most contemporary, like Karl Barth, C. S. Lewis, Josef Pieper, and Max Scheler.[4] Before moving on to consider both scriptural accounts of love and engaging the secondary literature on the topic, I want to make clear that it is not my intention to approach the concept of agapic love *theologically*—that is, from a position of faith—but, rather, *phenomenologically*, as an appearance in the world, if it does so appear. It is not necessary then to treat all of these thinkers, but only a sufficient number to establish the claims and debates central to the Christian concept of agapic love.

THE VERTICALITY AND HORIZONTALITY OF AGAPIC LOVE

Of course, in the spirit of phenomenology we should begin by going back to things in themselves, as it were, by addressing the use of and claims concerning agapic love in the New Testament. And, there is perhaps no better starting place for such a task than 1 Corinthians 13, wherein Paul provides what is one of the richest descriptions of the term. There he writes, starting with verse 4, that "Love is patient; love is kind; love is not envious or boastful or arrogant or rude. It does not insist on its own way; it is not irritable or resentful; it does not rejoice in wrongdoing, but rejoices in the truth. It bears all things, believes all things, hopes all things, endures all things," and finally, ending in verse 8, "Love never ends." From this account any number of concrete traits can be culled concerning the nature of agapic love, but none yet to single out the particularity of the nature of *agape*. Quite to the contrary, what Paul describes here appears to be little more than an idealized account of what our contemporary society might already take to be the nature of romantic love. Perhaps this is why it immediately evokes memories of countless wedding ceremonies. And this association is not unjust. After all, it is with *agape* that Paul admonishes husbands to "love their wives as they do their own bodies" (Eph. 5:28) and to "never treat them harshly" (Col. 3:19). From this we would have to conclude that agapic love seems at the very least to work in concert with erotic romantic love (*eros*).

And it is with this same agapic love that Jesus commands his followers to "love one another" (John 13:34, 15:12) and to love "your neighbor as yourself" (Matt. 22:39; Mark 12:31–32; Luke 10:27). It is through this love for the Other, neighbor, husband, or wife, the Scriptures suggest, that one approaches the divine. It is for this reason that the Gospel writers always accompany this command to love one another with the command to "Love God," and remind the reader that so long as these commands are kept one will "abide" in the love of God (John 15:10). This is, after all, the novelty of the Christian narrative, that through the love of the neighbor, husband, or wife, one can love God. What this immediately seems to suggest is a harmony between the more quotidian understanding and experience of love and the Christian exhortation to agapic love. There is not, it seems according to the Scriptures and contrary to the prevailing view, any real disjoint between the erotic love for one's neighbor or peer and agapic love for God.

THE CONFLUENCE OF *EROS* AND *AGAPE*

Augustine likewise testifies to the harmony between Christian agapic love and everyday erotic love. Agapic love, he claims in his *Enchiridion on Faith, Hope, and Love,* "embraces both the love for God and the love of our neighbor" such that it entails the erotic within its transcendence toward the divine. The lust typically associated with the erotic, Augustine claims, "diminishes as [agapic] love grows." Faith, he suggests, is the catalyst in this transformation, working within the erotic to transform it into a site for religious transcendence.[5] In this way, erotic romantic love for Augustine seems to be the fertile soil upon which agapic love takes seed, draws nourishment, and grows. Agapic love thus expresses for him a redeemed or fulfilled erotic love. Expanding upon this claim, Augustine argues in his *Confessions* that it is only in God that the heart finds satisfaction for all of its restless desires.

This early Christian view of the theological harmony between erotic love and agapic love is not merely something of historical interest. It remains alive today as the official doctrine of the Catholic church, as was expressed recently by Pope Benedict XVI in his first papal encyclical, *Deus caritas est.* There, drawing from Augustine, Benedict stresses the intimate interrelation between *eros* and *agape,* writing that "love is a single reality, but with different dimensions," at times expressed horizontally in the romantic love for another, while at other times expressed in the vertical transcendence of worship. The two, he seems to claim, mutually fuel one another, *eros* transforming into *agape* when disciplined, and *agape* reverting into *eros* when directed toward the Other. "Even if *eros* is at first mainly covetous and ascending, a fascination for the great promise of happiness," he thus concludes, "in drawing near to the Other, it is less and less concerned with itself, increasingly seeks the happiness of the Other, is concerned more and more with the beloved, bestows itself and wants to 'be there for' the Other." In this way, *eros* and *agape* appear not as two separate and distinct forms of love — indeed, Benedict claims, they "can never be completely separated" — but as different expressions of the same love.[6]

In this interpretation of the harmonic exchange between *eros* and *agape,* Benedict and Augustine both seem to draw from a Platonic account of the nature of erotic love, especially as it is presented in the *Phaedrus* as a kind of mania, bestowed from above which carries the lover beyond him or herself toward the divine, as will become more clear later. Indeed, Benedict's claim that for the ancient Greeks *eros* was conceived "principally as a kind of intoxication, the overpowering of reason by a 'divine madness,'" which was "celebrated as a divine power, as fellowship with the divine," is, though unacknowledged, a direct reference to Socrates' second speech concerning the nature of love in the *Phaedrus*.[7] It seems, then, if we are to properly understand the nature of agapic love as a religious expression of erotic love, we must first endeavor to understand the nature of erotic love. This requires our returning to the origins of this understanding, Plato's account of erotic desire in the *Phaedrus* and *Symposium*, respectively.

THE MADNESS OF PLATONIC *EROS*

As is well known, the *Phaedrus* contains two different Socratic discourses on the nature of *eros*, the second of which is generally interpreted to serve as a kind of penance for an error committed in the first.[8] From this we may safely assume that the second speech is offered by Socrates with a bit more humility and sincerity than his first one, which he declares in the text to have come from a man overcome with ambitions and thus incapable of attesting to the true nature of the phenomenon. While this may or may not be the case, depending on the hermeneutic with which one approaches the Platonic texts, there can be little doubt that a profound difference does exist between the two accounts given by Socrates, and that it is the second one that he, at least, recognizes as the more authentic of the two. In any case, by exploring the friction between these two accounts, the sin and its accompanying penance, the nature of Platonic *eros* becomes clearer.

Socrates' "sin against Deity" in the first speech essentially amounts to his having borne false witness against *eros* and consequently denigrated its status. But it is the nature of *how* exactly he bore false witness that is of such consequence to us. Socrates began his first speech by defining *eros* as a kind of "desire" ("Phaedrus," 237d). But one should be cautious here, as this is not a neutral assertion, for the "desire" that Socrates binds to *eros* here has a very specific and determinate meaning.

The word he uses here to identify *eros* as a kind of desire is ἐπιθυμία (epithumia), which is perhaps better translated as *lust*.⁹ The consequences of this association will become immediately apparent. First, says Socrates, "we must observe that in each one of us there are two leading principles…one is the innate desire for pleasure (ἐπιθυμία ἡδονων), the other an acquired opinion which strives for the best (ἐπίκτητος δόχα, ἐφιεμένη του ἀρίστου)" ("Phaedrus," 237d–e). And, he goes on, it is the first of these two that, overpowering the latter, guides us and takes the name *eros* (238c). Thus, *eros* is reduced to nothing more than the "innate desire (ἐπιθυμία) for pleasure"! So what appears at first and in translation to be a seemingly benign identification is actually wrought with significance. This definition of *eros* as a kind of lust is maintained throughout the rest of the first speech, ultimately leading Socrates to condemn erotic desire as base.

This is, of course, not the first time that ἐπιθυμία appears within the Platonic oeuvre. The *Symposium,* which is considered by those interested in dating the Platonic texts to have been composed earlier than the *Phaedrus,* also contains the word ἐπιθυμία. There it is used by Aristophanes to identify the sexual hunger of erotic movement.¹⁰ In fact, almost every time that *eros* is addressed by Socrates as something to be avoided, it is referred to as a kind of ἐπιθυμία.¹¹ But ἐπιθυμία and *eros,* though often related to one another, cannot be absolutely identified. That is, *eros* need not be the expression of a kind of ἐπιθυμία. Nevertheless, the equivocation of these two terms dominates the reading of the Platonic texts.

According to Drew A. Hyland, much of the confusion within Platonic studies on the nature of "desire" emerges from the obfuscation of the difference between *eros* and ἐπιθυμία, resulting in the confusion, in the classical sense of the word, of two fundamentally different terms. According to Hyland, "ʾΕπιθυμία we know to be the lowest faculty of the soul, the brute desire to possess what one lacks. ʾΕρως (*eros*) also desires, but unlike ἐπιθυμία, which only desires, ʾΕρως both desires and loves. The difference between ʾΕρως and ἐπιθυμία, then, must lie in this 'and loves.' "¹² This confusion is understandable of course since, as we have seen, Socrates himself at times identifies one with the other. Nevertheless, Hyland is right to decry it for, as we will see, it is an identification that Socrates himself also denounces in introducing another term by which *eros* can be oriented. In fact, the nature of Socrates' "sin against" *eros* seems to be wrapped up in this identification of it with ἐπιθυμία. His error was thus not committed in his condemnation of *eros*, but in his false identification of its nature. After all, if *eros* truly is nothing more than a kind of ἐπιθυμία, one cannot help but reject it if one is to maintain a Socratic perspective on the world. The sin of his first presentation of the nature of *eros* thus consists not in his *condemnation* of it, but in the *misalignment* of it to ἐπιθυμία, which precipitated this condemnation. His redemption must then proceed through a realignment of the nature of *eros* to another kind of desire.

Socrates begins his more faithful account of *eros* by invoking the name of "Stesichorus, son of Euphemus (man of pious speech) of Himera (Ἱμεραίου) (town of desire)" ("Phaedrus," 244a). Under this guise Socrates immediately renounces his previous teachings and begins to praise *eros* as a kind of madness (μανίας) by which one is inspired by the divine and propelled toward it. *Eros* is still identified as a kind of desire here, except that it is not associated with ἐπιθυμία any more, but with ἵμερος (*himeros*). His "pious speech" thus begins with the rebaptism of *eros* as a sojourner from Ἱμεραίον.

This identification of *eros* with ἵμερος remains consistent throughout this second presentation on its nature. Thus reassociated, Socrates goes on to account for the nature of *eros* as a kind of transcending desire that motivates the soul's movement toward the eternal good. Likening the soul to a winged beast, Socrates accounts for how through *erotic* appreciation of earthly beauty "the wings of the soul are nourished and grow" ("Phaedrus," 246e). According to Socrates, one is overcome by this madness when one "sees the beauty of the earth, remembering the true beauty, feels his wings growing and longs to stretch them for an upward flight, but cannot do so, and like a bird, gazes upwards and neglects the things below" (249d).

Before the demarcation of mortal time, claims Socrates, the soul traversed the heavens in a holy throng led by the 12 great gods of the pantheon. In that primordial procession every human soul, immortal like the gods, followed in tow, each in the train of one of the gods. When the soul takes flight through the inspiration of *eros* it flies upward to join again the path it once pursued. Thus, the followers of *Zeus* are carried upwards as philosophers while devotees to Hera "seek a kingly nature," and so on. So it is that through the flight inspired in the erotic appreciation of earthly beauty, the soul is elevated toward the transcendent and restored to its long home in the celestial throng.

If we are to follow the early Christian interpretation of the scriptural injunction to love (*agape*) as harmonious with the ancient Greek account of the nature of *eros*, then it must be this later form of erotic love—*eros-himeros*—with which *agape* accords. The untamed manifestation of erotic desire warned against by both Augustine and Benedict must, in contrast, be that erotic desire which appears as *epithumia*. If we can take this first alignment to be true, that agapic love appears to be contiguous with himeric erotic desire, then Plato's account contributes significantly to identifying a kind of phenomenal reality to the nature of agapic love. Agapic love, it would seem, is a love that appears alongside, in and through, something resembling Plato's erotic love, in as much as it is portrayed here. Thus, in addition to manifesting as a never-ending patience and kindness, which is "not envious or boastful or arrogant or rude," *agape* would also appear as a kind of restless striving that pushes the lover through the beloved toward the divine. Following Plato's account of *eros* in the *Phaedrus*, then, agapic transcendence should also be accompanied by a kind of restless pain that identifies the lover's climb toward the divine.[13] This claim explains the aforementioned restlessness of Augustine's desire, and it reveals the Platonic roots not only to his understanding of agapic love, but to the contemporary Catholic Church's as well. More important, recognition of this inherent tie between the agapic and erotic love seems to collapse any artificial distinction that might be constructed between religious transcendence and what could be termed social or ethical transcendence, blurring the lines irreparably between the love of God and our love for one another.

THE DISJUNCTION OF *EROS* AND *AGAPE*

Not all would agree with this coupling of *agape* with the erotic, however. Many contemporary theologians would argue that such synchronizations fail to recognize the originality and particularity of agapic love. To understand the radical nature of agapic love, they claim, one must begin not by *comparing* it to erotic love, but by *contrasting* the two. Perhaps the most famous of these is Protestant theologian

Anders Nygren, who in his 1932 theological classic *Agape and Eros* goes to great pains to separate and distinguish between these two concepts.

According to Nygren, Plato's *eros* is not only different from *agape* in degree or in expression, as Benedict would claim, but in kind.[14] *Agape*, he argues, expresses an entirely different *type* of love (210). This difference, for Nygren, hinges on what he sees as the disparate origins and aims of the two drives. *Agape* is distinct, he thinks, in the following ways: (1) It is "spontaneous and 'unmotivated,'" that is, it has no grounds or justification for its pursuit of the beloved (75). (2) It is "indifferent to value" (77). Indeed, claims Nygren, inverting the Nietzschean phrase, *agape* is the "transvaluation of all ancient values." It is not motivated by what it perceives to be the good, but is freely given. (3) It is a "creative" force that imbues the beloved it pursues with value. In this regard, though unmotivated by value, *agape*, thinks Nygren, "is a value-creating principle" (78). Agapic love is thus not motivated by an absence, by some lack within the lover, but expresses itself as something new, its own positive force. (4) It is "the initiator of fellowship with God" (80). As this mediator, Nygren asserts that ultimately, *agape* does not represent a human phenomenon, but a divine one. That is, *agape*, he claims, does not originate in the human desire for the Other, but expresses a divine desire for the human. In his words, "Agape comes down. Agape is God's way to man" (210).

By contrast, Nygren identifies the movement of Platonic *eros* as follows: (1) It is first and foremost "acquisitive" (177). "Hence love, as Plato sees it," claims Nygren, "has two main characteristics: the consciousness of a present need and the effort to find satisfaction for it in a higher and happier state" (176). Motivated by such a need, *eros*, Nygren claims, does not express a creative force that introduces something new into the nature of the lover, but manifests as an entirely negative transcendence. That is, it is motivated out of a privation within the lover. Furthermore, its interest is not to inaugurate a value, but to acquire and possess a preexistent value. In this regard, Nygren claims, *eros* manifests primarily as a "will-to-possess,"—it is not freely given, but wants something for itself in the beloved. (2) As such, thinks Nygren, *eros* expresses a movement that is primarily "egocentric"—a movement that aims at self-fulfillment and happiness (180).

"Everything" in the Platonic account of love, he claims, "centres on the individual self and its destiny" (179). As an expression of a self-interested transcendence, Nygren claims that *eros* is ultimately not attributable to God, but to man. (3) Indeed, he asserts, it expresses "man's way to the divine" (177). Thus, whereas in *agape* we witness God's descent to man, "*Eros* is the way by which man mounts up to the Divine" (178). *Eros,* Nygren thinks, is a wholly human endeavor originating in human interests, proceeding actively through human actions, and ultimately aimed at human possession of the happiness promised in union with the beloved. *Agape,* by contrast, expresses for Nygren an almost entirely Divine endeavor that proceeds from God's love for humanity for the purpose of creating value. Note that Nygren's claims imply that humanity is entirely passive in this experience, entirely subject to the love of God, overwhelmed as it were, with God's generosity. The love of God is not precipitated or solicited, thinks Nygren, by any human action or trait. It is entirely a free gift that humanity receives without warrant or justification.

Perhaps most significantly, Nygren argues, erotic love is ultimately aimed at self-fulfillment. In contrast, "*Agape* is sacrificial giving," which "seeketh not its own" and gives itself away unselfishly and unafraid of losing itself (210). In this distinction, Nygren draws upon the Johannine gospel claim that "No one has greater love than this, to lay down one's life for one's friends" (John 15:13), and Paul's argument in the letter to the Romans that "God proves his love for us" in his self-sacrifice on the Cross (Rom. 5:8). In this regard, Nygren's account of the nature of agapic love seems accurate. Indeed, Jesus' command to "Love your enemies and pray for those who persecute you" seems to establish agapic love as a love that is not interested in return or acquisition (cf. Matt. 5:44; Luke 6:27–35). But does the affirmation of this aspect of agapic love truly distinguish it from erotic love? After all, Paul in his letter to the Ephesians, when admonishing husbands to agapically love their wives, uses the model of self-sacrifice: love them, he declares, "just as Christ loved the church and gave himself up for her" (Eph. 5:25).

Like Nygren, Karl Barth insists that "in New Testament usage" *agape* "has acquired the well-known meaning and content of a love opposed to ἔρως," and argues, furthermore, that the heart of this difference is the self-sacrifice and self-transcendence enabled by agapic love. Thus, whereas *eros* "is the experienced and self-attained turning from [the human] being down below in darkness and return to [its] being up above in light," according to Barth, "*Agape* consists in the orientation of human nature on God in a movement which does not merely express it but means that it is transcended, since in it man gives himself up to be genuinely freed by and for God, and therefore to be free from self-concern and free for the service of God."[15] Notice that, for Barth, *eros* is oriented around the self and the self's interests—it is motivated by the self's desire to transcend its current state through the other in order to attain a higher level of satisfaction. In contrast, he claims, *agape* circulates entirely around the divine, and thus promotes a sacrifice of self, not for some eventual reclamation of a higher or purer expression of the self, but for the sake of the divine. Though this self-sacrifice is not motivated by the self's desire for a higher mode of being, this is, Barth claims, nevertheless, what results from such an agapic transcendence. The difference is that the truer self discovered through agapic transcendence is not what is sought therein. It is, instead, merely an incidental accompaniment to it. Fundamentally, "in *agape*-love a man gives himself to the other with no expectation of a return, in a pure venture, even at the risk of ingratitude, of his refusal to make a response of love, which would be a denial of his humanity." Nevertheless, he argues, through such a self-sacrificial transcendence, one "gives a true expression to human nature" and discovers his or her true self. Given the irreconcilable difference between the interests and aims of *eros* and *agape,* Barth concludes, they must be conceived as two entirely different types or kinds of love. As a result, he argues, in contradistinction to the claims of Augustine and Benedict, "*Agape* cannot change into *eros* or *eros* into *Agape.*"[16]

From Nygren's and Barth's insistence on the singular difference of agapic love, we discover that *agape*, in addition to being patient, kind, long-suffering, humble, and never-ending, must also express itself as a passivity in man, motivated not out of an active self-interest, but from a movement that flows from the divine. As such, it does not express a movement that rises up, as Nygren put it, but one that "swoops down" (178). As a desire that originates in the divine Other and is directed toward the Other, *agape* must furthermore manifest as a self-sacrificial love—one that eschews the self's desire for happiness and commits itself entirely to the good of the Other without any expectation of possible return. Finally, emergent from the divine, from whom it is passively received, *agape* must manifest as something positive. That is, it should appear not as the expression of some lack or privation within the subject, but as evidence of some surplus—it should appear as if from nowhere, as something new, testifying to the fact that it is expressive of new creation within the subject.

From this we are beginning to catch a glimpse of what purports to be the singular nature of agapic love. But does this truly distinguish it from the Platonic conception of *eros*? Is it true that *eros* is entirely self-seeking—motivated out of an active self-interest and aimed at a higher expression of the self? Or can *eros* likewise appear as a passivity in man—one in which he may become caught up by the Other? And might this erotic transcendence promote a self-sacrifice that does not hope for return? To investigate these claims, we should perhaps return, once more, to the Platonic texts themselves.

PLATONIC *EROS* REEXAMINED

Let us first address the directionality and motivation of erotic transcendence as accounted for by Plato. In the *Symposium*, Diotima suggests that *eros* appears to be some kind of "halfway," as it were, between the beautiful and the ugly. Just as right opinion is deemed by Socrates in the *Meno* and other texts to be "halfway" between truth and ignorance, so too must *eros* be considered "halfway" between the beautiful and the ugly (Plato, "Symposium," 202a–b). The curious mixture that composes *eros* is not, furthermore, the result of the fact that it *lacks* a portion of goodness or beauty. *Eros* is neither the result of a temporary displacement of some fullness nor is it representative of some *absence*. Instead, the "halfway" that *eros* inhabits expresses the very way in which *eros is*. It is the being of *eros* as such, and thus expresses a strange kind of *presence*.

Eros, it seems, *is* between: between ugly and beautiful, good and bad, etc. This *between* must not be understood as a Hegelian middle ground, the resolution of two opposing forces. The mediation between ugly and beautiful, or good and bad, is not one of compromise. Nor is it some fixed position—some chartable or measurable mixture. It is, rather, a dynamic movement between two poles. *Eros* is, in a sense, the current that runs between these two extremes. It is between, then, as one in transition. By personalizing *eros* as a daemon (δαιμόνιον), as a messenger between the mortal and the divine, Diotima accounts for *eros* as anything but a placid and resolved middle ground. There is no resolution in *eros*. It is, instead, the very principle of movement, of movement away from the ugly, the base and temporal, and toward the beautiful, the good and the divine. *Eros* is "in-between" *only* in this sense. This trait Diotima explains by way of *eros*'s curious parentage.

Eros, by Diotima's account, was born the child of Resource (Πόρος) and Poverty (Πενία). In his very essence, then, *eros* is the union of an inexhaustible *Lack* (Πενία) and *A Way* (Πόρος) out of that lack, a way across into abundance.[17] Combining in his being the lineage of both parents, *eros* is eternally in a state of transition between absence and presence, striving after fullness and yet ever denied its acquisition. *Eros* is thus at one time:

> ever poor, and far from tender or beautiful as most suppose him: rather is he hard and parched, shoeless and homeless; on the bare ground always he lies with no bedding, and takes his rest on doorsteps and waysides in the open air; true to his mother's nature, he ever dwells with want. But he takes after his father in scheming for all that is beautiful and good; for he is brave, impetuous, and high-strung, a famous hunter, always weaving some stratagem; desirous and competent of wisdom, throughout life ensuing the truth; a master of jugglery, witchcraft, and artful speech. By birth neither immortal nor mortal, in the selfsame day he is flourishing and alive at the hour when his is abounding in resource; at another he is dying and then reviving again by force of his father's nature.[18]

As a daemon, *eros* is not unidirectional. *Eros* does not move exclusively from the absence of indigence to the presence of resource. Instead, its being is maintained in the passage between these two—it *is* in a sense the path uniting them. *Eros* thus unites in its being abundance and absence in such a way that it expresses a kind of superabundant absence and completely indigent abundance.[19] Thus, in the words of Robert Lloyd Mitchell, "*Eros* is always needful, always seeking and devising a way out of need, always on the way—toward beauty, goodness, wisdom, deathlessness, but never in final possession of any of them."[20] Its trajectory is thus not from incompletion, unfulfillment, and privation to satisfaction, but from a presence that manifests *as* an absence and an absence that appears *as* a presence.

Furthermore, as a daemon, *eros* does not express exclusively humanity's self-transcendence toward the divine, but simultaneously the divine's condescension to the mortal. *Eros* is a messenger between these two worlds, the channel by which humans may mount up and by which the divine may descend. This claim is further supported by the *Cratylus*.[21] There the mixed nature of *eros* is alluded to through an etymological reading of the word *Hero*. Hero (HEPOΣ), claims Socrates, is derived from *eros* (EPOΣ) because a hero is one who is born out of a love that bound a god to a mortal—a love that inspires the divine to leave the holy seat of Olympus and descend amongst the mortals.[22] In this regard, Nygren's characterization of *eros* as solely the means by which man transcends is wholly false. Furthermore, it seems to suggest that what he attributes exclusively to agapic love might also be attributable to erotic love. Already at this point the distinctions made by Nygren and Barth between *eros* and *agape* begin to fall apart. The artificiality of their dichotomy becomes all the more apparent the further we probe the activity or passivity implied in erotic transcendence.

Remember that according to Socrates in the *Phaedrus* one is *possessed* by erotic madness when one "sees the beauty of earth, remembering the true beauty, feels his wings growing and longs to stretch them for an upward flight, but cannot do so, and like a bird, gazes upwards and neglects the things below" ("Phaedrus," 249d). Notice the way that time moves here. Socrates claims that it is only *after* seeing the "beauty on earth" that one remembers "true beauty." One cannot remember true beauty until temporal beauty has awakened it. So it seems as if temporal beauty solicits within the subject the memory of something of which it was previously unaware. It is thus a desire that arises passively within the subject, set in motion by that which lies outside of and beyond the subject. Erotic love, it seems for Plato, is the inward response to an external stimuli.

Moreover, according to Socrates, the erotic possession can enter someone unawares—it can place within someone a desire that would not have naturally arisen therein. Near the end of the first major part of the *Phaedrus*, Socrates introduces a curious anecdote about the power of the gaze and the role it plays in the subject's participation in the transcendence of erotic madness. According to Socrates, when one is overwhelmed with *eros* through the perception of a beautiful other, such as a young boy, the power of his or her *mania* can at times overflow the bounds of the perceiver and enter into the soul of the perceived ("Phaedrus," 255c). In this way, the perceived, though consciously unaware of the admiration he or she received, can feel him or herself drawn toward another not of his or her choosing.

While Socrates initially relates this phenomenon on behalf of the lover who *affects,* he quickly expands it into an analysis of what happens within the beloved who *is affected.* The perceived and admired, he claims, enraptured by the gaze of the other can him or herself become a lover and share equal part in the effects of erotic madness, though he or she "knows not with whom," and "does not understand his [or her] own condition and cannot explain it" ("Phaedrus," 255d). In other words, not only does it seem that *eros* reveals a kind of passivity within the subject, but also reveals the limits of what can be known by the subject, the limits of what it can understand. Furthermore, this is a passivity that, though perhaps driven toward heavenly beauty and rising upward toward the eternally Good, is mediated through the gaze of another and introduced from outside the subject. Socrates likens this aspect of erotic love to infection, a disease passed through the eyes or gaze of another.[23] This note on the possible passivity of the soul is far from *hapax legomenon* within the Platonic oeuvre, especially within the *Phaedrus.* Instead, this concluding observation serves only to punctuate and elucidate that which he earlier named as the aim of his endeavor: namely, to understand "the truth about the soul divine and human by observing how it *acts* and *is acted upon*" ("Phaedrus," 245c; italics mine). Notice the forthright recognition that the soul not only acts, but also is passive; it can be *acted upon.*

This is also brought forth in the *Cratylus* where, in his etymological exploration of the word Socrates claims that *eros* ('ἔρως) "is so called because it flows (ἐσρεῖ) in from without, and this flowing is not inherent in him who has it, but is introduced through the eyes."[24] Again we see *eros* figured as being introduced from outside of the subject and not pertaining inherently to him or her, but coming from the outside "through the eyes" or gaze of another.

This notion of *eros,* as an expression of a presence within the soul which is introduced from outside it and reveals its fundamental passivity, is also presented in the *Theaetetus*. There Socrates addresses young Theaetetus's inability to find "any satisfactory answer" regarding his questions concerning the nature of knowledge.[25] This dissatisfaction, claims Socrates, is not the result of any indigence—it does not derive its poignancy from any object of knowledge that Theaetetus lacks. Instead, says Socrates, it is the same kind of "suffering" one undergoes when in "the pains of labour."[26] It is thus not the expression of some absence within Theaetetus, but of some presence. Theaetetus, it seems, has been made pregnant by philosophical questioning and, accordingly, has become filled by its significance.[27] His relation to the pain and suffering of his erotic striving for answers is not the result of his own agency, therefore, but of something that, like pregnancy, is initiated by the introduction of something other.[28] Thus, though it resides in him and when emerging appears to have sprung spontaneously from him, it is not something that in the final analysis could have spontaneously originated in him alone—after all, one cannot make oneself pregnant without at least the tacit help of another. Pregnancy always involves the introduction of the Other. Socrates' role as midwife, then, is to help into the world that which has been placed within his interlocutors by this Other.

So it seems as if Nygren and Barth—though perhaps accurately addressing the nature of agapic love as emergent from the divine and a creative positive force that passively takes up man in its movement—have again misled us with regard to the singularity of agapic love and its difference from erotic love. Still, we have not addressed what both Nygren and Barth take to be the real hard core of the singularity of agapic love, namely, its trajectory away from the self, toward self-sacrifice. Can erotic love promote such a radical self-transcendence?

Remember that the *Symposium* is composed of a number of different speeches on love, each one building upon, nuancing, or differing slightly from its predecessor, each nevertheless circulating around a few central traits leading finally to Socrates recounting of his lessons in love at the foot of Diotima and ultimately to Alcibiades' interruption of the game. Among the interlocutors present at the preceding is Phaedrus, for whom the previously commented-upon dialogue is named, who is distinguished from the others present as the one who proposed the theme of discussion and the first one to present his ideas, laying the metaphorical groundwork for all that would follow.

Of course, a number of interesting themes surface through Phaedrus's speech, all of which lead to his conclusions that *eros* should be iden-tified as a great power. And "what shall I call this power?" he asks, "the shame that we feel for shameful things, and ambition for what is noble; without which it is impossible for city or person to perform any high and noble deed." This shame, inspired by *eros*, Phaedrus goes on to argue, functions to buoy up the lover, preventing a fall into reprobate acts of self-preservation and instead driving him or her toward noble and heroic deeds, specifically the willingness to sacrifice him or herself for his beloved, which Phaedrus fleshes out through mythological history.[29] So it seems as if *eros* was not seen by the Greeks to be an entirely self-serving drive, but one instead that inspired shame and demanded a radical self-sacrifice.

Clearly, *eros* appears to be a power that can encompass even the seeming singularities of agapic love pointed out by Nygren and Barth, leading us to conclude with Augustine and Benedict that indeed *eros* and *agape* are contiguous loves. Perhaps Nygren's and Barth's con-fusion has to do with a subtlety we have already pointed to in the Greek language itself. Remember that *eros* can appear ordered under at least two different forms. It can present itself either as bound to the mortal and earthly under the form of ἐπιθυμία or as tied to the divine under the form of ἵμερος, wherein it can be ordered either accord-ing to ἵμερος *as* proper and occasioned by abundance or according to the derivative form πόθος, as arising from a lack and absence. In either case, it is clear that *eros* should not be understood as an inde-pendent term, but one that must be modified by other forms to have any real determinative power in language. That is, it seems to be something that derives its meaning from the superstructures to which it is attached, either ἵμερος or ἐπιθυμία. By associating ἵμερος with divinity, Socrates has in a sense made it the perfected expression of *eros*, what becomes of *eros* when it is purified of its earthly dross. Remember, in the *Symposium, eros* was described not as a god, but as a messenger, a daemon (δαιμόνιον) uncannily caught between the divine and the mortal. When ordered among the mortal, *eros* seems to present itself under the form of ἐπιθυμία, but when it approaches its divine nature *eros* thus seems to be a kind of ἵμερος. Ἵμερος, it seems, is a kind of perfected *eros*, purified of the earthly, ἐπιθυμία, and thus too the "innate desire for pleasure." As such, it appears as a positive love that inspires the lover from without, moving it beyond itself and freeing it to sacrifice itself for the Other in its transcendence toward the heavenly good.

TOWARD A PHENOMENOLOGY OF AGAPIC LOVE

From this investigation on the nature of erotic love in the ancient Greek world, we can finally venture some conclusions concerning the nature of the agapic love exhorted in the Scriptures with which it appears to cross. Like its erotic cousin, agapic love must first *manifest as a passivity within the human*. That is, agapic love must be a desire that is not motivated from any active interest of the will or the subject—simply put, it is not self-initiated. Instead, it must be a desire that comes from without—sweeping the subject up in its movement. As such, agapic love must be a positive and creative movement within the life of the subject. It will not be the manifestation of an absence or privation within the subject, but will instead serve as evidence of the fact that something new has been introduced—*it must reveal an abundance*. Nevertheless, this abundance will not appear as any kind of presence, or being—but, as tied to lack (*penia*), *agape* will shine forth as the present, positive expression of a primal absence.

It is important to remember, however, that though *agape* must express a power that pours into the subject from without and overflows the limits of subjectivity, it will be experienced by the subject as an aching and restless desire that seeks satisfaction. Indeed, as we saw, it was for this reason that it is all too easily reverted into a kind of self-serving lust that seeks determinate satisfaction in the beloved's flesh. Still, this reversion does not express the primal trajectory of agapic love. For, as we have seen, agapic love must not aim at self-satisfaction. Quite the opposite, it must inspire a kind of shame for such self-interested occupations and demand in turn the lover's self-sacrifice for the good of the Other. Nevertheless, this agapic service promises a new self, one reoriented and redefined through this possibility for self-sacrifice.

Finally, agapic love must be a love that is directed toward the neighbor, the husband, the wife, the poor, the suffering, etc., and must forge through this love a relationship with that which lies beyond the mortal pale, the divine. In this regard, agapic love must be, as we saw with Paul, not something that ceases with the death of the subject, but something that stretches beyond the limits of human finitude, into the realms of the infinite. It will appear as a love that is "never ending."

These are, of course, strange claims: that in *agape* something appears which, in a sense does not appear. Or, put another way, agapic love must be the expression of a kind of positivity that falls outside the bounds of appearance and being and, in so doing, explodes the limits of one's finite being, directing the lover infinitely outward toward the neighbor. Just what such claims could mean must still be addressed. But even more crucially, the question of whether such a love actually exists such that it can stand as an object for phenomenological inquiry must be answered. If it cannot, then the uncanniness of such claims is of little consequence for they remain shrouded in mystery as tenets of faith, a foolishness to the world but a great wisdom to the believer. But if such a phenomenon does appear and can be addressed as a determinate phenomenon, then it carries with it profound consequences for how we understand ourselves and our world, and, more relevantly to this volume, how we understand the core element of the Christian faith tradition.

Certainly, elements of this love can be observed in everyday erotic love. But how often does this erotic love call for such a radical self-transcendence? How often does such an erotic love sever the ties of self-interest and solicit the subject into a relation with the Other that transcends the finite, introducing a new self-understanding in light of the infinite? According to Emmanuel Levinas, much more often than we would think.[30]

LEVINAS'S PHENOMENOLOGY OF LOVE

Throughout his oeuvre, Levinas identified what he termed a "metaphysical desire" at work within the life of the subject. To understand Levinas's notion of metaphysical desire, one must first correctly accent the phrase. In this case, the accent should fall on the first word, *metaphysical,* and not, as one might initially think, on the second. The notion of the metaphysical is in many ways the central theme in Levinas's works. It is in fact the subject of the first three lines of his most famous work, *Totality and Infinity.* There, he writes, quoting

Rimbaud, "'The true life is absent.' But we are in the world. Meta-physics arises and is maintained in this alibi" (*TI* 33). Metaphysics for Levinas, then, consists in what he terms the "'elsewhere' and the 'otherwise' and the 'other'" (ibid.).

Metaphysical desire, then, is a desire that "tends toward something else entirely, toward the *absolutely other*" (ibid.). It thus expresses for Levinas a kind of transcendence. Not transcendence in the simple sense. The transcendence present in metaphysical desire is more than a mere noncoincidence with the self, although this, too, is part of it. It is, more importantly, a transcendence directed toward that which is "other than" and "exterior" to the subject (*TI* 292). Indeed, the whole of *Totality and Infinity* is labeled an "essay on exteriority." As exterior, the metaphysical expresses that which is always *beyond* the subject.

But the metaphysical for Levinas is more than *merely* exterior. Its identity is not maintained in its relation to the subject as that which is simply exterior. Not everything outside the subject carries the weight of the metaphysical for Levinas. Instead, he claims, the metaphysical proper bears a specific positive meaning and ethical value. Thus, it represents for him not only that which is "elsewhere" and "other-wise," but also that which is superior and above us. The metaphysical is, he claims, situated on a *height* (*TI* 34–35, 200, 297; *BPW* 12, 18). The transcendence initiated in metaphysical desire is thus directed toward that which is *transcendent* proper. Hence, drawing upon the work of Jean Wahl, is Levinas's nomination of the movement that typifies metaphysical desire as a trans*ascendence* (*TI* 35). In meta-physical desire, one feels him or herself elevated, lifted up, over and beyond the immediate.

For this reason, Levinas not only avoids employing the French *nos-talgie* to typify this desire, but in fact pointedly distinguishes it from metaphysical desire. Nostalgia, Levinas claims, understood as a kind of desire, is ordered by the structures of need (cf. *BPW* 51). "As com-monly interpreted need would be at the basis of desire; desire would characterize a being indigent and incomplete or fallen from its past grandeur. It would coincide with the consciousness of what has been lost" (*TI* 33). Residing as they do on the basis of need, all desires thus ordered become "essentially a nostalgia, a longing for return," he claims (ibid.).

Need, Levinas goes on to argue, involves the consumption, absorption, and integration of the desired object such that "the forces that were in the other become *my* forces, become me" (*TI* 129). Arising as it does from an absence in me, and venturing toward the renewal of me, need is not a movement motivated by or directed toward that which is other or properly transcendent, but is structured instead entirely around the immanence of a subject. It orbits entirely around the subject's interests and is aimed at the subject's satisfaction. The only kind of transcendence expressed in such a movement arises from the temporary displeasure a subject feels with him or herself when lacking the object of some need—when hungry or thirsty, for example. This is not a kind of vertical transcendence as occasioned in metaphysical desire, but a merely horizontal one. Once the desired object is attained, this transcendence immediately ceases and the subject is returned to a state of complacent equivalence with him or herself. This return is thus accompanied by enjoyment or pleasure. Hence, Levinas claims that need is essentially about the *enjoyment* of the subject (116). In this regard, for Levinas "need" seems to resemble *eros* when ordered under the species *epithumia* as a self-serving lust for one's own good, whereas his account of metaphysical desire appears to be a kind of *himeric eros*. Indeed, *eros* remains an essential part of Levinas's account of this metaphysical desire of the Other.[31] But it is an *eros* without need. For within such an economy, claims Levinas, there is no recognition or affirmation of the otherwise for its own sake. Any determinate other encountered therein is immediately interpreted in terms of the subject's interests. As such, its status is reduced solely to that of an object of possible consumption or use. Its otherness is not what is aimed for, as in metaphysical desire, but is merely an obstacle that must be overcome for its integration into the subject's life. The object of one's needs thus never rises to the status of the metaphysical proper, but remains always something that is merely at hand for the subject, a mere prop in the epic narrative of the subject's life.

In contrast, metaphysical desire and a truly metaphysical *eros*, Levinas claims, appear as a desire "that cannot be satisfied" and that does not aim at self-fulfillment (*TI* 34). Metaphysical desire is not merely the reassertion of an "unsatisfied need" (179). It is not merely the result of an incomplete transcendence, one that, though striving for satisfaction, is eternally denied or delayed in arriving. It is fundamentally and by nature *insatiable*. It is thus marked by a transcendence that is wholly otherwise than the one present in nostalgia. Nor is there any promised unity between the desiring subject and the aim of metaphysical desire as there is in the religious desire of Augustine. Instead, metaphysical desire ties the subject to an aim that is maintained at an insurmountable distance. Though metaphysical desire may be directed toward some presumed *end*, the metaphysical as such, this end never becomes an *object* for the subject, never becomes a determinate aim categorized as a source of possible satisfaction (99). It is not the case, then, that were the subject of metaphysical desire to somehow reach the metaphysical itself, presuming such things can even be talked about in such a way, the subject would find him or herself placated. To the contrary, metaphysical desire, claims Levinas, only grows stronger in one's pursuit of it. Thus, he asserts, once one is caught up in the movement of metaphysical desire and pursuing the metaphysical in its own right, one does not find him or herself in any way satiated, but instead even more desirous—even more restless (*CPP* 121). Metaphysical desire is not a movement that once aroused can be bedded down, but one that instead grows increasingly intense the more it is pursued. It is thus a movement that is by design incomplete, and not merely because in our finitude we fail to attain it (*TI* 63). It is, claims Levinas, "situated beyond satisfaction and nonsatisfaction" (*TI* 179).

To Levinas, this metaphysical nature of this desire "is enacted where the social relation is enacted—in our relations with men" (*TI* 78). Our metaphysical desire, it seems, propels us toward a responsibility for the Other, an Other who can never be reduced to the status of an object by the subject (*TI* 75, 211). Again, according to Levinas, the Other "does not enter entirely into the opening of being where I stand" (*BPW* 9); he is never "wholly in my site" (*TI* 39). This is not to say that the Other stands entirely outside of one's field. If he did, then the subject could not even feel the pull that the Good exercises through the Other. What Levinas aims to say is that the Other cannot be conceptualized within the powers of consciousness—that he emerges from the "hither side of consciousness" (*BPW* 83). It is Levinas's intention in making this assertion to radically restructure the powers of consciousness and in so doing further pull the rug out from underneath the authority of the subject.

According to Levinas, the subject's powers are manifest, in part, through his or her ability to objectify the world, and in so doing, lay claim to it through conceptualization. This power is grounded, he argues, in the subject's mastery over all that is presented visually (cf. *TO* 97). On Levinas's reading, the subject establishes and maintains dominance over the world by illuminating all that appears therein and attempting to control those appearances by reducing them to objects of possible knowledge (cf. *TI* 44). As such, "vision measures [the subject's] power over the object" (*BPW* 9). This results in the subject's misapprehension of the origin of appearances. Mediated through the power of vision, one encounters something that appears as something that can be possessed—as something that *belongs* to the structures of subjectivity. The appearance of the Other on the scene, however, changes all of this. The Other, bearing the power of the Good, arrives on the scene as a kind of super-bright phenomenon that outshines all the intelligible powers of the subject. Thus, once a subject is brought into relation with another, the origin of visibility is reversed. A subject's power to perceive is revealed therein not to have originated in him or herself, but in the Other. The appearance of the Other reveals that it is not I who measure the world but he who "measure[s] me with a gaze incomparable to the gaze by which I discover him" (*TI* 86).

The Other exceeds the bounds of one's comprehension. He cannot merely be illuminated as an object of possible categorization. His appearance thus reveals that illumination itself cannot be accounted for solely by the powers of the subject, but must emerge from elsewhere, namely, from the Other. The subject can see not because of his own powers, but because the Other illuminates the scene for him. The Other is, in a sense, the light in which things appear—it appears, says Levinas, in its *own* light (*kath auto*). In this light, the world is revealed not to be ordered and structured around the subject's needs, but primordially oriented toward the otherwise—and available for use *for the sake of* the Other. Clearly Levinas draws here from Plato's allegory of the cave, wherein the Good, which remains for him always beyond both appearance and reality, figures as the illuminative power by which both appearance and reality, as well as the difference between them, appear.[32]

Levinas names the illuminating power of the Other the *face* (*TI* 51). Borrowing the light of the Good, this face "*signifies* otherwise" than my powers according to Levinas (*BPW* 10). It signifies precisely the limit of those powers. "The face is present," claims Levinas, "in its refusal to be contained. In this sense it cannot be comprehended, that is, encompassed" (*TI* 194). Yet, this face still expresses itself in that which is present, according to Levinas. But, in expressing itself "the face resists possession, resists my powers. In its epiphany, in expression, the sensible, still graspable, turns into total resistance to the grasp" (197). It is this face, which stands as a *refusal* of my powers in the world, that absorbs the power of the Good, according to Levinas.

Furthermore, claims Levinas, the responsibility for the other that I am called to by my metaphysical desire, though it liberates me from the tyranny of myself, *does not*, in the final analysis, alienate me. Instead, he argues, it brings me across the limits of my existence into a "beyond being," that I could not have attained on my own. In a sense, it inspires within me the birth of a new selfhood, not hemmed in by the confines of my own being, but elevated into the realm of responsibility (cf. *OB* 114). Thus, claims Levinas, "no one is enslaved to the Good" (11). Instead, through the responsibility for another mediated by metaphysical desire, one is in fact *liberated* into the curious condition of "finding oneself while losing oneself" (11).

According to Levinas, though the power of the Good binds us to the Other in an ethical relationship, this restriction must be understood as a kind of emancipation (*TI* 88). The Other's appearance on the scene does not leave the subject unchanged, but instead draws the subject up short and inspires a kind of shame by revealing not only the limits of his or her powers, but the way in which those limits confine, the way in which the subject can do naught but his or her own will (cf. 75). In doing so, Levinas suggests, the Other reveals to the subject the rut of his or her own existence and provides for the subject another way of living, a way out of the selfish servitude to his or her own being.[33] The Other reveals that instead of succumbing to the whims of one's own being, one is free to devote oneself to the Other. One must no longer be subject to the call of *need*, but can now follow the course to which one is solicited through metaphysical/ethical desire. In this way, metaphysical desire can be read as awakening a subject from the slumber of ontological actuality to the true life of ethical potentiality. Thus the trans*ascendence* initiated in metaphysical desire is not only an elevation out of oneself *to the Other;* it is also an elevation out of oneself *to another level of selfhood,* a level that was hitherto unavailable to the subject, and yet a level that was primordially placed within the subject by the Good. So, claims Levinas, "It is only in approaching the Other that I attend to myself" and "am brought to my final reality," "[my] final essence" (178–79).

As we have seen, metaphysical desire for Levinas, defined in contrast to need, is not seen as arising from some *absence* within the subject but instead from some determinate *presence,* namely, the trace of the Good and the entrance of the Other. Levinas names this *presence* within the subject the *idea of the infinite.* Drawing from the work of Descartes, he describes the idea of the infinite as "exceptional" and distinct from all other ideas "in that its *ideatum* surpasses its *idea*" (*TI* 49; *CPP* 54). It is thus an intuition *within* the subject that cannot be conceptualized *by* the subject—contained by the powers of ratiocination. "In thinking infinity the I from the first *thinks more than it thinks.* Infinity does not enter into the *idea* of infinity, is not grasped; this idea is not a concept" (*CPP* 54). As such, the idea of infinity is the expression of a *presence* within the subject of something that *exceeds the bounds of subjectivity itself*—a presence that, despite our attempts to master, grasp or comprehend, will perpetual evade its powers, remaining "radically, absolutely other" (*CPP* 54). Even the determinate other, on whom the power of the Good collapses and toward whom metaphysical desire is directed, "*infinitely* overflows the bounds of knowledge" (*BPW* 12). Since by its very nature the idea of the infinite defies any finite attempt by the subject to wrap his or her mind around it, and yet nevertheless resides within the finite subject, it expresses, for Levinas, a kind of openness within subjectivity—a breach within the totality of interiority that exposes the subject to exteriority and the beyond. As such, the idea of the infinite expresses wonderfully the curious relationship metaphysical desire establishes between the subject and the transcendent proper: though it emerges in and through a finite subject, its infinite insatiability enunciates the presence of something within the subject that is superior to it. As such, both metaphysical desire and the idea of the infinite serve as proof for Levinas of the subject's openness to the metaphysical—that his or her interiority is not complete, but has always already been breached by the Good. In the idea of the infinite and metaphysical desire, the Good lays claim to the subject, *possesses* it (*TI* 50).[34]

Possession is an apt analogy for detailing the way in which the Good operates within the life of the subject, for possession is something that comes over a subject and takes hold of him or her, driving the subject out of his or her customary paths. The passivity implied in this kind of possession is the salient point for Levinas. Since "the finite thought of man could never derive the Infinite from itself," the Infinite expresses something *within us* that could not have been produced *by us*, that could not have originated with us (*CPP* 160). Thus, claims Levinas, "the idea of the Infinite, *Infinity in me*, can only be a passivity of thought" (160),[35] and must therefore be understood as having "been put into us" (54). The gaze of the Other through which the infinite and the Good are mediated "slip[s] into me, *unbeknownst to me*" and without my assent, but, as quoted before, without enslaving me (145).

THE UNREASONABLE REALITY OF AGAPIC LOVE

It seems that we discover in Levinas's phenomenological analysis of the nature of the subject a love resembling *agape*—a love that reveals itself as a creative passivity within the life of the subject and functions to call the subject away from him or herself toward a radical self-transcendence in sacrifice for the Other—a self-transcendence that exceeds the very bounds of the subject's finitude, calling the subject out beyond even his or her mortality to be willing to lay down his or her life for the Other, a love furthermore that seems to encompass in this movement the erotic movement to our peers.[36]

If this connection can indeed be made, we can conclude that something like agapic love is indeed apparent in the world, but not in a way we traditionally think. That is to say, it seems as if agapic love is not merely a prescriptive, nor merely a possibility, but an active force always already at work in our everyday encounters with the Other. Our failure to recognize it as such has less to do with its mode of appearance than with our expectations concerning it.

Following Levinas's account of the nature of metaphysical desire, we can assert that agapic love is not manifest in spontaneous altruism or a kind of generous goodwill toward others. It is not necessarily apparent in the spirit of the humanitarian do-gooder or the generous hand of philanthropy.[37] This is because *agape* is not directed toward some vague idea of mankind or humanity in general. Instead, agapic love arises before concrete specific Others and manifests as the accompanying sense of compunction. Following Levinas's and Phaedrus's observation in the *Symposium,* we could conclude that more often than not *agape* appears in the embarrassment and shame, and subsequent apology, which follows, for example, from the beggar's request for aid. It is that spontaneous sense of being turned out and exposed before his or her gaze—measured up. *Agape* appears in the feeling that we must give account for our wealth, our comfort, indeed for our very existence, and the subsequent sense of responsibility to which it calls us. It is manifest in the conviction that we should not, and indeed cannot, simply walk away unchanged from an Other who looks to us for comfort—but that we ought to and must respond to his or her demands. *Agape* appears in this spontaneous power of the Other to interrupt our projects and demand something from us—it shows itself in this power the Other has to insert him or herself between us and our own interests, and to call us away from ourselves into an ethical responsibility. This is agapic love, to be ruptured from one's own complacency and being—to feel ashamed for one's own comfort and power and to feel called away from it not for one's own sake, but for the sake of the Other.

In this way, *agape* functions to initiate a new way of being for the I, one cast not in the light of its own interests and projects in the world, but one illuminated by the look of the Other before whom it must give account. And this reorientation is experienced in the affectivity of shame and the accompanying responsibility we have for the Other—the sense that to him or her, we must make an account and give a response.

The demand of the Other is unreasonable, as was God's request for Abraham to sacrifice his son Isaac, and yet it still affects us—that is, it still inspires a sense of shame, a conviction that we *ought* to give/sacrifice, even if we do not have enough for ourselves. What is revealed here is that the agapic love, the love evoked by the look and demands of the Other, goes deeper than self-interest and rational self-concern. Love does not aim merely for our excess, a perfectly reasonable request, but aims for our very being, demanding from us a kind of unreasonable sacrifice, one that cuts right to the very marrow of our existence. It requires that we substitute ourselves for the other, offering ourselves up in their place, exchanging our wealth for their poverty, our abundance for their lack and our clothes for their nudity. This is love, "to lay down our lives for one another" (John 3:16).

This is after all what we see in Jesus' command to love your enemies, to "do good to those who hate you, bless those who curse you, pray for those who abuse you. If anyone strikes you on the cheek, offer the other also; and from anyone who takes away your coat do not withhold even your shirt. Give to everyone who begs from you; and if anyone takes away your goods, do not ask for them again" (Luke 6:27–30). Agapic love is not about giving out of one's surplus, but giving unto one's very deficit. It is thus not merely to clothe the naked or even the unrighteous, as we see in Jesus' example of the robber, from out of one's excess (giving them our coat), but to clothe the naked from that which is our very own, that which we seemingly cannot live without (our shirt, our undergarments). Love, it seems, requires of us a kind of sacrifice, it requires that we go beyond the seemingly reasonable request for our excesses into the demand for our very own. It seems to consist, then, in a kind of substitution, for example, we must make ourselves naked to clothe the nakedness of the neighbor, we must make ourselves hungry to feed the hunger of the poor. Love is what Levinas called "taking the bread from out of one's own mouth." This sacrifice from out of one's very own is exemplified in the love Abraham shows for God in his willingness to sacrifice his son Isaac (Gen. 22) and in the widow who sacrifices her last mite to the coffer designated, ironically, for the poor (Mark 12:41–44; Luke 21:1–4), and is a pervasive theme throughout the Scriptures.

For example, consider Cain (Gen. 4:1–8), who offended the Lord by only giving out of his excess, the "fruits of the ground," in contrast to his brother Abel, who gave from his "first fruits," offering the "first born" of his flock, and in doing so pleased the Lord (remember that it is the result of this difference in treatment that Cain murders Abel, drawing an obvious parallel that to merely give from one's excess is tantamount to murder of one's neighbor). Remember as well that this practice of sacrificing from one's own most, from one's first fruits, became Levitical Law in the Tanakah (cf. Deut. 18:4,

26:1–11; Lev. 2:12–14, 23:9–14), the idea being that the first fruits of every harvest would be set aside either to be burnt as an offering to God or to be consecrated to the poor (note here that love of God is a blessing to the poor/neighbor). Throughout the Scriptures love is exemplified in this way, as a sacrifice, as a demand upon us that goes beyond our reasonable self-interest. It calls upon us to give to the point of our suffering.

AGAPIC SERVICE AS TRUE RELIGION

What is revealed from this investigation is that agapic love, though certainly prescriptive and carrying within it a very definite ethical demand, is equally an active reality always already at work within the life of the subject—one available to us through *a decidedly* phenomenological description. We are always already exposed to the neighbor—he or she is always already a part of us. The love to which we are called is not something in excess to our existence; it is inexorable from it. This does not mean that we all equally respond to it. Many of us deny it, choosing to flee it and our very nature for the cold comfort of material objects. Few of us give ourselves over to the love we feel pulling at our heart in the face of the poor and the suffering, the orphan and the widow—but all of us are always already initiated into this kind of love by the sheer fact that we exist. None of us are spiritually isolated. None of us are closed off to the demands of the poor, unaffected by the sufferings of the downtrodden. But not all of us are good lovers. Very few of us are saints. Most of us are accountants, busy counting the costs of the demands put upon us by a love we cannot escape. Still, it is only through recognition of the nature of this love, recognition of the way in which it appears in our lives in this sense of compunction and responsibility, that we can begin to attune ourselves more closely to the demands of faith; demands that cannot be appropriately acknowledged either through the dead precepts of a static religion, nor through the open question of a religion without content, but only through a rigorously hewn, openly determined, living *religion with religion.*

This then, it seems to me, is the real core of any such *religion with religion:* not the confession of doctrine or affirmation of ontological claims, but the active commitment to an agapic service of the Other.

Such a love in action must be the heart of any postdeconstructive expression of the Christian faith, a faith that expresses itself more clearly in active attendance to the neighbor than in any spoken pontification or written proclamation. Only in an engaged affirmation of the agapic solicitation of the Other will a true postdeconstructive Christianity emerge. Thus, it seems, can the Christian avoid the static rigidity of the kind of catechism critiqued by Derrida without sacrificing any core foundational content. To borrow a phrase from Nietzsche's Zarathustra, it seems to me we can only trust a religion "written in blood," one that is declared in the bodily sacrifice for and service to the Other who appears to us with a face: the concrete and determinate neighbor, orphan, widow, peer, colleague, husband, or wife. This is, as we have seen, the true heart and fundamental content of Christianity, that "true religion," as it were, must be asserted in love, confessed in deed, and disclosed in action.

A Tale of Two Logics
Some Further Questions about *Agape*
— A Response to Drew M. Dalton

Jeffrey Hanson

Drew Dalton's engagement with the issue of agapic love limns what I take to be absolutely key issues that are provoked by this doubtless crucial theme. I would like to offer some questions in the spirit of continuing our shared conversation; they are not meant as criticisms but calls for further cooperative inquiry. Three areas will be of concern to me in what follows: (1) the distinction between the love of God and the love of neighbor; (2) the origin of *agape;* and (3) the place of reciprocity.

With respect to Dalton's analysis of a possible compatibility between love of God and love of neighbor, there is an ambiguity here that is hardly surprising but calls for further reflection. As Dalton rightly shows, the Christian tradition hardly speaks with one voice on this issue. He justifiably opposes an Augustinian school with the interpretations of Barth and Nygren, proof enough that there has not been unanimity on the relationship of erotic and agapic loves. Dalton himself, in examining the scriptural basis for his claims, asserts that it is "through this love for the Other, neighbor, husband, or wife, the Scriptures suggest, that one approaches the divine." And this seems uncontroversial, as God's nature is love, and our loves rightly oriented are a taste of the divine itself. Perhaps open to more in-depth discussion, though, is his assertion that the novelty of the Christian narrative consists in the radical idea that "through the love of the neighbor, husband, or wife, one can love God," such that at the end of the account there is no "real disjoint between erotic love for one's neighbor or peer and agapic love for God." This does not seem to me to be the same claim.

While there can be compatibility between the loves, and again, I use the qualifier "rightly ordered" advisedly, as the tradition does seem to agree that not just any love will do, so to speak, compatibility does not mean identity. Dalton comes close to saying that love of neighbor is the same as love of God. Though I take it from his argument overall that this is not what he is asserting, there is a hairsbreadth of difference between saying that love of neighbor is the means to love of God and maintaining the opposite; both perspectives would agree on a possible accord between the loves but would stress the priority of one or the other.

This distinction is identifiable between two titans of our shared conversation, Levinas and Kierkegaard. As Merold Westphal has pointed out, this question of priority may be the only substantive pivot on which turns the differences between the pair, otherwise so much in harmony. Westphal writes,

> They agree that the transcendence and alterity that deserve to be called divine are not to be found in the realm of theoretical knowledge as interpreted by major strands of the western philosophical tradition; they rather occur in the decentering of the cognitive self by a command that comes from on high. But they disagree in that Levinas insists that the neighbor is always the middle term between me and God, while Kierkegaard insists that it is God who is always the middle term between me and my neighbor. This is their fundamental disagreement; perhaps, in the final analysis, their only one.[1]

Indeed, it is not difficult to find texts from Kierkegaard that support Westphal's characterization. To quote one particularly apposite passage from *Works of Love:*

> *Worldly wisdom is of the opinion that love is a relationship between persons; Christianity teaches that love is a relationship between: a person — God — a person, that is, that God is the middle term.* However

beautiful a relationship of love has been between two people or among many, however complete all their desire and all their bliss have been for themselves in mutual sacrifice and devotion, even though everyone has praised this relationship—if God and the relationship with God have been omitted, then this, in the Christian sense, has not been love but a mutually enchanting defraudation of love. *To love God is to love oneself truly; to help another person to love God is to love another person; to be helped by another person to love God is to be loved.*[2]

Kierkegaard, I take it, is arguing for precisely what Westphal has called God as the middle term in human relations. I have contended that without this middle term we cannot appreciate one of the central messages of *Fear and Trembling,* namely, the revolutionizing of human love in the light of divine love. Without this middle term, no matter how gratifying love is, it remains only an intimation of what is fully possible for our mutual associations. It is for this reason that Christian love according to Kierkegaard cannot help but appear to worldly thinking as only self-love and the absence of love.[3] Indeed, how else could Abraham's actions appear to one equipped only with a human understanding? If love is manifested as the most common thing, the constitution of our day-to-day relations as Dalton argues, then how does it present itself as a scandal, and under what conditions does it do so? We know certainly that the case of Abraham as Kierkegaard interpreted it struck Levinas as scandalous.[4]

So part of what I think our conversation shows us needing to continue to wrestle with is the priority of the loves, or if even such neat divisions can be drawn.

The second concern I have orbits around the question of the origin of the agapic movement, whether from without or from within. Dalton is clear in his final contention that agapic love is not "self-initiated" and is instead "a desire that comes from without—sweeping the subject up in its movement." There is ample reason to accede to this description. Yet I wonder whether agapic love does not speak to something in the subject all along, and again I think Dalton has given us indications of this in his treatment of the idea of infinity in Levinas and in the subtle and powerful reading of the *Phaedrus.* The subject is in a way prepared for *agape*—though perhaps we could explore the conditions for the possibility of what *agape* fulfills in the subject—even though the subject may at first only emptily intend what *agape* ultimately saturates. Without this groundwork being laid in the subject, I suspect the analysis may drift too close to the Nygren-Barth pole for Dalton's own comfort. On the other hand, Dalton also writes, "Our failure to recognize [agapic love] as such has less to do with its mode of appearance than with our expectations concerning it," and I agree that this could very well be the case. But an unintended consequence of situating the indiscernible character of the agapic in the poverty of our own expectations is that Christian revelation on this reading will have accomplished little more than giving coherent expression to an incipient possibility in human love that was there all along. But would that truly count as an advent, as a movement originating decisively "from without"?

It is likely that thinking the immanent and the imminent together is a more difficult task than it first appears, and it is clear to me that Dalton is fully appreciative of the difficulty. For I suspect we would want to say that the agapic is not originary to the subject, but at the same time something would have to be in the subject such that when the agapic appears it can be recognized as in communion with the erotic. Can a transformation be cognized as a transformation without some awareness, however dim, of what is being transformed? Again I refer to Kierkegaard, who in his journal wrote,

> The basis for erotic love is a drive, the basis of friendship is inclination, but drive and inclination are natural qualifications, and natural qualifications are always selfish; only the eternal qualification of spirit expels the selfish; therefore there is still a hidden self-love in erotic love and friendship.... To be permitted to love this one person is the gratification of infatuation and of preference, but at bottom also of self-love; to despair if it is denied is the very proof that the erotic love was self-love. But precisely because this escapes erotic love, it is able to come up with the giddy expression: to love another person more than oneself; alas, because the lover still has not learned to love himself in the truth and earnestness of eternity.[5]

A similar dynamic is at work in *Philosophical Fragments,* where Kierkegaard analogizes the passion of reason as it abuts the paradox to the passion of erotic love when it is overmastered by the agapic. There paradox, too, comes "from without" and so "The understanding certainly cannot think it, cannot hit upon it on its own, and if it is proclaimed, the understanding cannot understand it and merely detects that it will likely be its downfall. To that extent, the understanding has strong objections to it; and yet, on the other hand, in its paradoxical passion the understanding does indeed will its own downfall. But the paradox, too, wills this downfall of the understanding, and thus the two have a mutual understanding, but this understanding is present only in the moment of passion."[6] So, too, when I love another I love her in part because of my own self-love: She attracts *me*, she makes *me* laugh, her interests are also *my* interests. But to truly love her I must overcome the self-love that is in part the basis of my love for her; and the same could be said of her love for me. I must love her more than I love myself or throw her away. Insofar as we both want to love each other more than we love ourselves we can be reconciled in "mutual understanding" and "passion." Only then do I discover that it was not my self-love I wanted all along but love for the Other,[7] but it is nevertheless true that the former was the basis for the latter, though the latter was always its secret desire. Such is the happiness not of the overthrow of the erotic by the charitable but of the consummation of the erotic by the charitable.

And if this represents an exceptional moment in human experience, can it be right to inscribe the logic of the agapic at the level of the quotidian? Dalton follows the examples of the French thinkers he and I both appreciate so greatly and conflates the exceptional possibility, the rare moment of mutual understanding and impassioned joy, with the general experience of any openness to the Other. If charity is already the covert logic of all our dealings with one another, then what would the wholehearted affirmation of the Good look like? This last challenge is one that surpasses the possessive desire certainly for my own good but may also surpass the desire for the Other. As Kierkegaard points out in *Works of Love*, the exchange of rings at a wedding ceremony in a way is a poor symbol, for all it gestures toward is the swapping of "mine" for "yours," a simple reciprocity.[8] The real union that is realized in marriage, in the consummation of erotic love by its being caught up within agapic love, is the union of "ours," which is in turn more than the simple exchange of yours for mine. This seems to be a qualitatively different experience from that of any incident of genuine openness to the Other, rare as that admittedly is.

This leads me to my last concern, and that is with the place of reciprocity. What I have said in my second consideration explains why there is value to Barth's recognition that, in Dalton's words, "the truer self discovered through agapic transcendence is not what is sought therein," and yet in that transcendence we do indeed discover our true selves. Sometimes Levinasian rhetoric invites the charge that the ethical life is one devoid of reciprocal reward. But if in my relation to the Other I do discover my true self (and I do believe this is so), then is that not an extraordinary reward and a form of overwhelming reciprocity? The talk of taking the bread from my own mouth and giving it to the Other leaves the impression that in my giving I neither retain nor receive back anything for my effort. While we all agree acting for the sake of a reward is not especially worthy, I do not think *agape* leaves us without our own recompense. Those who seek the reward and those who do not are united in their ignorance of what reward would be, as surely as the person who consents to marry cannot fully know what he or she is getting in to, but once having got in, realizes that it was what they wanted all along.

It is certainly the case that "we must make ourselves naked to clothe the nakedness of the neighbor" and that "we must make ourselves hungry to feed the hunger of the poor," but do we then stay naked and hungry ourselves? I suggest that just as *agape* overcomes and fulfills *eros,* so too does the logic of charity overcome and fulfill the logic of scarcity. According to the logic of scarcity, if I have a cloak that means you lack one, and if I have something to eat you by definition do not have that something to eat. *Agape* proclaims that there is enough for all, but only if what we have is shared. I think of the one miracle of Jesus reported by all the evangelists: the feeding of the five thousand. The boy who takes the bread from his own mouth does not see it merely consumed by the mouth of another; he does not exchange "mine" for "yours." His seemingly ludicrous gesture, to offer up so little of his own in the face of bottomless need and indigence, is transformed into a miracle. When the gift is consecrated and distributed it satisfies not just the Other but another and another and another and another besides with a shocking quantity left over. But in order for the bread to be multiplied—let us not forget this—it must be torn to bits. *Agape* calls us to submit to this discipline but it does not leave us without the promise of reward—an unforeseeable reward, to be sure. If we will offer up ourselves, our souls and bodies, we will be torn to pieces. But thanks to the one who gives nothing that he did not receive from the Father, there will be more to give—precisely for its having been given up—than there would have been had we never given at all.

Chapter 4, Reply 2
True Religion
— A Response to Drew M. Dalton

Bruce Ellis Benson

was more than a bit dismayed when a Google search for "true religion" came up with this number one item: "jeans." Perhaps in our capitalist culture in which everything becomes a commodity I should not have expected any more: but *jeans*?[1] The occasion for the search was that I remembered there was a verse somewhere in the New Testament in which true religion is named and described. Given that I did not have a concordance at hand, I thought I would rely on the Internet. Fortunately, it did land me (further down the list) at the right verse: James 1:27.

Yet this got me thinking about *exactly* what is being omitted in "religion without religion." Slavoj Žižek is (in)famous for the following observation: "On today's market, we find a whole series of products deprived of their malignant property: coffee without caffeine, cream without fat, beer without alcohol. . . . And the list goes on: what about virtual sex as sex without sex, the Colin Powell doctrine of warfare with no casualties (on our side, of course) as warfare without warfare?"[2] It does not take much thought to realize that "religion without religion" could quite naturally be added to this list. But this immediately raises the following question: what is the "malignant property" that would lead anyone to want a religion that has somehow been deprived of that property? Put otherwise, and more completely: on the one hand, why is religion so "bad" that we want it purged and, on the other hand, valuable enough that we want it somehow still preserved? Would it not be simpler to jettison the whole thing, and thus bypass the extraction process?

In what follows, I want to answer that question. It will not be immediately obvious that my response to Drew Dalton is truly an engagement with his chapter. However, the tie to that chapter will become amply clear. Thus, what I say should be read as thinking alongside of Dalton, situating his point in a wider context.

Although Derrida does not speak explicitly of a "malignant property" when he raises the possibility of having a religion without religion, he does speak of the alternative as being a "nondogmatic doublet of dogma."[3] The offending term here, "dogma," can be benignly defined as "that which is held as an opinion" or, less benignly, as "a belief, principle, tenet; *esp.* a tenet or doctrine authoritatively laid down by a particular church, sect, or school of thought." But surely what Derrida also has in mind is what the *OED* lexicographers go on to add: "sometimes, depreciatingly, an imperious or arrogant declaration of opinion."[4] Given this definition, there are two aspects to the problem of dogma. On the one hand, it has positive content—whether a belief, principle, or tenet—that (by its very nature) is more or less definitive. On the other hand, it is held in a way that declares it absolutely true and the proclaimer thereof absolutely right. It is *both* the content and the way in which it is presented that offend. In Derrida's and Caputo's versions of "without," each of these is diminished. The content is reduced to a secret or to that which cannot be named or to a mystery. Each of them sees this new version of religion as moving away from a rigid system of beliefs and any kind of magisterium that would give us anything like final pronouncements. Explicitly, Derrida speaks of "religion" as "a set of beliefs, dogmas, or institutions."[5] As a way of escaping from this definitive content and prescribing a way to "hold" the much less defined content, Derrida speaks of "faith." Having "faith" means both that what one believes in is not readily defined or mastered and also that one lacks certainty and naturally would then avoid the arrogance of insisting that one's way of belief is truly normative for others.

Such a move makes perfect sense as long as we assume that this definition of religion is correct—that the Christian religion is composed of a particular set of propositions, a particular body of believers, and various institutions to regulate and define the boundaries of said religion. Yet what if "religion"—at least in Christian terms—is *something else?* Consider how the book of James defines religion: "Religion that is pure and undefiled before God and the Father is this: to visit orphans and widows in their affliction, and to keep oneself unstained from the world" (James 1:27). The word translated as "religion" here is θρυσκεια" [*thrêskeia*], which could also be translated as "worship." But the standard translation is indeed religion, and normally this passage is taken to be the biblical definition of "true religion." Yet, if that interpretation is correct, then suddenly pursuing "religion without religion" seems a far less obvious path. For James makes it clear that "religion" actually is something much more like "faith." If James is right, then religion is not a set of doctrines, a group or sect, or an institution. Rather it is something that one *does*.

Admittedly, this point needs some qualification. The book of James is known for its emphasis on putting faith into practice. Given that emphasis, Martin Luther is famous for referring to James as "a right strawy epistle" precisely because it so focused on works. Indeed, James's definition of true religion comes on the heels of a definition of "vain" religion in the previous verse: "If anyone thinks he is religious, and does not bridle his tongue but deceives his heart, this man's religion is vain" (James 1:26). Not surprisingly, some Christians attempt to downplay the gravity of this text. The Anglican bishop Richard Trench writes that James was "not affirming…that these duties are the sum total or even the great essentials of true religion, but declared them to be the body, the *thrêskeia*, of which godliness or the love of God is the animating soul."[6] However, this is not exactly what James says. Instead, Trench gives us an interpretation that makes this a much tamer verse. This is the only place in the New Testament in which we get an explicit definition of what the Christian "religion" is about, and there is good reason to take James at his word. While keeping "unstained from the world" is included as part of this definition, I find it particularly instructive that James gives us the "formula" of caring for widows and orphans *first*. In placing such emphasis on right practice, James does not mean that there are no "beliefs, dogmas, and institutions" that are part of Christianity. Instead, his point is that Christianity is first and foremost about *living* rather than *believing*.

In this sense, Trench is right that James is picking up on Micah's summation of the law as "to do justice, and to love kindness, and to walk humbly with your God" (Mic. 6:8). The word "orthodoxy" is instructive here, since it can mean either "correct worship" or "right belief." Without doubt, James is emphasizing the former over the latter. Of course, one must bear in mind two things. First, at the time of the book's composition—perhaps as early as AD 45, which would make it the oldest book in the New Testament—there simply *was not* a clearly established set of Christian beliefs or an institution. Second, apart from Antioch, where followers of Christ were first termed "Christians," what we today call Christianity was initially known simply as "the way." This emphasis on following Christ is not only true for the early church but also—I would insist—for Christianity today. To be a Christian is not primarily about beliefs. James reminds us that "even the demons believe" (James 2:19), so clearly belief is not sufficient (even if it is *necessary*). Of course, to develop this point adequately would require far more space than I have here. But, in sum, I think James has the emphasis exactly right.[7] And it would seem that Cardinal Ratzinger (now Pope Benedict XVI) would agree: "Christianity is not an intellectual system, a collection of dogmas, or a moralism. Christianity is instead an encounter, a love story; it is an event."[8]

It is this emphasis that returns us to Dalton's meditations on agapic love, particularly to three aspects. First, Dalton reminds us of the true radicality of agapic love—its sheer gratuitousness and inexplicable "logic." We are called to love the Other simply because the Other is there: no further reason can, need, or should be given. Further, as Dalton puts it, "the demand of the Other is unreasonable." We are asked not to give from our excess (as Cain did) but from our "first fruits," in such a way that we ourselves become needy. Dalton rightly brings in the command by Jesus to return evil with good—whether it is to those who hate and curse us or to those who mistreat us. These are truly radical demands and, as a result, Dalton notes, "very few of us are saints"; instead, "most of us are accountants" who are all too worried about keeping a crisp and clear balance sheet. Yet such a posture is radically out of keeping with what James is suggesting. Second, though strongly related, the widow and orphan are precisely those who cannot in any way adequately repay us. It is a standard measure of true spirituality in the Hebrew Bible whether the widows and orphans—the least of society—are being cared for. So, very much in line with traditional Jewish teaching, James has picked caring for the least of society as constituting true religion. Third, James makes it clear that this caring for the widow and the orphan is not some kind of general concern for humanity (a point that Dalton notes), but rather is concerned with concrete others. Indeed, it is James who gives us the figure of the person who looks in the mirror and does nothing about what she sees (James 1:24–25). Similarly, our encounter with the Other who is in need should compel us to do something about that need.

And that, finally, leads us back to the connection of *eros* and *agape* that is at the heart of Dalton's chapter. What Dalton—in line with no less than Augustine and Pope Benedict XVI—suggests is that *eros* provides *agape* with a sense of being utterly drawn to the Other. Although we often think of *eros* in terms of sheer desire or lust, that is really only ʽεωπιθμια. In contrast, ερως denotes a desire that also loves and, when connected to ίμεπος, gives us the idea of a love that transcends. Thus, Benedict is able to argue that, as *eros* draws near to the Other, it increasingly becomes *agape*. Or, as Phaedrus would have it in the *Symposium, eros* moves us to heroic and self-sacrificial deeds. This is very much in keeping with what James says about true religion. In fact, it would not be too much to say that, for James, anything less than *putting love into practice* is simply not *agape*—for we are called not merely to be "hearers" of the word but also "doers" (James 1:22).

Yet if being active lovers of the Other is what constitutes *true religion,* then there is no need for a religion without religion. Instead, we should have an *eros* for religion itself, desiring nothing less than to be utterly filled with religion and to embody that religion in all that we do. Or perhaps we could put it as follows: instead of "religion without religion," what we really want is *plus de religion*—with a strong emphasis on the "s."[9]

FIVE

"You Are Not Far from the Kingdom"

Christianity as Self-Disruptive Messianism

Bruce Ellis Benson

"Then the scribe said to him, 'You are right, Teacher; you have truly said that "he is one, and besides him there is no other"; and "to love him with all the heart, and with all the understanding, and with all the strength," and "to love one's neighbor as oneself," — this is much more important than all whole burnt offerings and sacrifices.' When Jesus saw that he answered wisely, he said to him, 'You are not far from the kingdom of God.'"

— Mark 12:32–34

Thereissomethingquite remarkable about this passage, though it is an aspect that is generally overlooked by many readers of the text. On the face of it, Jesus seems to give the scribe a great compliment. But, read more closely, Jesus' reply was probably not exactly what the scribe would have anticipated. "Not far" is complimentary—as far as it goes. Indeed, Jesus' answer must certainly be judged to be affirming, even though it is somewhat ambiguous.[1] Yet having given such an excellent answer, surely the scribe would have been expecting a response more like "well done—you have answered aright and thus you have *reached* the kingdom of God." Instead, the scribe gets an enigmatic answer that proves unsettling. We are not told how the scribe responds, or indeed if he responds at all. But we can easily speculate that the scribe would have had in mind something like the following questions: "What do you mean by 'not far?' " or "If I'm not already there, exactly *what else* do I need to know or do to get there?"

That Jesus' answer would have been rather unsettling to those listening would at least seem to be confirmed by what the gospel writer adds after those words: "After that no one dared to ask him any question" (Mark 12:34).[2] It is this unsettling structure that interests me here, for I take it to be at the heart of the Christian message. Put simply: at first glance, Christianity (or following Jesus) *seems* to be this relatively clear thing that can easily be comprehended and perhaps even mastered. Indeed, Jesus himself puts things in apparently straightforward terms at certain points. Yet even these relatively simple notions or metaphors that Jesus uses to describe the kingdom or salvation inevitably turn out to be deeper, more complex, and more paradoxical than they at first appear. Thus, read in one way, the Christian Bible can seem relatively uncomplicated and straightforward. Yet read more closely, the passages that seem most simple often turn out to be among the most difficult.[3] Thus, despite what many believers often think about their faith, the content of it is considerably more complex and paradoxical than is normally admitted—whether by those believers themselves or by their pastors or even by some of the theologians who are influential in forming the views of the faithful.

In following this complexity, I mean to attend to what I think lies at the very heart of the Christian Gospel itself. That is, I think that the very Gospel message does not merely *contain* but is *essentially composed of* tensions and complexities at its very heart. One might say that Christian existence—following Jesus—just *is* tension and complexity. Or one might put it as follows: Jesus is not in the business of making the Christian life simple. Of course, these tensions and complexities are all too often overlooked or explained away. It is not too much to say that many Christian believers are conditioned to read the New Testament and the sayings of Jesus—*if they read them at all*—with a certain kind of "Prozac hermeneutic" that simply blunts the force of what the texts themselves actually say, allowing those texts to become thoroughly domesticated.[4] My response to such readings is simply: have you *really* read the text? The title of Marcus J. Borg's well-known book—*Meeting Jesus Again for the First Time*—nicely gets at the complication of thinking that one has read and understood what Jesus is saying and then discovering that one is *at best* "not far from the kingdom." Thus, the more one reads what Jesus says, the more one realizes that "not far" all too well sums up what it is like to be a follower of Jesus. One is never (or seldom, as we will see) *there;* instead, one is always on the way. The moment one thinks "ah, now I finally get it" easily turns—with further reflection—into the moment of "I still don't quite get it."

While it would be fruitful to consider these tensions in the New Testament as a whole, in the logic of Christianity itself, and in competing versions of Christian theology, I will limit myself here to attending to what Jesus himself says.[5] As shall become apparent, these complications themselves are already far more than enough to occupy us.

Given the context of this book, it should not be difficult to see why I would want to make the point that Jesus' own comments (and, by extension, Christianity) prove self-disruptive. Jacques Derrida is hardly alone in thinking that determinate messianisms like Judaism, Christianity, or Islam often do violence—whether literal or figurative—in the name of messianic certainty.[6] Without doubt, fervent believers (whether Protestant, Roman Catholic, or Eastern Orthodox) often claim a kind of finality—a typical word used by some is the qualifier "absolute"—about their teachings (which often take the form of "X is the absolute truth"). Further, they often believe that their access to this "absolute truth" gives them a privileged place from which to judge others. Yet merely making such claims does not necessarily make them truly "absolute" (nor is it clear exactly what possessing "absolute truth" would look like in practice if one truly *did* have it). In pursuing what Jesus actually says, I have in mind Jacques Derrida's point that he makes about religions and their own internal logics: "For me, there is no such thing as 'religion.' Within what one calls religions—Judaism, Christianity, Islam, or other religions—there are again tensions, heterogeneity, disruptive volcanos, sometimes texts, especially those of the prophets, which cannot be reduced to an institution, to a corpus, to a system. I want to keep the right to read these texts in a way which has to be constantly reinvented. It is something which can be totally new at every moment."[7]

The point Derrida is making here seems quite right. Certainly it is the case in the religion that we call "Christianity" that there are multiple tensions and heterogeneity that are extensive. Christian believers often speak of "historic orthodoxy"—what orthodox Christians throughout the years have always believed—as if this has been a relatively uncontested and uniform thing. To be sure, we have the historic creeds, such as the Nicene Creed, that provide a genuine continuity. I have no intent to dispute that. While I could point out that *arriving* at the Nicene Creed was no small task and the extent of disagreement involved was substantial (even *after* its formulation), that is not my concern here. Instead, I simply want to focus on what Jesus says. Although Derrida specifically mentions prophets as being disruptive, Christianity has the distinction of a founder who is even more disruptive than the Hebrew prophets (and that is saying quite a bit). Of course, Derrida would say that all systems and texts are characterized by "*différance*" and thus are self-deconstructing. While one might question the extent to which this is true, the claim seems generally correct. Yet it is one thing to make such a general—even an *abstract*—sort of claim; it is another to *follow that logic* empirically. Here I am interested in pursuing the latter with the goal of illuminating the complexity of much of what Jesus says.

So here I pursue the logic of the "not far" as it gets worked out in different ways.

"What Must I Do to Be Saved?"

It is a very typical evangelical Protestant belief that there is some sort of thing you need to do and believe in order to become a Christian—or to be "saved."[8] No doubt, other Christian believers have some version of this, though that is not my concern here. Often this Protestant conception is put in terms of "asking Jesus into your heart" or "asking Jesus to become your personal savior."[9] While there are many aspects of both of these ideas that could be considered, I am more interested in the general belief that *something* must be done and believed in order for one to be—how shall I put this?—*in*. Exactly what one thinks is needed to be "in" depends on how one views salvation. For many, salvation mainly equals "getting to heaven." While it no doubt includes that, what Jesus calls the "kingdom of God" or "kingdom of heaven" really means something like "Jesus' movement." Thus, when he says to the scribe that he is "not far," Jesus is saying "you are not far from being part of my community of followers." In any case, that there truly is such a set of things that one must do and believe in order to "become a Christian" is so obvious to many conservative Christians that it is simply taken for granted. Of course, as some former colleagues from the theology department at my institution discovered over the years, when they asked students to spell out exactly what these things were, there was considerable discrepancy. For many students, being asked such an explicit question about something for which they had long assumed they knew the answer turned out to be somewhat akin to Augustine's problem with the nature of time. As he puts it, "Provided that no one asks me, I know. If I want to explain it to an inquirer, I do not know."[10] Specifying exactly what it is you must do and believe in actual practice to be a member of the household of faith turns out to be considerably harder than what fervent believers often believe in the abstract.

I begin with this general observation because I think it gets at a problem that is all too well exemplified in the Gospels. Specifically, Jesus himself is so difficult to pin down on what exactly is necessary to be part of the kingdom of heaven. Now, what I have just said will strike many believers as simply wrong. Indeed, the most likely response will be: "Jesus is quite clear that you must be born again" (and born again is parsed out in terms of what one must do and believe). The passage in which Jesus uses this beautiful and moving metaphor is in John chapter 3, a passage that for many conservative Christians is a central text of Christianity. Now, there are a number of questions or problems that can be raised concerning this passage. One might begin with the fact that only certain English translations use the locution "born again."[11] As it turns out, while "γεννηθῇ ἄνωθεν" [*gennāthā anōthen*] *could* mean born again (or "born anew"), the most likely translation is actually "born from above" (which is not nearly as memorable).[12] But there is a much more difficult problem with the passage. Despite the fact that this formula has become *the central metaphor* of what it means to be a Christian for many, there is something quite odd about that fact. The oddness is this: the occasion is that a Pharisee named

Nicodemus comes to Jesus in the dead of night and so this turns out to be (from every indication) a *private* exchange.[13] In other words, as far as we know from Gospel reports, Jesus only uses this formula of faith *one* time for *one* person. Yet, if this truly is *the* formula of faith, would there not be multiple instances of Jesus using this formula? Indeed, one would expect that it would be something like a campaign slogan, one repeated not merely by Jesus but by all of his followers. Yet such is not the case.

There are two further complications. First, Nicodemus is quite confused by this notion, even though Jesus thinks he should simply "get" it. Jesus first answers Nicodemus by saying the following: "Very truly, I tell you, no one can enter the kingdom of God without being born of water and Spirit. What is born of the flesh is flesh, and what is born of the Spirit is spirit" (John 3:5–6). While this answer is hardly simple, what Jesus goes on to say is particularly remarkable, leading us to a second complication: "Do not be astonished that I said to you, 'You must be born from above.' The wind blows where it chooses, and you hear the sound of it, but you do not know where it comes from or where it goes. So it is with everyone who is born of the Spirit" (John 3:7–8). So Jesus provides Nicodemus with an answer that is challenging in two ways. On the one hand, the whole metaphor of being born from above is hardly easy to understand. What exactly does this mean? On the other hand, Jesus' point in verses 7–8 is precisely that the Spirit works as it wills and so (as one conservative commentator puts it) "we can neither control him nor understand him."[14] Thus, we must be born of a Spirit that *we do not control or understand*. Such a requirement deals a heavy blow to anyone who thinks that the power of Christianity is something that we can master or control. No, says Jesus, it is quite the other way around: *you* are the one who is mastered.

One has the distinct impression that Nicodemus is at best "not far" from understanding what one needs to do to become part of the kingdom. If one takes this complexity and puts it together with the metaphor's single appearance (and, to make matters more complicated, neither this story nor the phrase is found in any of the other Gospels), it becomes hard to understand how one might think that the writers of Scripture (or even simply John) could have intended that this become the central, defining metaphor of Christianity. To be sure, it is hardly an unimportant one. Jesus speaks of being "born of water and the spirit" (John 3:5) and historically Christians have understood this as referring to baptism. Further, the writer of the First Letter of Peter speaks of being "born anew," which could also be translated as "born again" (1 Pet. 1:23), and begins his epistle by speaking of a "new birth" (1 Pet. 1:3). So the use of this metaphor certainly has biblical support.

Yet Jesus does not make everything simple by using merely one metaphor or one way of speaking about what one must do to be saved or become part of the kingdom. Indeed, it is as if he is trying to pull out all the stops and come up with as many metaphors as he possibly can in describing salvation and what the kingdom is like. There are so many of these that we will be forced here to examine only a few significant ones.

One of the more remarkable examples is the miracle of the paralytic who is let down to Jesus from the roof of the house where Jesus is speaking. Jesus says to the paralytic: "Son, your sins are forgiven" (Mark 2:5). In one sense, this seems like a relatively straightforward miracle, though usually the startling feature is taken to be that Jesus forgives the man's sins first and then heals him later. Yet consider exactly *why* Jesus both forgives and heals this man. The entire story actually revolves around this man's *friends*. For it is they who are intent on bringing this man to Jesus. It may well be that the man is more than happy to be brought to Jesus; it may even be that it was he who begged them to bring him. But we are never told *anything* about this man — whether about his motives, his belief, or his relation to Jesus — other than his paralysis. Instead, we are told about the motives of these friends. Specifically, we are told that "when Jesus saw their faith" (that is, the faith of these friends), it is at this moment — and due to *their* faith — that *his* sins are forgiven. And yet the opposite is not true: there is nothing said about the sins of the *friends* being forgiven, despite the fact that *they* are the ones with the faith. Simply put, this is not the way faith is normally assumed to work: the seemingly apparent logic of faith is that the individual believer exhibits faith and thus is saved. The whole notion of justification by way of faith (Rom. 5:1) is premised on the basis of individual faith. Indeed, there is good reason for thinking this way. When the woman suffering from hemorrhaging touches Jesus' cloak, he responds to her by saying "your faith has made you well" (Matt. 9:22). So, if we take it seriously, the example of the friends of the paralytic leaves us a bit in the lurch. What do we need to do to be saved? Is our friends' faith sufficient for us?

The story of the paralytic would be enough of a complication were there not at least two other instances in which the formula of faith, again, sounds quite different. The first of these is that of the story of one who is usually identified as "the rich young ruler." This is a story that has very much the air of "you are not far from the kingdom" about it. The young man approaches Jesus and asks him specifically "what good deed must I do to have eternal life?" (Matt. 19:16). To this Jesus replies: "If you wish to enter into life, keep the commandments" (Matt. 19:17). And the young man then asks "which ones?" (Matt. 19:18) Jesus then reels off the more or less standard list from the Ten Commandments, adding "you shall love your neighbor as yourself."[15] And this is where the story gets interesting, in two respects. First, the young man claims "I have kept all these." That he (at least thinks) that he is honestly able to say this—and Jesus does not contradict him—is remarkable. Who can truly say that he has successfully loved his neighbor as himself? But, even given this confidence, he still goes on to say "what do I still lack?" (Matt. 19:20). What is remarkable about the second aspect of this response is that the young man makes the assumption that he *lacks* something. Somehow he too is "not far" but also still not there. At this point, Jesus prescribes what he needs to do to finally have eternal life: "If you wish to be perfect, go, sell your possessions, and give the money to the poor, and you will have treasure in heaven; then come, follow me" (Matt. 19:21). This story, however, turns out rather badly. This was not what the young man wanted to hear. The result was that "he went away grieving, for he had many possessions" (Matt. 19:22). Yet why does Jesus require such a thing of this particular person? A typical answer to this story is that Jesus here puts his finger on exactly what is keeping this young man from being fully "perfect" (to use Jesus' own word). Thus, so the explanation goes, the requirement of selling all is a specific command and so only applicable to this young man. Were such a convenient way of dealing with the text only possible!

Unfortunately, it fails in at least two respects, one minor and one much more significant. In the first respect, it assumes that we know enough about this person to know that Jesus picks this requirement because this is the one thing *he* lacks. Yet this is mere conjecture (even despite the fact that Jesus goes on at this point to say to his disciples "truly I tell you, it will be hard for a rich person to enter the kingdom of heaven," Matt. 19:23). The second respect is that, elsewhere, Jesus actually makes this a requirement of *everyone*, saying: "None of you can become my disciple if you do not give up all of your possessions" (Luke 14:33). This is truly one of those "hard sayings" of Jesus. The problem with this passage is that—at least in its literal sense—it seems *far too clear*—for it speaks of "none" and "all." Jesus does not say this is the formula only for some people (say, those who are particularly materialistic), nor does he say that one should just have relatively few possessions. But, of course, one can soften this requirement, in two ways. First, we can note (as some commentators do) that Jesus uses the present tense and thus can conclude that one only need be "ready at any moment" to give up one's possessions, in the event that God asks. Second, we can conclude that "giving" them up means handing them over to God. In this case, we retain them in a practical sense but *theoretically* they belong to God, and so we do not hold on to them *as* possessions. We "have" them, but they are not really "ours." These are, to be sure, much "easier" readings. On the other hand, Luke has already quoted Jesus as saying much the same thing: "Sell your possessions and give alms" (Luke 12:33). Again, this is simply something that Jesus says in a general way, rather than limiting it to any particular audience. But, again, this passage can have much less of a sting if we conclude that what Jesus really means is that his disciples must (as one commentator puts it) "inwardly be quite free from their worldly possessions and must regard and use these as gifts of God's love to them, to be consecrated by them to His service by bestowing them on the needy and on the promotion of the work of the Lord in general."[16] Again, the requirement now becomes a kind of "mental" giving rather than an actual, practical one.

Is this what Jesus is really saying—something so much less demanding? It strikes me that these "softer" and less difficult interpretations are ones that we naturally want to be true. Needless to say, very few Christians over the centuries have taken these injunctions in a literal way. Indeed, most Christians would see selling all of one's possessions as an act of supererogation—something far and above what is actually required. Yet, for the sake of argument, let us assume here that these milder ways of interpreting these passages are actually correct. Even then, one is still left with a rather demanding commandment after all: for *truly* having let go of one's possessions even *mentally* is already quite an undertaking. How many Christians are really at this point of letting go—that is, where they could quite literally "let go" of everything they possess? On the other hand, there is good reason to think that some sort of a "harder version" is what Jesus really intends. Note that the passage continues with Peter saying to Jesus: "Look, we have left everything and followed you" (Matt. 19:27). So Peter, at least, takes Jesus quite literally.

One might conclude from these three passages that there really is no choice: selling all is what one *must* do. And yet the story of Zacchaeus—found a little later in Luke—complicates this conclusion. Zacchaeus is labeled as both "a chief tax collector" and also "rich" (Luke 19:2). In ancient Israel, tax collectors not only worked for the Romans or for Herod (which made them conspirators with the oppressors) but also were not known for levying fair and equitable taxes on their fellow Jews. Tax collectors made their money by adding a cost beyond what they collected for the Romans. We meet Zacchaeus when he climbs up a tree to see Jesus and then Jesus calls to him and says: "Zacchaeus, hurry and come down; for I must stay at your house today" (Luke 19:5). Zacchaeus's response to Jesus is startling. Without any prompting, he immediately says: "Look, half of my possessions, Lord, I will give to the poor; and if I have defrauded anyone of anything, I will pay back four times as much." To which Jesus responds: "Today salvation has come to this house" (Luke 19:9). This is remarkably good news for Zacchaeus, yet it is hard to reconcile Jesus' enthusiastic and quite explicit comment that Zacchaeus has finally "made it" with that of the rich young ruler. Both of them are rich, but Jesus obviously thinks that Zacchaeus's promise to give merely half of his possessions away is sufficient, whereas the demand on the rich young ruler is that he give everything away. Why the difference? What makes these passages difficult is that there is no explanation either way. Perhaps one could say that Zacchaeus's willingness to quadruple the payback to anyone he might have defrauded brings his "half" closer to a "whole." But there is nothing in the passage to indicate any such "logic."

So, taken together, what we have are four very different versions of what "one needs to do to be saved." The first, and most familiar, is that one must be "born again"; the second is that the faith of one's friends proves sufficient; the third is that one must sell all; and the fourth is that selling half is quite good enough. As "salvation formulas," these hardly jive with one another. Further, it seems impossible to pick out any one of these formulas and select it as "the one." True, Jesus says to Nicodemus that "no one can see the kingdom of God without being born from above" (John 3:3). So there is a universality to this requirement. Yet that same universality is found in "none of you can become my disciple if you do not give up all of your possessions." Conservative Christians have no problem generalizing the first, but the second—far from being generalized—is largely ignored, or else "softened" to the point where it loses any real difficulty or sting.

Yet these four accounts are, in effect, trumped by that of Matthew 25, where Jesus provides a rather startling explanation of how "all the nations" (Matt. 25:2) will be judged "when the Son of Man comes in his glory" (Matt. 25:31). There are at least two unusual aspects to this account. First, the ones who hear the words "Come, you that are blessed by my Father, inherit the kingdom prepared for you from the foundation of the world" (Matt. 25:34) are described as doing the following: "I was hungry and you gave me food, I was thirsty and you gave me something to drink, I was a stranger and you welcomed me, I was naked and you gave me clothing, I was sick and you took care of me, I was in prison and you visited me" (Matt. 25:36–37). There is no mention here of being born again or having faith or giving all of one's possessions to the poor. There is also no indication of a doctrinal requirement, such as believing that "Jesus is Lord." Instead, there is one very simple test: did you take care of those of the least of society? If so, you're "in." If not, you are "accursed" and destined for "the eternal fire prepared for the devil and his angels" (Matt. 25:41). This passage is certainly a problematic one for a universalist (one who believes that all go to heaven), but it is even more problematic for anyone who thinks that some kind of "propositional belief" is necessary to enter the kingdom. For here it is merely a question of what one *does.* However, a second aspect of this text is even more startling. The people whom Jesus welcomes into the kingdom and about whom he says that they have cared for him are surprised, for they have no memory of doing any of these things for Jesus. Indeed, they do *not* see themselves as being "the righteous ones." It is almost as if the left hand did not know what the right hand was doing, which Matthew has already relayed Jesus as saying regarding how one should give alms (Matt. 6:3). Yet Jesus insists that "just as you did it to one of the least of these who are members of my family, you did it to me" (Matt. 25:40). Here we come to a complication regarding the phrase "members of my family." The Greek wording is actually "ἀδελφῶν μου" [*adelphôn mou*], which literally translates as "my brothers" and which Matthew consistently uses to mean other Christians, specifically other Christians who are out spreading the Gospel. There is something rather strange about this interpretation: God is judging the entire world by how they treat Christian emissaries? That, at least, has been a traditional interpretation. And, if we put this together with the Luke passages, there seems to be a kind of fit: for if one has sold all of one's possessions and given them to the poor, then one is now oneself "the least of these"—hungry, thirsty, and likely something of an outcast. Perhaps something along these lines is what Matthew actually means. It certainly would put Christians in a very different place than they often are at least today in the western world: instead of being in places of privilege and authority, they would have renounced both to become humble and needy. Of course, it has become the more common interpretation to take what Jesus says as applying to all who are hungry and thirsty, alien or naked, sick or in prison.

HARD SAYINGS

Let us dwell for a while with the interpretation that it is Christians who are meant by "my brothers" and turn back to an even more famous passage in Matthew, the Sermon on the Mount. There are multiple features of what Jesus says here that frustrate any kind of conquering, mastering messianism. Indeed, the logic Jesus puts forth is one that is considerably more disruptive than the passages that we have so far considered, for here we come to what could be called the "mother lode" of disruptive passages. One way of describing the logic that drives this passage is by way of the refrain "you have heard it said...but I say to you" that accompanies many of the reversals that Jesus continually provides. Those reversals certainly can be found in such commendations of being poor in spirit, of mourning, and of being meek (Matt. 5:3–5), especially when we consider what Jesus means by these strange sayings. To be "poor in spirit" is to realize that one has no righteousness of one's own and thus is fully dependent upon God. Similarly, to be "meek" means that one has given up any pretentions of righteousness. Obviously, being poor in spirit and meek are the very opposite of thinking one is privileged or has the corner on truth. But where things really start to get interesting is when Jesus tells his listeners not to resist the one who does evil,[17] to turn the other cheek, to give one's cloak to one who only asks for one's coat, and to go the second mile (Matt. 5:39–41). All of these commands to do that which seems so utterly "unnatural" could be seen as summed up when Jesus says to "love your enemies and pray for those who persecute you" (Matt. 5:44). Even if we only took this one commandment—and left all of the others behind—Christianity could not be anything other than a messianism that simply could not lead to any kind of triumphalism. What could be more disruptive to any triumphalistic intentions than a command to love and even pray for one's enemies?

It is important to realize that "love" here does not necessarily involve a feeling. True, if one is really to love another, there must be some kind of change of heart. But if one is only at the beginning of moving in this direction, the practical results of such love is that one *do* that which is loving—to lend the other (in this case, the enemy) a helping hand. Yet if I truly love my enemies, then something remarkable happens. Structurally, these enemies will no longer be "enemies" in the same sense as they were before. For even if they remain against me, and even if I in whatever way find them disagreeable or dangerous, they are no longer "simply" enemies. My relationship toward them—and thus my comportment toward them—can no longer remain the same if I am not merely to *pray for them* (which is the easier thing to do) but actually to *love* them. What would it really look like to love my enemies? Since really *doing* this is hard even to imagine, if this is part of what it means to follow Jesus then one is surely some ways off from the kingdom—perhaps even more than "not far." In any case, it is far beyond the scope of this paper to work out this change exactly (and, of course, it will vary from situation to situation).

If we couple these passages with those of Matthew 23, things get even more complex, for this is where Jesus says, no less than seven times, "woe to you, scribes and Pharisees" (i.e., the religious establishment). Jesus begins his litany of their failings by saying that "they do not practice what they teach" (Matt. 23:3) and, in the list that follows, some version of hypocrisy is connected with most every charge. The scribes and Pharisees put heavy burdens on the common folk, "but they themselves are unwilling to lift a finger" (Matt. 23:4). Jesus calls them "blind guides" who nevertheless make themselves out to be great spiritual examples. They care immensely for the comparatively unimportant tithe of "mint and dill and cummin" while neglecting "justice and mercy and faith" (Matt. 23:23). Jesus calls them "whitewashed tombs," for they seem clean and beautiful on the outside "but inside they are full of the bones of the dead and of all kinds of filth" (Matt. 23:27). What makes this critique so important is that these very scribes and Pharisees are the ones who prescribe moral and religious law and thus are presumed to be exemplars of that law. Jesus' point is clear enough: these "keepers" of the law in one sense are anything *but* "keepers" of the law in another sense. In disrupting the very religious establishment itself, Jesus gives reasons for any of us who think we are "exemplars" of the law to pause and look deep within ourselves, as well as to consider how well our deeds match our teachings. Jesus' message is clear: the more you think you are truly fulfilling the law — or truly living the life of the kingdom — the more you need to be circumspect.

And this point very naturally leads us to what may well be the most disruptive passage in the Sermon on the Mount:

> Do not judge, so that you might not be judged. For with the judgment that you make you will be judged, and the measure you give will be the measure you get. Why do you see the speck in your neighbor's eye, but do not notice the log in your own eye? Or how can you say to your neighbor, 'Let me take the speck out of your eye,' while the log is in your own eye? You hypocrite, first take the log out of your own eye, and then you will see clearly to take the speck out of your neighbor's eye. (Matt. 7:1–5)

There is something particularly alarming about this passage. Basically, if it is taken seriously, it stops one in one's tracks. Of course, some take this admonition—do not judge—to rather simplistic conclusions. Yet Jesus can hardly be saying something as simple as: "stop judging altogether." Making judgments is part of what it means not just to be an intelligent being but also necessary to living aright. We make judgments all the time about various things, including others (not to mention ourselves). Not to do so would be simply foolish. So Jesus must have something much more nuanced in mind, and that becomes clearer once we look at this entire passage. It is obvious from the context that Jesus has in mind judging other people. But what he says ends up being much more about ourselves.

Consider the way in which Jesus sets this up. First, he warns against judging. The admonition not to judge clearly is a stark warning that judging is dangerous. Jesus is more or less saying: "You really don't want to get into the business of judging. It's difficult and it has consequences for *you* that you may not find so easy to live with." That leads us to Jesus' second point: that any kind of judging of others is going to have to be predicated on our judging of ourselves. He sets up a kind of reciprocity of judging: basically, I will be judged in the same way that I have judged others. Thus, before I get involved in doing any judging, I had better be sure that I am willing to be judged by whatever standards I am judging other people. However, there is something even more complicated at work here, and here we come to a third aspect. Jesus takes it for granted that our judging is inherently biased. We see the little things of which the other is guilty and fail to see the far more significant things of which we are guilty. That Jesus does not say "sometimes" this is the case and instead speaks as if this is the normal situation would indicate that there is something structural at work here. We *normally* are critical of the faults of others and tend to overlook our own faults. It does not take much introspection to establish that this is all too typical, at least for most of us. So Jesus calls us to deep self-examination before we even begin the business of judging others. And this is where his logic is most disruptive. If I am truly guilty of seeing the speck in the other's eye and simply missing the log in my own eye, then I have my work cut out for me. Now, put in the context of this passage, Jesus is saying: "before you even think of judging the other person, you had better have entered into a brutally honest assessment of yourself." It is this stage that is difficult, perhaps we might say *so* difficult as to make it a question whether one would or could ever be sufficiently "done" with this stage to be at the place where one is now "qualified" to judge. Why so? I think Friedrich Nietzsche gets at this in one of his comments on lying. Normally, we think of lying as something we do to others. Nietzsche would have us think exactly the opposite. As he puts it, "By lie I mean: wishing *not* to see something that one does see; wishing not to see something *as* one sees it. Whether the lie takes place before witnesses or without witnesses does not matter. The most common lie is that with which one lies to oneself; lying to others is, relatively, an exception."[18] As counterintuitive as this might seem, I think Nietzsche is right. That is, we are constantly working very hard not to see that which is plainly before us ("the log"). The result is that one lies *mostly* to oneself. If Nietzsche is right that lying to ourselves is the normal state of things, then at what point can we be sure enough of our judgment—sure enough that *finally* we are telling ourselves the truth—that we can now begin the process of judging others? This is not some academic question; rather, it gets at something that is highly practical. The problem here seems to be that, however much one might try to get that log out of one's own eye, one can never be *sure* one is really at the place of being qualified to judge others, rather than being at the place that is "not far." If Jesus had merely said "do not judge," he would actually have left us with a much easier command to follow. Instead, he leaves us with a command to *live* differently. First, we must engage in whatever level of introspection is necessary to identify the log in our own eye. Then we must actually *remove* it. If the first of these is difficult, then the second is even more so. For identifying the bias (or, more probably, *biases*) that keep us from seeing aright is one thing; truly overcoming them is another.

Conclusion

So at what point can one say one has "arrived" at the kingdom of God—or arrived at the place where one is fully confident in one's ability to judge others? Given all that we have seen, it would seem difficult for one to say—with any real confidence—that one is truly "there." Indeed, by this point it would seem that "not far" now sounds like a relatively high compliment. But, if "not far" is probably descriptive of the *best* of us, then who is left standing to "pronounce" with clear and unwavering certainty about the other? And then exactly what sort of messianic violence can really be done by anyone who takes these words of Jesus seriously? Again, I do not mean to suggest that no judging is possible or desirable. Nor do I mean to suggest that there are not certain things that are required for following Jesus. If anything, it is not that Jesus has given us *too few* pointers but *too many*. As to formulas for salvation, perhaps the reason it is hard to reconcile these is because Jesus does not intend there to be anything like "the formula." Instead, following him is something that cannot be reduced to the formulaic and thus is always both concrete and provisional. In some ways, that is quite discomforting, for our tendency is to want to *know* "the formula" and then be sure that we have fulfilled it. But from what we have seen, Jesus does not seem to be in the business of giving anything like certainty that we are "right." What he calls his followers to is a life that is *constantly disrupted*, one that is constantly showing us that the "logic" of the kingdom of God is simply not of this world. Thus, these disruptions—far from being simply confusions—are instead intimations of a new kind of human existence. That those intimations often throw our systems and formulas into confusion only show how far and above the logic of the kingdom of heaven is. And so we are always "not far."

The Liturgy of Hermeneutics
Midrash as Open Religion *with* Religion
— A Response to Bruce Ellis Benson

Drew M. Dalton

In his extended mediation on the enigmatic "not far" of Mark 12:28–34, Bruce Benson invites the reader to think of the truth of the kingdom of God not as some propositional content but as emergent within the strife and tension such difficult statements as the "not yet" evokes. The Gospel message, he assures us, is therefore not one that closes off discussion or debate. It does not operate like a period, finalizing, defining, and completing discourse. Instead, it operates like a question mark. It functions to open a cognitive space and invites the reader to still more discussion and interpretation.

The truth of the kingdom of God, it seems then, is not so much an ending, some final home or resting place, as a beginning — an aperture that does not invite rest but provokes movement within the reader. Jesus' statement in the passage in question is not the promise of some eventual satisfaction for the scribe concerning his query, but the transference and eternal postponement of that satisfaction.

This, of course, should come as a troubling message to those who turn to the Gospel looking for peace and satisfaction—those who are washed up on the shores of the kingdom exhausted from the tribulations of life and looking for a safe haven, for, claims Benson, the routes to the kingdom are not broad and easy, but narrow and difficult. It is a journey, then, that will continually frustrate those who begin it with the hopes of finding easy answers or programmatic formulas. For the truth of the Gospel cannot be boiled down to the statements contained within it. Instead, this elusive truth seems to lie, Benson suggests, between these words, precisely in the tension that the sometimes conflicting statements create — hence Benson's assessment that Christianity, understood properly, is an inexorably self-disruptive transcendence.

Understood thus, the Scriptures could be read as somehow radically incomplete — pointing always away, beyond themselves to something still about to come, something not yet here though "not far" off. This is the messianism of the scriptural truth and the kingdom of God, one might say. But if this is the case, where are we to look to find this messiah? How are we to orient ourselves in the disruptive (should we read "deconstructive"?) space that is the Gospel message? Or are we left utterly directionless by these tensions, disoriented and lost within the shifting sands of a contentless "religion *without* religion"?

At this point, it becomes difficult to know how to read Benson. On the one hand he seems to affirm with someone like John Caputo that given the inherent tension the Gospel invites, "there is no such thing as 'religion,'" and that nothing resembling an "institution" or "system" can adequately testify to the disruptive movement of the kingdom. We are simply "not there" and can never hope to "get there" — can never hope to construct a creed or cult that can properly give voice to the tension of truth. In this regard he seems to point to precisely the kind of "religion *without* religion" to which this volume critically responds. But, of course, this is not the final word of Benson's essay, for he concludes the essay by reminding us that though we are "not yet there" we are still "not far" — that though we may never achieve some final "formula" that can contain the truth, we are not left entirely floundering. We are instead invited to a new way of being, one that recognizes and welcomes this disruption. Perhaps this is the "religion *with* religion" hinted at in the title of this volume. But at this point Benson leaves off, refusing to formulate what this "new kind of human existence" to which we are invited might look like — refusing, in other words, to give the reader some final answer or definitive recipe. Instead, Benson's essay leaves us asking our own questions.

But questions are not meant to throw us into dumbstruck apoplectic awe—they demand answers (at least provisional ones). They are not meant to provoke worship, necessarily, but discussion and debate. And perhaps it is in this recognition that some provisional answers to Benson's questions lies. So let us honor the questions posed in his essay by offering some tentative answers to what such a religion *with* religion, such a religion that allows space for disruptive questions, might entail.

It seems to me that the content of such a notion lies in something we already witness at work in Benson's essay, something that could be called, for lack of a better phrase: the liturgy of hermeneutics, or the interpretive discipline.

The fact that the truth of the Scriptures cannot be boiled down into a propositional imperative does not mean that there is no demand or exigency to their message. Quite the opposite: the opening they create solicits, and indeed obliges, the reader to discourse. One must try to make sense of these enigmatic statements that entreat us to pursue their meaning just as much as they hold us at bay, remaining elusively "not far" off. One must attempt to forge an answer to the questions they impose. And, moreover, this activity must be pursued in the company of others, for discussion always requires at least two (one cannot discuss where there is no difference, nor indeed where there is no discord—no language is private, after all). Perhaps this explains the strange formula for worship found in Matthew 18:20, "wherever two or three come together" there we find the church, the body of Christ.

Faith, as a practice, it seems, requires the possibility of discourse, disagreement, and discussion. It is something that takes place publicly in the space between those who have been challenged by the questions asked by the Scriptures as they each attempt to answer them together. It is the liturgy of hermeneutics; what for the Jews is called Midrash, the communal act of interpretation forged through debate and dialogue. Faith in this understanding is never a private thing. It can be conducted neither in the privacy of our own thoughts nor in the solitude of our studies. "Two or three" are required. Debate and discussion are demanded. For only in the discursive space present between those who come together to interpret the meaning of the kingdom of God can we do justice to the questions asked by it.

The practice of faith is indeed a necessarily self-disruptive process then, as Benson asserts, for it is a practice that demands subjecting our ideas to the scrutiny of others who will most likely disagree with us. It requires opening ourselves in this way to the claims and criticisms of others. It is not narcissism and does not flourish in the intellectual vacuum of homogeny. It is exposure, analysis, and argumentation. It is not smooth and easy, therefore, but rough and abrasive.

The Spirit, which Benson correctly identifies as the origin of the disruptive movement of faith, this Spirit that we do not control nor cannot truly understand, announces itself in the voice of debate and discussion. It speaks through us in Midrash, the liturgy of hermeneutics, and can be heard in the tension that emerges between two opposing minds and taut vocal chords. The truth of the kingdom thus appears in this communal tension. Its seat is the thinking and debating body of questioners. It thus manifests wherever tough questions interrupt false union and debate unsettles the ease of complacency.

Note, then, that this Spirit is not the Spirit of Hegel's dialectic. The liturgy of Midrash does not aim at enveloping those who question in some final completion or resolution. It is not directed toward totality. It needs space, difference, and otherness to thrive and thus works against forming a consensus. The kingdom of this Spirit is thus never completed, never closed off or finally settled, but always under question, always a point of contention.

In this regard, the messianism pronounced in the "not far," though never filled out completely, is nevertheless "present" in some way amidst those who come together to debate and interpret its meaning. Jesus, who has died and who is proclaimed risen by his followers, has thus always already come again amidst those who open themselves to this process. And yet this same risen messiah remains, in this very process, forever "not far" off, always still about to come. Look not then to the heavens to see this messiah, look instead to the other person, the neighbor, the one who questions you and who questions with you.

In this way we arrive through engaging Benson's questions with answers at a new picture of religion—an open religion that testifies to the free play and difficult contradictions of the kingdom of God;

a religion that invites the disruption of an Other who calls us into question and blossoms in the insecurity and uncertainty of a forever incomplete and nontotalizable message. And yet we find in this same picture a religion that does not sacrifice determinate content, which neither gives way entirely to the free play of sign and signifier, nor becomes lost in the infinite proliferations of possible interpretation. For such a religion remains intractably rooted in the text and resolutely committed to the rigorous study and debate of these infinite possible meanings. In this way we catch site of a religion that, while testifying to the forever unfinished phenomenon of the "not far" of faith, remains coherent *as a religion*. And, in the end, perhaps it is precisely such a notion of religion that this volume announces and invites continental philosophy to consider as a religion *with* religion.

Perhaps Still a Bit Farther Off Than We Think

— Engaging Bruce Ellis Benson

J. Aaron Simmons

"The person who turns one of his ears to the prophetic unmasking word of the gospel and the other to the cries of those who suffer deprivation and oppression is not likely to suffer from the illusion that he is engaged in pure theory when in fact he is working to shore up his own position of privilege."
— Nicholas Wolterstorff,
Reason within the Bounds of Religion

P rivilege is a funny thing in that it is most problematic when it is most invisible. Much of continental philosophy has been a sustained attempt to unmask the unacknowledged privilege that operates (often invisibly) in philosophical discourse, political theory, and historical social praxis. So, when Nietzsche describes the "prejudice of philosophers" he does so with an eye toward challenging the dominance of objectivity and neutrality so prominent in much of Western philosophy. This challenge is most vividly and powerfully expressed in a simple question at the beginning of *Beyond Good and*

Evil: "Suppose that truth were a woman—and why not?"[1] Nietzsche's question anticipates various trajectories in twentieth century philosophy including the work of such feminist thinkers as Simone de Beauvoir, Luce Irigaray, Iris Marion Young, and Martha Nussbaum, the race theory of Cornel West, Frantz Fanon, and Houston Baker, and also the queer theory of Michel Foucault, Eve Sedgwick, and Judith Butler. Despite the fact that these thinkers come from a variety of philosophical traditions (Anglo-American analytic, American pragmatism, French existentialism, poststructuralism, etc.), what they all share is a commitment to giving voice to those individuals and groups who have been historically marginalized by those who would claim epistemic certainty, absolute truth, or theological absolutism, even when such claims are offered internal to philosophy itself. We might say that all of these thinkers contest philosophy's traditional privilege to be unreflective about the privilege that sometimes functions in its own theoretical discourse and professional practice.

Perhaps no movement in twentieth century philosophy is more deeply defined by the task of unmasking and disruption than the deconstructionism of Jacques Derrida. Ironically, perhaps, it is for this reason that Bruce Ellis Benson sees Derrida as a resource for Christian philosophy/theology. According to Benson, a Derridian appreciation of the Christian Gospel leads to the recognition that the "Gospel message does not merely *contain* but is *essentially composed of* tensions and complexities at its very heart." As such, a close reading of the words of Jesus leads Benson to claim, "Jesus is not in the business of making the Christian life simple." Now, even if this is true—that is, that the Gospel has been traditionally misread (or, as Benson claims, there has been a silent "Prozac hermeneutic" operative in much of Christian history)—it might seem that this disruptive reading of the sayings of Jesus is a far cry from the type of disruption one finds in the feminism of Irigaray or in the queer theory of Butler, say.

Yet Benson demonstrates that once the Gospel is not seen as a static (and simple) account of "how to be saved," the supposed privilege that underlies much of Christian triumphalism is radically contested. The result, Benson contends, is that Christian existence is itself disrupted because it becomes impossible to claim the status of having achieved or "arrived" at the "kingdom of God." In this sense, Benson's essay implicitly asks a version of Nietzsche's question: Suppose that Jesus' words disrupt much of what is recognized as "Christianity"—and why not? Asking this question leads Benson to put forth three basic theses: (1) Jesus is disruptive, (2) Certainty about "having arrived" is problematic internal to Christianity, (3) There is no soteriological "formula" for Christian life found in Jesus' own words. In an attempt to engage Benson (or better, think *with* him), I will investigate how his theses might stand in relation to contemporary continental philosophy of religion and political theory.

One of the main limitations of continental philosophy is that the task of "unmasking" privilege is often taken to be an end in itself. If unmasking is, by itself, enough, then it is unclear how one would even argue that such unmasking is something that one "ought" to do. For would one not need to unmask the privilege of those engaged in the task of unmasking? But then, what would be left? Assuming that the answer to this question is "not much," some scholars have emphasized the negative component of deconstruction (*de*-construction), rather than the positive part (de-*construction*). This has led many, in a variety of traditions (from analytic philosophy to process theology), to claim that deconstruction is primarily (or even exclusively) "destructive." What is needed, some claim, is a "*constructive* postmodern" corrective.[2] However, the very notion of "constructive postmodernism," as opposed to "deconstructive postmodernism," depends upon a particularly bad interpretation of Derrida, I believe. As I read Derrida, deconstruction should be interpreted as always already constructive because it requires three moments, as it were. First, there is a critique of privilege in order to clear the way for moving forward differently. Second, there is an affirmation of what such an alternative way forward might look like. Third, there is a critique of any assumptions that this new way forward is the *final* word on the matter. None of these three moments can stand isolated from the other two. *De*-construction is always already de-*construction*.

Thus, Derrida, like Levinas, recognizes that unmasking must be done in the name of something else. For Levinas, this something else is variously termed "charity," "the ethical," or even the call/command of the Other. For Derrida, this something else is termed "justice," which he famously says is "undeconstructible." The third deconstructive moment, though, challenges all claims to have come finally, completely, or totally, to know what "justice" is and, further, what it would involve if enacted in history. Hence, even while attesting to the undeconstructibilty of justice, Derrida always inserts a phrase to mark the importance of the third deconstructive moment. Derridean references to justice are usually accompanied by the qualifier, "if there is such a thing," as a way of reminding his readers (and perhaps himself?) of the constant temptation to allow triumphalism to show up in one's own thought even while engaging in the process of challenging the triumphalism of others. The "if there is such a thing" reinforces the idea that assuming to know exactly how justice is to be brought about in the world is tantamount to *forgetting* justice. As Levinas and Derrida both so powerfully remind us, justice is only just insofar as it continues to recognize that it is never just enough.[3] However, the impossibility of ever being just enough does not mean that all options are equally unjust. For example, any account of the political that would make it impossible to celebrate civil rights as more just than slavery should be abandoned. *Disruption might need to be perpetual, but that need not mean that progress is impossible.*[4]

In his attempt to demonstrate the disruptive tensions that are constitutive of the Christian Gospel, Benson focuses on destabilizing the privilege of Christians (especially in the Evangelical tradition) that err on the side of arrogance when it comes to theological understanding and ethical life. The claim that "Jesus does not seem to be in the business of giving anything like certainty that we are 'right,'" is Benson's way of challenging the privilege of any one particular account of Christianity that might view itself as *the* Christian account. If Jesus "calls us to . . . a life that is *constantly disrupted*," then surely he contests our belief that we have got it all figured out—that is, that one has "arrived" at the kingdom of God. Now, I imagine that most continental philosophers (whether "religious" or not) will applaud Benson's claim here. For all those who have felt oppressed and marginalized by the dominance (or privilege) of the Christian tradition in both American society and also in the history of philosophy, the unmasking of Christian arrogance is surely something to be celebrated. Accordingly, I find Benson to be in agreement with John Caputo that the answer to the question "what would Jesus deconstruct?" is "Christianity itself!"[5] But, uncritical enthusiasm at this point is problematic. Just as we would be wrong to read deconstruction as only negative, if the "message" of the Gospel is *only* disruption, then it would appear to lack any positive content of its own—it would stand as just one big "no" to whatever content one might propose. Similar to the problems faced when unmasking is taken to be an end in itself, it is not clear how the disruptive "content" of Christianity would even make sense unless it operates in the name of something else—e.g., God's grace, God's charity, or God's kenotic relation to the world.

Despite the three deconstructive moments articulated above, when it comes to the notion of "religion without religion," it is difficult to figure òut exactly what the constructive alternative might entail (or even could entail) internal to such a framework. As many of the essays in this book contend, Derrida's lack of a clear alternative is especially problematic when it comes to religious belief and practice. What exactly is the "positive content" to a deconstructive account of religion? If Derrida is only a philosopher of the "without," then it seems that he would be guilty (at least when it comes to religion) of the very sort of thing that the "constructive postmodernists" contend—all negation and disruption. Benson recognizes this potential problem internal to deconstruction. After quoting Derrida as saying about religious texts, "I want to keep the right to read these [them] in a way which has to be constantly reinvented. It is something which can be totally new at every moment," Benson adds a crucial footnote: " 'Totally new'—what could that *possibly* mean? The rhetorical point is clear enough. Yet the statement is quite easily dismissed as hyperbolic." Benson rightly pushes back against what could be viewed as the *purity of the without* that sometimes seems to show up in Derrida's work.

In contrast to the frequent hyperbole so often found in the work of Levinas and Derrida, Benson suggests that within the Gospels, "these disruptions—far from being simply confusions—are instead intimations of a new kind of human existence" that serve to "show how far and above the logic of the kingdom of heaven is." Accordingly, Benson does not present Christianity to be *merely* disruptive (for if it were it would be self-defeating), but instead argues for its being productively *de-constructive* (with all three moments in play: critique, affirmation, and critique of claims to finality for one's affirmations). As with deconstructive justice and the importance of naming some

things as more just than others, claiming that the best we can hope
for is to be "not far" from the kingdom of God is not to say that
everyone and all perspectives are *equally far* away. Indeed, Jesus'
statement to the scribe is reminiscent of the sort of thing one might
hear fans cheer as a runner gets near to the end of a marathon: "Not
much farther, you are almost there." Being "not far" from the finish
line of a race requires that there is a distinction between the starting
line and where one is now — that is, one is closer to the end than one
was. Even if you are not yet where you want to be, you are closer
than you were. Similarly, being "not far" from the kingdom of God
requires that there is such a "thing"[6] as the kingdom of God. Jesus
disrupts claims to have reached the kingdom, but he does so in light
of the truth that the kingdom should serve as the goal toward which
we strive. However, affirming such a goal must itself be done recur-
sively in light of the disruption itself.

Even Caputo, perhaps the most prominent proponent of the
Derridian "without," recognizes the importance of the affirmative
moment. The "poetics of the kingdom," writes Caputo, "lays claim
to us and…calls for a 'transformation into existence.'"[7] Yet transformation must be change from one thing to something else. In this
case, Caputo's call is for the aporetic logic of the kingdom to be
made manifest in historical, social, and political structures. Such a
manifestation would require a change in the current structures such
that the transformation *into* existence would amount to a transformation of the shape *of* existence itself. If Caputo and Benson are right to
advocate a particularly "Christian" account of what the transformation should look like, then there must be some content by which the
change is normatively evaluated as worth undertaking. Even though
we may not have it all figured out, if the "kingdom of God" is simply
an empty concept, then such evaluation would be impossible.

However, *epistemic certainty* is not required for what might be
termed *existential confidence*.[8] While claims to certainty often lead to
arrogance, confidence allows for the dialogical honesty required for
real conversation. Certainty resists revision; confidence admits of revision while recognizing the stakes and costs of it. The deconstructive
lens Benson brings to bear on Jesus' words simultaneously challenges
claims to finality, certainty, and objectivity, but quite sensibly leaves
in tact the notion that some interpretations are better than others.

Indeed, Benson should be committed to the fact that his particular Derridian-inspired reading of the Gospels provides a *better way* forward than do the other interpretative approaches that dominate so much of evangelical theology. Similarly, Caputo is right to support the disruptive "poetics of the kingdom" rather than the deadening literalism so often found in some appropriations of Christianity. In this way, Benson and Caputo are both not far off, I believe, but part of what it means for them to be "not far off," here, is that they continue to realize that they are *not there yet.*

Accordingly, while never forgetting the essential revisability and fundamental fallibilism of all human accounts of the kingdom of God, Christians should remain existentially confident that there are *some* notions of the kingdom in which we should invest ourselves—that is, Christians should continue to claim that Christianity matters; Jews should continue to defend Judaism as meaningful; Muslims should continue to think internal to an Islamic worldview, etc. In the attempt to be inclusive and invitational in light of the important unmasking of privilege that deconstruction enacts, one should not loose the ability to continue to affirm the importance and truth of the narrative in which one finds oneself; though *how* one affirms that importance and truth is likely to be dialogically hospitable and critically reflective.

Similar to Cornel West's notion of "prophetic pragmatism"[9] and Merold Westphal's notion of "prophetic philosophy of religion," Caputo claims that the kingdom "provides a *politica negativa,* a critical voice rather like the voice of a prophet against the king." Importantly, Caputo recognizes that it also requires "the hard work of concrete political invention, the cleverness of inventive political structures."[10] I agree with Caputo on this point and, as such, think we should push back against "religion without religion" when it begins to overemphasize the *de* and underemphasize the *construction.* Accordingly, I wish Benson had gone a bit further and filled in some of the possible attributes of the kingdom that could serve to inform what Caputo terms "concrete political invention."

Though I am unable to give anything more than just a sketch of what such invention might look like, I want to propose seven characteristics, which I take to follow from Benson's interpretation of the Christian Gospel, that are likely to be found in social institutions as well as individual persons who attempt to live on-the-way-toward the kingdom of God, as it were:

(1) Epistemic humility
(2) Hermeneutic charity
(3) Personal hospitality
(4) Dialogical honesty
(5) Solidarity with the "least of these"
(6) Critical relation to power structures
(7) Service orientation

Of course, all of these characteristics are vague abstractions that still call for substantial development relative to theological and political praxis, but even as a loose framework in which to operate, these traits are more compatible with a "religion *with* religion" than a "religion *without* religion." Though the interpretative difficulties continue and the temptations to triumphalism continue, the words of Jesus do not leave Christians stranded in relativistic quietism. The very tasks of continuing to read deeper, to understand more profoundly, to challenge former conceptions, to be a better listener, etc., require that one be committed to displaying such characteristics in one's own life as a positive manifestation of a life well lived and yet still on the way.

When considering these characteristics in relation to political theory, it is not surprising that some have suggested a profound link between Derrida's notion of the "democracy to come" and the Christian Gospel. Derrida himself writes the following: "More than any other form of democracy, more than social democracy or popular democracy, a Christian democracy should be welcoming to the enemies of democracy; it should turn them the other cheek, offer hospitality, grant freedom of expression and the right to vote to antidemocrats, something in conformity with a certain hyperbolic essence, an essence more autoimmune than ever, of *democracy itself,* if 'itself' there ever is, if ever there is a democracy and thus a Christian democracy worthy of its name."[11] Benson and Caputo both note that the kingdom of God does not rise and fall with the interpretations that are offered of it. Similarly, despite occasional proclamations from within American evangelicalism, no specific historical democracy should ever be viewed as having instantiated what Derrida names the "Christian democracy."

Like the kingdom of God, the democracy to come is an ideal toward which we continue to strive. Nonetheless, what the disruptive words of Jesus demonstrate is that these are ideals that are structurally "im-possible," and so are best thought of as eschatologically situated. Said a bit more theologically but, as Benson demonstrates, still deconstructively, we are all in need of God's disruptive (and redemptive) grace. This claim need not lead to theological vacuity under the guise of continental opacity, though it certainly does invite a temptation to such apophatic excess. Rather, it should call Christians to take seriously the assertion that being a Christian involves more than simply living in this or that way, and more than simply believing a specific set of propositions about God, though as I argued in chapter 1, it surely involves a transformed existence and believing some things rather than others. Accordingly, religion *with* religion, and the political visions opened along with it (see Stephen Minister's chapter), should never lead to rigid formulas, but to intentional religious and political existence in a postmodern world.

In the end, Benson's essay is compelling because it *explicitly* critiques Christian arrogance and also, albeit with a bit of charitable expansion, *implicitly* critiques the problems that accompany claims to know that deconstructive religion must be "without" determinate religion. As I said earlier, privilege is most problematic when it remains invisible. Accordingly, I want to conclude by turning to the passage from Nicholas Wolterstorff that I used as an epigraph: "The person who turns one of his ears to the prophetic unmasking word of the gospel and the other to the cries of those who suffer deprivation and oppression is not likely to suffer from the illusion that he is engaged in pure theory when in fact he is working to shore up his own position of privilege." When one continues to listen intently to the "wretched of the earth" (as Fanon and West both would say), it is impossible to become arrogant about one's own position and complacent about the positions of others. Benson helps us see that, while Christianity has far too often turned its ears away from the suffering of those with whom it shares the world (both human and nonhuman),[12] continental philosophy might also have too often turned its ears away from the "word of the gospel." Again, my point here is not exclusively a Christian one. I mean this as a defense of the legitimacy of determinate religious belief within deconstruction, regardless of one's particular religious tradition. Indeed, when deconstruction is conceived as allowing for "religion with religion," I take it to be a critical resource for fostering substantive and mutually transformative interreligious dialogue.

Nonetheless, *Christians* must always remember that certitudes about Christianity must be disrupted if Christianity itself is not to become forgetful of the very "least of these" with whom Jesus identifies. Similarly, *continental philosophers* must always remember that certitudes about the deconstructive critique of determinate religion must be disrupted if deconstruction is not to slide into the very thing it warns against. As I argued in chapter 1, *a Christian can be deconstructive while still being a Christian and a deconstructionist can be Christian while still being a deconstructionist.* Those who are Christian deconstructionists have dual reasons for never allowing theory (whether philosophical or theological) to "shore up [one's] own position of privilege." Though Benson is surely right to say that the best we can hope for is to be "not far" from the kingdom of God, I propose that Christianity helps deconstruction to see, and deconstruction helps Christianity to see, that *we are all perhaps still a bit farther off than we think.*

Part Three

RESPONSES TO RELIGION WITH RELIGION

SIX

Conversations on Religion with or without Religion

Merold Westphal

With one exception, all the contributors to this volume are either friends of mine or former students (and friends too). Among these the longest and deepest friendship is with Jack Caputo. We have deep agreements and deep disagreements on the matters under discussion here, and we have often discussed these both in private and in public. Most recently I had the privilege of being a commentator on his work at the 2009–2010 Siena College Symposium on Living Philosophers, where he was featured. On matters substantive I tend to be more in agreement with other contributors to this volume, but I am enormously grateful for the friendship Jack and I have had over the years, in spite of our theological and philosophical differences. While he is a major advocate of religion without religion, my practice and commitments are to religion with religion.

I have learned a great deal from deconstruction, often with Jack's help, but I am not persuaded that it requires such a thin and indeterminate theology as his; nor am I persuaded that it requires his politics, although I am far more sympathetic to it than to his theology. Following Derrida, he always says that undecidability calls for decision, and it seems to me that there is more decision than deconstruction in both his theology and his political ethics. The postmodern critique of reason that is deconstruction forbids certain epistemic aspirations and alleged achievements that we now label "modernity," but I am convinced that it allows decisions other than the ones Jack makes and that the relation between his choices (and mine, for that matter) and deconstructive theory is a contingent one. I sometimes put it this way: deconstruction as such places no constraints on what we can say but rather on the meta-claims we make about what we say, such as "we are objective in the sense of presuppositionless," "we speak from the Center or from some Alpha (Descartes) or Omega (Hegel) point," or "we are the bearers of absolute and final truth."

The spirit of our friendship is perhaps best revealed in this incident: After he published *More Radical Hermeneutics* as a sequel to *Radical Hermeneutics,* I suggested that he follow the Hollywood example and write a prequel, *Not So Very Damn Radical Hermeneutics.* He responded immediately. "No need. You've already written that book." In that spirit of fraternal provocation I am grateful for this opportunity to carry on our conversation with others who have joined it along the way and who are making their own important contributions to "continental" or "postmodern" philosophy of religion and in particular to the question of religion with or without religion.

When I hear slogans like "religion without religion" or "messianicity without messianism," I naturally ask about the "without" and find the following four items heuristically helpful:

- Without God, not necessarily without the name "God," but without a clear affirmation of the reality of a personal God, one who performs speech acts such as making promises and issuing commands. Without such a God we are back with Spinoza, called to love a God who could not conceivably love us first.
- Without church (synagogue, mosque, temple—"church" in the sociological sense as the community of shared religious belief and practice).[1] Like the institution of marriage, the institutional church is often a disaster. Hence this "without." But like marriage it has both possibilities and actualities that are quite wonderful and worth working for.
- Without Scripture, that is, without sacred texts that are perceived both as a great treasure and as the highest norm for personal and communal life. If one assumes that possession of some Scripture gives one immediate access free of inter-

pretation, or that my (or, more likely, our) interpretation is the one and only right one, that shows the spirit of modernity and not postmodernity. If deconstruction is a phenomenology, it is surely a hermeneutical phenomenology (radical, more radical, or not so very damn radical). So Scripture as norm is not unproblematic. On the other hand, if one quotes some Scripture freely but only selectively and only to illustrate theo-political positions that do not rely on the authority of that Scripture (in which case one would have to give up being so selective and treat the text as a divinely given whole)—one is still operating "without Scripture."

- Without a fairly determinate morality. "I'm for love and peace and justice" is too vague to count. Sometimes, of course, there is a very specific politics attached to the very vague theology, but the link is far from clear and does not seem to be a deconstructive necessity.

In summary, without commitment and its concomitant risks. But do we become more radical by making our commitments and thus our identities more abstract, less determinate? Do we come closer to whatever degree of truth is available to finite, fallen creatures? Is the resulting soup too thin to provide real nourishment for the soul?

It is worth noticing that while this "without" has been developed with great sophistication by Derrida, Caputo, and a good many others, it is by no means restricted to the academy. On close examination, "I consider myself spiritual but not religious. May the Force be with you" turns out to be pretty much the same "system" of withouts.

It seems to me that both Hegel and Feuerbach give some worries to those who take the path of "without," whether in the academy or on the street. Hegel is speaking about trust or mistrust in Science (the System) rather than some commitment to religion with religion that does not arrogantly purport to be Absolute Knowing, but his question can be raised just as well in relation to the latter: "why we should not turn round and mistrust this very mistrust. Should we not be concerned as to whether this fear of error [a determinacy we cannot finally justify] is not just the error itself? Indeed, this fear takes something—a great deal in fact—for granted as truth." In this case, Hegel fears, "what calls itself fear of error reveals itself rather as fear of the truth."[2] Or, we might ask, does fear of commitment cut us off from the truth?

But are we necessarily committed to anything that could deserve to be called "the truth" in which we might participate in some measure? No. But *nota bene:* to presuppose that there is such truth (whether this is defined theologically or not) is no more a presupposition in need of support than to presuppose that there is not. If there is an undecidability here, what Kierkegaard's Climacus calls an "objective uncertainty," the call is for a decision that is a risk, even if it functions as an axiom in some language game.

It is worth noticing that we sometimes use "truth" talk when we mean the weaker claim that this view is better than that one, truer or more nearly true, minus the claim that the better one is final, absolute truth. Then, if we feel free to say that this politics is better than that one, what possible reason can be given for refusing to claim that this theology is better than that one and refusing others the right to do so? I have never understood the widespread habit of rather dogmatically affirming the superiority of this politics to that while rather dogmatically denouncing those who affirm the superiority of this religion to that. The answer cannot be violence, for surely politics is and has always been *at least* as violent as religion.

Feuerbach poses a nastier question, one that belongs to the hermeneutics of suspicion. He worries about the motivation behind an omnivorous apophaticism. He worries that "the proposition that God is unknowable or undefinable" so easily becomes a fixed dogma.

> On the ground that God is unknowable, man excuses himself to what is yet remaining of his religious conscience ... his absorption in the world: he denies God practically by his conduct, — the world has possession of all his thoughts and inclinations, — but he does not deny him theoretically, he does not attack his existence; he lets that rest. *But this existence does not affect or incommode him;* it is a merely negative existence, an *existence without existence* ... a state of being, which, as to its effects, is not distinguishable from non-being.... The alleged religious horror of limiting God by positive predicates, is only the irreligious wish to know nothing more of God, to banish God from the mind.[3]

The question here is whether dogmatic apophaticism is morally innocent or arises, at least in part, from latent motivations that are not acknowledged. Masters of suspicion like Kierkegaard, Marx,

Nietzsche, Freud, Foucault, and Karl Barth raise similar questions that must be taken seriously no matter how thin or how thick one's theology is.

SIMMONS / BENSON / MINISTER

"Apologetics"

I welcome Simmons's defense of my "epistemological" or "methodological" postmodernism over against Caputo's "metaphysical" interpretation of deconstruction as radical hermeneutics.[4] I think that Jack gets what he considers radical over against my "not so very damn radical hermeneutics" by (mistakenly) attributing substantive metaphysical exclusions to deconstruction. But I have to confess that I am allergic to the term "apologetics." I am sympathetic to the claim by Kierkegaard's Anti-Climacus that "the first one to come up with the idea of defending Christianity in Christendom is *de facto* Judas No. 2: he, too, betrays with a kiss"[5] and to the longer version of this idea that Simmons quotes from the *Journals and Papers.*

One reason is that the Christian thinkers who are most likely to describe their work as apologetics are those least likely to abjure the yen for objectivity, universality, and neutrality, aspirations and claims that Simmons clearly disavows. They tend to be stuck in modernity and to see postmodern philosophy only as a threat to Christian faith. Simmons cites a number of Christian philosophers in the analytic mode who make a break with modernity's arrogance about its knowledge. In so doing he points to possible bridges between analytic and continental philosophy of religion, despite their obvious differences. But what he does not call attention to is the fact that these thinkers whom he praises almost never describe what they are doing as apologetics. They may well be "defending" theism in general or Christianity in particular by clarifying what they mean and seeking to defuse theoretical objections to them, but I prefer to leave the term "apologetics" to those who have more grandiose ideas of what they are doing.

A second reason why I am allergic to "apologetics" is that those who like the term typically speak all too complacently about a "rational defense" of theism or of Christianity and of the "truth" of religious beliefs, as if the concepts of reason and truth were not doubly problematic. But, on the one hand, quite apart from postmodernism, philosophers mean many different things by "reason" and "truth," and we cannot assume that when we use those term we all mean the same thing and everyone knows what it is. On the other hand, postmodern philosophers have raised very pointed questions about various ways in which philosophers have used these terms, and someone, like Simmons, working within postmodern horizons has a particular duty to specify very clearly what his postmodern understanding of "reason" and "truth" is.[6] It seems to me that Simmons fails to do this and that he thereby mirrors those "modern" or "rationalist" apologists from whom he otherwise seeks to distance himself. Would it not take a whole lot more than "epistemic humility" to clarify what would make a defense of theism or Christianity, the attempt to show them to be worthy of assent, "rational"?[7]

In the section "Positive Apologetics in Continental Philosophy of Religion," Simmons makes some gestures toward saying that he means by these terms by saying primarily what apologetics is not. The problem here is that this section, taken as a whole, seems to undermine his claim, just before this section, that "*apologetics should be aimed at truth and not simply persuasion.*"

Selfhood and Identity

I turn to Minister's important discussion of identity and the self as a multiplicity of voices. My view of the matter is the following, and if in my earlier discussion with Jack Caputo I gave a different impression, I failed to express myself clearly.

(1) I agree with Kierkegaard that "purity of heart is to will one thing."[8] Ideally speaking, my identity is a unity (with difference, as it will turn out).

(2) By virtue of human finitude I am, as Gadamer would put it, a confluence of various traditions, some religious (believing) and some secular (unbelieving); or, as Caputo would put it, I am a multiplicity of voices. I have been shaped by and continue to think and speak in the plural.

(3) By virtue of human sinfulness *some* of those voices, *both religious and secular,*[9] represent failures to will and love the Good, the one thing willed by purity of heart in Kierkegaard.

(4) Becoming a unified whole is the task of a lifetime. Only in insufferable arrogance can I claim to have completed it and gone beyond it to something else. On the one hand the task is to minimize to the point of elimination those formations and voices that are sinful, at odds with the Good. On the other hand, the ever ongoing task is to integrate the "innocent" formations and voices into a hierarchical, organic whole in which the better is always given hegemony over the merely good, and the best (the Good) is the organizing principle that gives to everything its proper place. Kierkegaard's own account of the relation of the stages or spheres of existence, the aesthetic, the ethical, and the religious, is one very general map of such a complex unity.

(5) Frankfurt's analysis of how we can care about what we care about and desire to desire differently, strengthening this desire, weakening that one, and even eliminating that one altogether, can be helpful here.[10] What it leaves out of account, theologically speaking, is the role of the Holy Spirit in the conversion process by which we become less sinful and less incoherent.

Let me make this more concrete. I sometimes pray what I call the prayer of Elvis, "I want you, I need you, I love you with all my heart," addressed to God rather than the original referent of these words. I almost gag on the last four words because I know them to be false if taken at face value. I can only say them when I mean by them: "I recognize this as my task, I desire to be more nearly able to love God wholeheartedly, and I desire that this desire may become stronger, subordinating other desires to it in appropriate ways."

In short, my identity is always a plurality of traditions, desires, voices, etc., more or less coherently organized, and more or less structured with reference to the Good. For the Christian theist, of course, this Good is the God of the Bible. So it is appropriate for Simmons to ask about the coherence of his Christian beliefs and his postmodern beliefs. To argue that they are not incompatible is not to claim that his heart is pure in Kierkegaard's sense but only that he is not *ipso facto* incoherent by virtue of his C-beliefs and his P-beliefs.

MINISTER / HANSON / SIMMONS

Apophaticism

I would like to address three themes raised by Stephen and his commentators. First, apophaticism. Minister cites Avicenna, Aquinas, and Maimonides as three theologians with both a very strong apophatic recognition of the inadequacy of our God-talk to God and a willingness to talk about God within the horizons of their religious communities and on the basis of their Scriptures, noting that many names could be added to the list. My own list would include the Cappadocians (and virtually the whole Eastern Orthodox tradition), Augustine, Pseudo-Dionysius, Aquinas, Luther, Calvin, Kierkegaard, and Karl Barth.[11] They all have a strong apophatic streak, a deep sense of the incomprehensibility of God. What they also have in common is a willingness to decide, to take a risk, to say that this way of speaking about God is better than the (current) alternatives. Their apophaticism does not eliminate determinate theological claims but rather serves to qualify the epistemic status of such claims. They speak of a God who is absolute, but they do so as relative, as mere mortals, reminding us that one does not have to be purple to speak about pansies.

Pseudo-Dionysius, sometimes seen as the patron saint of "negative theology," is an interesting and instructive case. He writes a very little book, *The Mystical Theology*, seven pages in translation, in which the inadequacy of language about God gives way to silence. But he also writes a book twelve times as long, *The Divine Names*, in which he tells us how to talk about God based on biblical revelation; and he writes two other books, *The Celestial Hierarchy* and *The Ecclesiastical Hierarchy*, in which, following his own advice in *The Divine Names*, he speaks freely about God.[12] Taken together, the latter three works are 28 times as long as the first. One is reminded of the Buddhists who speak endlessly about the Unspeakable.

What is needed here, to make sense out of the possibility of talking meaningfully about what we cannot describe adequately, is Aquinas's theory of analogy, or something very much like it.[13] So it comes as no surprise that Thomas quotes Dionysius more often than anyone but Aristotle.[14] The point is quite simple: the insight that human language is never adequate to the divine reality need not lead either to absolute silence or to letting the name of God loose in an endless flux of substitutions. The latter is a choice, for which a rationale is needed, just as determinate discourse about God that makes no claim to adequacy represents a risky choice. So far as I can see, nothing about deconstruction as such makes that choice for us or provides the rationale for either choice.

Minister finds Caputo saying that our language about God, or rather "the event," a very abstract and indeterminate substitute, is never adequate. Simmons attributes to Caputo the even stronger view that "all discourse about God *is entirely inadequate* to 'the event.'" What we need to notice here is that on this point Caputo is no more than a good Thomist, drawing on his early study of the *doctor angelicus*. In Aristotelian-Thomistic context, "adequate" is a technical term in terms of which truth is defined. Truth is the *adequatio intellectus et rei* when the form in the thing is (nonnumerically) identical with the form in the intellect. In other words, truth is defined as the perfect mirroring of the real in the mind. The mathematical overtones of *adequatio* evoke an equation in which what is on one side is perfectly equal to what is on the other side.

The apophatic dimension of Aquinas (and all the theologians mentioned above) is the denial that human discourse about God is ever adequate in this sense. God surpasses human comprehension. When I say that *strictly speaking*, for Thomas nothing we say about God is true, it makes my Thomist friends uncomfortable; but none of them has ever shown me that this is not the case. Truth is adequation, and human God-talk is never adequate, in the clearly if technically defined sense, to its object.

Of course it does not follow that we should not commit ourselves to any determinate descriptions of God, so long as we do not forget their status as human, all too human. We might make the risky claim that this way of talking about God is better than another way, that it is in this sense truer or more nearly true than the other way, and that while not adequate in the technical sense of the term, it is adequate for our faith and practice.

I suspect it is this weaker claim that Minister and Simmons have in mind, and the stronger, Thomistic definition of truth that Caputo has in mind. If so, the dispute rests on an equivocation. I think both Minister and Simmons would accept the Thomist point while drawing conclusions from it that differ from Caputo's conclusions. Just as deconstruction does not entail or justify either the thin or thick theologies that place themselves within its horizon, so here the meta-physical-epistemic principle of inadequacy does not tell us whether or not apophaticism should be the tail that wags the dog to the exclusion of any thick theology.[15]

Violence

All of this sets the stage for my second and third themes: violence and idolatry. Caputo suspects that any thick theology will inevitably be violent and idolatrous. Here again we need some conceptual clarification, especially in the light of the unfortunate inflation of the notion of violence in so many postmodern discourses. When everything is violent, nothing is violent.

I suggest we distinguish three things. First, there is literal, physical violence. Second, there is psychological violence, although I prefer to call it rhetorical violence, since its weapon is language. Finally, there is the exclusion involved in any claim that this view or this practice is better than that one, for all other views or practices are excluded from being the best. In making such a claim, one can say very different things about the theories or practices excluded, all the way from saying (1) that they are good or even very good, but not the best available, to saying (2) that they are not all bad but not very good, to saying (3) that they are pernicious and dangerous.

Once again, parties to the discussion need to be clear about what sort of violence they have in mind. Hanson wants to deny any necessary connection between religion *with* religion (and, presumably, *with* thick theologies) and violence. With reference to both literal violence and rhetorical violence, he is on firm ground both conceptually and historically, in spite of the undeniable fact that religion with religion has all too often been physically and linguistically violent. The wars of religion and the anathemas of too many creeds must not be forgotten; but neither must the religion of the likes of Jesus, Gandhi, the Mennonites, and Martin Luther King, Jr.

But is exclusionary discourse not a form of rhetorical violence? Well no, not unless any claim that this theory or this practice is better than the alternative(s) is to count as violence, no matter what one says about the alternative(s). But why inflate the concept of violence to this level, making it all but meaningless? In any case, Minister and Simmons point out that Caputo cannot make such a claim because of the exclusionary character of his politics. What he says about the religious right is not only exclusionary but at times seems to evoke the spirit of creedal anathemas. We might add, it is not only his politics but also his theology that is exclusionary in its repudiation of the thick theologies he wishes to be "without." My claim is that there is nothing wrong with this, per se, so long as one avoids literal and rhetorical violence, granted that what constitutes the latter is not nearly as clear as what constitutes the former.

Idolatry

We might distinguish two ways in which thick, monotheistic religion can become idolatrous while professing to worship the one true God: intrinsic and relational. Intrinsic idolatry occurs when the human interpretation and understanding of (what purports to be) divine revelation is given the status of absolute, divine knowledge.[16] If idolatry is the worship of what is made by human hands (or minds), then the (purported) fact that one is responding to divine revelation does not keep treating one's theology as absolute and final from being idolatrous.[17] Relational idolatry occurs when the alleged epistemic absoluteness of one's theology becomes the warrant for physical or rhetorical violence.

Minister sides with Caputo in acknowledging that "at their worst" determinate religious traditions "become ends-in-themselves, replacing God as the object of our love." Hanson demurs. "I do not know that this ever actually happens, and I certainly find it strange to claim that anybody 'worships a religious tradition.'" It seems to me that Hanson needs a more suspicious hermeneutics. Of course, people do not say, "I worship the Catholic Church" or "I worship the Reformed tradition." But it does not follow that they do not as a matter of fact treat what is human, all too human, as if it were divine, being careful not to notice this. So I side with Caputo and Minister in holding that "at their worst" determinate religions (but not indeterminate ones?) become *de facto* idolatrous. I would only insist that neither conceptually nor historically is there a necessity to succumb to this temptation. Determinacy in theology is not inherently idolatrous, but thin theologies become idolatrous when their anathemas (explicit or implicit) take on the aura of absolute authority.

HANSON / DALTON / MINISTER

A Confession and a Challenge: Is There Filler in "Fear and Trembling"?

Fear and Trembling is one of my very favorite books, but Hanson focuses on the two portions of the text that I have found most nearly opaque and least helpful, the four false starts, which I agree are examples of how not to tell the Abraham story, and the third problem, the one about silence. I often tell my students to avoid "filler" in their papers like the plague, material that may be true, or important, or interesting, but which fills up space without contributing in any significant way to the overall thesis of the paper. I confess that I have treated these two portions of the text like filler. The four false starts seem to me entirely unnecessary.

Of problem 3 I sometimes say that the romantic side of Kierkegaard had been too much the lit major and that he threw in a lot of stuff without tying it clearly enough to his general argument. When Silentio says that Abraham was silent because no one could understand him, it seems to me pretty clear that he does not mean that Sarah could not have understood the statement, "I am going to go and sacrifice Isaac," spoken in whatever was their native tongue. Against the background of the distinction between the Ethical and the Religious in problems 1 and 2, it seems clear what Silentio means: because Sarah did not have access to the divine revelation to which Abraham was responding, she could not understand how he might be doing the right thing, even if he told her that God had told him to do it. A second-hand report of a revelation is no substitute for hearing the voice of God for oneself, which is why sermons are no more than a motivational speech or a political harangue if the human word does not become, in a kind of transubstantiation, the divine word, if the hearers do not hear God speaking directly to them.[18] While there is no semantic problem with understanding what Abraham might have said, there is the spiritual problem of not being able to understand how what he says is true or right.[19] As I read part 3, it is a lot of sound and fury signifying very little for this problematic. Kierkegaard's next book (not counting *Upbuilding Discourses*), *Philosophical Fragments* throws far more light on the secret and the silence of Abraham.

I do not necessarily recommend my dismissive attitude toward these portions of the text. As I already said, I confess it. I am grateful to Hanson and those on whom he draws, who take these texts more seriously than I do; at the same time, I wish they would make it clearer, if they can, how the literary texts of problem 3 fit in with the claim, repeated throughout the text and not just at problem 3, that Abraham cannot speak because Sarah, Isaac, and Eleazar cannot understand, *for reasons developed in problems 1 and 2.*

Derrida and Silence

Hanson's essay is not just in dialogue with Derrida's. It is downright Derridean. It is a reading. I kept waiting for Hanson to draw the moral of the story, what all this signifies for continental, or postmodern, or deconstructive philosophy of religion. He never does. Like Derrida in so many texts, he simply gives us a (very careful) reading and stops.[20]

Hanson worries that Derrida's thoughts on silence as univocal cannot illuminate the difference between demonic and divine, that is, faithful silence. Another way to put the point is that there are two radical individualisms in Kierkegaard, not to be confused. In each, the individual stands outside and above the universal (the ethical in the sense of *Sittlichkeit*, the social order, the laws and customs of one's people).[21] In the aesthetic mode the individual stands alone because neither society nor God is recognized as a higher authority to which the individual is responsible. In the religious mode the individual stands alone—before God—because while society is recognized as having legitimate authority, God is taken to be a higher authority. In both spheres the ethical is denied ultimacy, but for very different reasons that might be described as demonic or divine (faithful).

There is, I think, in Derrida what we might call a structural silence. It is analogous to the Heideggerian claim that unconcealment is always inseparable from concealment. To put Derrida's point in the language of Levinas, we might say that for every saying the said emerges out of and against the background of the unsaid, which remains the secret about which speech is necessarily silent. Any claim to transcend this dialectic, to say it all, as it were, would be a claim to full presence, which human finitude and temporality preclude. Here we have a silence without a secret, for while Abraham knows the secret (God's command) about which he finds himself necessarily silent, on this model the speaker is no more in possession of the unsaid than is the listener.[22] This account, it seems to me, is too formal and abstract to distinguish aesthetic from religious silence, which is not to say it is unimportant.

But there is more than this in Derrida's readings of *Fear and Trembling*. He has a substitute for Kierkegaard's God, the Levinasian Other, the human other of which it can be said that "every other is wholly other."[23] Levinas can say that aesthetic silence, always potentially demonic, is solipsistic in that it lacks the responsibility inherent in this relation to the Other,[24] while religious silence (without religion) is relational, responsible, and, at least in principle, transformative. The silence here involves the relation to the impossible, which Hanson nicely describes as "that which happens in a way that cannot be comprehended but only lived." In relation to their respective Others, Kierkegaard and Derrida can say that the relation and its responsibility have this form.[25] Amoral silence is thoroughly different from transmoral silence[26] both for Kierkegaard and for Derrida, whose concepts of silence are not univocal.

Tragedy or Teleological Suspension

Hanson wants to make Abraham the paradigm of faith by saying that each person's trial must be "equally unprecedented." Later he seems to gloss this strange idea by speaking of "the *inevitable* heartbreak, separation, and loss, symbolized by the weaning narratives"[27] (emphasis mine). He speaks of "the *most common experience*," of being "confronted with the disappointment of our hopes and dreams," of the time "when the ones we love most of all die in our arms" (emphasis mine). But this is to reduce *Fear and Trembling* to the dialectic of the knight of infinite resignation and the knight of faith. The belief that in the face of death, whether our own or that of a loved one, all things are possible for God, even personal resurrection, places faith in the context of what is both "inevitable" and "most common." That is *part* of Silentio's account, but he emphatically labels it "preliminary." That is because the heart of the story is not about losing a son but about killing a son, not about tragedy but about trespass and the question of whether this trespass is murder or sacrifice. The crucial contrast is between the tragic hero and the knight of faith.

There is nothing "inevitable" or "most common" about Abraham's trial in its specificity. He can be the father of the faithful only if there is some more general feature to his trial that is shared by those who are never commanded to kill a child. Here I think we need to read *Fear and Trembling* in the light of *Works of Love*. The central theme of the former, it seems to me, is that for faith there is a higher criterion of the right and the good than the laws and customs of one's people, that faith is always in principle countercultural. Abraham's trial and Dietrich Bonhoeffer's conviction that it was his Christian duty to join a plot to assassinate Hitler make this point dramatically. But in *Works of Love* the general principle of a socially transcendent norm is put to work in the *neighbor*hood where all of us live, we who may never be called to some knightly heroics. The command to love our neighbors as we love ourselves signifies "Our Duty to Love the People We See,"[28] to be sure. But since absolutely everyone is our neighbor without exclusion, this command is to find ways to love (since it is about works of love) those whom we do not see, whether they be those whom our *Sittlichkeit* has rendered invisible or those who are geographically rather than culturally invisible. Moreover, this unconditional universalism means, quite explicitly, that or enemy is our neighbor, and we are to love our enemy as we love ourselves. On these two points, at least, loving those we do not see and loving our enemies, we have a teleological suspension of the ethical. What ethos, what society, what culture would dare to make this demand on us?

In short, our "trial" is in the command to love, not, at least not in any universal sense, in a command to kill. Perhaps there in some sense in which our trial is as "equally unprecedented" as Abraham's. But this description seems to me more likely to lead us to misread *Fear and Trembling* than to understand it and the frightening claim it makes on those who claim to be children of Abraham.

Faith as Fiction? As Lie?

Abraham's faith is always future oriented. He believes that he will have a son, that all people will be blessed through this son, and that God will keep this promise even if Abraham has to sacrifice this son. Dalton suggests that when Abraham says to Isaac, "God will see to the sheep for His burnt offering, my son," this is "*not* immediately true. It is an invention, a fiction. In a word, it is a lie." This strikes me as a bad example for a bad idea. It is a bad example because, as a claim about the future it does not claim to be already true. On the basis of what is already true, that God has promised, Abraham is confident that the denouement will be God's doing. Perhaps he has guessed how God will let him off the hook. More likely he thinks he will have to go through with it; but at least for Christian readers the notion that the Lamb of God might be a human son and that such a sacrifice is indeed God's doing should not seem strange. It is at the very heart of the Gospel.

But Dalton is thinking about eschatological hope more generally. Thus a better example, because it is not already stated in the future tense, is the notion that on the basis of baptism a believer might claim to be a "new creation," "born again," "washed clean," and "made blameless." In most Christian theologies there is some sense in which these claims are indeed already true in spite of the fact that there are obvious senses in which they are not and await a future fulfillment.

But is it helpful to calls such claims inventions, fictions, or lies? I think it is a bad idea. They are not inventions or fictions because they are not, at least not for faith, products of human creative imagination that make no claim to actuality. They are rather understood as responses to divine revelation and expressive of divine action that has already taken place. Nor are they lies, for faith does not understand them as false claims that one will try to put over on the unsuspecting. They are rather instances of the "already/not yet" structure of eschatological hope. On the basis of what has happened, faith takes the completion to be a sure thing and speaks of it in the present tense. Oscar Cullman's famous example is pertinent. On the basis of the success of the Normandy landings, it was possible to say that the war was already won and Hitler defeated although fighting and dying did not immediately cease.[29] Such a claim is neither a fiction nor a lie. Here faith is the evidence of things not seen (Heb. 12:1). Kierkegaard expresses this temporality nicely. "Faith is not an eternal struggle, but it is a victory that is struggling. Consequently, in faith that higher actuality of the spirit is not only becoming but is present, although it is also becoming."[30]

DALTON / HANSON / BENSON

Phenomenology

Dalton takes a phenomenological approach to his theme, agapic love. But this needs to be specified more closely in the present context.

After all, there is transcendental phenomenology as developed by Husserl in some of his most widely read works. It belongs to modern rather than the postmodern philosophy in two important ways: in its Cartesian quest for certainty expressed in the ideal of rigorous science (the end) and in its locating of the transcendental ego outside the world and thus free from contamination by anything historically contingent (the means).[31] The idea that by bracketing the real existence of the objects of our investigation we "purify" ourselves from prejudices that distort our interpretations and cover over the thing itself (*die Sache selbst*) strikes me (with apologies to my Husserlian friends) as simply laughable.

Phenomenology moves from modernity to postmodernity only when it takes the hermeneutical turn with thinkers like Heidegger, Gadamer, and Ricoeur. All understanding is interpretation, and no interpretation is presuppositionless. We are immersed in historically contingent and particular languages and traditions, and much of our presuppositional location is mediated by texts, which are muddier than clear and distinct ideas and more nearly nominalistic than *Wesensschauen*.

It is far from clear, at least to me, that the turn to hermeneutical phenomenology throws any light on the issue of religion with or without religion. Heidegger, Gadamer, and Ricoeur can be and have been used in the mode of faith seeking understanding by believing thinkers whose faith is religion with religion. Deconstruction can be and has been read as hermeneutical phenomenology, but while thinkers like Derrida and Caputo opt for religion without religion, I cannot see that this choice is required by deconstruction. It strikes me, rather, that in the face of the undecidable they have decided. But the decision was not made for them by deconstruction, which is a powerful theory of the way human thought is "contaminated" by the particular and contingent.[32] The fact that we cannot be the Center, the Alpha and Omega points, the intuition of the totality, does not entail that no one else can be or that such a Someone cannot be a Speaker and an Agent in history, as claimed by the Abrahamic monotheisms, prime cases of religion with religion.

Locating Agape in Relation to Eros

While I think it is important to distinguish agape from a certain eros, as Nygren, Barth, and Kierkegaard do, I am very sympathetic to the argument that there is another eros that can "join" or be "contiguous" with agape. But here again I have a hard time seeing that Dalton's discussion throws any light on the question of religion with or without religion. In his opening paragraph he says he wants to investigate the possibility of a postmodern religion with religion, one not stripped of its content in the name of some philosophical theory. In his last sentence, he claims to have opened the way beyond "the dead precepts of a static religion" and "religion without content" to a "rigorously hewn, openly determined, living *religion with religion*."

But here is my problem: However interesting and compelling the "contiguity" of agape and eros might be, I simply cannot find anything in it that could not be affirmed by Derrida and Caputo and fitted into their religion without religion. The location of a higher (heavenly) eros in Plato and Augustine seems neutral. We might say that for Plato it fits into religion without religion and for Augustine it is part of his religion with religion.[33]

Nor does the turn to Levinas help.[34] There are strong Levinasian elements in Derrida and Caputo, and is it not clear that anything essential in Levinas has been left out when he is appropriated by advocates of religion without religion. There is a deep ambiguity in his philosophical writings. He keeps a lot of religious language, such as God, revelation, height, glory, etc., but it looks as if these get regularly retranscribed as human attributes.[35] He may well be himself an instance of religion without religion, but in any case he makes no clear contribution to the debate between "with" and "without."

So it seems appropriate to me that Benson asks about the "without." He suggests that dogma, at least in its content if not as an attitude, is the "malignant property" that religion without religion is without, and then notes that James defines true religion in terms of good deeds without reference to dogma. So maybe, he suggests, there is no need for religion without religion. "If James is right, then religion is not a set of doctrines, a group or sect, or an institution." It would seem that religion can safely be reduced to ethics.

But this makes the matter too easy. In the first place, there is a crucial logical difference between "faith is not a set of doctrines" and "faith is not merely a set of doctrines." In the first context determinate doctrines can be swallowed up (without loss) in an omnivorous apophaticism,[36] while in the second case they are an essential part of religion. To say nothing of the rest of the New Testament, James seems to adopt the second option when he says that faith without works is dead.

> But someone will say, "You have faith and I have works." Show me your faith apart from your works, and I by my works will show you my faith. You believe that God is one; you do well. Even the demons believe — and shudder... Was not our ancestor Abraham justified by works when he offered his son Isaac on the altar? You see that faith was active along with his works, and faith was brought to completion by the works... You see that a person is justified by works and not by faith alone. (James 2:18–24, NRSV)

There is no reduction of religion to ethics here. James clearly thinks that faith, which he does not identify with works but illustrates with the belief in monotheism (dogma), is an essential element in true religion. He is in agreement with Paul, who writes, "the only thing that counts is faith working through love" (Gal. 5:6, NRSV). The suggestion of religion without religion in James is further weakened in 5:14 (NRSV): "Are any among you sick? They should call for the elders of the church and have them pray over them, anointing them with oil in the name of the Lord." Here we find "organized" religion, a community of worship with designated leaders and what looks to be a religious rite. Here as elsewhere, biblical religion is religion with religion.

BENSON / DALTON / SIMMONS

Method

Bruce Benson's essay is in the tradition of hermeneutical phenomenology in two ways. It affirms that the task of interpretation is ongoing and never finally completed, and it turns specifically to the interpretation of texts. Dalton's reference to Midrash is appropriate. Some may feel uncomfortable about the fact that the texts are biblical. How is that philosophy? But to assume that, say, Derrida is doing philosophy when he gives close readings of literary texts, but that one abandon's philosophy when one turns to biblical texts is to beg important questions about where truth and insight are to be found. More especially, if one is reflecting on religion with or without religion one might do well to look at some religious texts.

But Benson also makes it clear that his hermeneutical phenomenology is deconstructive. Disruption and tension are key terms, and they are not imposed on the text by the reader but found in the text. We get four different answers in the Gospels to the question, "What must I do to be saved?," and they are not easy to reconcile with one another in a neat formula. They disrupt what Benson calls a "Prozac hermeneutics" that smoothes everything out to what is simple and comfortable. Then, just to make matters worse, Matthew 25 and 23 are thrown into the mix. There is good warrant for Simmons to suggest that Benson's answer to Caputo's question, "What would Jesus deconstruct?," is "Christianity," especially certain forms of conservative Protestantism.[37]

With or Without?

They tell of the preacher whose sermons always had three points: "first I tells 'em what I'm goin' to tell 'em; then I tells 'em; then I tells 'em what I told 'em." Just as I wished Dalton had been more explicit about the import of his reading for the "with" or "without" question, so I wish Benson had been more like the preacher, telling us more explicitly either before or after or perhaps both what he takes the upshot of his reading to be for that question. It is a nice irony that Dalton would also like Benson to be more expansive on this point.

Simmons assumes, rightly I suspect, that Benson is arguing that if it takes Jesus seriously, Christianity, a major instance of religion with religion, will always have a prophetic, deconstructive element, and he gives a nice sevenfold summary of the "how" of such faith without trying to spell out the determinate (but not final and absolute) nature of its beliefs and practices. On this assumption he thinks Benson lets Derrida off the hook too easily. Benson quotes Derrida as saying, with reference to the Abrahamic messianisms, "I want to keep the right to read these texts in a way which has to be constantly reinvented. It is something which can be totally new at every moment." Benson dismisses this "totally" as hyperbolically impossible, but expresses sympathy for this commitment to an open rather than a closed hermeneutics.

What needs to be seen here is that Derrida's "totally new" is not just hyperbole; it violates his own hermeneutical principles. In what

I take to be his most succinct statement of his hermeneutics, he writes:

> The produce this signifying structure obviously cannot consist of repro-
> ducing, by the effaced and respectful doubling of commentary, the
> conscious, voluntary, intentional relationship that the writer institutes
> in his exchanges with the history to which he belongs thanks to the
> element of language. This moment of doubling commentary should
> no doubt have its place in a critical reading. To recognize and respect
> all its classical exigencies is not easy and requires all the instruments of
> traditional criticism. Without this recognition and this respect, critical
> production would risk developing in any direction at all and autho-
> rize itself to say almost anything. But this indispensable guardrail has
> always only *protected*, it has never *opened*, a reading.[38]

This can be read as an expanded version of Gadamer's claim that
"understanding is not merely a reproductive but always a productive activity as well."[39] For both Derrida and Gadamer, a text has
a determinacy, Derrida's guardrail, that must be respected and an
indeterminacy that keeps interpretation from hardening into mere
repetition. But what is new and fresh in the ever ongoing process of
interpretation must keep faith with the determinacy that prohibits an
"anything goes" hermeneutic. When Derrida, in the passage quoted
by Benson, speaks of his "right" to reinvent, he neglects to honor
his own principle that this right comes with the "duty" to honor the
reproductive element, the "doubling commentary." This principle
applies to both scriptural and nonscriptural texts. It is not clear that
interpreting scriptural texts in the context of religion without religion
takes Derrida's guardrail principle seriously enough.

The Religion of Jesus

Benson is surely right to emphasize that when asked, "What must
I do?" Jesus does not respond by saying we should believe certain
propositions. But we need to remember that he is not inventing a
religion *ex nihilo*. He appears in the first instance as a Jewish prophet
in conversation with fellow members of a particular religion with
religion.[40] The Kingdom at the center of his preaching is the Kingdom of God, the God of Israel, maker of heaven and earth, the one
who elected Israel to be in covenant relation with God and thereby

to be a light to the nations, the God who delivered the Israelites from Egypt, who later delivered them into captivity in Babylon, and then brought them back to their own land. These beliefs are the context within which Jesus teaches and preaches.

Jesus also presupposes the "church" (in the sociological sense given above, and not, of course, the Christian church). He teaches in the synagogues and goes to the festivals. The Gallup Poll would list him among the "active church members" of his day.

Jesus also makes his appeal to Scripture. "It is written." Some of his interpretations are new, exciting, even frightening, but he treats the Jewish Bible as authoritative.

Finally, Jesus has a fairly determinate ethic. He is not just for love but for love of neighbor where the enemy is also the neighbor.

This all-too-brief sketch could be filled out in greater detail, but it should be sufficient to head off any suggestion that he practices a religion without religion or that he reduces religion to ethics. His pointing to practices rather than to propositions when asked, "What must I do?" evokes the Epistle of James. Assuming that his listener is a member in good standing of the local "church," sharing its beliefs and routine practices, he disrupts the complacency of what Kierkegaard will call in his own context Christendom, by pointing to the never completed, never neatly reduced to a formulaic demand that this God places on those who purport to worship this God.

Violence

Benson suggests that the tensions and disruptions found in the teachings of Jesus undercut the rationale for religious violence. I believe he is right and would only highlight the threefold path he sketches. First, there is the epistemic moment. In the absence of final certainty and human understandings that are absolute truths, the key nerve to religious violence is cut. Ideological violence, both religious and secular (Nazi, Soviet, Maoist), regularly presupposes that "we" are the bearers and embodiment of absolute truth and as such have a "divine" right to order the world as its masters. Those who oppose us are seen as evil and worthy of death.

Second, there is the ethical moment. Since "we" ourselves are always on the way to truth and goodness and have never arrived, we are in no position to judge others who deviate from our religious beliefs or practices. In particular, there is no place for violent rhetoric, demonizing and anathematizing those who differ from us. Our job is to worry about ourselves, to see whether we are living up to our own professions. Once we have finished that task once and for all (ah, there's the rub), we can set about straightening out everyone else. Jesus said something like this once, as Benson reminds us. This does not mean that we cannot bear witness to what we take to be the best interpretations, theologically, ethically, politically, and so on, but it does mean that we occupy no imperious absolute standpoint to which everyone else must conform or die. There is no need to abandon determinate commitments in theory and practice; what is needed is to abandon the arrogant assumption that these make us instead of God the judge of others.

Finally, there is the political moment. Since we are not the embodiment of absolute truth and since we always have our hands full learning to be faithful to our own faith, there is no rationale for religiously motivated or legitimized violence. The long, shameful, and ongoing history of religious violence stems not from personal and communal commitment to determinate content in faith and practice but to the self-absolutizing arrogance that is the expression of human sinfulness in communities religious and secular, right wing and left wing.

CONCLUSION

I have argued elsewhere[41] that apart from their atheism, Marx, Nietzsche, and Freud sound a lot like the biblical prophets, including Jesus, in their critique of religion and that, accordingly, religious people would do well to take those critiques seriously. Even if, as believers will hold, their atheism is false, what they say about religion in general and Christianity in particular is true, all too true all too much of the time. So the prophetic challenge that believers can hear in their writings is not to abandon the determinate content of their faith but to be more faithful to it by abandoning the arrogance and complacency into which it all too easily degenerates.

It seems to me that post-Nietzschean postmodernism in general and deconstruction in particular continue this tradition, partly as a hermeneutics of finitude and partly as a hermeneutics of suspicion. Having looked at religion and found it deeply unattractive, Marx,

Nietzsche, and Freud opted for atheism. But of course this conclusion is not entailed by the truth of their observations of what humans have done in the name of God. It just does not follow from the fact that believers are in various ways weak or wicked that God is unreal. Similarly, it seems to me that the option of religion without religion is just that, an option, a choice, a decision—as risky as the option of religion with (some particular) religion. For postmodern and deconstructive analyses, the limits of human insight and language simply do not require that our religion, if it be that, be without religion. Our theories do not make our choices for us, nor do they provide the kind of guarantees we would like. That is what modernity failed to understand.

On Not Settling for an Abridged Edition of Postmodernism

Radical Hermeneutics as Radical Theology

John D. Caputo

I am grateful for the invitation to address the questions posed by the other contributors to *Reexamining Deconstruction and Determinate Religion: Toward a Religion with Religion* and for the compliment they pay my work by taking it up, particularly in pairing me with my good friend Merold Westphal, from whose work I have learned so much. I am grateful for their kind words and for making me think through one more time exactly what I am getting at.

THE ABRIDGED VERSION OF POSTMODERNISM

The overarching difference between the other contributors and me can be seen as a debate between a postmodernism that descends from Kant and a postmodernism that descends from Hegel. We both take our lead from postmodern critiques of modernist rationality, but we strike out on different paths from that common point of departure. They think that postmodernism plays the role of Kant on the contemporary scene, whereas I think it plays the role of Hegel. They think postmodernism is the contemporary way to delimit knowledge in order to make room for faith. I think that it is a strategy they have come up for limiting the exposure of Christian faith to postmodern analysis and that postmodernism interprets Christianity more holistically and comprehensively by treating religion as an historical form of life. Although we all agree the only safe way to have faith is to appreciate that faith is not safe, the results of my analysis is to make it a good deal more *un*safe than in theirs.

They start out by asking, "How is faith possible in the postmodern situation?" I begin by asking, "What is the human condition?," to which faith like everything else is irrecusably subject. I think they are trying to build an umbrella for when the postmodern rains come, whereas for me postmodernism means singing in the rain. On the Kantian model, postmodernism provides a shelter in which believers can keep their faith dry; it is no more than a way to delimit atheism in order to make room for Christians to lay claim to representational truths about Christ and God. On my Hegelian model, postmodernism returns any given community of believers to the living-breathing, concrete-determinate, linguistic-historical form of life to which it belongs (which in Hegel is part of a metaphysics of *Geist*) and in which its truth is generated, nourished, and expressed. They think they are loyal to the concrete and determinate and criticize me for taking flight from the concrete. I think that they are using that as a cover—the best defense (apologetics) is a good offense—to assert their belief that their particular faith is exclusively true.[1] I think they are in fact avoiding the *contingency* of the concrete and determinate, which goes all the way down. On their Kantian model, postmodernism stakes out and patrols a space that allows them to claim not merely a unique but a privileged access to the truth. On my Hegelian model, you cannot get away with that, because whatever religious beliefs one holds are saturated by one's historical condition, which is the one "saturated phenomenon" to which I subscribe. The Kantian model results in an apologetics, not a classical-modern version but an updated postmodern one, which according to Simmons even has analogates in analytic philosophy. If so, we can all be grateful for that. We are also agreed that Merold Westphal is the exemplary practitioner of postmodern Christian apologetics. The Hegelian model, however, does not issue in apologetics but in a theology of the event that feels around for the underlying experiences to which concrete religious traditions give form and figure, nomination and actualization.

On the Kantian model, postmodernism is an epistemology that limits knowledge to make possible a faith in metaphysical-theological realities. But it would be a mistake to conclude, as do these contributors, that the Hegelian model of postmodernism is by contrast metaphysical. Of course, that was true of Hegel himself but my postmodern Hegelianism is suitably postmetaphysical. The impish Derridean way to put this is that deconstruction is not an ontology but a "hauntology," which needs a gloss. What I am proposing is neither an epistemology nor a metaphysics but a phenomenology, albeit of a post-Husserlian, radical or deconstructive variety (no transcendental subject). That is because an "event" is not a metaphysical hypothesis but a phenomenological experience. However, it is not a garden-variety experience but a limit experience, an experience *without* experience, having to do with phenomena *without* phenomenality, which Derrida calls an experience of the impossible, whose possibility turns on its impossibility. You can already see what happens if we try to do without "without"—things tend toward full presence. In the straightforward modernist and metaphysical Hegelian mode, religion is analyzed as the expression of the metaphysical notion of the Absolute Spirit. In its postmetaphysical, post-Hegelian, postmodern mode, religion is analyzed as the expression of an event, of some underlying limit experience. For example, on the Kantian model, postmodernism delimits knowledge in order to make room for faith in the God of classical Augustinian metaphysical theology and everyone crowds under the umbrella of "overcoming onto-theology." But for them that is a highly circumscribed expression limited to getting past "objectifying thinking," say a rationalist proof for the existence of God, so that it remains safe to retain faith without proof in the classical metaphysical theology of Augustine. For the most part, postmodernism for them means admitting that we are all fallible and finite, with an added corollary about the need for generosity toward and tolerance of others. But we do not need postmodernism to figure that out. I think that is damage control, an attempt to cut off the exposure of Christian faith to the postmodern critique of metaphysics, which goes much further than the abridged edition of postmodernism that is being served up in what they call "overcoming onto-theology." I am recommending that we have to read the whole unabridged edition if we want to see its point and that we cannot simply settle for an edited-down version cut to fit a preconceived apologetic framework.

While the Kantian model marches under the banner of the concrete and determinate, the analysis takes the form of largely decontextualized and ahistorical arguments about religion, faith and God that pay no attention to cultural and historical context (sometimes even launching a propositional calculus), an ever-present menace in analytic philosophy. On the Hegelian model, "religion," "faith," and "God" are historicized and restored to the play of traces upon which they depend. They are returned to their concrete historical matrix in the determinate linguistic and cultural traditions of the three monotheisms and, in this case, to the Greco-European traditions of Christianity, which is itself a way to give word and form to certain underlying events. These expressions cannot be treated as innocently as they are here, as if they dropped from the sky. It is a commonplace in the study of religion today that these terms cannot be simply and univocally extended beyond the monotheistic and Greco-European cultures in which they have been born. Outside this framework, these notions either do not exist or belong to a horizon that is profoundly different and does not match up one to one with Greco-European Christianity. In a theology of the event, there are multiple horizons, traditions, languages, and cultural frameworks, among which Christianity is but one. I am not saying that nothing is true, but that we have to use caution when we speak of truth. As an established historical form of life, each tradition has its own vitality, and it is by virtue of this vitality that each framework is true. The vitality of its truth is the truth of its vitality. That means that each tradition, holistically taken, gives word and structure to an enduring form of life. These horizons are certainly different but they can also be compared and contrasted and they can even learn from one other. Just because horizons are incommensurable does not mean they cannot be compared. But there is no sense in which one would be exclusively true (so that there is a big advantage to being born Christian), as is claimed by the Kantians, no more than one language or culture could be conceived to be exclusively true, even if they are not all saying the same thing.

On the Kantian model, what is made to pass for "overcoming ontotheology" is really a code word for a saying of Johannes Climacus, that "Existence itself is a system—for God, but it cannot be a system for any existing spirit."[2] This means that just because postmodern analysis severely rocks the boat of classical metaphysics, that does not stop us from believing it anyway as a matter of faith (which is what Kant said to the Newtonians about ethics). That is what nowadays is being criticized by Quentin Meillassoux as "fideism," and on this point at least Meillassoux is right.³ But on the Hegelian model, "existence," "system," and "God" are all made to tremble by being returned to *différance*, to their historical matrix in their concrete and determinate form of life to which they give words and cultural form. It is the underlying events that need to be examined, so that postmodern analysts reach much further than they think or are willing to concede. The Kantian model is defensive and apologetic, a retrenchment in the face of the latest wave of an ongoing series of Copernican revolutions, which takes the form here of a vigorous confessional apologetic. They want to insulate God from the play of differences, just the way Jean-Luc Marion wants to insulate God from what Heidegger calls Being. God is an infinite center independent of the play of traces for them and postmodernism is reduced to merely remarking that we are finite. This is a version of the God of the gaps, a constant retrenchment program that is trying to preserve an epistemological gap (Kant's "to make room for") in which faith may be sheltered. Kant's purpose, too, was largely apologetic—he started out with Newtonian physics and the Pietists he grew up with and asked, "How can they both be right? How can I keep them both safe?"

The Hegelian model is more robust. It does not start with faith as a given but it puts faith into question. It does not ask how faith is possible, but about what is going on in historical effects like faith, and whether there might be a deeper, more elusive, more uncertain and unsafe "faith" (*foi*) stirring restlessly beneath historical Christian "belief" (*croyance*). In that sense, we postmodern Hegelians could sneak into the Kantian camp one night and steal their slogan and say that we have found it necessary to delimit "belief" (*croyance*) in order to make room for "faith" (*foi*). I hasten to add that even though its range of "critical" analysis extends much wider than in the abridged version of postmodernism that the present contributors advance, the full version of postmodernism is also more deeply *affirmative*—and precisely of a more radical *faith*. But this faith is a much more restless and obscure thing and it can only make those who gather within the protective walls of an orthodox *croyance* very nervous, wary of a wider wave of critical analysis of the human condition. The contributors largely ignore this distinction between *foi* and *croyance* (while still claiming to speak of deconstruction), but they go on the attack. If anyone speaks of a more restless faith that takes full stock of its own contingency, they say the latter are afraid of the concrete and determinate. But I think they are wary of the full implications of the concrete and determinate, of the radical *contingency* that gives the concrete and determinate its bite. The contingency of the concrete withdraws the grounds for claiming privileged access to an exclusive truth—other than to say "but you can't prove we're wrong!" Of course, they do not come right out and say that. I think this confessional apologetics is philosophy in an abridged edition, which starts by assuming faith, whose credibility it wants to establish, and is content with a draw, with showing that it cannot be shown to be wrong. Even if that were true I would expect more from philosophy. They are fond of logic, and in logic this is called the *argumentum ad ignorantiam*.

I should be clear that by offering a hauntology, a certain heretical phenomenology that is not a metaphysics, the Hegelian version of postmodernism I advocate has no interest in or grounds for saying that their claims are "incorrect," that there is no such thing as the "God" described in the metaphysical theologies of Aquinas and Augustine, and even less interest in smoking out the present contributors as part and parcel of what Freud called "the future of an illusion." That is a bankrupt Enlightenment project that is today being carried on by Richard Dawkins. I am more interested in unfolding affirmatively the form of life that unfolds in religion, its affirmation of the impossible, the *foi* that is going on in *croyance,* which is why I have sometimes been mistaken for an orthodox Augustinian myself. This is not to say that I do not object to the position of these contributors. I certainly do and I will point this out.

While I think their Christian faith is whole hearted, I think their philosophy is half-hearted. They begin with a firm affirmation of the exclusive truth of the Christian faith, in the God beyond time, history, and the play of traces, and, while trying to provide a generous version of exclusivity (by allowing for some overlapping truths held by multiple faiths), they are (like Kant) content with a standoff. They are happy to filibuster their opponents: while they have motives inside their community of faith for believing as they do, nobody outside their community can falsify or refute them. That may be so. There are a lot of things we cannot disprove—like angels and alien abductions. But that is a very disappointing result, one that is rather less than one would hope for from a philosophical inquiry wherein everything is on the table. Such an exclusively defensive and apologetic undertaking is, frankly, not the most fruitful way to think philosophically. It produces results that are provincial campfire talk for other (American, mostly Protestant) Christians, of local interest only to fellow (*sic*) Christians. It tends to be inside stuff, church talk.

Although they are trying to help me out and I would never deny that I need help, I think this fellow they call "Caputo" needs a fresh introduction. The theology of the event I advocate is a good deal more hardy. It seeks results of a more universal and thoroughgoing sort, feeling about for the underlying events of life and death, joy and sorrow, love and enmity, hostility and hospitality, that can be proposed to anybody anywhere who has an interest in the human condition. It is deeply interested in the concrete communities of faith, not from a desire to defend their right to their private property, but from a desire to get at the underlying experiences to which they give expression. The real difference between me and the Kantians is that they are trying to avoid the implications of the fact that concrete and determinate historicality goes all the way down and I am not. If anybody has "universality" on their side, it is we radical theologians.

One of the main points of my fellow contributors to this volume is that the meaning of belonging to a tradition is to countersign its truth, to take its truth seriously. As Simmons says, either one believes what one is saying in church (or synagogue or mosque) or one does not.[4] That means that the multiplicity of religious traditions represents a multiplicity of different communities who believe different things and do not agree and cannot all be right, at the cost of the principle of the excluded middle. If people did not believe their religious tradition, they would be nonbelievers, outside the tradition. But you can frame the situation like that—as a logical problem about propositions—only if you think that religious truth is propositional truth and that different religious traditions are defined by different and competing propositional assertions. I treat that as a category mistake about religious truth. I am not arguing that religious traditions lack truth, but I am arguing that the truth of the religious tradition is not deposited in assertions, in propositional truths (even if you insist that propositions are vain without a corresponding praxis). I think religious truth is found in a more underlying "way" (which is another word for "religion" and was once the name of Christianity before that name caught on). The way is a "world" (a *Welt* in the phenom-enological sense), a certain world-disclosure, a form of life, which on my account actualizes the truth of the "event." World-disclosures are multiple, are not tied to privileged access, and are misunderstood if seen in terms of competing propositional assertions.

Then what about propositional assertions? I think the "way" underlies the assertions, which gradually accumulate into a kind of mission statement in which the way gets conceptualized as theology and imaginatively portrayed in its sacred Scriptures. But it is mistake to think that this self-articulation gives the way over to representa-tional truth. These assertions are how the community clears its head when it tries to spell out its liturgies, songs, and stories. So I do not speak of "beliefs" in which I make truth-claims, which is a way of thinking about religion that came to a head in modernity although it has its roots in late scholasticism, but of being-claimed by the truth of a faith that cuts deeper than beliefs, and this arises from a cri-tique of modernism that begins in Hegel's critique of Enlightenment *Verstand*. I think that if what Simmons calls "C-beliefs" are taken as anything more than a contingent community's self-articulation (faith seeking understanding of itself), they are inextricable from privileged access because they require (among other things) historical infor-mation—like saying that a young Jewish man back in Palestine two millennia ago is uniquely God incarnate—that would not be acces-sible before Jesus was born, for example. (Just as illiterate Christians in the American Midwest in the nineteenth century cannot be held responsible for not knowing that Vishnu is the supreme deity.) Such a requirement would mean that when people organize their lives in terms of the deep structure of their understanding of themselves and the world, the vast majority are disadvantaged by the unavailability of information crucial to this task. So the vast majority of humanity is at a disadvantage in matters that could not be more essential—the deep structure of their lives—while Christians at a special advantage. The next step—which the present contributors of course resist—is to say that the *Spolia Aegyptorum* are theirs for the taking. I am offering an account of things wherein this assertion is not even a temptation to be resisted.

A great work of art, in literature or painting, is true with a truth that cuts beneath representational or propositional truth. There may or may not have been a "real" Hamlet, but the disclosive power or

truth of Shakespeare's play is completely independent of that factual issue. This question of truth goes to the heart of this difference
between me and the other contributors to this volume. Although this
is the subject of another paper, I would displace Simmons's phenomenology of feeling comfortable with his confessional identity by way
of a hauntological phenomenology of "acknowledgment" that would
be quite discomforting (spooky), one in which even people with the
least amount of time or training to engage in complex philosophical
reflection on the nature of religious beliefs would see my point. On
my hypothesis, they would experience spooky moments—"we're all
in this together" moments, we all share a common fate—in which
they would be led to acknowledge that while their tradition is theirs,
the only one they can inhabit, there are many such traditions, each
having its own uniqueness, integrity, vitality, and "truth," but in
such matters as these no one really has privileged access. There are
moments when they step back, or when the step back is taken in
them, like it or not—like encountering the witness that is given by
a "saint" of a very different tradition with very different narratives,
or the saints who rightly pass for atheists—which leads them to this
acknowledgment. Religious truth is witnessed, not verified representationally. Only as hauntology is phenomenology possible.

I think we are being served up an abridged edited version of postmodernism in which various surrogates for postmodernism are being
made to do service for postmodern theory but fall quite short of it,
and we see this in Simmons's essay. We do not need postmodernism
to learn that we are finite and fallible things and that our knowledge is never adequate. We already know that and practically no one
nowadays would deny our epistemic limits in whatever tradition or
style they practice philosophy. "Fallibilism" still maintains a theory of
propositional truth while only requiring that we admit we are neither
God nor Descartes. For that we do not need postmodern theory,
which is not to be confused with postmodernism. What we need is
a different conception of truth itself and, in the case of the present
debate, a fundamentally different kind of analysis of what is going on
in religious traditions. Nor is this demand met with nonfoundation-
alism, which is also capable of functioning as an account of propositional truth. Nor is it met by saying we should be epistemologically
"modest" and admit our limits, which is a pious and innocuous
substitute for deconstruction. Nor is it met with "finitude," a point

that was widely recognized without the help of poststructural theory. I am not just a good Kantian asking that we all concede the obvious, that we are finite beings and have no supersensible intuition. If anything, I am a heterodox Hegelian who thinks that the finite belongs to *Verstand*, and I invoke the idea of the infinite, of infinite depth, infinite responsibility, in a theopoetics of an infinite secret. I am not trying to stake out critical boundaries for finite beings to observe with all due modesty, but trying to meditate an uncontainable event and affirm the possibility of the impossible.

Nor do we get anywhere by arguing, as Simmons does, that my position is caught up in a performative contradiction.[5] That is not a postmodern argument but a favorite of the Habermasians, logicians, and ontotheologicians. I have always found that a futile, lame, and reactionary objection against radical theory, an argument of last recourse and testimony to the poverty of formalism. Lest I be misunderstood, I hasten to point out that, having attended graduate school in the days before there were any "continental" programs to speak of, I had a completely traditional philosophical education. I have always been grateful for that training, especially for the work I did on axiomatization and formal systems,[6] which later helped me understand Husserl, structuralism, and the analogous use of the notion of formal undecidability in Gödel and Derrida. Because of that training, I have never suffered from the illusion that formal thinking can do service in matters that are profoundly phenomenological.

Of course I think that the second-order statements I make *about* religious discourse, and hence the series of assertions I have just made, are true. Even Heidegger—the great critic of "calculative thinking" and "propositional truth"—said, at the beginning of *Time and Being*, that what follows takes the risk of making assertions *about* something that is *not* a matter of assertions.[7] I am not saying that there are no propositional truths or that I do not make propositional claims. I am saying that treating the New Testament as a body of propositional truths is a category mistake, and that holds true *ipso facto* for theological conceptualizations of these narratives. I do not think that narratives like the raising of Lazarus are true with a representational theory of truth (*WG*, chap. 11). I do not think that this narrative should be understood as representing a state of affairs, as a record of some actual episode in the past. But I certainly hold that this claim *about* that story is true, and that there are good reasons for it, which are found in the massive literature of historical-critical New Testament research. There we can see that the movement from Jesus of Nazareth, a figure all but lost in the fog of history, to the Nicene Creed is a largely an imaginative theological construction, as even John Milbank admits,[8] which faith tries to underwrite as the work of the Holy Spirit, while being forced to admit that "faith" in the "Holy Spirit" is of course a *part* of the construction. That is where the force of "reason" is borne in upon confessional "apologetics," which the apologists try to blunt by saying that "reason" cannot see what the eyes of faith can see in these matters. (That, by the way, is why critical and historical work of this sort is usually best done outside the supervision of ecclesiastical institutions where the threat of losing one's job hangs over one's head.) So much for reason. Seen in these terms, if anybody is on the side of reason, of giving good reasons *all the way down*, enjoying the right to ask any question, it is radical theology, not confessional apologetics.

A phenomenology of the event, of the truth of the event, is then in a position to acknowledge what should be obvious, that we are all up to our ears in historicality (the Hegelian point) and the play of traces (the poststructural point). In a theology of the event religion is seen as a way to give evocative form to provocative events, to provide nomination and actualization to certain obscure but fertile, latent but underlying experiences or "events" by which our lives are nourished. It concedes the contingency of these beliefs in the name of a deeper faith in something toward which we are always already underway and for which we lack any guarantees. It is trying with all its heart not to be halfhearted and defensive, but more radically interrogatory, open-ended, and full throated about our contingent mortal lives. For that reason it is, and this is the heart of my reading of Derrida, more radically confessional, circumfessional, and in that sense more radically Augustinian. In a theology of the event, everything is on the table, including the contingency of the traditions we have inherited, which, by the way, jells very nicely with the contingency of the actual course the universe has taken since the Big Bang, according to the physicists, so that we post-Hegelians do not feel the need to fence off religion from science in order to keep faith safe from the physicists. The contributors to the present volume claim to be as radical as they need to be, whereas we post-Hegelians think the real challenge is to be as radical as we have to be, as radical as are the things themselves, which are always slipping away. But thinking is unconditional exposure to what is to be thought, which is risky business. It is not a limited exposure that stays in the water for a bit and then heads for the towels. For the cut in that more radical "circumfessional" confession, I think the present contributors lack a taste.

In the end, I regard the present volume as a missed opportunity. My fellow contributors underestimate my most Christian texts, my ongoing meditations on the theology of the Cross that culminate in *The Weakness of God*,[9] where my most sustained engagements with religion *with* religion interact with the logic of the *without*.[10] Furthermore, by neglecting the distinction between *croyance* and *foi*, between a position taken and a deeper affirmation, between a decision made (*doxa*) and a deeper decisiveness (*pistis*), which is central for me, the other contributors never notice that the work I do is aimed at undermining the distinction between "theism" and "atheism," with which they are preoccupied. For me, theism and atheism are opposed *croyances*, contrasting beliefs, positions posed against each other in a doxological dispute, in this corner Hitchens and Dawkins, in the other corner Reformed Epistemology, one more round of the fun but futile and fruitless debate back in 1948 between Bertrand Russell and Fr. Frederick Copleston on the BBC. If Russell or Copleston had switched "positions," were later on counted on the other side, that would make news, but it would not make philosophy unless it hit those two fine British chaps that there are underlying events or affirmations going on that run deeper than these positions and cut across their opposition. My own interest is focused on those affirmations, a more uncertain, troubling, restless, and unsafe faith, that may emerge in either camp, whether one rightly passes for an atheist or rightly passes for a Christian or a Hindu.

At its worst, what we get from the present volume is confessional apologetics, turning on the old rhetorical advice that the best defense is a vigorous offense against my views. That may be in part my fault. Like my good friend Merold Westphal, I try hard to be clear. But there is a certain amount of whimsy and a bit of the Kierkegaardian humorist in what I write, and that can sometimes cause me trouble. Like Kierkegaard and Derrida I am always laughing through my prayers and tears. At its best, the present volume raises a number of important points, starting with the question of the difference between the Kantian and Hegelian versions of postmodernism, a question that is worth our attention. So I need to do a little rehabbing of the word "without" and its venerable apophatic logic and also reintroduce the readers of this volume to another "Caputo," even though my fellow contributors and I have a good many things in common. Whether we will also meet continental philosophy of religion for the first time in my remarks, instead of a by-product of continental philosophy, I leave to the reader to decide.

In what follows, I will be almost exclusively considering and responding to the chapters by J. Aaron Simmons and Stephen Minister, because they criticize my work directly; I will also take note more briefly of the piece by Bruce Ellis Benson. In so doing, I have no wish to be dismissive of the other chapters.

RADICAL THEOLOGY: THE UNABRIDGED VERSION OF POSTMODERNISM

Stephen Minister's opening presentation of my work makes for an interesting counterpart to Martin Hägglund's *Radical Atheism*,[11] in which "Caputo" is staged as a conservative Augustinian theologian who treats Derrida's discourse on the impossible as an argument for the existence of God and of divine omnipotence. I am denounced by Hägglund for being too strong a theologian and by Minister for not being strong enough. I think both these commentators might in part have been misled by the whimsy with which I say certain things. Be that as it may, they and their critiques occupy opposing polar caps and to both I make the same reply. I am not an orthodox confessional theologian, a theologian if it pleases you, but neither orthodox nor confessional. I decided to use the word "theology" under the prodding of Charlie Winquist because I thought it might unsettle both the (confessional) theologians and (secular) ethnologists of religion! The "continental philosophy of religion" I do is the unabridged version, what we in the Syracuse University religion department call "radical theology," the full-bodied one coming down from Hegel and poststructural theory, not the decaffeinated version coming down from Kant. So I embrace the aporia that weak theology makes for full-strength postmodernism, while strong theology is a bit weak-kneed about putting itself in question.

In the view I take, confessional theology is a certain first-order discourse that reports back to the local community of the faithful (Jewish, Muslim, Christian, Hindu, Bahá'i, etc.). Here the community has every right to expect that it will be able to "recognize itself," which is a theme that runs through these papers. In antiquity, this recognition happened more or less automatically because then the classic functions of bishop and theologian were then joined—Augustine is the paradigmatic case of this—and theology was more closely linked to sermons and the existential life of the faithful. Simmons's account of Justin Martyr is also a good example of the way theology and life were joined in Christian antiquity, and so is Origen. Today, these two functions are divided and each is viewed by the other with suspicion. Bishops are bureaucrats who sometimes feel obliged to protect sexual predators from the law in the name of the corporation, while the theologians read unreadable papers to one another that only a couple of dozen people in the known universe can understand and that one thinks at times must pose a challenge to the divine mind itself.

Radical theology, on the other hand, is a second-order discourse interested in what I like to call, following Derrida and Deleuze, the "event" that is going on in theology. Deleuze once said that the event is not what happens (with its ordinary sense) but what is going on *in* what happens.[12] The event is the locus of the *truth* of what is happening. The truth of the event seeks to be nominated and actualized, strives to surface or actualize itself, to unfold, strives to come true, to become (true). The truth of the event is constantly insisting on existing. When I say "truth," you can already hear motifs from Hegel and Heidegger playing in the background (but without the *Seinsgeschichte*). To be sure, the truth of a thing is not written all over it. Like the Scriptures, it has to be read or interpreted, which is why "radical theology" is just a type of what I have been calling "radical hermeneutics" for many years now. Radical theology, accordingly, is not as interested in religion or theology as it is in what is going on *in* religion or theology, in its *truth*, in the *event*. So one of my first strategies in responding to the other contributors to this volume is to not concede the ground of truth to them. I am playing on my opposition's court, the crowd is against me, but I will not let them boo me for being against truth. Just as Jim Wallis advises the Democrats against conceding the ground of "religion" to the Right, I will not concede the ground of truth to the orthodox of any *doxa*.

But to whom, then, do the "radical theologians" report? To anybody who is interested, to anyone with an interest not simply in what happens but in what is going on in what happens, anyone who is interested in the truth of what is going on—in religion or politics, liturgy or sex, particle physics or metaphysics. That is the advantage of radical theology—more universal relevance—over confessional theology and apologetics, which have a local audience (the faithful, the believers, the card carriers). Intellectuals should be as interested in what a radical theologian is saying about religion as they are in literature or history, painting or politics. That is another part of my strategy in this response: I do not concede the ground of universality to the home crowd. That is why, when the other contributors to this volume, inspired by Alain Badiou, advise me to consider the universality of truth, I am nonplussed. I would have said that we radical theologians submit what we have to say to the length and breadth of humankind. They say they are widening the horizon of apologetics by bringing continental and analytic philosophy into conversation,[13] which is to their credit, but they are ultimately reporting back to their local confessional community whose faith they are trying to conceptually elaborate. As a second-order discourse reflecting on confessional theology, radical theology does not require local communities nor does it require that its readers be card-carrying Christians, Hindus, Bahá'ís, or anything else. They may be atheists like Martin Hägglund or not religious at all.

Its readers just have to be interested in reflecting on the human condition, on the inscrutabilities of human life and death, and maybe also animal life (since animals and the environment are not Christians, they get very little attention in this volume), on the moral law within and the starry skies above, as Kant put it (and everything in between). They just need to think there is something to be learned from reflecting on the religious and theological traditions, the way there is in reflecting on literature or any other important human activity. Until recently, of course, we radical theologians have had a hard time convincing secular thinkers that theology and religion are worth thinking about, because religious and theologically minded people behave so badly every time scientists make a new discovery or the religion of some chosen people gets unchosen (constitutionally disestablished or just ignored and abandoned). This situation has changed dramatically in recent years, thanks in no small part first to Levinas and Derrida and more recently to Badiou, Agamben, and Žižek, although the latter group are uncommonly ungrateful to the former for having shown them the value of thinking about religion and theology, about what Derrida called the "unavowed" theology in everything we do.[14]

I would, however, be the first to confess that the praise I am heaping upon radical theology is a bit of a fiction. Because radical theologians are usually not independently wealthy they have to make a buck as academic publish-or-perishers. They, too, read unreadable papers to one another at the American Academy of Religion (AAR), although I myself have tried in several books to speak over the head of my peers and write for a wider audience (*OR* and *WWJD*). As academics, radical theologians do indeed report to someone—to promotion and tenure committees, deans and university presses, and other such "normalizing" powers (in the Foucauldian sense) that keep them inside the borders of the academic form of life, borders I have tried to test from time to time (after I got tenure).[15] But it is also a fiction to think that this distinction between first-order and second-order discourse is airtight. The first-order discourse of the confessional theologies inevitably forms, informs, and deforms the second-order discourse of radical theology. That is because of what we in the "radical hermeneutical" tradition call the impossibility of pure reflection, the impossibility of the transcendental reduction or of the pure cogito, and it is why the pure messianic is also always another messianism (*PT* 139–43; *DN* 168–78), a point I have been making from the start. Inasmuch as we embrace, we insist upon, the "facticity" of human understanding, its "situatedness"—despite the picture of us drawn by the defenders of the abridged version— we concede there is no pure disengaging of radical theology from the concrete forms of life of which it means to provide a certain reflective awareness.

I find it excessively odd to accuse a radical hermeneut of a distrust of the concrete and factical. That makes one suspect that there is something else going on behind this accusation—and my hypothesis is that the rhetoric of the concrete and determinate is made to serve an apologetic argument for privileged access, where there is a not very subtle trade-off made between the "uniqueness" of Christianity and its "exclusive" truth. In the view of us radical hermeneuts, one is *always* reporting to some local community or other—the intellectual, social, linguistic, historical community to which one belongs more deeply than one can say or will ever know. Maybe after you are dead, if anyone still cares about you, they will be able to define exactly what community you were reporting to. So all we can do, the best we can do, is shoot for what Gadamer called hermeneutical universality, with the understanding that this does not result in an agreement upon some essence or other. Essences are always provisional and local, always *somebody's* essence, always an essence for this time or place, which is why when we hear a case being made for religion *with* religion we have to worry about "*whose* religion?" Essences contribute to tribal conflicts over one's favorite essence, like the "essence of Christianity." The only thing genuinely universal is singularity and the only community is "we're all in this together." So we aim at hermeneutic openness, a hermeneutic hospitality, a potential universal never actualized, according to which for beings of language like ourselves, there is nothing of human import that cannot be put on the table and discussed, nothing that cannot be set forth in terms somehow accessible to the other, that cannot be set forth in words. That even goes for words intended to express ineffability, which is an experience of an intralinguistic caesura that any speaker, and only speakers, can understand. That hermeneutic hospitality is the principal force behind maintaining the "messianic openness" (or religion "without" religion) of any confessional theology, which otherwise deals in strictly local goods for local consumption.

What I call radical theology is traditionally described as the "philosophy of religion," a discipline that is enjoying a renaissance today in conjunction with what is often called "the return of religion." Here is where the genealogy of radical theology from Hegel's *Lectures on the Philosophy of Religion* rather than from Kant's *Religion within the Limits of Reason Alone* is important. Hegel thought that Christianity is the absolute religion toward which all other religions tend. This is the reason that in secular departments of religion today the ethnographic approach to religion is rapidly displacing the philosophical approach. From its start with Hegel, the "philosophy" in the "philosophy of religion" tended to mean Western philosophy and "religion" tended to mean Christianity. Consequently, the "philosophy of religion" is code for the (Christian) philosophy of the (Christian) religion, that is, Christian apologetics, which is exactly what it is put forward in the present volume. One way secular universities have found to displace the hegemony that Christianity has traditionally enjoyed in this discipline is just to drop the philosophy of religion and leave it to church-related institutions or divinity schools. There it can come out of the closet, drop its pretense to being full-throttle philosophy, and simply concede that it is Christian apologetics. Far from dispelling these concerns, the other contributors to this volume rush to embrace them. Christian apologetics is unapologetically what "continental philosophy of religion" is reduced to. The most draconian solution of all available to secular universities is to drop the "department of religion" entirely and make it a part of the sociology department.[16]

But we radical theologians have another idea. While arguing that radical theology has Hegelian credentials, we keep a safe distance from Hegel's idea that "Christianity" is the consummate religion, religion itself, where religion converges *with* Christian religion, which is what the contributors to this volume share with Hegel. Of course, Hegel went on to say that religion is an imaginative figure (*Vorstellung*) of something that can only be conceptualized in and by Hegelian philosophy—that is the point at which these Christian apologists head straight for the door. That was Hegel's attempt to radicalize theology, the move in which we radical theologians recognize a radical gesture. This gesture was picked up by Tillich, the father of radical theology, who helped us clear our heads of supernaturalism and magic. That makes Hegel our grandfather. Old grandfather Hegel was feeling around for what I am calling the truth of the event. But if truth be told I only go along halfheartedly, half-heretically with Hegel. As I once argued, in the philosophy of religion, I am a heretical deconstructivist Hegelian.[17] I think religion is an imaginative figure, not of the Absolute Concept, but of the event, which is a phenomenological, not a metaphysical, occurrence. That is what Derrida calls the secret, the absolute secret that there is no secret, the secret of something-I-know-not-what, which alas for the (metaphysical) Hegelians also means of something-Hegel-knows-not-what. When it comes to religion there are only *Vorstellungen,* works of imaginative genius, and no burning through to an absolute Essence, Concept, Spirit, Will-to-Power or Divine Special Revelation. So when I speak of the truth of the event, I can just as well speak of its untruth, of its never quite seeing the light of day, of the endlessly altered ways in which this insistence insists on existence.

Thus, notwithstanding his Christocentrism, Hegel made the crucial, I would say defining move in the formation of a radical theology and of a distinctively continental approach to the philosophy of religion. Hegel upbraided the rationalists of his day for leaving out of consideration the characteristic doctrines of the Christian religion—in particular, creation, the Trinity, and the Incarnation—and restricting themselves to the bloodless and barren exercise of the abstract "understanding" (*Verstand*), like proving the existence of God or the immortality of the soul.[18] He would certainly have been no less critical of what passes for the "philosophy of religion" in the textbooks and books of readings assembled by analytic philosophers and Thomists. In its place, Hegel put the work of "reason" (*Vernunft*), which consisted in the wider work of feeling around for the form of the Spirit that was unfolding in these determinate and particular Christian doctrines. I recommend we replace "Spirit" with "event," or the Truth of the Spirit with "the truth of the event" (no caps). That is exactly what I am recommending in *The Weakness of God: A Theology of the Event,* which is an extended meditation upon the logic of the Cross, upon Jesus as an icon not of God's omnipotence but of God's weakness. (As Catherine Keller shows so nicely, the tradition wanted a more testosterone-rich God than that!)[19] There is no text in which I am more concerned with their "with." Far from shying away from the concrete and determinate, I am like a good Hegelian (of a somewhat heretical stripe) who prefers *Sittlichkeit* to *Moralität* and recommends a meditation upon what is happening in very determinate traditions, like the Christian one, which is the one in which I am least incompetent. That is why Simmons will find in *The Weakness of God,* just as in Hegel's lectures on the philosophy of religion, an ongoing discussion of the "C-beliefs" he and his congregation hears in Pentecostal services, even as I know for a fact of the occasional sermon, maybe in a university chapel, or among Bruce Benson's progressive Episcopalians, that would mention P-beliefs, since the best sermons are not only haunting but haunted. Indeed, it would be impossible to undertake what I call a "theology of the event" except by closely analyzing the concrete confessional religious traditions, of which radical theology is a second-order analysis. In the very best traditions of deconstruction, radical theology is a parasite.

In other words, in this Hegelian schema, the philosophy of religion is distinguished from confessional theology formally, by the point of view—taking religion as imaginative thinking (*Vorstellung*), not conceptual thinking (*Begriff*)[20]—but not materially, by sorting out theses knowable by the use of natural reason, say the existence of God, from doctrines that have been supernaturally revealed, say the Incarnation and Trinity. On the contrary, for Hegel, what is most interesting of all are Creation and Incarnation, the Trinity and the Holy Spirit, the concrete, determinate, distinctive, and defining doctrines of Christian life and theology, even as what interests me in *The Weakness of God* is the Crucifixion, which of course also greatly interested Hegel. That is a defining mark of radical theology, which reflects upon and takes up the distinctive themes of the confessional theologies, the concrete religious traditions, and feels around for their events, for what is going on in them, which certainly cannot be done by restricting oneself to rational proofs of philosophemes. That is why the vast majority of *The Weakness of God* is given over to reflecting on Christian texts and doctrines and very little or no time at all is spent in the rare air of the "pure messianic" or, God forbid, with proofs for the existence of God or the Platonic idea of the "immortality of the soul." I do not distinguish between natural and supernatural truths, but between the prosaic and poetic sense of truth, between matters for representational truth (governed by logic and rules of empirical evidence), and matters of the truth of the event, a point to which I will return. My "poetics" of the event is a phenomenology of religion but, once again, a heretical and hauntological quasi-phenomenology that questions both the classical idea of "philosophy" and the Western Christian Latin idea of "religion."[21]

Now I am not saying that radical theology and confessional theology belong in principle to two different levels of discourse that pass each other like ships in the night. On the contrary, I am interested in examining exactly how they interact. My thesis has been, and I am very grateful to Minister for pointing this out to Simmons, that radical theology "spooks" confessional theology, that it provides a ghost that haunts the confessional theologies, and that deconstruction is "undead." I take the trope of the "undead" from Žižek in order to unnerve him—as if anything could!—about his hasty proclamation that the time for deconstruction is over and that now is the time for, well, in all modesty, Žižek. There is some of that in the present volume, too, whose other contributors are also telling us that the time of indecisive deconstruction is over and that now is the time to assert the exclusive truth of Christianity (as if that program has not already had quite a run over the last two millennia). As Johannes de Silentio would say, I wish them and their omnibus well in bearing the spirit of the present age. But I am here to haunt them, like the ghosts who spooked old Scrooge, to whisper in their ears, to visit them in their dreams, and to say, however often you kill off deconstruction and its logic of the "without"—the very "without" these contributors are trying do without—you will find it will come back to haunt you. So when Žižek says that the time has come for the democracy-to-come to become the democracy-to-go, he should know, first, that that is exactly what the democracy to come is, if it "is," and, second, by his own logic of the undead, that if deconstruction goes it will come back to haunt him like a *revenant*.[22]

The task of a deconstructive or a radical theological point of view is to spook the confessional theologies, to whisper in their ear that, according to a very elementary rule of the determinate and concrete character of factical life, were they born in another time and place and had never so much as heard the name of Jesus, they would be singing songs to some other form or figure of the event, some other way to be, some other position, with equal decisiveness but—and this is the point—with presumably no loss to their powers of affirmation or the earnestness of their faith (even though their beliefs would be different) or the integrity of their lives. This is why religious truth is not a zero-sum game. Radical theology whispers the unnerving thought in the ear of confessional theologies that, unless they are careful, they are producing goods for local consumption, writing stories for local campfires, producing texts with a limited market, singing hymns to an accident of birth.[23]

A Phenomenological Excursus

To a great extent, debates like this boil down to the dexterity by which one side is able to frame the other side, to restate the arguments of the other side in one's own terms, and then declare oneself the winner and march home in triumph. I hope it is possible to break out of that and find the terms in which we each recognize the other and ourselves. To that end, let me offer the following attempt to cast all this on a more experiential level in order to get down to the matter itself.

Simmons is concerned about his Pentecostal "identity." I understand that (I was raised a pre-Vatican II Catholic under Pius XII!), and I wish him well. But I think that he should understand and experience his identity as an identity *without* identity, that he should not be identical *with* himself. I think that for his own good he would be better off were he more uneasy about his identity, about what he believes, a little spooked about what he believes he believes, when he and his Pentecostal community gather in assembly. I recommend that Simmons say what Graham Ward says (and I do not often cite Ward for support) in what is I think is one of his best moments:

> We do not know how the story ends and we do not know how far we have come in the plot. We do not know how many other characters have yet to appear, have appeared, appear already. We do not know whether we are a leading player or in a supporting role. We do not know what we say when we say "Abba," "Lord," "Christ," "Salvation," "God." We see so few of the connections which make up our lives, and so few of our connections with other lives.... Our certainties are persuasions; our facts are selections from the data available; our dogmatisms speak more about our fears than our aspirations. There is no room for Christian imperialism.[24]

We each of us try as best we can to be in good faith, trying not to deceive ourselves or others, doing the best we can. But when I speak of good faith, the faith in good faith is *foi*, not *croyance*, a deep faith I have in the course of things, in the future, in others, in the work I do, in those I love, in myself, in the joy of life, in love, etc. Those, I would say, are all workings of the event. I was delighted to read of Mother Teresa's life-long doubts, not because I am happy to see a good woman tormented but because I think what she is confessing is important.[25] Suppose Mother Teresa decided to change or give up on her beliefs (*croyances*)? There would not be the least reason for her to give up on her faith (*foi*), on the work she did, or on our faith in her. I distinguish deep decisions, the deep resolve that makes us who we are, or rather who we are trying to become, from the resolutions we make because of the time and place in which we live and die.

That means I have to face up to the ghosts that haunt me, the thought that I do not in any deep and fixed sense know who I am or what I desire, and that there are others very far from here, in space or time or both, whose *croyances* are very different from mine, and that were I there, I would be one of them, lest I unwittingly absolutize my date and place of birth. One of the crucial ingredients in the idea of the other, as Husserl said so simply and so fatefully, is that "were I there, 'there' " would be 'here,' " and the faith of the other would be mine.[26] Then my apologetics would start out from a different belief, and I would be hard at work erecting an apologetic wall of defense around something else. In my view, the levels of *foi* and *croyance* interact with each other and it is precisely deconstruction that keeps the lines of communication open between them. Beliefs are deconstructible, but faith in itself, if there is such a thing, is not deconstructible, and deconstruction is faith. The faithful represent a wider world than the communities of belief. I do not want to reproduce the two-story theory of nature on the first floor and supernature on the second. I want one house but the whole house haunted. Hence, I look around in confessional theologies for the way these two bleed into each and the one shows up in the other. And that happens all the time, as when Mother Teresa throws a scare into the faithful (*les croyants*) by expressing her doubts about her beliefs (not her *foi*). It also explains why church authorities often distrust their own confessional theologians, calling them a "curse and a plague upon the church," and this because the critical spirit of theologians exposes the thin underpinnings of the ecclesiastical doctrines up above, something which has often cost them their jobs.[27] It also shows up in the famous logic of the *sine*, of the *sans*, which is proposed to us by apophatic theologians who are, I think, pressing against the limits of confessional theology, which is why Buddhists can hear themselves talking in what Meister Eckhart says and why the Inquisition went after Meister Eckhart. Eckhart was the first theologian in whom

I looked for traces of a more radical theology, although I had no idea at the time that that is what I was looking for (the only way to really be searching for something is to search *without* knowing what you are searching for).[28]

Try this imaginative variation: Suppose according to some speculations of the more speculatively minded cosmologists (not to mention the creators of the TV show *Lost*) time travel is indeed possible, and we go back and check up on Yeshuah of Nazareth only to find that he was quite a charismatic fellow, quite courageous and with quite a silver tongue, but he was not quite up to Council of Nicene speeds. Or suppose tomorrow a Dead Sea Scrolls type discovery is made of a large set of manuscripts of contemporaneous reports of the life and death of Jesus that show John Dominic Crossan is basically right and this man of flesh and blood, Yeshuah of Nazareth, would have only understood the first and last lines of the Nicene Creed (provided it was translated into Aramaic), the bits about God creating heaven and earth and the resurrection of the body, and would have been utterly nonplussed by everything in between, would have rejected it outright, would have considered it Greek polytheism and blasphemy against the One God, and furthermore that the story of the Virgin Birth would have reduced Miriam of Nazareth to peals of laughter? If we find our *croyance* is in trouble, does that mean that our faith (*foi*) is in vain, that our life has been proven meaningless? Or would one not in such a situation fall back upon a deeper, more irreducible affirmation that does not depend upon the (representational) truth of Christian beliefs? I think that there is a kind of unconditional affirmation of justice, of peace, of joy, that one finds in people like Gandhi, Mother Teresa, Martin Luther King Jr., Dorothy Day, and Nelson Mandela, which is not even to mention people long dead and forgotten whose names have disappeared into the night of history, like now nameless Native Americans who stood up against the slaughter visited upon them by the visitors from Christian Europe, who thought that at the name of Jesus every knee should bend or else every head should roll. I think the uncontainable force of *foi* does not stand or fall with Hinduism or Christianity, which are *croyances* that tap into but cannot contain the life of faith. Were you driven to such a point, you would not be driven into nihilism. You would simply find that like the God devised by traditional theodicy, our lives too are sometimes written straight with crooked lines. As Heidegger says in *Being and Time*, "The certainty of the resolution signifies that one *holds oneself free for* the possibility of *taking it back*."[29] Sometimes we have to take back a resolution in order to remain loyal to our deepest resolve, or take back a *croyance* to be loyal to a *foi*, as they put it on the *rive gauche*.[30]

Or finally one more way: imagine several people—a Christian, a Buddhist, a native American, and a Hindu, say—earnestly sunk in what we call in Christian Latin "prayer," each practice steeped in its own protocols and background beliefs (which make us wary of using the same word "prayer"), and then try to determine which person is praying truly, which one has the true prayer. That, I submit, is impossible, and it is impossible because it is incoherent, and it is incoherent because prayer is not that kind of thing, not true in that kind of representational sense of truth. It is impossible to deal with the event in that way, and it is at best a misunderstanding and at worst *hybris* to try to pass such a judgment.

Simmons's Missed Opportunity

Aaron Simmons and I share in the aim of trying to set the tensions between the "with" and the "without," but we do not set them at the same point. Of all the contributors to this volume, Simmons does the best job of framing (the pun is inevitable) the present debate. To a certain extent, I do not have to respond to Simmons because Minister already has. When Minister brings up the hauntological principle, that is exactly the right point to make, including the point that Minister makes at the end, with which I also agree, that we *also* need to have a practical working identity. Minister's remark is missing only the footnote to Derrida on having an identity *without* identity, an identity in which one is not self-identical, not identical *with* oneself.[31] I describe this by saying that the idea of the self is not to be jettisoned—I do not even know what that would mean—but redescribed, so that the self looks like a chairperson making a report for a committee which, behind closed doors, is at odds with itself. In what follows I will address the concerns Simmons voices on four points: formalization, metaphysics, the "how" and the "what," and a/theology.

Formalization

First, a word about the attempt made by Simmons to proceed by way of an analysis of formal and enumerated propositions. I will forgo this procedure and stick to the slipperiness of English prose. I think this kind of excessive formalism is the defining characteristic of analytic philosophy—it makes no difference to me whether it is foundational or nonfoundational, whether it deals with proofs for the existence of God or the Incarnation.[32] While formalized discourse certainly has its place, I think it is obfuscating here, although I appreciate the good intentions behind it (see note 5). Simmons's calculus proceeds from the mistaken assumption that C-beliefs have representational force and are propositional claims, which I regard as a category mistake such that they are prevented from being treated as elements in the same calculus. Furthermore, a calculus works with propositions, which are ideal constructions, which are self-identical unnuanced elements in the system. As the entire point of deconstruction is lodged in the search for and valorization of the singular, the idiomatic, the idiosyncratic, that is, for the unprogrammable and nonformalizable, this undertaking, while well intentioned, is doomed to fail. Formalization is a useful practice in certain contexts, but it is of minimal use in a deconstructive analysis of religious traditions. That is the perduring mistake of rationalist and analytic thought, which Merleau-Ponty painstakingly deconstructed long ago in *Phenomenology of Perception* in the name of "ambiguity." It assumes that the matters we are discussing can be formalized and translated into some sort of calculus—and if they cannot, then they must be purely "emotive." In such a calculation, nobody gets a chance to say that they think they might believe, that they believe they believe, but sometimes like Mother Teresa they think they do not, and in truth they are often not sure what they think, and that it depends on whether you mean now or last weekend, which is what Mother Teresa was talking about with her father confessor. Everybody in the calculus (if there is anybody there at all) *is* a Christian, not merely trying to become one. This kind of cognitivism affected Husserl himself, a mathematician by training, and it was just the thing to which Heidegger and Merleau-Ponty objected. Had they not reformed Husserlian phenomenology in the way they did, the name "Husserl" would be, like that of Ernst

Cassirer today, known only to historians specializing in early twentieth century German neo-Kantianism.

This sort of formalistic thinking is ham-fisted when it needs to be delicate, or too pointed when it needs a smoother touch. It has a good use in purely formal matters, but Stephen Toulmin spent a lifetime trying to explain the difference between formal logic and how people actually think about concrete and determinate things. (For a professed lover of the concrete and determinate, this is an odd discourse to adopt.) That is why so much of what Richard Swinburne writes seems so futile to many of us. This is a good example of the distinction that Heidegger insisted upon, between thinking and calculating, and of Whitehead's comment that the advantage of the propositional calculus he and Russell invented was that it eliminated the need for thinking. That analytic philosophers are capable of laying aside this formalized style and of speaking from their heart I have never doubted, and nothing I have ever said implies that I doubt it. That continental philosophers are beset by their own stylistic devils and write in a way that is so exotic and hypernuanced that hardly anyone can understand a thing they say, is also something I have never doubted and something about which I issued daily bulletins to my graduate students. Merold Westphal and I have tried to earn a living by earnestly resisting that tendency among continentalists.

I have already pointed out that Simmons's argument is vitiated by assuming a univocal sense of the English word "beliefs" when in fact everything that I am saying depends upon distinguishing and following the interaction between two different kinds of belief signified by Derrida's distinction between *foi* and *croyance*. That makes it impossible for me to disentangle what Simmons is saying by sticking with his calculus. A similar ambiguity besets other words in Simmons's chain. Take the word "revelation," which he is using in the traditional sense of a supernatural gift and which I am rejecting on Tillichian grounds. For Tillich the distinction between "supernatural revelations" and "natural human" experience is a recourse to magic. I have redescribed this distinction as a distinction between the prosaic (representational, so-called "natural" knowledge) and a poetics (nonrepresentational, the so-called "supernatural"). I redescribe "revelation" as a theopoetics, a certain of way being laid claim to by the events that happen to me, which accordingly unfolds into a form of life, a complex of narratives and figures, parables and paradoxes, institutions and practices, histories and traditions, liturgies and art forms. I think there are many such revelations, as many as there are languages and historical traditions, just as there are multiple poetic revelations; and it is a conceptual category mistake to try to classify or rank order them in terms of propositional truth and falsity, which would launch a debate about whose sacramental practices are "true" and whose are "magic." The way to protect religious traditions from the charge of "magic" is to drop the supernaturalism and take sacramental practices as an element in a theopoetics, like a dramatic performance, a "theodrama."

I am not saying that all religious traditions at bottom say the same thing or share a common essence. I think they are irreducibly different. Sometimes the differences are about matters we can rationally debate, like the treatment of women, and when they are, we can argue and see if we can learn from one another. But the deeper differences are the differences of different paths, standpoints, and attitudes toward things as a whole and on this level are largely incommensurable. These differences cut deeper than the question of evidence for propositional beliefs or differences of opinion about where certain ethical practices will take us. I think there is something to be gained from exposing them to each other, in the hospitality each extends to the other. I endorse Richard Kearney's image of a scene in which Jesus and Buddha meet and bow to each other in a respectful expectation of hoping to learn from each other.[33] But nothing is to be gained from fusing traditions into a common essence or treating them as different versions of the same thing, in the mode of classical comparative religion, or ranking them in terms of true religion and the rest, even in the spirit of generosity subscribed to by the other contributors to the present volume, who admit that not everybody gets everything right or wrong while reserving for themselves the right to be right about the most important things. I do not think genuine pluralism comes at the cost of truth but rather that religion pluralism is the form truth takes. The pluralization or multiplication of truth, the multiple forms of religious truth, is the form the event takes. The truth of the event is the multiple and irreducible truth of a poetics, even if saying this is not going to get me elected President of the Society of Christian Philosophers.

Metaphysics

Simmons thinks I am doing a covert metaphysics, so let me say a word about metaphysics. Before Kant "metaphysics" represented a kind of final word about the nature of things in themselves, a highest science, not in the modern epistemological sense of the science of science (*Wissenschaftslehre*), which is what it became in Kant, but in the classical sense as the logos of the really real, the word itself about how things really are. Kant showed that every time someone made a metaphysical move of the classical sort, it was possible to construct an equally persuasive argument that things were not that way at all, that in fact they were completely the opposite. If that is so, how is it that people would come to decide on one side or the other of two equally probative but antinomical arguments? That, said Kant, is decided by one's "interests." Fichte followed up this point by saying that while determinist materialism and idealist freedom fought to a speculative draw, the actual choice between them was made by the character of one's will, whether one had a heart for moral combat or one were willing to reduce one's will to a wheel in a turning machine. That is pretty much what the other contributors to this volume think. Since classical metaphysical arguments all result in a speculative draw, my colleagues here cannot be proven wrong in holding themselves the beneficiaries of an exclusive revelation deposited in their laps by being born Christians, a choice they make on the grounds of their interests, that they would rather be Christ-like than Nietzsche-like. I object to the "exclusive" bit because I think it is an illusion that can lead to inhospitality and bloodshed, and this potentiality is my interest. My colleagues in this volume certainly share this interest, but their answer is to try to blend privileged access with hospitality to the unprivileged. I think we can do better than that.

In general Kant's critique has held up and only a minority of major philosophers still try their hand at metaphysics, although there is a growing movement among younger continentalists today to return to metaphysics under the impetus of Badiou and Meillassoux, but this a highly materialistic metaphysics. The most notable up until now have been the process metaphysicians, Whitehead and his followers in the United States and Bergson and Deleuze in France. But in my opinion, if we look closely at theologies that come equipped with a metaphysics, what they offer us in fact turns out to be a "metadiscourse." A metadiscourse is the overarching story that a community tells itself when its members try to work out the community line. It is their (local) big story, the account they tell one another about how things "are." Up to a point, I think that is fair enough, as long as they admit they are just explaining things to themselves and do not entertain the illusion that anyone outside the community is going to buy it.

That explains why the metaphysics of Thomas Aquinas—if I may introduce a Catholic into this rather Protestant assembly—has almost without exception remained the private property of Catholic Christians and is rarely examined elsewhere except as an object of historical study. Practically no one outside that community buys it, despite the assurance of every pope from Leo XIII to Benedict XVI that it is all a matter of "reason." John Paul II penned an encyclical entitled *Fides et Ratio* (1998) which proclaims to the city (maybe) and the world (no chance), *Urbi et Orbi,* that Christianity (well, Catholicism) is the true faith (that is the "*fides*" part), while the philosophical metadiscourse Catholics favor when they articulate their faith (Thomistic metaphysics) is "reason" itself (*et ratio*). In general, I am not to be numbered among those who were reassured by this encyclical! Of course, the metaphysical arguments embedded in the extensive writings of Thomas Aquinas represent a majestic, subtle, and interesting account of the nature of things from a Catholic Christian point of view. I grew up with Aquinas and wrote a book about him.[34] But the claim that this is "reason" itself—rather than a pretty good reason that a particular community of Christians chiefly of the Catholic flavor give themselves to go along with their faith in Catholicism—is dead on arrival with virtually everybody else. Aquinas employs a strictly local, premodern, and highly teleological sense of "reason" that goes along with a number of largely dualistic assumptions inherited from the metaphysics of Plato, Aristotle, Augustine, and Neoplatonism about time and eternity, body and soul, etc. One of the evolving features of the work of John Milbank is the regrettable tendency he shows nowadays to speak less of a Christian "metadiscourse," as he did in *Theology and Social Theory,* where he was trying to take seriously the Hegelian point that historicality goes all the way down, and more and more of the (medieval) "metaphysics" of Aquinas, albeit with a controversial spin.[35]

Those who want to put out a larger story that will be accepted beyond the borders of the local community do have a few good choices. They might make a contribution to "world literature" that will outlast them and their times, because great literature has a way of slipping past the guards of doctrine and getting at the events behind religious positions. Or, if they do not feel quite up to that, they might do well to follow Heidegger's turn to phenomenology, which Heidegger conceived as a means of thinking Being while "overcoming metaphysics," or the later Merleau-Ponty's radical meditation upon the "flesh of the world." Heidegger's idea of "overcoming metaphysics" (rationalism) and overcoming "humanism" (anthropocentrism) had a mystical and religious tonality that appeals to theologians.[36] In fact, it was one of the discourses Derrida mentioned when he spoke of "religion without religion," that is, a discourse that reproduces religion but without the dogmas of religion.[37] The religious philosopher who was the most serious about taking Heidegger's advice to turn to phenomenology as a way to "overcome metaphysics" is Jean-Luc Marion. Marion puts phenomenology in the service of the mystical *sans* or *sine* that was the subject of my first book, *The Mystical Element in Heidegger's Thought*.[38] Unfortunately, Marion and the school that has formed around him (and their common ancestor Michel Henry), by whom some authors in this volume are impressed, have produced a phenomenology of such a transparently confessional sort that its central features stand no chance of making sense to anyone who is not a Christian. Not even Milbank puts any stock in it.[39] While this school is intent on "overcoming metaphysics," it simply reproduces in phenomenology the same dead end of being a strictly local discourse driven by the same local confessional interests. It faces the same problems as Pope's claim that Thomistic metaphysics is "reason" itself. That fodder is purely for local consumption; it is strictly a phenomenology for Catholic campfires. Nobody outside the community circle is about to swallow it, which is the fatal shortcoming in the "new phenomenology," a shortcoming that my fellow contributors to the present volume should face up to. To boast that today phenomenology in France is "Catholic" is to announce that today in France phenomenology is a cul-de-sac, that nobody except Catholics do phenomenology any longer.[40] It is to the credit of the present contributors that they want to expose continental and analytic philosophers to their mutual other. But even if they succeed in doing this, still, by continuing to think within the frameworks of a Christian apologetics, they are constructing a conversation to which no one who is not Christian is going to pay any heed. We radical theologians have a wider aim.

But Simmons still thinks I am doing metaphysics, a bad and negative metaphysics, making a negative ontological argument against the God of metaphysics. He thinks I am a bad Kantian, speaking about the *Ding an sich* after I promised not to, by saying or strongly suggesting that there is no God, which is what Jacques Derrida thinks. While I am certainly not doing metaphysics, I do think that some notions of God are better than others and I certainly am trying to make the traditional Augustinian God look bad as a phenomenological matter and I have good reasons for doing this. I hold that the name of "God," what we in the Abrahamic traditions call "God," is as deconstructible as any other name. Given the way that signifiers work, every signifier is deconstructible, historically constituted in historical languages according to linguistic rules, recontextualizable, substitutable, and so on. We cannot stop the process at one name and declare it a transcendental signified which stands as an exception—whether that name be "God," "Love," "Justice," the "Church," the "Party," "Capitalism," "Democracy," and the like—and declare it off limits. When someone claims to have a transcendental signified, they are not pointing out where the play of signifiers stops; they are just telling us where they stop. But as Žižek says, the therapy is over when you realize there is no Big Other. This is not to say deconstruction is a Big No. No, no, it is a double affirmative, a *oui, oui,* and that *oui oui* goes hand in with a crucial *peut-être,* a perhaps, which is also not a no.

So I am not a bad Kantian but a good (heretical) Hegelian and (heretical) phenomenologist. I think that whenever religious "revelations" come adorned with "metaphysical" explications, they run into the problems that Kant points out, so that metaphysics ends up being the meta-discourse of the local community, with no credibility outside the community (*Extra ecclesiam nulla credibilitas est!*). As Simmons points out, I have argued in two different papers on

Merold Westphal's work, which I have been privileged to present, that Westphal's adaptation of postmodernism is strictly epistemological in a Kantian mode.[41] That does not make my position metaphysical by contrast. The contrast, as I see it, is between an epistemological position that makes use of an abridged version of deconstruction and other postmodern resources, the strategically limited and apologetic use we find in Simmons and Westphal, and an unabridged version, a deconstructive-phenomenological one. But I have taken pains to make plain that there is nothing about deconstruction that would permit one either to affirm (Reformed Epistemology) or deny (Martin Hägglund) the existence of God in the metaphysical sense either of a supersensible personal causal being of the sort found in Augustine or Aquinas or in the more heterodox panentheistic traditions of process metaphysics. I simply say that there are no such proofs that cannot be countered with counterproofs in just the way Kant predicted. So successful have I been in denying that one could deny such a being that Martin Hägglund has attacked me for mounting a defense of the existence of God in its classical Augustinian version. Perhaps the best thing for me to do is get Simmons and Hägglund in the same room and engage them in an intellectual shootout in which each finishes off the other (in a strictly intellectual sense, that is).

I do not think there is anything about deconstruction as a body of theory that refutes the existence of the God of Augustine in a metaphysical sense. I think deconstruction makes it look bad, but I do not think, as a methodological matter, it "refutes" it. Deconstruction is an account of how things are constructed in the first place, that is, constituted in the spacing and timing of *différance*, and as such it is both incapable of and has no interest in declaring that nothing happens outside space and time. It is restricted to pointing out, as Heidegger did, that "outside" space and time is itself a construction constituted within and by means of space and time and that anything we might have to *say* about such a sphere is subject to the conditions of space and time, so that as soon as we *do* say something of that sort, that *saying* is subject to *différance* and hence deconstruction. But I think Aquinas would say something like that, too, on the basis of Aristotle and the primacy of the sensible order as the basis of speaking about the supersensible. The difference is that this is not merely an epistemological point but a phenomenological one.

That is, deconstruction says that like any ideal object these are constituted effects, effects of *différance,* and we have no reason or grounds
for saying that they precede their constitution.

Deconstruction is a "how" and as such it has been put to use by
others in a way that is quite consistent with orthodox Christianity.[42]
I am thinking in particular of an intensely careful and good reader of
Jacques Derrida like Kevin Hart. Hart once asked Derrida about the
"gift" of "theological faith" made possible by "sanctifying grace" in
Catholic theology. Derrida said that "deconstruction has no lever on
this." That is, it has no leverage, no authority, no basis for affirming
or denying it. "In relation to this experience of faith, deconstruction
is totally, totally useless and disarmed," and that is not a weakness in
deconstruction because such a faith belongs to the structure of the
Kierkegaardian "secret." But Derrida went on to add that deconstruction has something to say only when this faith begins to speak,
when it becomes a discourse, an institution, a theology, a church,
for all such constructions are deconstructible.[43] But let us look more
carefully at this how/what distinction.

The "How" and the "What"

Simmons is complaining that there is a surreptitious slipping from
the "how" to the "what" in my work since it is obvious that *I think*
the God of Augustinian metaphysics (a *what*) is clearly not a good
idea and that I strongly recommend giving it up in *The Weakness of
God* for another weaker "what," so to speak, the subject of a (weak)
theology, which is also what interests Minister. That is all true and
this is what Simmons wants me to explain, because he thinks I am
blurring the distinction between the how and the what and making it impossible to use deconstruction and be an orthodox Christian. Simmons is raising an important point. I have indeed moved
from the how to the what, and this certainly needs to be clarified,
and that can be seen in the fact that, unlike *The Prayers and Tears of
Jacques Derrida* (1997), and this is important, *The Weakness of God*
(2004) is not a book about Jacques Derrida. It is about God. There
I am engaged in what is nowadays called in the American Academy of
Religion (with or without the capital letters) "constructive theology"
or what we Derridean-types would call a "repetition" of theology

conducted *without* the supervision of ecclesiastical authorities, one of the most precious senses of *sans* that I can think of!

So here I can kill two birds with one stone, so to speak, that is, answer both Simmons on the how/what, and Minister on calling this "theology." Let us differentiate three levels of discourse. (1) The first-order beliefs and practices of the concrete historical religious communities and their theological conceptualization, the confessional theologies that I label "strong" theology. This is a "what," let us say, the "first what." (2) The second-order body of theory found in deconstruction, which is metadiscursive, a discourse about beliefs and practices. Deconstruction in and of itself, if there is such a thing, is a "how." (3) Then there is *doing* deconstruction, what one does with it, which produces a wide range of unprogrammable results. There are first the authorial results, what Derrida himself did with it, which was to produce a concretely identifiable contextually embedded body of work where this body of theory is deployed in specific analyses of works of art, literature, philosophy, architecture, laws, politics, and so on—including religion. That concrete body of work I call still another concrete messianism, meaning that it represents a particular actualization of deconstruction by Derrida himself. Then there are the death-of-the-author effects, the work done with deconstruction by others, putting it to work in ways that Derrida did not, the repetition of deconstruction, where deconstruction achieves iterability, twisting free from Jacques Derrida himself. That is where *The Weakness of God* belongs, as does Hägglund's *Radical Atheism*. As regards Christian theology, *The Weakness of God* constitutes a kind of "second" what, a "weak" theology, a "repetition" of Christianity, a deconstructive reopening of Christianity.

In Jacques Derrida, the theoretic impulses of deconstructive analysis are enmeshed with his own interests as a particular person living in a particular time and place. In the *Weakness of God* those impulses are enmeshed with my interests and concerns, and hence are brought to bear upon certain salient biblical texts, both Jewish and Christian, and the mainstream Christian theological tradition, in a way not found in Derrida, but which Derrida himself welcomed.[44] This issues in what the AAR calls "constructive theology," a version of what we used to call "philosophical theology" and what I like to call a "weak" theology. I call it weak, first, because it represents a nondogmatic repetition of theology in terms of the weakness of events rather than strong superbeings like "God" (what Derrida calls the "unconditional without sovereignty") and, second, because, in taking its cue from the event that bears the name of Jesus, it is a theology of "weak" moves like forgiveness rather than retaliation.

So I am in this very precise way both making propositional assertions (which are not metaphysical assertions) and doing theology. I maintain the Scriptures are to be construed as a theopoetics and not as providing a series of propositional assertions. Of course, maintaining that claim is an assertion, which I defend. In setting forth deconstructive theory one makes numerous propositional assertions about language, history, time, etc. although—in order to bear witness to itself—that constative mode of exposition typical of "philosophy" or "theory" that deconstruction tends to take at this level must be constantly upset or offset by performative, or perverformative, interventions that signify there can be no pure theory. *The Weakness of God* is found on the third level, where there are plenty of propositional assertions but the heart of it is to *do* a theopoetics, to *produce* a performative theopoetic effect, to *repeat* Christianity, the event that is harbored in Christianity, with results likely to scandalize the orthodox since I am trying to talk the orthodox out of Augustinian Christianity. In that sense it certainly is a theology made up of intentional acts (in the Husserlian sense) directed at events, a theology of events, which is what I said in my subtitle, but I need ways to keep it clear of strong or confessional theology. It is, accordingly, also a certain and more complex second "what," a second theology. Second theology is a ghost that haunts first theology—like those annoying "ghosts" we used to see on the old CRT screens picking up faint signals through its "antennas"—keeping orthodoxy up at night, worrying it half to death that this is "what" is going on words like "God," "theology," and "Jesus." By inscribing these words in the play of traces—and not "simply" settling for a negative theology that happily concedes our finitude and God's infinity—deconstruction taken in its full-throated sense unsettles orthodoxy in a way orthodoxy finds intolerable, whereas negative theology is ultimately orthodox. If you keep those three levels of discourse separate, you will find I have not violated the trust shown in me by my logic teachers.

As to Augustinian Christianity, I try to discourage it. I think that it is dualistic and inevitably caught up in a denigration of the "flesh," that it is a kind of soft Gnosticism at odds with a theology of In-*carn*-ation. I think that Augustine's God belongs to a two-worlds theory inherited from Neoplatonism, and hence to a dualism of time and eternity, body and soul, and that the whole thing leaves us up to our ears in problem-of-evil-paradoxes. I think that without a radical theology of events it cannot finally be cleanly insulated from "magic." Without a theology of events, without getting rid of the propositional theory of religious beliefs, what is a "miracle" in the Christian tradition will be "magic" in another tradition (and conversely); what is an "icon" in Christianity will be an "idol" in another tradition (and conversely), even if for reasons of "charity" and "tolerance" some Christians may actually refrain from saying so out loud. I do not think one can honestly admit the sacramentality of practices in other traditions when you think, as a matter of propositional truth, that sacramental power in invested in the apostolic succession within Christianity. I think Christians are just being polite (when they are polite) in not saying so. But I concede that Kant is right, you cannot settle metaphysical debates, and so I concede that there is no stopping someone from holding views like these (the way you cannot stop someone from believing in alien abductions). All you can do is try to discourage such views by making them look bad and by offering a more cogent alternative, a way of reimagining God and reinventing Christianity, of thinking the event that is harbored in the name of God and Jesus, which is what we radical theologians are trying to do by seducing the orthodox with a "theopoetics" of "events."[45]

So I think that the force and tendency of full-throated deconstruction is to lure us away from orthodoxy and to encourage us to reimagine God, to give "God" and "Jesus" a future that will make the orthodox nervous, to inhabit orthodoxy from within and reinvent it, letting it reconfigure without the Neoplatonic metaphysics and without the supervision of hierarchical authority, whether the latter originates in Nashville or the Vatican. But if you are hell-bent (so to speak) on orthodoxy, you will likely cherry pick postmodern theory and retreat into treating it as an epistemology, backing off from the post-Hegelian claim that it is a comprehensive quasi-phenomenological reinterpretation of experience and the Derridean reinscription of Christianity in the play of traces. Then you will have missed the opportunity presented by postmodern theory to expose what is going on in Christianity to the event by which it is nourished, which means

to expose it to its future. Then this attachment to propositional correctness will have proven to be a block to thinking and to questioning
another "truth," just as continentalists from Heidegger on have been
predicting.

Consider just two of the effects of allowing the camel nose of
deconstruction under the tent of orthodoxy. First, even from a strictly
Scriptural point of view, Augustinian metaphysics is foreign to the
Hebraic world to which Jesus in particular belonged whereas deconstruction (which has Jewish ancestors) is an invitation to rethink that
God in more time-bound and earth-bound ways, a lot more like the
earthy terms in which the Jewish Scriptures thought. Jesus knew
nothing of the Greek theory of the immortality of the soul adopted
by Augustine and the tradition of Christian metaphysics, but he
shared the faith of the second Temple Jews in the resurrection of the
body. Secondly, as N. T. Wright has shown, the rule of God that was
expected by the early Christian communities from which the New
Testament emerged meant that Jesus would come back down to *earth*
and *stay here,* where he would preside as Lord—not abide on high in
a Platonic eternity. Deconstruction would move Christian theology a
good deal closer to its Scriptural moorings on both those points, to
thinking in terms of space and time, the body and the earth.

Second, deconstruction would encourage theology to undertake
micrological histories of the multiplicity of Christianities—the best
way to deconstruct something is to write a microhistory of its construction—of the multiple and diverse communities that grew up
under the impact of the event that took place in Jesus, long before the
church became a corporation, before it adopted the imperial structure of Rome and the language in which Jesus was condemned to
death, long before "orthodoxy" tried to boil down the event that
took place in multiple, diverse and endlessly autodeconstructive
forms. That provides an entrée for Pentecostalism. Far be it from me
to tell Evangelical or Pentecostal Christians what their business is, but
it seems to me that what deconstruction does is encourage them to be
even *more Pentecostal.* After all, my affection for hauntology is happy
to cohabit with ghosts, including holy ones. Deconstruction would
encourage loose communities without community, not as propo-
sitionally stabilized in C-beliefs, but more open-ended and "Holy-
Ghost driven," as "The Apostle E. F." says in the Robert Duvall film

The Apostle. Deconstruction would return us to the uncontainable "events" by which Christian life is nourished and endlessly reinvented in innumerable "scribblings"[46] (unregulated sayings, texts, practices, liturgies, and spontaneous para-liturgies in free assemblies unregulated by an ecclesiastical hierarchy), before they were strangled by heresiology, before they were collapsed, condensed, contained, and congealed into propositions that bore the seal of the corporation. It would encourage them to return to these events and reinvent Christianity, repeat it, as must be done again and again in any living tradition, and forget about trying to exercise an epistemological supervision that seeks to contain events with C-beliefs. Far be it from an Italian Catholic from Philadelphia to tell Simmons (who is from Tennessee) what Pentecostalism is, but is his abridged version of deconstruction not a sustained missed opportunity—for Pentecostals? Deconstruction would encourage the faithful to pay attention to events and to lay off the metaphysics. Deconstruction would open up a play of traces, an imaginative and liturgical play that would take place without the propositional police. It would keep the future open in the only way that a future can really be open, can really be a future, that is, by putting itself at risk, which is impossible when propositions hold sway over the experiences of which they are the secondary articulation. That would be my contribution to the cause of Parisian Pentecostalism.

But, after pointing all this out, it would remain true that there is nothing in deconstruction that would actually *refute* Augustine's metaphysical God. That does not represent an "exclusionary" gesture toward metaphysics but a rebuttal of it, first, on Kantian grounds (its antinomies), and second by trying to make it look bad on deconstructive-phenomenological grounds and so giving some good reasons to kick this metaphysical habit.

As Merold Westphal likes to say, postmodernism reminds us that we are not God and that we do not take on divine powers by believing in God. Amen to that. That should be posted on every billboard in the Bible Belt. But we already knew that without deconstruction. Deconstruction goes on to add that "God" is not God, that the name of God is, like other every name, inscribed in the play of traces, which as I read them is the point at which Simmons and Westphal drop out of the parade. What is called "God" in the Jewish, Christian, and Islamic tradition of monotheism is an historically constituted and deconstructible name, as subject to an endless play of substitution as any other name, so that we do not know what we mean when we speak of God. That "God" is not God was already recognized in apophatic theology, when Meister Eckhart said he prayed God to rid him of "God."[47] But while the pope concluded that there is something unnerving to orthodoxy in what Meister Eckhart was saying, and he was right, apophatic theology for its part is actually trying to be reassuring. It is trying to say that God is greater than "God," that God is even more than anything we call "God," so that the deconstruction of the name of God in apophatic theology is a form of praise, a way to affirm the hypereminence of the *hyperousion,* of the Godhead beyond God.

But the deconstruction of the name of God in deconstruction is undertaken in a less reassuring manner than in apophatic theology, a more unnerving "khoral" sense than negative theology is prepared for. What we are calling God, what we are affirming in and under the name of God, is exposed to the play of traces; it may go under other names; it promises something which is promised but not being delivered in the name of God, and what it promises is also a threat. We did not need deconstruction to instruct us that we are not God. That is certainly true as far as it goes and I will vote for it every time it is put on the floor for adoption. But it does not go very far. Not only because it does not go as far as deconstruction, as if that were some kind of end in itself, but because it does not go as far as the things themselves, as far as we are pressed by the things themselves. It is a question of going as far as one "needs" only if one's purposes are merely apologetic. In philosophy, it a question of going as far as one has to, as far as we are driven to go by *die Sache selbst,* as far as the autodeconstructibility in our beliefs and practices takes us, as far as we are taken by the event, whether we want to go there or not, whether we like it or not, even if it is a disruptive force at Pentecostal suppers. It is a question of trying to get to the bottom of things (which is not the same as foundationalism), which is what genuine philosophical questioning is all about. It is a question of releasing a "Christianity" to come, which I think is genuinely unnerving to orthodoxy, whose concern to protect the Christianity that "is," that pretends to "be." The metaphysically infinite personal causal being of orthodoxy is *finite* by the standards of deconstruction, a limited region in the infinite play of traces. This "necessary being" refuses the "impossible." It is an historical construction that is being protected from the radical future that puts it at risk, by going to a place where "metaphysical," "infinite," "personal," "causal," and "being" would all be displaced, and that is a place that apophatic theology itself will not go. Deconstruction means to go where you cannot go, to the impossible.

Simmons plants his feet firmly on the ground of a classical Christian faith and invokes postmodern theories as far as they are useful to him in an apologetic effort to defend a propositional digest of his faith against critique. He begins with a position and calls up the troops of postmodernism to defend its propositions. I do not object to that as far as it goes, but I think we should go further, because I think it is too local a movement. The opposite movement, beginning from experience itself, is more radical and wide-ranging, not because it takes flight from the local and determinate, but because it acknowledges the multiplicity of the local, of the multiple "heres" in any "here I stand." But I am on record as saying that we would all be better off, and Christianity would be better served, if every Christian would do at least that much, if every Christian were at least minimally Westphalian, putting an end to religious wars by signing a Westphalian treaty, adopting postmodernism in the abridged version, which disposes of fundamentalism and the worst forms of intolerance. If that were the most conservative version of Christianity around, we would be far better off than with what presently calls itself conservative Christian faith. If you insist on having an apologetics, at least it is a postmodern version of apologetics. But it is apologetics nonetheless.

I am making a plea to go further. I find it amusing that in the abridged version, postmodernism is a sinner—but that would mean that it is something with which Jesus would have associated—that is, it is shrunk down to a "hamartiology," as Simmons says, a delimitation of the inability of our fallen-by-sin faculties to get to the truth. I reject that for two reasons. First, the limits under which we labor are hermeneutical, not sinful (that is such a distressingly Augustinian lament). They are well described by Aristotle when he explains that all the knowledge we embodied beings have is gathered from the sensible world in which we are firmly planted with all its attendant limitations, which is why Heidegger's "hermeneutics of facticity" started out as a commentary on Aristotle, not on original sin. Second, this is just too grim, too Calvinist, a view to take of deconstruction, for the latter has the twinkle of an impudent rabbi in its eye. Deconstruction is affirmation; deconstruction is love; deconstruction is justice—that joyful wisdom is where I start. So deconstruction is to be read in conjunction with the "good, good" of the first creation story (the one the redactors put first), not the bad, bad of the second one, which has won the sad swooning hearts of the Calvinists. That being said, I have always maintained that deconstruction is "bad" in the Michael Jackson sense, diabolically and sinfully impudent—particularly in the face of orthodoxy.

By sticking to a thin rather than a robust version of deconstruction, the abridged version fails to expose Christianity to the truth of the event, to the event of truth. It starts and stops with an untranslatable term, asserts a name above every other name, and puts a transcendental stop to the chain of translatability or substitution, for which there is no philosophical warrant. It does not show that the play of signifiers stops here; it shows that I stop here. It announces a conversation stopper but it does not stop the play of signifiers. It simply says, I am starting, stopping and standing here, *hier ich stand, ich kann nicht anders.* But that is not good enough. Maybe I cannot do otherwise but what is it to say that something other cannot do otherwise in me. Wishing to stay here does not make it so. It does not hold up; it does not arrest the play—just like when Luther said "here I stand," the earth (and Luther with it) kept on moving. It is not up to Simmons or Westphal, or to Kierkegaard or Luther, or to Derrida or me to arrest the play. The "here I stand" sounds pretty undeconstructible, until one recognizes the irreducible universalizability of "here," as Hegel said, or until one realizes, as Husserl pointed out so dispassionately, were I there, "there" would be "here," which is an "imaginative variation," as he put it so dryly, that rocks our world. Luther should have added, here I stand *now*, and I do not in any deep way know where I am going, no more than when he took his first here-I-stand stand, when he professed his "vows" as an Augustinian friar, did he know where he would stand later on, when he had to "take back" his resolution (religious vows) in order to stick to his resolve (reformation), which he himself called a *destructio*, which is probably where Heidegger got the word *Destruktion*, which is where Derrida got the word *déconstruction*.[48]

The play is inscribed in the discourse, in the beliefs and the practices, in the texts and the institutions, in the historical coming to be and passing away, in the endless recontextualizability, in the play of traces, in which "Christianity" too is inscribed, which poses the possibility of a Christianity to come and what Derrida calls the coming God. That is why we speak of autodeconstructibility. No one, not even himself (Jacques Derrida), nor anyone else, deconstructs anything; things are autodeconstructing and deconstructors are at best good detectives or the first reporters on the scene. As contingently woven complexes or constructions, the concrete and determinate are deconstructible; what comes to be may pass away. When I say that the name of God cannot be protected from endless substitutability I am not saying that the God of Saint Augustine cannot exist. I am saying that the belief (*croyance*) that takes the form of what the monotheisms call "God" in their metaphysical theologies cannot be protected from the chain of substitutions and insulated with a lining of exclusivity, and that that metaphysical discourse is getting away from the event that takes place in Yeshuah, a name I favor because it defamiliarizes the overwrought name of Jesus. Getting clear about that can only get done in radical theology. We cannot issue a special exemption to the name of God, or Jesus or the Holy Spirit, and hold them exempt from translatability, or recontextualizability, no matter how deeply underground, and no matter under how many rhetorical layers of "concrete and determinate," we try to plant it.

A/theology

The missed opportunity in Simmons's essay is nowhere more palpable than in his treatment of Derrida's atheism, where there is a detectable indignation typical of the scene *before* Derrida and Levinas opened the way to a new way to think about religion, before the "without." Of course Jacques—actually the name on his passport was "Jackie"—Derrida is, by the standards of the local rabbi (or Pentecostal preacher), an "atheist." I think there is an interesting case to be made that Levinas was, too.[49] Derrida tells us that he stopped accepting the Jewish "faith" (*croyance*) of his childhood home when he came of age as a philosophy student in Paris, that he stopped observing Passover in his earliest visits to New York City, that he married a gentile woman and his sons were not circumcised. *That atheism is all part of his path, part of his faith.* In any given situation that would be the common background assumption of the leftish French intellectuals among whom he spent his life, just the way "Jesus is our personal savior" is an unexpressed background assumption at Pentecostal suppers. That is hardly worth remarking.[50] In his early writings, he tended mostly—and this is far from simple[51]—to treat the name of God as the paradigmatic example of a transcendental signified (a conversation stopper). What is far more interesting is what Derrida said when he *thematized* the name of God. In the early works, this occurs in quite exotic ways, but the later works contain a number of haunting reflections in which (under the influence in part of Levinas) the older man, recalling his origins in a Jewish home in Algeria, repeats his beginnings. (Don't we all!) In so doing he helped create the environment ("open the space," as we say in continentalese) in which the present volume itself works. He began to "think" (in the transitive sense) the "name of God," to "save/except" the name of God (*sauf le nom*). But that, too, is too simple, for this meditation, it turns out, is not just "late," but goes all the way back to a very early exchange he had with a young Jewish Algerian woman (also an "atheist"), who sent him the manuscript of her first book, *Le prénom de dieu*, in which the two meditated upon how this name fluctuates between a proper name and common noun, in which, I am tempted to say, all the mysteries of the present debate are condensed about whether and how anyone other than Christians speaks truly of "God." The exchange between these two young *pieds noirs*, Algerian French-speaking Jewish atheists, Jackie Derrida and Hélène Cixous, was a brilliant beginning of what I regard as a meditation upon the event that is unfolding in the name of God, upon what is happening in that name, whether or not one puts any stock in what is happening in a synagogue, church or mosque, one that shows the way for theology to reinvent itself.[52]

Simmons misses the opening lodged in Derrida's remark that "I quite rightly pass for an atheist"—symbolize *that*—a wonderfully nuanced comment in which Derrida declines to say outright that he *is* an atheist—*c'est moi, je suis*—a point upon which I and others loved to press him. "Why do you put it this way?" we asked him. "Because I do not know if I really *am* an atheist," he said. Why not? Because he was at odds with himself, not identical *with* himself, because beneath the (pro)positional reports made by the "ego" (*je suis, c'est moi*), behind its closed doors, there sat a disputatious committee that gave him no peace, in which the position of one is contested by the oppositions of the others.[53] The things that I will I do not, the things that I do I will not. The very structure of my heart is restless with a desire beyond desire, so that I am dissatisfied with satisfaction and satisfied only by dissatisfaction, as Mark Taylor says. *Quaestio mihi factus magna sum.* One of the things that interests me about religion is that great religious geniuses like Paul, Augustine, Pascal, and Kierkegaard have been much more keenly conscious of the restless, unsettled, and unclear heart than are the philosophers who, in an effort to make things clear, make the mistake of thinking that things are clear.

In one of the countless conferences over the years that I have had the pleasure to attend with Merold Westphal, someone who evidently did not know him well asked him if he were a Christian. With characteristic wit Merold answered without missing a beat, "I rightly pass for one." I do not know if he ever worked this out in print, but his answer took the form of an exquisitely Derridean formula. He did not mean that sometimes he is confused with a Hindu but that he is doing his best to become a Christian. So this formula is also exquisitely Kierkegaardian—which is why I sometimes speak of Danish deconstruction—like that of Johannes Climacus, who declined to accept the honor of *being* a Christian and said he was spending his life trying to become one, trying to get as far as faith. What is going on in this expression is that Christian *croyance* is here structurally exposed to a deeper *foi*. On another occasion, when we were presenting together, I asked Merold if, having now found it necessary to deny knowledge to make room for faith, it would in principle be possible that at some point in the future he would find it necessary to relinquish his Christian faith, and he said he certainly could not exclude that possibility in principle. That means that what would rightly pass for a "lost" faith (*croyance*), here and now, would then and there be viewed as a step forward, so that the change of course in *croyance* would represent a painful movement forward in *foi*. He could foresee such a move in principle, however improbable in fact, without a loss of face or *foi*, and no one who knows him would think the less of him. In my rewrite of the Kantian formula, he would find it necessary to delimit *croyance* in order to make room for *foi*. Or as Heidegger said, the necessity of staying underway, of staying resolute, requires the possibility of taking back a given resolution.

The whole idea behind the event is that something is being affirmed in the beliefs to which we assent and the practices we embrace, and that affirmation is advanced even with, or rather precisely by, shifts in our beliefs and practices, which are occurring and must be able to occur without doing injury to the deeper affirmation by which we are constituted. Christian belief is a historically constituted and constructed complex which is structurally revisable, reformable, and deconstructible, all with a view to what it is being affirmed there. What is affirmed is its event. What is that event? An inner impulse, not an overarching transcendental condition; a pulsating desire, not a regulative ideal. I have tried to sketch the phenomenology of its form of life in the second half of *The Weakness of God*, which I treated in terms of what I called "weak" forces like forgiveness, hospitality, and the simple joys of everyday time emblematized under the figure of the lilies of the field. But the deeper point is that I do not know what the event is, or if there is *one*, which is to say that I do not know what I desire, what I desire with a desire beyond desire. Beyond any given assignable and identifiable desire I do not know what is finally being desired in this desire, and that is the defining stuff of the human venture, the definition being undefining and unconfining, what Augustine called the *cor inquietum*. The point is not to reduce the *foi* to the *croyance* but to allow the *croyance* to tremble in the winds of the affirmation by which it is carried, which is also the air it breathes, and to understand that there are multiple *croyances*, and that as Husserl said, "were I there, 'there' would be 'here.'" Were I there—born in another time or place or both, were I at another time or place in my own life—"there" would be "here," with no necessary loss of face or *foi*.

This is all a way of saying that the most interesting outcome of deconstruction for this debate is to undermine the distinction between theism and atheism, which is relegated to a polemics, a competition among apologists, a debate about positions and how one positions oneself, about whether (right now) one is here or there, about what position one has here or now but not about justice, joy, or desire. It is for the most part a tiresome and to me, at least, a not very interesting debate, which is superseded as soon as its terms are more closely scrutinized, and as soon as one appreciates that the best answer one can give to such positional interrogations is that one rightly passes for one or the other. Johannes Climacus said the name of God is the name of a deed, so that a bishop or a theologian with his positional and propositional ducks in order but who leads a corrupt life has not understood the name of God, has not grasped *what is going on* in the name of God (the event), as opposed to a person of simple and completely unlearned faith who worships a graven image in spirit and in truth. I am reminded of the admiration expressed for Albert Camus—another Algerian atheist who wrote about Augustine—by a very young Michael Novak. (Somebody should write a book about the religious genius of Algerian atheists.) Novak, who was once a member of a radical religion department at Syracuse University before he switched "positions" with his own conversion (to the Right), wrote about how much Christians had to learn from the (Christian) witness to justice exemplified by the atheist Camus.[54] The sort of truth embodied by biblical texts is witnessed, not verified, as witnessed by the witness/martyr Justin.

Whether or not the affirmation one makes of flesh and the body, of the lilies of the field and the birds of the air, of other animals, our companion species, and of other persons, our human companions, of the worlding of the world in the widest terms—I completely reject the reduction of religion to ethics—whether that affirmation takes place under the name of one or the other of the three great monotheisms, or what is there called "God," or under other names altogether, is a matter of local interest and local practice. I am not saying that local interests or local practices are not important; their importance is to be the actualization of our desire, the existence which our insistence takes. Perhaps Martin Luther King Jr. or Gandhi would not have felt equally summoned to pursue justice without their Hindu or Christian faith—or perhaps they would have. But I am saying such commitments and such faith are not reducible to these beliefs and that these beliefs and practices must be kept open, exposed to the events that they actualize, and that these events have the structure of an open-ended desire and expectation. That is also why "secular" or "atheist" writers like Derrida (or Lyotard or Heidegger) can produce such compelling and unorthodox readings of Augustine's *Confessions,* and why it is really not interesting to point out that these readings diverge from orthodox readings by orthodox theologians, which are more "correct representations" of Augustine. These "atheists" undertake a meditation upon the event that is unfolding in the *Confessions.* That is much more productive than a confessional polemic, an apologetics defending the turf of Christianity. Events are singularities that overtake us in the singularity of our existence, while essences, like the "essence of Christianity" (a short list of enumerable C-assertions), are the subject matter of *croyance.* Without the "without," essences fuel the fires around which communities warm themselves but they also tend to fuel the fires of tribal allegiances and the searing conflicts of tribalism.

At this point, I recommend a reading of the contribution to this volume by Bruce Benson, who is the one writer in the collection who displays a taste for the style of deconstruction, who approaches matters with a deconstructive stylus, where the rhythms of the "without" are detectable and who is not beating tribal drums. Like the "not far," a superbly deconstructive phrase,[55] the response Jesus gives the Scribe, the words of Jesus, Benson shows, are often ambiguous, unsettling, paradoxical, structured by their complexity and tensions, self-disruptive, beset by the ambiguity of translation (including the translation of Aramaic into Greek). Jesus gives us multiple accounts of what we need to do to be saved. We are told that we are personally justified by faith, but the paralytic lowered through the roof is saved by the faith of his friends. The rich young man in Matthew 19 is told to rid himself of his entire fortune, and in Luke 14 we are told that everyone, not just the rich, must give up all their possessions. Zacchaeus, on the other hand, wins approval from Jesus for volunteering to give up only half his possessions. Furthermore, does Jesus mean this literally or could we continue to hold on to our possessions while not being attached to them in our hearts? In still another narrative, Matthew 25, the famous story of giving the master to eat and drink when he was hungry and thirsty, those who do meet this requirement, in perfect accord with Derrida's logic of the gift, did not know they doing any such thing. Add to this mix, as Benson does, how we are to understand the hard sayings, like loving our enemies, not judging others lest we be judged ourselves. The multiplicity and impossibility of the ways to arrive at the Kingdom testify to the point that there is no formula, just because there are too many formulae. The task is not to arrive at the certitude of being a Christian, but, not arriving at all, to stay underway in the task of trying to become one, of rightly passing for one, where the Kingdom is not far away. To that I would only add that what is true within the Christian way is true of the broader multiplicity of ways, of which Christianity is just one way, depending on wherever one happened to be born. The story of giving the other to eat and drink *without* knowing the identity (without knowing the *identity*) of who in fact that other one is, has a special ring of truth, the truth of the "without," of the truth without disclosure, of the phenomenon without phenomenality, of the religion without religion.

Minister's Dangerous Supplement

In Stephen Minister's view, the deconstruction of theology results in another theology but of a thinner and more indeterminate sort. In my view, that is half true. The deconstruction of theology results in a radical theology that spooks the confessional theologies by describing the conditions under which they labor and the ghosts that haunt them. In Minister's view, the deconstruction of ethics results in another ethics, but of a more confused sort. In my view, that is half true. The deconstruction of ethics results in a hyperbolic ethics that describes the conditions under which ethics labors and unsettles its tabulations of good and bad behavior. Minister, Simmons, and I are all agreed about the need to strike the right balance between the "with" and the "without," in theology and ethics, and Minister is trying to help me out. In appreciation of that I will try to help him out, thereby annulling the gift, on five points.

1. *The Pure Messianic*

Before turning to these two issues allow me to single out something I find particularly helpful in his remarks. Simmons poses the central issue for me, whether we start with Christian faith and enlist deconstruction in a subordinate capacity to aid in its defense, or whether we start with the human condition, submit it to a radical analysis, and see Christian faith as a stand taken by some people in the midst of a secret we do not understand, realizing the deep contingency of the stand we have taken. Minister sees this issue clearly and comments on it intelligently in his response. When he says that "the names given to the event are not themselves given by the event, but are *our* response to the event," he sees exactly what is on my mind and condenses the whole issue crisply. I was very pleased indeed to see Minister, at the end of his essay, cite my "A Number of Messianisms" in *Prayers and Tears* (139–43). I would have made this text the point of departure of the analysis, because in it the issue that concerns him and Simmons is addressed directly and in terms that they should have found of some interest, the point of intersection of with and without. Right from the start I expressed concern about Derrida's distinction between the formal messianic and the concrete messianisms, because it too readily conformed to the form/matter, essence/fact distinction. The distinction implies everything that deconstruction is out to deconstruct, and exposes deconstruction to slipping back into a straightforwardly transcendental, rather than quasi-transcendental mode. Of course Derrida himself tried to put this distinction into question, posing to himself a kind of which-came-first question, but his question is too easily answered by an equally classical distinction between the order of knowledge and order of being (*DN* 168–78).

Worst of all, I feared, a distinction like this is just going to fuel the complaint circulating among orthodox confessional theologians that deconstruction dallies with structure without content, with the empty and the indeterminate, and is fearful of the concrete and determinate (exactly the opposite objection inspired by the early Derrida). That complaint I regard as a red herring. To deny that any particular concrete and determinate religious tradition has access to an "exclusive" truth—if you do not believe it, you are wrong or in the dark—that has not been "revealed" to others is not to encourage a love affair with the indeterminate but to embrace the contingency of the determinate and the multideterminate, and it implies a practice of hospitality among the multiple traditions, where traditions are invited not to close themselves off from their own future or from one another. That complaint threatens to become an alibi for confessional theologians to call in sick when asked to deal with deconstruction. I was worried then, and the present volume confirms my worry, that by making this distinction Derrida was bringing this criticism down on his own head. Of course, we should remember that the distinction was meant to apply only to the three religions of the Book, that it was not proposed as the defining mark of "religion" in general (there is none such for Derrida), and in a way had almost the opposite intention, namely to show how porous is the distinction between the religious messianisms and the "philosophical" messianisms of Hegel, Marx, and Heidegger, how easily the messianic migrates between the two, and to show the sense in which they, too, practiced a religion sans the dogmas of the monotheisms.

Given this distinction, I said, deconstruction, too, would have to be counted as another concrete messianism—a fourth (added to the three monotheisms) or a seventh (counting the three philosophical messianisms), viz., the concrete deployment of deconstructive style in concrete circumstances by Derrida and others. That is because, by the very terms of deconstruction, the messianic does not exist. The messianic is an event, an insistence not an existent, neither a being nor a hyperbeing, neither a past-present nor a future present being. The only thing that exists is the concrete messianisms in the sense that the only thing that exists is the particular historical beliefs and practices upon which human communities settle, which form and deform us all, and that goes for deconstruction, too. I do not believe in the existence of the messianic (or of deconstruction, for that matter) but in its insistence. The aporetic situation is that deconstruction is a second-order theory of the messianic, but it also cannot help but be itself another first-order concrete messianism, just by virtue of the fact that you cannot have a pure transcendental disengagement from or reflection upon anything. If on one side deconstruction is a "how," on its other side the particular views, commitments, positions, and dispositions adopted by any given work of deconstructive analysis, any "application" of deconstruction, will always take a concrete form. Of course, the theory/application distinction is eminently deconstructible: one does not apply events to cases; one actualizes events in words and deeds.

That is why I said, and this is a central part of my argument, the "pure" messianic is better regarded as what the young Heidegger called a "formal indicator." Heidegger came up with this idea in connection with his interpretation of Aristotle, where for example the schema of justice that the *phronimos* possesses is considered not as a universal concept under which particular cases are subsumed, but as a potency that is actualized in the concrete performance, where the actualization is higher and more perfect than the schema. That is especially true here, because the coming of the event is the advent of the possible, or rather of the possibility of the impossible that exceeds the horizon of possibility or expectation. Making a first-order religion out of the pure messianic is like a musicologist who would rather study a score than hear the music actually played; but closing off the pure messianic is like claiming that one performance is definitively and exclusively correct. Every performance is haunted by the ghost of alternative performances, of the *tout autre*. In the order of existence, the concrete messianisms are higher and more perfect than the messianic, which is but a weak force, what Derrida calls something "unconditional without force."[56] It a wisp of a thing—a mere ghost—which keeps the messianisms structurally open to what is otherwise. But the pure messianic is higher in the realm of ghosts, where possibility, the ghost of a chance, the *peut-être,* is higher than actuality, especially when it is a question of the possibility of the impossible. (What the young Heidegger calls a formal indicator gets a little more charge if you call it a ghost, a specter.)[57]

2. Hyperbolic Ethics

Minister says that the deconstruction of ethics is an ethics all the same. I say that is half true, that the deconstruction of ethics is at best a hyperbolic ethics, by which I mean an ethics of singularity and responsibility beyond or without ethics in the conventional sense. Ethics wants to know what is good and bad, while hyperbolic ethics is not a theory of the good or of the bad but of our unconditional responsibility to the *tout autre* without (*sans*) knowing whether the other is good or bad. Structurally speaking, the *tout autre* may be an axe murderer or a homeless orphan. The *tout autre* as such is a singularity and a secret about whom we cannot know in advance whether it is good or bad (not until the "moment" of encounter). That is why you will never find me or Derrida saying things like, "the *tout autre* is good" or "the good in itself," as Minister appreciates.

From the *tout autre* no determinate ethical prescriptive can be derived; nothing can be *dérivé* from the *arrivé* (*WWJD*, chap. 2). Deconstruction is not in the business of writing ethical prescriptions. Of itself, it urges responsibility to the singularity of the other. It undertakes multiple strategic reversals, but these are not to be construed as "rules" that the one who is "out" is always "good" or that the one who is "in" is always "bad," which are just more rules and as such would relieve us of our responsibility, which is always singular. In deconstruction, the ethical business of prescriptives has been suspended, but it has not been suspended because deconstruction fails to get as far as ethics but because ethics does not get as far as deconstruction. Deconstruction is not satisfied that responsibility is met by ethics, because in ethics responsibility is not exposed to the impossible. In deconstruction, ethical rule making is suspended for the sake of the impossible. In deconstruction, where everything turns on the impossible, the possible means the same, the regular, the rule bound—not the *tout autre*.

The suspension is teleological and the model is the religious suspension of ethics in *Fear and Trembling*.[58] The role played by the religious for Johannes de Silentio is played by the impossible in Derrida, and that is why for both of these authors ethics is a "temptation." If you turn to ethics in deconstruction, it is because you have suffered a relapse, having turned back from the abyss of the impossible to the *terra firma* of the rules governing possible experience. The reason that deconstruction is structured like a religion is that, like religion, deconstruction turns on the possibility of the impossible, according to which the smooth plane of a normalized and routinized life is disturbed and interrupted by the advent of the impossible. It would take an earthquake (read "event"), Johannes Climacus quipped, to awaken drowsy Christendom from sleeping through the Paradox. That parallelism of the impossible in religion and deconstruction is my central claim. The impossible in Derrida is the subject matter not of a logic or a calculus of the possible, but of a poetics of the impossible, which is not so much a logical contradiction as a dream, while our relation to it is like someone whose eyes are blinded by prayers and tears. That is behind what I am always arguing.

Hyperbolic ethics lies prior to and cuts deeper than garden-variety ethics. That is a lot like Levinas, who while always singing the praises of "ethics" disappoints the "ethicians" by failing to come up with a list of rules and ethical prescriptives and turning instead to the being, or rather the hyperbeing of responsibility. Ethics pursues prescriptive rules meant to manage the fluctuation of factical life and to keep things well within the range of the possible. In hyperbolic ethics, rules are a way to avoid responsibility, to fall back upon the universal, to apologize and say, it's not me, it's just the rules, and I don't make the rules. (Somebody does!) Hyperbolic ethics, on the other hand, pushes beyond the possible, or pushes the possible beyond itself, toward the impossible—the impossible hospitality, forgiveness, love—and ends with a poetics of risk, of the promise/threat, of the impossible. So what you find in hyperbolic ethics is not ethical theorems but hyperbolic evocations and parabolic provocations of the impossible—a point Minister himself recognizes—like the account of pure hospitality or the pure gift, strategic reversals and displacements that display the workings of the impossible in order to displace the workings of the possible, in a way that is strikingly reminiscent of the parables in the New Testament, which would be quite clumsy to transliterate into rules. The moment of decision is constituted by the event, and the event is constituted by its exposure to the impossible, by the solicitation of the impossible that bids the possible beyond itself, lest the moment sink back into the routines of presence, of rule-governed life. The event is always the impossible and hyperbolic ethics is a hyperethics of the event. Hyperbolic ethics is marked by a preferential option for the impossible on the grounds of the *tout autre* character inscribed in everything (*tout autre*)! It undertakes a teleological suspension of the ethical because: (1) the ethical as such is the universal but the *tout autre* is higher than the universal: (2) we have an unconditional responsibility to the *tout autre;* and (3) ethics has to do with disclosedness (transparency) while the *tout autre* is structured by a secret. The attentive reader notices that hyperbolic ethics thus reconstitutes in its own way the three problemata of Johannes de Silentio.[59]

Given that the *tout autre* is *tout autre,* the deconstructive thing to do is to feel about for the possibility of the impossible embedded in the singularity of the encounter. If the *tout autre* turns out to be someone in need, then the deconstructive move is to reinvent the rules of the gift and make an impossible expenditure without return.

If the *tout autre* turns out to be someone bent on doing us harm, then the deconstructive move is to feel around for the impossible thing to do, perhaps to greet aggression with kindness, or forgiveness, or love. There lies the suggestive similarity I see between deconstruction's notion of forgiving the unforgiveable and the Sermon on the Mount's idea of loving those who hate you, or comforting those who have come to harm us. That is why Sister Helen Prejean's *Dead Man Walking* showed up on Derrida's syllabus for his course on capital punishment. It is the same poetics of the impossible at work in both. As Edith Wyschogrod pointed out years ago, this is the poetics of the "saints" who are famous not for keeping the rules of ethics but for being impossible, for making moves beyond the possible, taking *le pas au-delà*. But it is structurally and necessarily the case that we do not know who is coming, and that whatever rules we have acquired up until now will require reinvention, being pushed beyond themselves. The alternative is to be content with reducing the singular to a particular to be subsumed under the universal, content with playing it safe, instead of being responsible in the deconstructive sense.

So you fail in the deconstructive sense when you fail to take a risk, when you evade responsibility by remaining under the protection of the rule. In deconstruction, ethics is the temptation. You fail by being ethical. Minister, on the other hand, thinks in the traditional style, that you fail by failing to be ethical, and by failing to come up with a rule. He is so enamored of the idea of writing an ethics of rules that covers all the counterexamples he can think up that when he reads an author who has declared himself against ethics he decides that author could not possibly have meant it. He then proceeds to "supplement" the author by the standards of an ethics book—what is the rule for this counterexample or for that? He works very earnestly, in the spirit of analytic ethics, to come up with as many counterexamples as he can think of to counter the theorems the author has proposed, although the author has proposed no theorems. I am very grateful that he is trying to clear things up for me, but a harsher critic than I might say that this shows that analytic philosophy has no ear for singularity and to what extremes it drives people to substitute excessive contentiousness for thinking through the things themselves. This same harsh critic might say that it shows a bit of a tin ear when Minister reduces the capacity that literature has to disclose the truth of the human condition, a truth more universal than history, as Aristotle said, to "having a favorite novel." Once we discover that Constantine Constantius and the young man are fictions, that the whole thing is a farce, should we return *Repetition* to the library and look for something more serious? The truth of "fiction" expands the disclosive power of truth beyond representational assertions, just the way nonrepresentational painting expands the power of art to disclose the world beyond realistic depiction. Are we to abandon our hope that the analytic philosophers would have learned something from Stanley Cavell, Richard Rorty, Stephen Toulmin, and others — our hope that we were entering a "postanalytic" period, an end of the analytic conception of philosophy as a calculus, as a contest in coming up with counterexamples, as a calculation machine, a competition over the validity of inferences about symbolically coded propositions? I fear that in trying to keep itself safe from literature, the conception of philosophy as a calculus keeps itself safe from — thinking.

Minister worries that I have failed to write an ethics, whereas for me it is ethics that constitutes the failure. For me, ethics is a way to evade perplexity and responsibility, a way to give a guide to the perplexed and offer guardrails, prescriptive rules, and norms of action that relieve one of the singularity of responsibility and decision and stills the fetching voice of the impossible. Still, Minister is of goodwill and proceeds to offer to help me out, by offering several suggestions, no doubt well intended, about how I could make his work into an ethics book, even though I have declared myself against ethics. This is like the good intentions of a driver who stops to offer a jogger a lift, which while reflecting a generous spirit does not reflect a good sense of what the jogger is trying to do. What is to protect me if my next reader is interested in writing a book on French cooking, or on the history of China, or who knows what?

The improvements Minister suggests will tighten the screws on my "ethics," clear up the ambiguities, set up some rules for an unruly situation, whereas the deconstructive point is to become wary of rules in favor of the unruliness of the singular. I should be grateful although I cannot shake the feeling that if Minister had been in the crowd listening to the parable of the laborers in the vineyard, his hand would have shot up just when Jesus got to the bit about the last being first and the first last, "surely, Rabbi, one can think of many eminent people, religious and political leaders, who were just men all their lives long and deserve a high place in the Kingdom!" Minister is offering a "supplement" but I have learned to be wary of the logic of the supplement. He says very sensibly that the aporias I single out are strategic reversals and are not to be treated as ethical theorems to be interpreted literally, but he worries that tensions and ambiguities remain: (1) We need to distinguish the sinner from the sin. Perhaps, but the deconstructive point would be not to fall back too quickly on such a sensible distinction; it is more "impossible" than that. Not only might this distinction prove to be a disguised way of not forgiving the sinner, but, and here I am following the analysis of E. P. Sanders, there is good evidence that the scandal Jesus was giving because of his association with sinners went further than such an easy distinction would suggest (*WG,* chap. 10). (2) We need criteria to distinguish who is "in" and who is "out," because this shifts with the circumstances—pederasts were often abused as children, the Roman centurion was not "out" of power. I agree that in singular cases we need to closely analyze the singularity of the circumstances; that is the point of a hyperethics of singularity. What constitutes the alterity of the other is that the other is *tout autre,* a singularity, at whatever point on the social or ethical scale the other is found, in all the complexity of the situation. That does not alter the fact that for the most part, of course, the "preferential option" is for the ones on the bottom, who most require redress, which is fairly clear from Jesus' own ministry. Or as Minister himself says of Levinas, in an eloquent response to his own point: "Levinas sometimes seems to treat 'the widow, the orphan, and the stranger' as privileged others, but this simply reflects the fact that we are more likely to be aware of our responsibility to others when confronted by those clearly in need." (3) "While Caputo at times recognizes that there can be no justice without law, I worry that his seemingly disproportionate focus on the fact that law can never achieve justice discourages us from recognizing the ways in which the powers-that-be may already be serving justice." Then do not be discouraged! Have faith in the impossible! The impossible only discourages the dangerous complacency that justice is here, now, right here among us, in Christianity, in the USA, wherever you are. (For what it is worth, I have never been charged with "deep pessimism" from any critic other than Minister!) Besides, if I were such a *literal* anarchist, I would not have Slavoj Žižek on my back denouncing me as a mere reformer and not a revolutionary. I say power is dangerous, not evil, and I counter it with the dangerous memory of injustice, with the weak power of mercy, love, and forgiveness, exemplified in the Christian tradition in the figure of Jesus.

Most of Minister's advice comes in the way of suggestions about how to transform a hyperbolic ethics into a more practical ethics, with a covering rule for every case. He thinks I risk causing confusion, but I think he risks putting the exposure to the impossible at risk. But when Minister cites me as saying power is "disastrous," he does not mention the context of my statement, that is, in a discussion of the powers of this world in the New Testament that are responsible for the death of Jesus. Power is disastrous when power is absolute, sovereign, or indivisible, so I say power is to be divided as widely as possible, but it cannot and is not to be eliminated. When Minister says my notion of the inviolability of the *tout autre* "seems to curiously retain the modernist conception of autonomous agency," I am at a loss for words (almost). My idea derives from the Franciscan tradition of haecceity, from Derrida's notion of the decision of the other in me, and from the apophatic idea of God as the *tout autre*. So central is the apophatic gesture of inscribing a zone of respect around the *tout autre* that Derrida says he does not trust any discourse that does not pass through apophatic theology but then goes on to universalize it into the one universal that I think can be defended in a philosophy of singularity, *tout autre est tout autre*. When Minister says, "Though it may be entirely contrary to Caputo's intended views and practices, justice begins to sound like an exotic adventure for bored suburbanites," I respond that that this is not a particularly helpful way to argue. It invites responses in kind, like "Though it may be entirely contrary to Minister's intended views and practices, his justice begins to sound like an exercise in defending fundamentalist extremism." That game can get nasty. I admire urban mystics and I think—like Charles Sheldon—that the focus of a postmodern liberation theology inspired by the ministry of Jesus should fall squarely on the blighted ghettoes in the United States and in underdeveloped nations that are the product of late capitalism. When he says that we do not need "an ethics built around the concept of powerlessness or alterity, but one inspired by humanity's positive potentials," I would say the very idea of the "potential" of "humanity"—and of quite a few other species, too, not to mention the natural world—turns on not restricting the potential to the possible but on exposing our potential to a visitation by the impossible. It turns precisely on the notion of keeping the future open, which requires the notion of the *tout autre*, for the *tout autre* is the event, the possibility of the impossible, the very structure of the "to come," the way to say yes to the future without fencing in it with universals that are inevitably local favorites. The most radical notion of the future turns on its radical unforeseeability, *beyond* "our potential." The most radical possibility is the possibility we cannot foresee or know is out there, which is the point of my analysis of "postmodern paths" in *What Would Jesus Deconstruct?*

3. Religion, Reason, and Fundamentalism

Ministers says that the deconstruction of theology results in another theology but of a weaker, fuzzier sort that no one can believe. I say the deconstruction of theology results in a radical or second theology that spooks the things believers believe they believe in the confessional theologies. Religion, as I have explained above, is a first-order set of beliefs and practices, whereas my work on religion is a second-order analysis of religious beliefs and practices. In my view, the symbolic and narratival forms religion takes in sacred Scriptures, creeds, and liturgies give form and substance to its underlying events. These events circulate around "the possibility of the impossible," a structure that is common to both deconstruction and religion, by which I mean Abrahamic religion. When I say that deconstruction is structured like a religion that is what I mean. I could also say that religion is structured like a deconstruction. In fact, I would say that the Abrahamic motif that "with God anything is possible" is the unavowed theologeme of deconstruction—except that it is explicitly avowed by Derrida. This structure lies at the heart of our "heart," of our Augustinian *cor inquietum*, what psychoanalysis calls "desire," what the New Testament calls *kardia*. (Whether the disdain with which Minister greets this deeply Christian concept (*kardia*) is testimony to overdosing on analytic argumentation, I cannot decide.) I should add that I am less confident that deconstruction so conceived could have emerged outside the cultures of the Abrahamic religions. The question of the event, in particular of the possibility of the impossible, outside the Abrahamic traditions is more complicated and I have hesitated to address it, although I will say a few words about it below. That is why the very idea of a pure messianic already bears the stamp of the Abrahamic traditions.

My overarching point, then, is that religious Scriptures, narratives, traditions, and creeds are not to be conceived as representing facts of the matter but instead as giving form and substance to events, above all to the events that circle around the possibility of the impossible. The most famous story of the possibility of the impossible in the west is the story of the Annunciation, which, as such, is an important and meaningful one that has inspired endless commentary and works of art. Its capacity to nourish our imagination is its truth, its vitality. This vitality is its truth. But the notion that it records a conversation written down many years later although witnessed by no one, that took place one day between an archangel and a young Jewish girl named Miriam in the dusty little town of Nazareth, is misguided. That story was unknown to Paul, Mark, John, and I dare say to Miriam. It would have induced a broad smile in her, her son Yeshuah, and his brothers, and no doubt a still broader one in their father. The object of my critical analysis of religion—and it is not merely critical—is orthodoxy itself, insofar as orthodoxy lays claim to offering representational truths about things like the virgin birth or the Trinity, two representations about which Jesus himself seems to have been quite innocent. I am not saying, as Minister wants to say, we must have "faith" that things like this conversation actually took place even though no one knows for sure, and hence we must have a humble orthodoxy. I am saying it is a conceptual mistake. I think it a misconception to take this as the record of an episode, to think that this narrative is describing a factual state of affairs. On the proposal I am advancing, the understanding that faith is seeking proves unnerving to confessional faith (*croyance*) resulting in a deeper but more ambiguous *foi*.

Minister has a special interest in fundamentalism, which I find revealing. While my position is not defined by the exclusion of fundamentalism, as he claims, it is deconstructively parasitic upon existing religious traditions, because it is an analysis of them, and without them there would be nothing to analyze, nothing to spook. My concern, then, is obviously much larger than "fundamentalism," which is not normally what is on my mind, although I tried to approach it with some sympathy in *On Religion*. I have a Roman Catholic culture, and when I criticize theories of the supernatural or of omnipotence I am not thinking of fundamentalism but of the major figures of mainstream theology, of Augustine and Aquinas and nowadays of the "strong" theologies of Milbank and Marion, and when I criticize authoritarianism I often have the Vatican in mind.

He says I consider fundamentalism irrational but I never said fundamentalism is irrational. I said it is impossible (*OR*, chap. 4), and there is a difference. I am not Habermas, and I have never been confused before with Habermas.[60] It belongs to my anarchic conception of things that a democracy is composed of variously and irreducibly adversarial groups, including the fundamentalists, in which consensus is not only impossible but also undesirable. I always liked the idea of Paul Feyerabend—who is something of the Derrida of philosophers of science—that anything, even voodoo, could prove a valuable resource for science (*RH* 211–12). So when I said the fundamentalists are impossible people, not irrational, I was speaking quite precisely. Impossible—for better and for worse. For *worse*, as a social and political phenomenon: its theocratic ambitions, its desire for a Christian empire and a war with Islam pose a dangerous threat, not only to people who do not share its extreme views, but to the very institution of democracy itself, as both Laclau and Derrida think. But unlike Habermas, we deconstructionists do not think that all the players in a democracy have to reach consensus, even about the rules of the game, even the rules of reason. They think a democracy is marked by what Derrida calls an "autoimmunity" to the antidemocratic, which it harbors within itself *structurally*, and must simply outwit its darker forces. The most famous case in point of this for Derrida was the Algerian elections of 1993. Minister's notion, by the way, that my anarchy is *opposed* to law and to institutional structures, is on the short list of misguided things he says about me and deconstruction. Deconstruction, I have said, and here I am merely repeating Derrida, is a philosophy of institutions (*DN*, chap. 2), above all a radically democratic one, which exposes it structurally to the risk of anarchy.

I do not mention fundamentalism much, if at all, in the works of my right hand, the books written for a professional audience. I only bring it up in the works of my left hand, the ones written for a wider audience, because it plays such an unfortunately prominent place in American culture, though thankfully such extreme views have little purchase in western Europe. I am gratified to receive weekly, sometimes daily, e-mails from readers thanking me for my roasting of fundamentalism in *What Would Jesus Deconstruct?* The deconstruction, since it seems to have slipped right by Minister's analytic eye, was to take Charles M. Sheldon's book *In His Steps: What Would Jesus Do?*—the source of one of the Right's favorite bumper stickers—and to argue that if you actually read this book and take its question seriously instead of using it as a stone to throw at (those whom you pronounce) sinners, you would be led to exactly the opposite conclusions drawn by the Christian right. If you take a *pharmakon* you may get poisoned, not cured.

For *better:* I introduced fundamentalism into *On Religion* as testimony to the bankruptcy of secularism (and my critique of secularism is ignored by Minister). In *On Religion,* one of the books of the left hand, my presentation of fundamentalism was far from an unqualified attack. It was an exploration of its ambiguity. I proposed it as massive and palpable evidence that "religion" was far from "dead." As Peter Berger himself would tell us, contrary to all the prognostications of the inevitable secularization of America by academic sociologists of religion back in the 1960s, God is dead only in the academy. Religion is back not only in American fundamentalism, but worldwide, in the resurgence of Islam, in the triumph of the Solidarity movement in Poland, in the sympathetic attention paid around the world to the persecution of the Dalai Lama, and among intellectuals, and so on. I turned to fundamentalism to buttress my contention that the modernist critique of religion fails—in fact, it has provoked the opposite reaction—because it replaces a religious understanding of the world with nothing, with the "heartless" "logic" of secularism that is bound to fail, not only philosophically but also politically, as Jim Wallis has been telling the Democrats for a while now. Far from repudiating the faith of fundamentalists, as Minister says, I referred to the social service of Pentecostalists and evangelicals as "the better angels of our nature," warned that I do not "dismiss fundamentalist spirituality as so much nonsense," and then proceeded to search out what I saw as the conflicted and very fetching "heart" of "The Apostle" — played so memorably by Robert Duvall in the film of that same (Pauline) name. One of the reasons I treasure this film is its use of "real people," not only professional actors but "real" born-again Christians who give us a vivid sense of the warmth of its spiritual life, just the way HBO producer David Simon uses real street people (*The Wire*) and real victims of Katrina (*Treme*) as an effective way to draw us into these worlds. I think that the Sunday morning meetings of the church of the "One Way Road to Heaven" and the extravagant energy of their spontaneous liturgy, of their extraordinary song and dance, are testimony to an event that secularism cannot comprehend, as well as flying in the face of the solemn liturgies of the orthodox. I take religious people seriously and I am trying to find out what is happening there, or what's going on in what happens in churches like "The One Way Road to Heaven," which goes beyond offering an apologetics for a *croyance*.[61]

Minister's defensiveness about fundamentalism is revealing, since he professes not to share its views and I have no doubt that he does not. Then exactly what is he defending? Their irreducible voice in a postmodern conception of things where there is no overarching standard of who gets to say what is on their mind? I agree. This same is true of "rationality" — because then we postmoderns would just ask, "*Whose* rationality?" On that we are agreed. But I suspect that there is more to Minister's defense than this. He would agree that fundamentalists go too far, are too scripturally literalistic and doctrinally inflexible, too politically reactionary and obnoxious, etc. — *but* they are so about a common core of beliefs he shares with them. Like what? The two worlds theory of Augustine (temporal-sensible and eternal-supersensible), the notion that Christianity is the one true religion, and the belief that the narratives of the New Testament, the conciliar creeds, and the mainstream theology constitute a body of representational truths picking out things *extra mentem*, like angels, devils, virgin births, water-walkings, heavenly assumptions, resurrected and resuscitated bodies, etc.? Fundamentalism is mostly a harassment to the rest of us but it is an embarrassment to the orthodox. It shows what happens when people take what orthodoxy believes in the simplest way and carry it to its final decimal point, to its more extreme conclusions, without nuance or sophistication or critical analysis. But fundamentalism and orthodoxy share a lot of core beliefs up to and including a common understanding of religious truth as representational. It is precisely that common understanding I am criticizing. But Minister wants to make sure that we do not have any arguments to prove fundamentalists are "irrational." (Although we need to explain why so few of us would want to expose our children or, for some of us, our grandchildren, to the biology curriculum in school districts with fundamentalist school boards.) But that is the *argumentum ad ignorantiam* that I claim runs quietly in the background of the present volume: we have arguments to prove that you cannot actually prove that we, or the fundamentalists, are "irrational."

I certainly object to fundamentalism. But as I also have been contesting the idea of an ahistorical "rationality" ever since *Radical Hermeneutics,* wherein I replace it with the distinction between "good reasons" and "bad reasons," as suggested by post-Kuhnian philosophers of science, "irrational" is not on my list of complaints. Nor do I think fundamentalists should keep their religion in private. I reject the notion that religion is private, and I affirm the right, the need, for religious communities to be counted among the public voices in a democratic debate, as Jeffrey Stout argues. (I grew up in the age of the *Reverend* Martin Luther King Jr.) I am just complaining that their reasons are bad and their voice has been deplorable, and, as Rorty says, the idea in a democracy is to make bad things look bad (the alternative is to have one's political opponents disappear in the night). My complaints are both political and theological. My political complaint is this: After the Supreme Court rulings in 1963 about the racial integration of universities caught up with Bob Jones University, these conservative Christians mobilized as a political force—hitherto they considered politics the work of the devil—so that they would not have to send their children to school with black children, and this in the name of Jesus. (Suffer the little white children to come unto me.) Flying under the "antiabortion" flag came later, after *Roe v. Wade* (1973), and while a certainly a legitimate issue (*WWJD* 112–16) it also provided a cover for what they were up to (racial segregation); that was clever strategizing, not "irrational." I gave "good reasons"—I did not advise burning their books, rounding them up in camps, or setting the secret police on them—that their political intervention has proven to be mean, greedy, sexist, racist, homophobic, and xenophobic. Or: not exactly what Jesus would do. Minister—who otherwise criticizes me for not making determinate judgments—concludes from this that I am intolerant! Theologically, I complain that fundamentalism has a misguided understanding of religious truth, but I also think that it shares the core of that misunderstanding with orthodox philosophers of religion like Minister, which on my hypothesis is for him the baby that may get thrown out with the bathwater in *What Would Jesus Deconstruct?*

I do agree that fundamentalism can be critiqued in many other ways and that that espoused in *What Would Jesus Deconstruct?* is only one way, although I am happy it has its audience. But if I thought fundamentalism and conservative evangelicals generally issue in an irrational and incommensurable discourse, I would not have written *On Religion,* would certainly never have bothered to write *What Would Jesus Deconstruct?* and publish it with an evangelical press, or would never have lent a hand to the work of the "Emergent Church" people whom I so much admire. Far from being irrational, I think evangelicals, fundamentalist or not, have been understandably stampeded by modern secularism. Minister thinks it ironic that I would attempt a sympathetic understanding of fundamentalism, and I think there are cracks in its surface showing signs of light. By this I mean the young evangelicals who voted in larger numbers for Obama, who do not trust the emphasis of the elders of the movement on homosexuality at the expense of peace and justice, many of whom have proven to be a receptive audience for *What Would Jesus Deconstruct?* just as I intended. But it also needs to be critiqued from the inside, by "recovering" fundamentalists, or by progressive evangelicals who would—initially at least—have some "credibility" with them. Brian McLaren was such a figure for a while, but I think he is now becoming suspect to them. Maybe there is room for Minister and Simmons to move in here.

It is also important for me to point out that Minister misunderstands me when he suggests that I am trying to sort out a common universal true religion focused on the underlying truths—like the "love of God"—that all religions share with particular contingent determinate and idolatrous religions. This is a conclusion one might be tempted to draw from *On Religion,* which is meant for a wider audience, rather than from the more specialized accounts in *Prayers and Tears* and *The Weakness of God*. I am suspicious of "identity" unless one means the identity of the different, and of "community" unless one means the community of non-knowers. But I am less suspicious of particularity. I affirm it, and as Eckhart liked to say, I go further: I call it singularity, and I say singularity is the one true "universal" for me. I say that is all there is. So I am not a Spinozist who thinks that "determination" is a "negation" but a deconstructionist who thinks singularity is affirmation, the actualization of an event. To observe an "ironic distance" on the actualization is to keep an eye on the virtuality and to keep the future open. So my point, as Žižek loves to say, is exactly the opposite. I am engaged in a work not of comparative religion (which I reject) but of universalizing (meaning "open-ended") hermeneutic phenomenology, albeit of an aberrant stripe (a phenomenology of "events," *without* transcendental subjectivity, hence quasi-transcendental and a radical hermeneutic).

My idea—were I qualified to undertake such a thing, which I am not—would be to expose what I take to be the events that circulate through the "religions," that is, what we in the Western-Abrahamic traditions call in Christian Latin *religio,* to their non-Abrahamic other, to what is "impossible" from the Abrahamic horizon. The result would be not a fusion of a horizons but the shock of alterity, of worlds with very different senses of time, death, and individuality, where the shock of that difference would be the event, the impossible. My claim is that a careful exposure of Christianity and Buddhism, to take an example referred to by Minister, would result not in "comparative religion" or the study of universal principles of "world religions"—there is a reason that Huston Smith has constantly criticized postmodernists for not affirming these universal principles—but a mutual shock of deeply different and deep-set "takes" on, by which I mean "receptions" of, the world that are moreover embedded in different languages, cultures, and traditions. This shock would be an event itself, one of proximity (Buddhists love Meister Eckhart) and of distance. It would produce something new, quite in the way Picasso revolutionized art a hundred years ago by contemplating African masks, which were for him the visual impossible. That was exactly the terms in which Cubism was denounced by the critics of the day, who still played by the old rules of representational art and complained that it is "impossible" to make out the figures! Thinking in terms of events would get us past the tunnel-vision Christocentrist misunderstanding of saying what Pope John Paul II said (in *Crossing the Threshold of Hope*), that the Buddhists are atheists—which is like criticizing football because in football you cannot steal third base. The result of such mutual exposures would be an ever-widening sense of the impossible—the event is always the impossible—and the ever-deepening sense of the mystery that we ourselves are, of the mystery of the event that is contained, or rather uncontained, in the name of (what in the Abrahamic traditions is called) God. The result would spook and unnerve the confessional religions with an unnerving hermeneutic openness to the event.

Religion is a first-order practice. The second-order radical hermeneutical reflection on religion that I undertake is not a rival religion. It has no national or international headquarters, is not a new entry in the marketplace of religious worldviews. It is a parasite or a spook that—in matters of "religion"—inhabits the only thing that exists, the concrete religious traditions that are the depositories of our religious memories and aspirations. My spooks do not "exist" they "insist," and with their spectral help I try to spook these traditions. That is also why the spooks will inevitably look like the spooked; there is no pure reflection, only endless hermeneutical exposure, which is why the very word pure "messianic" means it is Abrahamic all the way down. To spook these traditions is to provoke them into taking into account the Husserlian imaginative variation, the subversive subjunctive, "were I there, 'there'" would be 'here.'" My appeal takes place entirely on the phenomenological plane. I am betting that in that midnight hour when one is alone with oneself, one sees, with a shudder, but perhaps also with relief, that "Christianity" or "Judaism" or "Islam" is one's tradition, one's inherited form of life, which gives symbolic and narratival form to a form of life but that there are multiple forms of life. That, as I said above, is what I suspect happened to Mother Teresa: she suffered a blow to her *croyance* with no injury to her *foi*. In such moments the creeds and creedal assertions of *croyance* tremble. Perhaps for only a moment, perhaps for a sleepless hour, perhaps from time to time in the midst of busy waking life, like Heidegger's "call of anxiety" which we are anxious to silence by having quick and ready recourse to the comforts of the universal. In such moments I think we are running up against what I am calling "events," the promise/threat, the hope/fear, the riskiness and open-endedness of our lives from which we are constantly tempted to take shelter. Such experiences bring us up short, help us understand that we are all in this thing together, fellow travelers in a night of unknowing, companions in the same dark night in a community of non-knowers. That is what I call, following Derrida, a community *sous rature*, a community *without* community, without a common creed, a common set of beliefs and practices, only a common destitution, and a common prayer, a common faith in the possibility of the impossible.

I do agree with Minister that religious truth bears an important resemblance to political beliefs, that they are inherited, rooted in our flesh and blood and bones, not in bloodless reflection, and like deep political differences are not settled by abstract argumentation but by transforming existential experiences. But without denying all the important ways that religion and politics communicate, a point that is gaining increasing attention these days — Linda Alcoff and I recently organized a conference on the "politics of love" based on the recent work of Hardt and Negri — I think religious beliefs differ from political beliefs in an important way. Politics like everything else must have a taste for the impossible and immeasurable, but its special mission is to find the measurable and the possible, possible measures for what can be done, for ways in which people can get along that ensure the least violence. It seeks to find manageable structures, measurable procedures, and definable institutions that will allow people with very different points of view to coexist peacefully. That is why, like Minister, I admire the theory of radical democracy, inspired in no small part by Derrida, in the writings of Mouffe and Laclau, with its refusal of the ideal of consensus and its affirmation of irreducible plurality (see my *AE*). Religion, on the other hand — and religion is missing from Laclau and Mouffe — is rather more focused on the immeasurable and the impossible, on the possibility of the impossible, on dreams, which gives imaginative form, or what Hegel called a *Vorstellung*, to our desire, to our *cor inquietum*. When I say our desire, I mean not our desire for the possible but our desire beyond desire for the impossible, our desire not for the containable but for the uncontainable, not for practical measures but for the immeasurable. Religion is indeed the heart of a heartless world. The mistake, I am contending, is to treat these dreams as representations of facts of the matter, which is where the trouble starts. The difference is between the measurable truths of political theory and the poetics of the immeasurable in religion. The difference between the stories of Jesus in the New Testament and the tales of Lord Krishna is, importantly, *unlike* the difference between the views of a free-market individualist and a socialist, for the latter has to do with adjudicable and measurable differences. The "were I there, 'there' would be 'here'" notion is in play in both cases, but in politics it is much more vulnerable to criticism and adjudication. That is why closed societies resist the exposure to open societies afforded by the internet. But religious differences are at their heart, not the adjudicable differences between two competing representations of facts of the matter, between different economic systems or political structures, but the difference between two different hyperbolic and parabolic evocations of the impossible, two different ways to sing the world, to give it word and deed, song and form, *ergon* and liturgy. And my liturgical advice is to take care about singing songs to accidents of birth.

4. *Badiou and Saint Paul*

Minister thinks to help me out by adding a bit of Badiou to my mix. "Alterity," Minister says, "cannot be the basis for ethics, not because it is a figment of our imagination," but because it is (as Badiou terms it) "the banal reality of every situation." "What we need is not an affirmation of difference," Minister adds, "nor the exaltation of one type of difference, but the formation of identities that are more significant than the differences." Before going any further with this remark, let me say that I do agree with a certain notion of "identity," and that is the identity of the "we are all in this together," and in politics with universals that are provisional and pragmatically assembled unities in which we form political coalitions. We are all siblings in the same dark night, none of us has privileged access to the secret, and in the matter of religious truth in particular we share a common lack of having any special advantage over anyone else. There is thus a community of non-knowers, whose identity is lodged in the multiple differences among them, which is why Duns Scotus said that the highest form (universality) is *haecceitas* (this singular thing), Deleuze said the highest repetition is the repetition of difference, and Derrida said *tout autre est tout autre*. That should make us wary of locating the "formation of identity" in anything local. Our "identity" is still in the making, always coming, in a forward repetition, and its ultimate condition of possibility is the confession that we do not know who we are. Identity is what we all will have been when we are long dead and gone. Our lack of knowing who we are is not a lack but the only way to have a future.

So it is more than curious that for such a model of a universal identity, Minister follows Badiou's turn to Saint Paul, whom he takes to be the apostle of universality, because, as Minister says, "the *oneness* of Christ…transcends ethnic, socioeconomic, and gender differences. Only in this way can we establish a positive conception of the Good worthy of commitment, or in Badiou's preferred terminology, *fidelity*." That I think is a tellingly bad choice, on both Badiou's and Minister's part. As I said, I accept the notions of truth and universality, but the only thing I accept as genuinely universal is singularity, and I think that truth is the unfolding of the event. The only thing truly the same is difference. When anything else is put forth as truly universal, my hypothesis is that it will turn out to be *somebody's* universal and hence a pretender to the throne.

I think Badiou's idea that Paul proposes a new universality that transcends ethnic identity, the identity of the Jewish people is, as Dale B. Martin argues, "transparently false."[62] Paul's idea of universality—to the Jews first, then to the Greeks—is a perfect example of why we should back off from universalist claims of this sort and particularly from taking religion (with religion) as a model of universality. As Paula Fredriksen puts it in her own memorable way:

> Paul the "radical" has gotten a lot of mileage out of the sound bite in Galatians 3:28: "There is neither Jew nor Greek, there is neither slave nor free, there is neither male nor female; for you are all one in Christ Jesus." This sentence about radical equality reverberates so much with what we want to think of as the best in all of us. But when we get down to it, what was he saying about the people who were traditionally religious in terms of majority Mediterranean culture (a.k.a. the idol worshippers)? He didn't respect them. He didn't embrace their alterity. He said that, come the end of the age, they were going to fry. And

what was Paul demanding that his gentiles, his saints, his "believing ones" do? They had to cut themselves off from their own roots. Why? Because Paul based his argument about Jesus on an unsystematic reading of his own sacred Scriptures. *Paul is not obligated to history* because he is so convinced that he's right about the eschatological time-table on the strength of the fact that he thinks he has seen the risen Christ. Paul's indictment of majority Mediterranean culture in the first chapter of Romans is horrific. These people—most of the humanity whom he is acquainted with—are given to unnatural sexual practices, he says; they are morons, because they look at the sky but they do not infer anything about the God of Israel who made the sky, and so on. And Paul has seen a second miracle that confirms to him that he is absolutely right about what time it is on God's clock. He is getting people from this wicked pagan group to quit their low-down heathen ways and to do something that only one other people in the empire do, namely, the Jews...Paul makes a *ritual* demand of his gentiles: no more idol worship. Finished. And the fact these gentiles are able to do this, despite the debilitating environment of their own native culture, confirms for Paul yet again that the kingdom of God is going to arrive in Paul's own lifetime.[63]

Paul's idea was precisely not to *transcend* identitarian-ethnic differences but to cut these different ethnicities—the wild olive trees—off at their roots and *graft* them on to the tree of Israel, the cultivated olive tree (Rom. 11:17–26). Israel is the *one true identity*, the privileged identitarian difference, the one true people of the one true God—and those who do not agree with you will "fry." "The exaltation of one type of difference," before which every knee should bend, which every tongue should confess (Rom. 14:11), is *precisely* Paul's apostolic mission. The *last* thing Paul wanted to do was to transcend the identity of the specially chosen people, the tree of Israel, the identity handpicked by the God of Abraham who chose Abraham (that's a surprise) and his descendants. Paul did not want to transcend this identity but fulfill it, confirm it, extend it, and thereby universalize it. He was not trying to transcend Israel in order to attain a non-ethnic universal; he was trying to universalize Israel. Paul's universalism did not get its traction from subtraction but from an additive incorporation. It was not achieved by "subtracting" identitarian difference and ethnic divisions but by "grafting," by declaring one divided-off ethnic division the *winner*, the one and only one that was *chosen*. The choice that poses for everyone who was not chosen—the gentiles—is to choose to sign on or fry, and it grieved him to say that even his own people, those who were chosen, the blood descendants ("according to the flesh") of Abraham, were confronted with the same choice to accept Christ—or fry. His so-called universality was achieved by dropping the idea of blood descendants and circumcision, a bold apostolic strategy resisted by the more conservative followers of Jesus back in Jerusalem (his family and the ones who actually knew Jesus), in order to carry out the incorporation of all the different bloodlines into the one true handpicked body.

I am sure that the Palestinians, that Islam in general, would draw great comfort from knowing their salvation lay in being incorporated into the tree of Israel, just when they thought it was the opposite. In my view, Paul's apostolic mission to the gentiles is the prototype of the Western Christian colonial project of grafting the nations and native populations everywhere on to the tree of Israel. By the tree of Israel, as Dale Martin points out, Paul meant the tree of Israel, since Paul never heard of "Christianity" and had no intention of founding a new religion—"such notions would destroy his vision entirely"[64]—but of bringing the old one (Israel) to a happy conclusion as the end time rapidly descended upon everyone. But by the tree of Israel Christians mean Christianity. By the time "Christianity" comes about as a term and a movement, "the Jews" had become a term of contempt in the gospel of John, a mutation that would have grieved and astonished both Jesus and Paul. Grafting the nations onto the (symbolic) tree of Israel has had a long run from Constantine to the present, and the time has come to try something else. If I may quote a passage of Minister to a somewhat different end, "This self-contradiction is so blatant that...the only surprising thing is how widely it is ignored."

Oneness and universality will always turn out to be *somebody's* oneness and universality. That is why when we hear talk of religion *with* religion we should ask, according to my hypothesis, "religion with *whose* religion?" It will always turn out—it never fails—to be *somebody's* religion, meaning, *ours,* because *we* are the ones who were lucky enough ("grace") to be standing in the right place at the right time when the divine motorcade went speeding by and we caught sight of the god ("special revelation"). Of course, every "revelation," every distinctive "religious" tradition is "special" in the sense of being singularly and idiomatically itself and not something else, and that is why it ought to be treasured. But I deny it is exclusive, that it comes at the cost of the equal claim to—or rather, experience of—truth in other revelatory traditions. Why does this not ever happen to someone *else?* Why do the advocates of "special" revelations (by which they mean exclusively true in a zero-sum game of representational truths) never say, alas, there was a special revelation but we missed it? We were *not* chosen! It landed over *there,* it belongs to *the others,* and we were left out! Then it would gain some credibility in my eyes and it would make for a wonderful example of the hyperbolic ethics of the *tout autre!* The irony is so blatant that the only surprising thing is how widely it is ignored! That is why I think that the only thing that is genuinely universal is singularity, singular existence, not essential universals or universal essences, which always turn out to be locals, "favorite sons," as they say in politics. That is also why the only universal "discourse" I trust is hermeneutic universality, which consists in saying the event is always coming and therefore there is not anything we cannot talk about, no question we cannot ask, lest we foreclose its coming. The matter for thought, *die Sache des Denkens,* as Heidegger would put it, is not the universal we think we know but the unforeseeable, not the universal we think we understand but the impossible, whoever or whatever that may be.

I also find it odd that Minister thinks that the insults Badiou directs at Levinas—as a morose, morbid, or moribund dwelling upon the victim—should be directed at me but not at Levinas. I am not a (John the) Baptist: I prefer piping to mourning. When my "tears" are not tears of laughter, I am laughing through my tears. Before reading Minister, I would have supposed that anyone who has read my books would have noticed that, like Derrida, I make a cautious use of Levinas for that very reason. The logos of the Cross, the dangerous memory of the suffering of Jesus, the brutalized body of a victim of imperial power, is salient and irreducible. Furthermore, I find it obscene for a Christian to side with Badiou's arrogant mockery of beaten bodies against the central emblem of Christianity and to dismiss *kardia* for Badiou's *nous,* which I find excessively formalistic (is that not what Minister and Simmons are criticizing *me* for?), mathematicizing, and dualistic.

Still for me, for Derrida, for the New Testament, this is only one figure of the "other." The other is no less the beloved, where deconstruction is love, where love is the relation to the other. The other is the lilies of the field, the children, the neighbor, the stranger, the past, the future, the text, the whole length and breadth of our experience of other persons, of time, of history, of nature. The other is the staggering alterity of the cosmos, in space and time. The other is also the animal, the one from whom Heidegger, Levinas, and Badiou are insistent we be radically differentiated. The similarity of apes and humans, the reminder of our flesh, haunted Heidegger and it seems to be the source of no less unease to Levinas and Badiou, who are eager to make sure "we" are not taken to be "animals," we invisible, infinite, immortal ones. The other is for me, in addition, the length and breadth of the natural world, and here the later Heidegger's meditations on *physis* and the later Merleau-Ponty's lectures on nature are particularly valuable. This in contrast to Levinas, one of the objects of criticism in *Against Ethics,* where the transcendence and majesty of the natural world seems to have gone entirely unnoticed, except to be denounced as "paganism"—in which case, as Catherine Keller shows, there is a good deal of paganism in the Jewish Scriptures—a part of "being," and "being" is "evil," a point that Elohim seems to have gotten wrong (Gen. 1).[65] But Derrida saw transcendence where Levinas saw none, not simply in the other person but in *physis,* and he saw a transcendence in *physis* that Heidegger failed to see, the transcendence of the animal, and indeed the singularity of each and everything, all creatures great and small, which is why *tout autre est tout autre.*

I have criticized Levinas for his *anthropocentrism*—the only other that matters is the other person; and for his *ethicism*—the only relation to the other person that matters is ethics. This culminates in a grim preoccupation with obligation that borders on self-persecution and the pathology of being held hostage, which led him to suspect even art itself. Deconstruction, on the other hand, is the double affirmation, *viens, oui, oui,* the affirmation of the impossible, of the beloved, of the work of art, of the world, of the flesh of the world, of what solicits us in the name of God, of the coming of the Kingdom. The chapters in *The Weakness of God* in which I take up the "kingdom of God" bear titles like "Making All Things New," "Keeping Time Holy," "Rebirth and Resurrection." I work constantly upon "constructing"—my adaptation of deconstruction is a work of "constructive theology"—a conception of the Kingdom not in terms of Pauline notions of sacrificial death but of Paul's notion of the "new creation," the "new being," which is I think Paul's better side. I reject ethicism for a much wider range of experiences—*tout autre*—which I try to evoke under the name of a poetics. I applaud Badiou for prying open the event to include four categories, not just ethics, but I encourage him to keep on counting until he hits the innumerable (an infinite set!), which is never, for the event is unforeseeable, uncontainable, and certainly not limited to one (ethics) or four or numerable at all.

I cannot resist adding that Minister worries that I am going to cause confusion but he expresses no concern over the proposals that Žižek and Badiou make concerning what to do about global capitalism. (1) The Bartleby plan: Badiou recommends withdrawal from participation in the political system although he himself engages privately in political action. Žižek has a better idea! Blessed are those who prefer not to, who just say no, who do nothing, who stay out of the political system, who do not help, not just publicly but privately; let Africans die of AIDS, be tough, practice a cold merciless justice, do not lift a finger, which is only helping a bad System work better.[66] (2) Blessed are those who also cut a few throats here and there, those of really bad people, if they think they will not get caught (which of course is the same principle behind killing abortion doctors and bombing their clinics).[67]

Apart from such bankrupt "practical" advice—and Minister wants to make my poetics more "practical"—what do we finally get in the way of "theory" from the new universalism? A notion of the event as that which emerges locally in some element that has not been counted, that has been left out of the "subset" (preferably someone *suffering*, by the way, an astonishing irony). (Nobody notices that human life is not well described by "set theory," which turns on aggregates of atomic elements, and that, if you like logic and mathematics, experience is much better matched by "mereology," part/whole" theory (thus giving the "not all" a new cast), a movement that gained cache in twentieth century mathematics and logic and makes a good deal more sense for thinking about the "field" of human experience. It is part of the impetus that Husserl gave contemporary thought that he was in fact one of the predecessor figures of "mereology.") Be that as it may, this local element disturbs the established order, so the story goes, and precipitates a new accounting, a reconfiguration in things, by galvanizing subjects of responsibility around a new universal. But as it happens (just as post-structuralism predicts), this new configuration can never be final, because things are not totalizable and there are no true universal types, ones that are not coercive, since singularity is the only true universal. You do not want consensus because that closes off the future and you want to keep things open-ended. In short, once Žižek and Badiou get done distorting and bashing postmodern writers like Derrida, and after Žižek tells a few lewd jokes, they refute postmodern writers by way of repeating what Derrida, Levinas, Lyotard, Deleuze, and Foucault have been telling us for 40 years, only this time they repeat it accurately. Then they declare victory, crown themselves the new generation of truth, decision, and universality, and march home in triumph, a posture that the contributors to *Reexamining Deconstruction and Determinate Religion: Toward a Religion with Religion* would do well to avoid.

In point of fact, although Minister emphasizes the notion, I use the word "victim" sparingly. Not because it is not a fine word, and not because I do not honor it. Above all today, what better word to describe the children abused by clergy entrusted with their care in a church more concerned with the effect of this abuse on its corporate image than on the children—the victims, *pace* Badiou and Minister. I use it sparingly because it is part of a right wing Swift Boat rhetoric aimed at smearing people who are concerned with the common good—if it catches on it may mean a rise in taxes. Badiou's discourse on Platonism and his haughty disdain for animality go hand in hand with the dualism of Plato, about which Minister expresses no reservations at all. We brave immortal ones, we soldiers of the good and the true, we do not think in terms of victims and beaten animal bodies. We are tough; what does not kill us makes us immortal. We are the knights of fidelity to the truth. Those are fighting words, for the left or the right. Today the Right, Christian or secular, loves militant talk like that—it helps keep down taxes for social welfare programs.

5. The Politics of Truth

A core problem that is being addressed in this volume is simple, dangerously simple: when Christians affirm that Jesus is the Incarnate Son of God and other people deny it—or at least decline to believe it;

let us abstract, if you can, from people who never even heard of Jesus, the vast majority of the history of the human race—the Christians are right and everybody else is either wrong or negligent or not as lucky as Christians who got it revealed to them. It is that simple, as simple as ~(p&~p). I do agree with one main solution they propose to this problem, the one that is more political than theological—democracy, for example, Chantal Mouffe's conception of democracy. In a parliamentary democracy we have devised a method whereby the *agon* of competing voices ("agonistics") may be adjudicated without violence ("antagonistics"), a democracy being a place where people disagree with each other and office holders are regularly replaced, all without killing one another. The underlying idea behind Mouffe's conception of democracy is the idea of difference, and the irreducibility of dissent; the multiplicity of people is the multiplicity of differences. In a democracy of irreducible difference it is neither possible nor desirable for the dissenting voices to be silenced. The desirable and necessary thing is to find peaceful ways—debates and elections—to adjudicate dissenting opinions, to let the flow of unpopular ideas run free, and get a regular but nonviolent turnover in the officials at the top. So on one level my fellow contributors to this volume are asking for their civil rights in a modern liberal-secular society; they want to be allowed the pleasure of believing that on at least a few important points about God and Jesus they are right and others are wrong, so long as this belief does not cause injury to others who disagree with or ignore them.

I am grateful for Minister's generosity in pointing all this out to me. As a token of my gratitude, I would only point out to him in return that this is the ethico-politico-theological position I first sketched out in 1987, in the last three chapters of *Radical Hermeneutics*, and that I continued this account under the influence of Lyotard in *Against Ethics*, where I argued myself hoarse on behalf of dissensus—hailing "Lyotard's love of the *agon*," and adding "Dissensus stirs the pot of democracy" (*AE* 120)—and that Chantal Mouffe and Ernesto Laclau are among the most important political thinkers in the Derridean deconstructive tradition. Mouffe and Laclau are advancing a view of democracy not at all unlike that of Isaiah Berlin[68]—the idea that a "consensus" is not even a regulative ideal in a community of differences. I hasten to add that a community of differences is what Derrida would call a community *without* community, where the "without" is what is needed to allow the dissent to occur, to allow the community to stay open (*DN* 106–24). So we see that one tinkers with the word "without" at great risk! Without "without" you tend to close things down. If you strike it here you lose the democracy. I have been arguing this political point in print since 1987 in my dialogue with Anglo-American philosophy of science (*RH* 209–35; cf. *PT* 48). I am fond of what Levinas says about affectivity rising up into calculations about distribution and equality. I am fonder still of the way that Merleau-Ponty shows in *The Visible and the Invisible* that understanding is a way we speak and write and think with our bodies, that thinking is nothing other the life of the flesh, that "matter" and "spirit" are abstractions siphoned off the concrete life of the flesh, where the invisible is the invisible of the visible, thus undermining the dualism of *pathos* and *nous*, which is resurfacing with a vengeance in the excessive formalism of Badiou (cf. *AE* 255n26, n28).

I think that Minister and Simmons are ultimately defending a logico-theological point. They want to be right about *p*, where *p* is a proposition like Jesus-is-God, or God-is-personal, or God-is-triune, to the *exclusion* (not just with the force of the excluded middle but with that of privileged access) of those who dissent. As I have been arguing, that is a category mistake, a bad way to put what is going on in religion; it proceeds from a bad idea of religious "truth," which is at the heart of our disagreement. To put it in Heideggerians terms, they are trying to make their belief in Jesus into something "correct" (*richtig, recht, rectus, orthe*), whereas it is true with a different sort of truth. Its truth is not "representational" but a matter of *Unverborgenheit*, of unconcealment or revelation (*without* caps on the latter, by the way). The truth of unconcealment, of what Heidegger calls the "event," admits of multiple forms, as multiple as are the forms of life. What gets opened up in the New Testament for me is not an airtight factual report for making a true assertion *p*, such that if *p* is true, and I believe it and you do not, then sorry to say, I am right and you are wrong, although I promise to be as "generous" with you as possible. What gets opened up is a religious "horizon," a form of life, an "open," an "unconcealment," which is not verified but witnessed, testified to in and by praxis, in and by the exemplary lives to which it gives birth, as in Edith Wyschogrod's "exemplars."

The *veritas* here is the *facere veritatem* of Augustine that Derrida likes to cite, the truth of praxis, of the form of life. Most important, such forms of life do not compete with one another, no more than Martin Luther King Jr. competed with Gandhi even though they had different beliefs. These differences are not entries in a zero-sum game in which the truth of one knocks out the truth of others, which is not to say that the all the differences are same.

The only work that "correct" can do, by contrast, is to operate *within* a religion, a religion *with* religion, where it is used as a rod to straighten out assertions made *inside* the horizon. Something is "correct" if it abides by the rules of the game it is playing. So it makes no more sense to say that one sphere of openness is "correct" and the others are not or are only partly correct, than it does to say that chess is the correct game and the others are incorrect. When the community gathers around the campfires and tries to collate its views, some beliefs (*doxa*) emerge as "correct" (*orthe*) while others are dropped because they are unpopular and an "orthodoxy" is "forged" (in several senses of that word). Then the faithful gather in councils and try to come up with a short list of "C-beliefs," that God exists, is triune, that Jesus is God Incarnate, which make up the creed (*credere, croyance*), which defines the irreducible "essence" of Christianity or whatever the orthodox faith being carved out is. So there can be correctness inside the framework or horizon, with the result that the incorrigible are usually shown the door. Correctness can function as a disciplinary technique, as an instrument of correction, fueling ominous "institutions of correction." A religious horizon as a whole is not correct or incorrect, but true in the sense of showing, unconcealing, or revealing a way that validates itself in the practice, in the paradigmatic figures it generates, in the fertile traditions in which it unfolds, in the forms of life that flourish under its sway.

In general, you might have guessed that I do not make regular contributions to the cause of orthodoxy. I treat it is a form of anxiety (more effectively treatable by psychoanalysis than argumentation), which tends to harden the lines of force inside the horizon, to freeze it up and insulate it against the event to which the form of life gives word and deed. The orthodox of their time did not think much of Jesus or of Paul, for example, and the orthodoxy of today is geared up to block the way of any future comparable revolutionaries.

I think "orthodoxy" goes against the grain of the community of "dissent" to which the other contributors to this volume otherwise pay tribute. Nietzsche said that the Renaissance church pleased him no end because in those days Dionysus sat on the throne of Rome and he could not forgive that grim friar Luther for ruining it all. My own perverse pleasure would be to discover that Mother Teresa was indeed a heretic on the level of the correctness of her "C-beliefs." My hypothesis is—this is my phenomenology of acknowledgment—that in that midnight hour when we are alone with ourselves, we are prone to admit that our beliefs are very much in doubt but that, no matter, we hope, we pray, something deeper is going on in our lives, that we have managed to tap into a vein of deep truth that cuts beneath belief systems, a way to be, that validates itself *in actu exercitu,* in the doing. The reason I love *A Diary of a City Priest* so much is that no matter how deep the doubt of Fr. McNamee grew, the work he was doing (he has since retired) in that desperately poor inner-city Philadelphia neighborhood continued to validate itself, like the work that "religious people" do in the most obscure hovels of the underdeveloped world among slumdogs who never become millionaires except in the movies.

The open ambient truth of the "religious" way to be is quite a beautiful thing to behold, and I have earned the wrath of my secular friends for befriending it quite overtly ever since *The Prayers and Tears of Jacques Derrida* and *On Religion,* which includes a little hymn to Christian fundamentalists. Orthodoxy in religious matters, on the other hand, is often not a pretty business. In general, the careers of those who do not sign on to the orthodox list of approved propositions do not advance very far in the corporation, the *corporatio Christi,* while those who do are protected from the laws that protect children against sexual abuse by those entrusted with their care. Christians who do not countersign the right list of C-propositions, which is the core concern of the other contributors to this volume, are not going to get any big jobs or big plumbs in the corporation and people will wonder why they are still hanging around. Christians who write unorthodox books will get a lot of rejection slips from Christian presses and bad reviews from Christian journals, not to mention what they will hear from Christian committees on tenure and promotion (*s'il y en a*). If they are not firm about *p,* they will never make it in the firm. If you can live with that whole orthodoxy thing, that is your business. That, I hasten to add, is not a continental-analytic thing, but a philosophy thing. As the present contributors appreciate, the surest way to clear a room full of philosophers, continental or analytic, is to shout "theology." But I myself prefer taking the principle of dissensus quite seriously, keeping the system off balance, at risk, open to its future, so that the meditation upon the tradition is *radical,* that is, everything is on the table and exposed to the truth of the event, to the event of truth, in virtue of which we confess that everything is deconstructible (*without* crossing our fingers behind our back.)

Notice the peculiarity of religious truth. If people disagree about something in mathematics, politics, or about some point in the history of Rome, there are in principle ways to get to the bottom of it, but it is a category mistake to think that a religious opening or revelation is like that. If at this point our contributors rush in to say "but this does concern a point in the history of Rome, events around 33 AD" (or would they say CE?), they will soon enough turn on their heels and rush right out again, pleading the excuse on the way out the door that, to be very precise, this is an historical point that cannot be established by the historians, and that they were merely fighting for a draw. All they wanted to say was that the historians cannot prove they are wrong, which is like saying you cannot steal third base in football. That is why, as I said above, the analogy between religious truth and political truth holds only a limited amount of water. The founding Scriptures of the great religious traditions do not even *claim* to be history (it is anachronistic to think what they did then is what we today call history) but rather "good news," songs to sing, narratives in which hearts are made glad, in which a certain way to be is being dramatized, poetized, put into verse and song, which is why the "Gospels" are a theopoetics that promise salvation, not factual consistency.

If there is something about them you cannot establish—like some central C-belief—that is irrelevant, as Kierkegaard showed us. Suppose someone from the Society of Biblical Literature (SBL) points out that it is a long way from Yeshuah of first century Nazareth, who is all but lost in the fog of history, to the multiple oral traditions of saying Gospels that were formed in his memory, and a long way from these traditions to the earliest written versions of the four narrative

Gospels, and from the earliest manuscripts of the four Gospels to the existing redactions with which we work, and from the extant redactions of the Gospels to the Nicene Creed, and finally pointed out that, except for *abba*, Jesus never spoke a word of what is recorded in the New Testament because the New Testament is written in Greek and Jesus spoke Aramaic. If someone pointed all that out to Kierkegaard, he would shrug it off. He would simply point out that on your death bed you are not going to send out for the latest issue of the *Zeitschrift für neutestamentliche Wissenschaft* to see what they are saying about the historical Jesus this quarter in order to decide how to make your final peace. A life is validated by the life that one has led, not by a set of correct beliefs. But the point is that life is not a quiz show in which we are expected to guess the correct answer. There is no "correct answer" because the truth at stake is not a question of correctness. Correctness is a category mistake, and the answer is the response that is given by our lives, not by the Councils or the catechism. (And *that* assertion is a second-order radical reflection *about* the first-order practices of religion.) The New Testament is "true" with a qualitatively different kind of truth, which Kierkegaard called existential (or "subjective," which was not the best choice of words) as opposed to objective truth, be the latter historical or speculative. Such truth is testified to in the living, not verified in the documenting, or demonstrated in the syllogizing. The same thing is true of any of the great religions, ways, or *dharmas;* each is sustained as a self-validating history of beliefs and practices, of founding texts and paradigmatic practitioners or saintly exemplars of its way, in each of which the multiple historical communities make their own way. Each has given form and figure to a certain way to be in which they can recognize themselves. These ways differ but are no way in competition with each other in a zero-sum game.

RECESSIONAL: A SONG TO SANS

I have long been singing a song to the logic of the without, of the *sans* in deconstruction and of the *sine* in Meister Eckhart and Augustine, and I will remain steadfast in my faith in the *sans,* even and especially when I am told that by a brave new generation that the time has come for it to go. I do not think we can do without "without." In point of fact, I think, the best solution to this problem was proposed a while back by James Olthuis, when he entitled a collection based on my work *Religion With/Out Religion*,[69] meaning both with *and* without, where with and without communicate, recognizing both that the "without" is irreducible and that, at the same time, we "always already" live and move and have our being in concrete factical and historical situations (the "with"), which I have constantly held. We are all agreed about that, more or less, but it is where the more and the less fall that causes the dispute. Olthuis's formula of "with/out" is a very nice way to put the hauntological point, which describes the way radical theology haunts the chambers of the confessional theologies and keeps them up nights (unless they only use the decaffeinated variety). Religion without religion means religion, yes, but not without reminding ourselves that the events harbored by the name of God show up under other names, even and perhaps especially under the name of atheism, and not without reminding ourselves that were I there, there would be here and I would be tempted as are the present contributors to throw up the tall walls of "with" around another contingent construction.

Religion, *oui, oui,* but not without with/out.

To deconstruct something is not to raze it to the ground but to read it closely and expose its porosity, which is not to be confused with contentious bickering and presenting endless counterexamples, but by pressing its exposure from within to its own without, to show how it itself tunnels out to its own outside and its own future, digging a wormhole from its within to its *without.* In this spectral spirit I propose a final gesture of deconstructing Christianity, a repetition of Matthew 25, which repeats the point that we are serving Jesus every time we serve the least among us *without* knowing (*sans savoir*) that it was Jesus. Carried by the event that stirs within this saying, I add that whenever we serve the least among us, even after we are told we are serving Jesus in them, we still serve *without* knowing whom we are serving, for what happens in and under the name of Jesus, happens under many names, with or *without* the name of Jesus or of God. The whole point of that parable is living *sans voir, sans avoir, sans savoir,* and I take that seriously, radically.

After all, life is not a game in which we are supposed to guess the secret word. And it is certainly not a rigged one, where a certain circle of elect have been tipped off about the answer.

1. See especially John D. Caputo, *The Prayers and Tears of Jacques Derrida: Religion without Religion* (Bloomington: Indiana University Press, 1997); *Deconstruction in a Nutshell: A Conversation with Jacques Derrida,* ed. John D. Caputo (New York: Fordham University Press, 1997), in particular Caputo's commentary; *God, the Gift, and Postmodernism,* ed. John D. Caputo and Michael J. Scanlon (Bloomington: Indiana University Press, 1999); *Questioning God,* ed. John D. Caputo, Mark Dooley, and Michael J. Scanlon (Bloomington: Indiana University Press, 2001); *The Religious,* ed. John D. Caputo (Oxford: Blackwell, 2002); *Augustine and Postmodernism: Confessions and Circumfession,* ed. John D. Caputo and Michael J. Scanlon (Bloomington: Indiana University Press, 2005); John D. Caputo and Michael J. Scanlon, *Transcendence and Beyond: A Postmodern Inquiry* (Bloomington: Indiana University Press, 2007).

2. Caputo, *Deconstruction in a Nutshell,* 166.

3. Ibid., 21.

4. Jacques Derrida, "Circumfession: Fifty-Nine Periods and Periphrases Written in a Sort of Internal Margin," in Geoffrey Bennington and Jacques Derrida, *Jacques Derrida* (Chicago: University of Chicago Press, 1993). For more on Derrida and religion, see *Derrida and Religion: Other Testaments,* ed. Yvonne Sherwood and Kevin Hart (New York: Routledge, 2005); Dawne McCance, *Derrida on Religion: Thinker of Difference* (Sheffield: Equinox, 2009); J. Aaron Simmons, *God and the Other: Ethics and Politics after the Theological Turn* (Bloomington: Indiana University Press, 2011). See also Jacques Derrida, *Acts of Religion,* ed. Gil Anidjar (New York: Routledge, 2002); *Religion,* ed. Jacques Derrida and Gianni Vattimo (Stanford: Stanford University Press, 1998).

5. See Caputo, *Prayers and Tears.* Derrida affirms that "religion without religion" is an accurate description of his thought in an interview with Mark Dooley (Mark Dooley, "The Becoming Possible of the Impossible: An Interview with Jacques Derrida," in *A Passion for the Impossible: John D. Caputo in Focus,* ed. Mark Dooley (Albany: State University of New York Press, 2003), 21–33, 32). For a sustained consideration of Caputo's postmodern religious thought, see Christopher Ben Simpson, *Religion, Metaphysics, and the Postmodern: William Desmond and John D. Caputo* (Bloomington: Indiana University Press, 2009).

6. Caputo, *Prayers and Tears,* 97.

7. Ibid., 103.

8. Caputo, *Deconstruction in a Nutshell,* 158.

9. Caputo, *Prayers and Tears,* 63.

10. Ibid., 64. For more on how a revised rhetoric of possibility might be compatible with Caputo's notion of impossibility, see Richard Kearney, "The Kingdom: Possible and Impossible," in *Cross and Khôra: Deconstruction and*

Christianity in the Work of John D. Caputo, ed. Marko Zlomislić and Neil DeRoo (Eugene: Pickwick Publications, 2010), 118–39. See also, Richard Kearney, *The God Who May Be: A Hermeneutics of Religion* (Bloomington: Indiana University Press, 2001). One might even make a case that Open Theism would also provide a constructive conversation partner on this front. See, for example, John Sanders, *The God Who Risks: A Theology of Divine Providence*, rev. ed. (Downers Grove, IL: InterVarsity Press, 2007); Gregory A. Boyd, *The God of the Possible: A Biblical Introduction to the Open View of God* (Grand Rapids, MI: Baker Books, 2000); and especially, Clark Pinnock, Richard Rice, John Sanders, William Hasker, and David Basinger, *The Openness of God: A Biblical Challenge to the Traditional Understanding of God* (Downers Grove, IL: InterVarsity Press, 1994).

11. Caputo, *Deconstruction in a Nutshell*, 159. Of course, the worry about triumphalism is not something only found in continental philosophy. Indeed, even Alvin Plantinga has suggested that triumphalism might be one of the greatest challenges to contemporary philosophy of religion (see "Response to Nick Wolterstorff," *Faith and Philosophy* 28, no. 3 [July 2011]: 267–68).

12. For example, consider the Postmodernism of Mark C. Taylor, the Radical Orthodoxy of John Milbank, Catherine Pickstock, and Graham Ward, the Radical Theology of Charles Winquist, the Process Postmodernism of Catherine Keller, David Ray Griffin and Roland Faber, the Radical *Political* Theology of Clayton Crockett, Jeffrey Robbins, and Creston Davis, the "nihilistic" Christianity of Gianni Vattimo, the aesthetic and hermeneutic approach of Richard Kearney's "Anatheism," the feminist approaches of Grace Jantzen, Judith Butler, and Ellen Armour, and even the deeply influential work of thinkers who resist easy categorization such as Slavoj Žižek, Jean-Luc Nancy, and Alain Badiou. For more on the different shapes of postmodern theology, see *The Cambridge Companion to Postmodern Theology*, ed. Kevin J. Vanhoozer (Cambridge: Cambridge University Press, 2003); Graham Ward, *The Blackwell Companion to Postmodern Theology* (Oxford: Blackwell, 2001); *The Postmodern God*, ed. Graham Ward (Oxford: Blackwell, 1997).

13. See Dooley, *A Passion for the Impossible;* Zlomislić and DeRoo, *Cross and Khôra;* and *Religion with/out Religion: The Prayers and Tears of John D. Caputo*, ed. James H. Olthuis (London: Routledge, 2002).

14. As just two examples of this continuing prominence, consider that in his book-length engagement between analytic philosophy of religion and continental philosophy of religion, Nick Trakakis focuses almost exclusively on the deconstructive phenomenological approach as representative of the continental tradition (*The End of Philosophy of Religion* (London: Continuum Press, 2008)). Similarly, the book series, The Church and Postmodern Culture, published by Baker Academic and edited by James K. A. Smith, has primarily focused on the way in which deconstruction and Christianity are important resources for each other.

15. In particular, see Drew M. Dalton, *Longing for the Other: Levinas and Metaphysical Desire* (Pittsburgh: Duquesne University Press, 2009); *Kierkegaard as Phenomenologist: An Experiment*, ed. Jeffrey Hanson (Evanston, IL:

Northwestern University Press, 2010); *Michel Henry: The Affects of Thought*, ed. Jeffrey Hanson and Michael R. Kelly (London: Continuum Press, 2012); Bruce Ellis Benson, *Pious Nietzsche: Decadence and Dionysian Faith* (Bloomington: Indiana University Press, 2008); Bruce Ellis Benson, *The Improvisation of Musical Dialogue: A Phenomenology of Music* (Cambridge: Cambridge University Press, 2003); *Words of Life: New Theological Turns in French Phenomenology*, ed. Bruce Ellis Benson and Norman Wirzba (New York: Fordham University Press, 2009); *Transforming Philosophy and Religion: Love's Wisdom*, ed. Bruce Ellis Benson and Norman Wirzba (Bloomington: Indiana University Press, 2008); *The Phenomenology of Prayer*, ed. Bruce Ellis Benson and Norman Wirzba (New York: Fordham University Press, 2005); Stephen Minister, "Forging Identities and Respecting Otherness: Levinas, Badiou, and the Ethics of Commitment," *Symposium: Canadian Journal of Continental Philosophy* 9:2 (Fall 2005); Stephen Minister, "Intersubjectivity, Responsibility, and Reason: Levinas and the 'New Husserl,'" *Philosophy Today* 50, no. 5 (SPEP Supplement 2006); Stephen Minister, "Derrida's Inhospitable Desert of the Messianic: Religion within the Limits of Justice Alone," *Heythrop Journal* (March 2007): 227–42; J. Aaron Simmons, *God and the Other: Ethics and Politics after the Theological Turn* (Bloomington: Indiana University Press, 2011); *Kierkegaard and Levinas: Ethics, Politics, and Religion*, ed. J. Aaron Simmons and David Wood (Bloomington: Indiana University Press, 2008).

16. Indeed, after the publication of *The Prayers and Tears of Jacques Derrida*, Caputo says the following in a 2002 response to the essays included in *Religion with/out Religion*:

> The idea is not to denounce the concrete messianisms utterly, or to leave everyone with the idea that they are "essentially poisonous," in Shane Cudney's felicitous formulation, or "by their very nature violent," as Ron Kuipers puts it, but to maintain the tension, to maintain them in their pharmacological undecidability, which is the structure of the Gift/gift, the poison/remedy. The failure to do this is the main rhetorical failure of [*Prayers and Tears*], which is *a serious failure for book that takes rhetoric and the flow of prayers and tears very seriously.* [*Prayers and Tears*] appears to have broken the tension, the undecidable fluctuation of the messianic/ messianism, which is what is truly productive in any concrete messianism.

See John D. Caputo, "Hoping In Hope, Hoping Against Hope: A Response," in James H. Olthuis, *Religion with/out Religion*, 120–49, 128; emphasis added. Despite recognizing this "serious failure," Caputo again can be read as saying that "the concrete messianisms are...essentially poisonous" in *The Weakness of God* when he describes the "God of religion and strong theology" as "an idol, a graven image, an instrument of institutional power, or moral melancholy, of top-down authoritarianism, and confessional and identitarian divisiveness" (*The Weakness of God: A Theology of the Event* [Bloomington: Indiana University Press, 2006], 35) and suggests that we move beyond conceptions of God as "a being who is there, an entity trapped in being, even as a super-being *up there,* up above the world, who physically powers and causes it, who made it and occasionally intervenes upon its day-to-day activities to tweak things for the better in response to a steady stream of solicitations from down below (a hurricane averted here, an illness averted there, etc.)" (39). For Caputo, such personalist accounts of God and petitionary prayer amount to "an essentially magical view of the world" (39). It is hard to see how this recent rhetoric would avoid the critiques that Cudney and Kuipers offered to Caputo's earlier work. If anything, it seems to give more weight to their initial concerns.

17. In Caputo's essay in the present volume, he affirms Olthuis's strategy.

18. See Dominique Janicaud, "The Theological Turn of French Phenomenology," in *Phenomenology and the "Theological Turn": The French Debate* (New York: Fordham University Press, 2000). For a set of essays responding to this "turn" see *Words of Life: New Theological Turns in French Phenomenology*, ed. Bruce Ellis Benson and Norman Wirzba (New York: Fordham University, 2010).

19. See Hent de Vries, *Philosophy and the Turn to Religion* (Baltimore: Johns Hopkins Press, 1999).

20. See Alvin Plantinga, "Advice to Christian Philosophers," in *The Analytic Theist: An Alvin Plantinga Reader*, ed. James F. Sennett (Grand Rapids: William B. Eerdmans Publishers, 1998), 296–315.

21. John D. Caputo, "A Game of Jacks: A Response to Derrida," in Dooley, *A Passion for the Impossible*, 34–49, 35.

22. As Caputo himself notes in his chapter in the present book, he is seen as too indeterminate by some (viz., J. Aaron Simmons) and as too determinate by others (viz., Martin Hägglund).

23. See also Nick Trakakis's worry about the lack of content in continental philosophy of religion (*The End of Philosophy of Religion*, especially chapter 4). Similarly, Stefan Stofanik expresses a worry about the lack of determinancy when he notes that Caputo's own theological gestures in light of religion without religion lead to "the 'dymythologization' of Jesus facilitated by a poetic reading of Scriptures; and second, the loss of the specifically Christian beliefs in Incarnation and Trinity" ("Introduction to the Thinking of John Caputo: Religion without Religion as the Way out of Religion," in *Between Philosophy and Theology: Contemporary Interpretations of Christianity*, ed. Lieven Boeve and Christophe Brabant [Farnham, UK: Ashgate, 2010], 19–26).

24. Kevin Hart, "Without," 80–108, in Zlomislić and DeRoo, *Cross and Khôra*, 80–108, 85. Consider also Hart's claim later in the same essay: "A phenomenology of Christianity that dos not find traction in worship and prayer does not adequately describe the Christian's life. This happens, I think, because Derrida and Caputo perform a phenomenological reduction of Christianity as 'religion'" (102).

25. Kevin Hart, "Without," 95. See also Lewis Ayers's account of "soft postmodernism," which he defines as postmodernism that maintains a basically modernist notion of liberalism ("A Reading of John D. Caputo's 'God and Anonymity,'" in Dooley, *A Passion for the Impossible*, 129–46).

26. When viewed in this way, religion without religion might not seem to be a very new idea at all. Kevin Hart suggests that religion without religion is one more move reminiscent of the "X without X" formulation: "Christianity without metaphysics (Ritschl), Christianity without myth (Bultmann), Christianity without religion (Barth), Christianity without the supernatural (Tillich), Christianity without religion (Bonhoeffer), Christianity without reliance on dogma (Rahner), even Christianity without God (Altizer)" (Hart, "Without," 94).

27. Ronald A. Kuipers, "Dangerous Safety, Safe Danger: The Threat of Deconstruction to the Threat of Determinable Faith," in Olthuis, *Religion with/out Religion*, 21–33, 22. Shane Cudney goes even further and suggests that Caputo's own project ends up being violent: "So even though Caputo has kept the philosophical dust from settling (something he does quite well), it seems to me that his 'neutered' universal, this demasculinized, gelded, more subdued Heideggerianism still cannot genuinely connect with or penetrate the surface of concrete religions, even if it can sing a little higher. Stripped of its aggressive, violent tendencies, the problem is that this docile, more manageable messianic is also stripped of certain very human, gonadian features, which also strikes me as violent" (Cudney, " 'Religion without Religion': Caputo, Derrida, and the Violence of Particularity," in Olthuis, *Religion with/out Religion*, 34–49, 41).

28. For example, in an interview, Westphal says: "It's possible to read him [Derrida] as simply saying, 'This is an analysis of human knowledge. Whether there's anything beyond that, I don't know; I'm agnostic about that'. He certainly isn't careful in making that distinction and restriction the scope of his conclusions, and he often will say things, which on the face of it certainly seem to be that non sequitur—'this is ours and that's all there is'. Someone like Nietzsche, of course, is completely explicit about that"; see B. Keith Putt and Merold Westphal, "Talking to Balaam's Ass: A Concluding Conversation," in B. Keith Putt, *Gazing through a Prism Darkly: Reflections on Merold Westphal's Hermeneutical Epistemology* (New York: Fordham University Press, 2009), 181–205, 184.

29. Richard Kearney, "*Khôra* or God?" in Dooley, *A Passion for the Impossible*, 107–22, 111.

30. David Goicoechea argues that the undecidability stressed by Caputo is, ostensibly, meant to keep in play the "with" and the "without," but that Derrida does a better job at keeping the "with" in play than does Caputo. However, in line with some of the other objections we have considered above, Goicoechea does note that Derrida certainly doesn't allow for the "with" in as substantive a way as does someone like Kierkegaard (who also challenges the dangerous absolutizing and triumphalist tendencies in determinable religions as well as, if not better than, Derrida and Caputo). See, David Goicoechea, "Caputo's Derrida," in Olthuis, *Religion with/out Religion*, 80–95.

31. Mark Dooley, "The Becoming Possible of the Impossible: An Interview with Jacques Derrida," in Dooley, *A Passion for the Impossible*, 21–33, 31.

32. I specifically mention Pentecostalism here because it is the specific religious tradition I consider in chapter 1. But others are also beginning to think at the intersection of Pentecostalism and Postmodernism. In particular, see

James K. A. Smith, *Thinking in Tongues: Pentecostal Contributions to Christian Philosophy* (Grand Rapids, MI: William B. Eerdmans, 2010). For a theologian who is also exploring such themes, see the work of Amos Yong.

33. Caputo also affirms this instability: "Deconstruction has not been sent into the world to settle the question of God, or of Jesus, of Christianity or of any of the other 'determinate messianism[s],' or of theological grace. No one has authorized deconstruction, and it would never authorize itself, to do so. Deconstruction is not a *what* but a *how*, not a set of propositions, theistic or atheistic, but a way of holding a faith or a knowledge—not an attempt to cut off possibilities"; and also, "Deconstruction is an account of *foi* but it has no lever or leverage on the determinate beliefs, the specific *croyances* of the several confessions, like believing that an angel announced the virgin birth of Jesus to Mary. Deconstruction simply claims that to hold to one or another of the various clusters of belief, like faith in the annunciation, is to 'rightly pass' for a believer of that sort, a Christian, for example. But, please note, the same thing holds for Derrida's own atheism, which is part of the furniture of his own personal more secular *croyance*." ("The Possibility of the Impossible: A Response to Kearney," in Zlomislić and Neal DeRoo, *Cross and Khôra*, 140–50, 142, 144).

34. John D. Caputo, "Only as Hauntology Is Religion without Religion Possible: A Response to Hart," in Zlomislić and DeRoo, *Cross and Khôra*, 109–17, 114.

35. John D. Caputo, "Hoping in Hope, Hoping Against Hope: A Response," in Olthuis, *Religion with/out Religion*, 120–49, 128–29.

36. John D. Caputo, "What Is Merold Westphal's Critique of Ontotheology Criticizing?" in Putt, *Gazing through a Prism Darkly*, 100–15, 115.

37. In reply, one might suggest that Caputo's own "theological turn," or better "theopoetic" turn, makes such disjunctions a matter of linguistic illumination and not of syllogistic logic. While I applaud the profoundly fecund readings that Caputo brings to theological archives and appreciate the distinctive voice that he adds to the postmodern theological landscape (in particular, his blend of radical theology, process thought, deconstructive philosophy, and Kierkegaardian social critique is something from which we can all learn regardless of our disciplinary identities or theological leanings), I lament that this theopoetic move can seemingly move Caputo beyond the pale of philosophical engagement and criticism. Indeed, sometimes it seems as if "theopoetics" were more a project of redescription (similar to Richard Rorty), than a project of reason-giving. However, as many have pointed out relative to Rorty, redescription can slide to mere cajoling if not accompanied by supporting reasons that make his arguments available for logical analysis. The same is true regarding Caputo's "theopoetics." Caputo's work demands philosophical consideration and criticism (as well as other modes of engagement). For Caputo's own thoughts on Rorty, see "Parisian Hermeneutics and Yankee Hermeneutics," in *More Radical Hermeneutics* (Bloomington: Indiana University Press, 2000). See also Mark Dooley's "In Praise of Prophecy: Caputo on Rorty," and Caputo's reply to Dooley, "Achieving the Impossible—Rorty's Religion: A Response to Dooley,

both in Dooley, *A Passion for the Impossible*. For those places where Caputo develops his "theopoetic" account, see especially, *The Weakness of God; What Would Jesus Deconstruct? The Good News of Postmodernism for the Church* (Grand Rapids, MI: Baker Books, 2007); *On Religion* (New York: Routledge, 2001); *Philosophy and Theology* (Nashville: Abingdon Press, 2006); and John D. Caputo and Gianni Vattimo, *After the Death of God*, ed. Jeffrey W. Robbins (New York: Columbia University Press, 2007).

38. I admit this point is ironic given Caputo's own claim that "Deconstruction is not a *what* but a *how*, not a set of propositions, theistic or atheistic, but a way of holding a faith or a knowledge—not an attempt to cut off possibilities" (John D. Caputo, "The Possibility of the Impossible: A Response to Kearney," in Zlomislić and DeRoo, *Cross and Khôra*, 140–50, 142.

39. For worries about apologetics from continental philosophy, see B. Keith Putt, "The Benefit of the Doubt: Merold Westphal's Prophetic Philosophy of Religion," in Putt, *Gazing through a Prism Darkly*, 1–19.

40. For more critical engagements with Caputo's ethics, see Kevin Hart who charges Caputo with a reduction of religion to ethics (Kevin Hart, "Without," in Zlomislić and DeRoo, *Cross and Khôra*, 18–108), and Merold Westphal who challenges the Nietzschean undercurrents of Caputo's ethics in "Postmodernism and Ethics: The Case of Caputo," in Olthuis, *Religion with/out Religion*, 153–70. Jeffrey Dudiak inquires into the practical social and political implications of Religion without religion ("Bienvenue—just a moment," in Olthuis, ed., *Religion with/out Religion*, 7–19). And Mark Dooley argues that the political liberalism of Richard Rorty is a resource for the ethico-political thought of Caputo ("In Praise of Prophecy: Caputo on Rorty," in Dooley, *A Passion for the Impossible*, 201–28).

41. See Drew M. Dalton, *Longing for the Other: Levinas and Metaphysical Desire* (Pittsburgh: Duquesne University Press, 2009). For other postmodern considerations of love, see James H. Olthuis, "Testing the Heart of Khôra: Anonymous or Amorous?, in Zlomislić and DeRoo, *Cross and Khôra*, 174–86; Patricia Huntington, "On Witnessing and Love: A Dialogue with Caputo," in Zlomislić and DeRoo, *Cross and Khôra*, 197–223; and the excellent collection edited by Norman Wirzba and Bruce Ellis Benson, *Transforming Philosophy and Religion: Love's Wisdom* (Bloomington: Indiana University Press, 2008).

42. For a related consideration of different ways of understanding "the kingdom of God" in line with different postmodern philosophers, see David Goicoechea, "The Kingdom and the Cross," in Zlomislić and DeRoo, *Cross and Khôra*, 61–73.

43. However, Reformed Epistemology tends to operate explicitly with a very specific set of Christian theological premises (drawing on John Calvin and Abraham Kuyper) while religion with religion does not.

44. Merold Westphal has been an example for how to speak across such divergent discourses. See also Neil DeRoo's essay " 'The Weakness of God': A New Theodicy?" in which he argues that Caputo's recent theological work can be put into conversation with contemporary debates in Analytic philosophy of religion

concerning the problem of evil (in Zlomislić and DeRoo, *Cross and Khôra*, 302–17). For other excellent thought occurring at the intersection of Continental and Analytic philosophy of religion, see the work of John Davenport, James K. A. Smith, and, especially, Nick Trakakis's *The End of Philosophy of Religion*. I have attempted such bridgework myself in *God and the Other: Ethics and Politics after the Theological Turn*. For an edited collection that makes significant strides in this direction, see *Self and Other: Essays in Continental Philosophy of Religion*, ed. Eugene Thomas Long (Dordrecht: Springer, 2007).

NOTES TO CHAPTER ONE / SIMMONS

The first epigraph is from John D. Caputo and Michael J. Scanlon, "Apology for the Impossible: Religion and Postmodernism," in *God, the Gift, and Postmodernism*, ed. John D. Caputo and Michael J. Scanlon (Bloomington: Indiana University Press, 1999), 18n1. The second epigraph is from John D. Caputo and Gianni Vattimo, *After the Death of God*, ed. Jeffrey W. Robbins (New York: Columbia University Press, 2007), 127.

1. I should note that, although I am going to be specifically concerned with Christianity, the same question could be asked for any determinate religion. Moreover, if what I will be claiming is correct, then an apology for atheism would also be potentially legitimate. I will argue that a rational defense can be given of determinate religious truth-claims (whether positive or negative) within postmodernism.

2. The worry about such arrogance is not found only in continental philosophy. In a recent essay, Alvin Plantinga claims that "triumphalism" is a pressing worry for philosophy of religion and that we "must reject" it ("Response to Nick Wolterstorff," *Faith and Philosophy* 28, no. 3 (July 2011): 267–68.

3. As explained in the introduction to this volume, not all CPR necessarily falls into this tradition. In particular, many figures associated with CPR are much more indebted to psychoanalysis and critical theory than to extending the legacy of Husserlian phenomenology. In this regard, consider especially the work of Slavoj Žižek. Moreover, many working in the area of "postmodern political theology" would fit better in the tradition of critical theory than with the figures associated with new phenomenology. In particular, see the work of Philip Goodchild, Eric L. Santner, Kenneth Reinhard, and Clayton Crockett. Alternatively, see work more in a neo-Nietzschean vein, for example, the work of Gianni Vattimo. See the following by Žižek: *The Puppet and the Dwarf: The Perverse Core of Christianity* (Cambridge: MIT Press, 2003); *On Belief* (New York: Routledge, 2001); *The Fragile Absolute* (London: 2000). See the following by Vattimo: *After Christianity*, trans. Luca D'Isanto (New York: Columbia University Press, 2002); *Belief*, trans. Luca D'Isanto and David Webb (Stanford: Stanford University Press, 1999). See also: Slavoj Žižek, Eric L. Santner, and Kenneth Reinhard, *The Neighbor: Three Inquiries in Political Theology* (Chicago: University of Chicago Press, 2005); *Theology and the Political: The New Debate*, ed. Creston Davis, John Milbank, and Slavoj Žižek (Durham, NC: Duke University Press, 2005). That said, the distinctions between these various traditions are not

hard and fast within CPR. Both Caputo and Derrida have published books with Vattimo (see Caputo and Vattimo, *After the Death of God,* ed. Jeffrey W. Robbins [New York: Columbia University Press, 2007] and *Religion,* ed. Derrida and Gianni Vattimo [Stanford: Stanford University Press, 1998]); and the books the Goodchild has edited in this area have contributors who cross traditions (see *Rethinking Philosophy of Religion: Approaches from Continental Philosophy* [New York: Fordham University Press, 2002] and *Difference in Philosophy of Religion* [Aldershot: Ashgate, 2003]). Finally, the work of Hent de Vries brings all of these traditions together (see *Philosophy and the Turn to Religion* [Baltimore: Johns Hopkins University Press, 1999], *Religion and Violence: Philosophical Perspectives from Kant to Derrida* [Baltimore: Johns Hopkins University Press, 2002], and *Minimal Theologies: Critiques of Secular Reason in Adorno and Levinas* [Baltimore: Johns Hopkins University Press, 2005]). Despite the work done extending CPR in these other directions, the present volume focuses specifically on the phenomenological/deconstructive tradition and so I will exclusively consider it in what follows.

4. This is neither to say that such claims are definitive of all Christian communities nor to say that they are necessary requirements for Christian belief as such. However, they are crucial to my community (or at least my understanding of my community) and, accordingly, to my religious identity.

5. I am not claiming that this is the only way salvation is possible. But simply that I do not think that affirming (4) requires me to affirm a particular view of soteriology.

6. For more on how this might work out in practice, see Bruce Ellis Benson's chapter in this volume.

7. Though I can certainly inhabit these different aspects of my identity in different ways, depending on the context. In particular, I think that the authority structures operative in CPR are not necessarily the same as in Pentecostalism. Accordingly, I can operate professionally in different ways (as a philosopher, or theologian, or sociologist, etc.), even though my personal identity remains plural as a Postmodern Pentecostal. Elsewhere I have considered the distinction between personal and professional identities (see my *God and the Other: Ethics and Politics after the Theological Turn* [Bloomington: Indiana University Press, 2011], especially chapter 7, and "On Shared Hopes for (Mashup) Philosophy of Religion: A Reply to Trakakis," *Heythrop Journal,* forthcoming.

8. Jacques Derrida, *The Gift of Death,* trans. David Wills (Chicago: University of Chicago Press, 1995), 108.

9. John D. Caputo, "Spectral Hermeneutics: On the Weakness of God and the Theology of the Event," in John D. Caputo and Gianni Vattimo, *After the Death of God,* ed. Jeffrey W. Robbins (New York: Columbia University Press, 2007), 47–88, 53.

10. John D. Caputo, *The Weakness of God: A Theology of the Event* (Bloomington: Indiana University Press, 2006), 13.

11. Just as with C-beliefs above, I do not mean to suggest that these P-beliefs are necessary requirements for being a postmodernist, but merely that they are fairly representative of many postmodern discussions of religion. In what follows,

I will have occasion to challenge whether these specific beliefs should have been adopted in the first place.

12. Søren Kierkegaard, *Concluding Unscientific Postscript to Philosophical Fragments,* vol. 1, trans. and ed. Howard V. Hong and Edna H. Hong (Princeton, NJ: Princeton University Press, 1992).

13. John D. Caputo, *The Prayers and Tears of Jacques Derrida: Religion without Religion* (Bloomington: Indiana University Press, 1997), xxi.

14. Here, "dogma" is not meant as a belief held dogmatically—that is, without room for revisability and critical distance—but rather, like the term is used by skeptical philosophers such as Sextus Empiricus, it is simply meant to indicate a truth-claim that stands as part of a particular tradition.

15. At this point it might be objected that P-beliefs would simply be a particular subset of C-beliefs (when expanded to include all necessary claims for Christianity). I have no problem with rephrasing the situation in this way because the problematic tension would be maintained; C-beliefs would seem to be internally inconsistent. I have chosen not to collapse the two sets of beliefs into one simply because I will later have occasion to pull them apart and rephrase P-beliefs such that the two sets (or the one large set) are coherent.

16. There may be many other reasons for denying the truth of C-beliefs, but all I am concerned with here is that it is plausible someone might reject C-beliefs solely because she is a postmodernist.

17. Crucially, I am *not* saying that this particular way of expressing the dilemma will be a problem for *every* postmodern philosopher who claims a Christian religious identity (John Caputo, for example, might take this as a productive rationale for why we should have "Christianity"—articulated according to P-beliefs—without "Christianity"—understood as C-beliefs), but it will at least be a problem for anyone who understands Christianity to, in one way or another, affirm truth-claims that postmodernism appears to make impossible to affirm.

18. As explained earlier regarding the two senses of being "after" objectivity, giving a "rational defense" does not mean operating by means of arguments that will achieve universal assent, depend upon objective evidence, or affirm absolute truth, but merely by means that are neither self-contradictory nor affirmed through foot-stomping—what C. S. Peirce would term the "method of tenacity."

19. As John G. Stackhouse Jr. notes, "Christians engage in apologetics because they want their neighbors to take Christianity more seriously than they otherwise might" (*Humble Apologetics: Defending the Faith Today* [New York: Oxford University Press, 2006], 86).

20. Merold Westphal, *Overcoming Onto-Theology: Toward a Postmodern Christian Faith* (New York: Fordham University Press, 2001), 189, hereafter cited in the text.

21. Here I insert "that" to replace "us," which I can only assume is a typographical error since it makes no sense in the context of the sentence.

22. John D. Caputo, "Methodological Postmodernism: On Merold Westphal's '*Overcoming Onto-Theology*,'" *Faith and Philosophy* 22, no. 3 (July 2005): 294.

23. Again, it is important to remember that even Alvin Plantinga is worried about such triumphalism (see "Response to Nick Wolterstorff").

24. Merold Westphal, *Whose Community? Which Interpretation? Philosophical Hermeneutics for the Church* (Grand Rapids, MI: Baker Academic, 2009), hereafter cited in the text.

25. See Kierkegaard, *Concluding Unscientific Postscript,* 118. A careful reader will realize that this is not exactly what Climacus says. Indeed, his claim is that "existence itself *is* a system—for God" (emphasis added). There are two possible ways of making sense of this "is" here: (1) it can be read as a rather straightforward claim about the epistemic perspective of an existing God; (2) it can be read as a conditional claim of the following sort—*if* there is a God, *then* we must assume that existence is a system for God. Given the decidedly non-Christian perspective of Climacus, I propose that the second interpretation is the most plausible. Accordingly, the antecedent to this conditional is granted by Climacus as a rather baroque thought experiment. As such, what we find in the *Postscript* is not a dogmatic claim about the ontological reality of a divine being, but a thoroughly fallible claim about the apparent epistemic constraints on human knowledge. Importantly, Westphal implicitly offers a similar interpretation when he paraphrases Climacus as saying that "reality *may very well be* a system for God" (*Overcoming Onto-Theology,* 190; emphasis added).

26. Caputo, "Methodological Postmodernism," 289.

27. Following Kierkegaard, perhaps one still might claim ecclesial authority or theological authority, but such claims would not be of the sort that philosophers *as philosophers* would be able to make and, as such, are not problems for this account.

28. Caputo, "Methodological Postmodernism," 292.

29. Ibid., 293.

30. Caputo, *The Weakness of God,* 16.

31. Ibid., 12.

32. Ibid., 32–37.

33. I consider this as well in the introduction to this volume (see esp. 357n16).

34. Caputo, *The Weakness of God,* 9.

35. When taken as a *descriptive* claim, of course, religious pluralism is quite uncontestable. I see the stakes of Caputo's affirming normative religious pluralism as having more to do with theological matters related to soteriology and eschatology, etc.

36. Caputo, "Methodological Postmodernism," 293.

37. Ibid., 294.

38. Caputo and Scanlon, "Apology for the Impossible."

39. It could be argued that (16) does not require metaphysical postmodernism, but only epistemological postmodernism with the supplemental qualification that MT-beliefs necessarily operate according to a strong evidentialism. As such, EP-beliefs could potentially include (16) because MT-beliefs would, by definition, be a model of just the sort of religious tradition that is problematic

because of how it holds beliefs and not simply because of what beliefs it holds. Though I think that Caputo's affirmation of (16) probably operates according to some such rationale, I do not find this approach convincing. When Caputo offers an account of what MT-beliefs entail, namely, "that God is an infinite eternal omnipotent omniscient creator of heaven and earth," this claim is unquestionably a matter of content.

40. The distinction between the two types of postmodernism depends quite heavily on exactly what one takes "onto-theology" to be and what "overcoming" it might mean. For essays taking up this question, see *Religion after Metaphysics*, ed. Mark A. Wrathall (Cambridge: Cambridge University Press, 2003), especially Adriaan Peperzak's "Religion after Onto-Theology?" (chapter 8). See also Merold Westphal, *Transcendence and Self-Transcendence: On God and the Soul* (Bloomington: Indiana University Press, 2004), and Jeffrey W. Robbins, "Overcoming Overcoming: In Praise of Ontotheology," in *Explorations in Contemporary Continental Philosophy of Religion*, ed. Deane-Peter Baker and Patrick Maxwell (Amsterdam: Rodopi, 2003), 9–22.

41. Merold Westphal, "Divine Excess: The God Who Comes After," in *God, the Gift, and Postmodernism*, 266.

42. Caputo, *The Weakness of God*, 5.

43. See Nick Trakakis, *The End of Philosophy of Religion* (London: Continuum Press, 2008).

44. Caputo, "Who Comes after the God of Metaphysics?" in *The Religious*, ed. John D. Caputo (Oxford: Blackwell, 2002), 1–19, 3.

45. Alvin Plantinga, "The Free Will Defense," in *Philosophy of Religion: An Anthology*, ed. Louis P. Pojman and Michael Rea (Belmont, CA: Thomson Wadsworth, 2008), 181–200, 189–90.

46. L. W. Barnard, *Justin Martyr: His Life and Thought* (Cambridge: Cambridge University Press, 1967), 26.

47. Ibid., 37–38.

48. Merold Westphal has also encouraged continental philosophers of religion to begin writing more often for the Church rather than solely for only the academy (see Westphal's "Taking Plantinga Seriously: Advice to Christian Philosophers," *Faith and Philosophy* 16, no. 2 [April 1999]: 173–81). See also "The Church and Postmodern Culture" series with Baker Academic Press, ed. James K. A. Smith, as well as the work of such popular authors as Brian McLaren and Peter Rollins.

49. St. Justin Martyr, *The First and Second Apologies*, trans. Leslie William Barnard (New York: Paulist Press, 1997), I, §1, p. 23, hereafter cited in the text.

50. At the beginning of the *Second Apology* we find the same motivation: "O Romans, what has recently happened in your city under Urbicus, and what is likewise being done everywhere by the governors unreasonably, have compelled me to compose these arguments for your sakes, who are of like passion and are our brothers, though you are ignorant of the fact and repudiate it on account of the splendor of your position" (II, §1, p. 73). I understand Justin's Second Apology

to be similar to what one finds in Derrida's "Open Letter to Bill Clinton" in which he offers evidence for why Mumia Abu-Jamal was falsely accused and is the victim of a great injustice (in *Negotiations: Interventions and Interviews 1971–2001,* ed. and trans. Elizabeth Rottenberg [Stanford: Stanford University Press, 2002], 130–32). For other examples of this same sort of argumentative motivation, see Derrida's essays, "For Mumia Abu-Jamal," and "Derelictions of the Right to Justice" in the same volume.

51. Emmanuel Levinas, *Otherwise than Being or Beyond Essence,* trans. Alphonso Lingis (Pittsburgh: Duquesne University Press, 1997), v.

52. After giving a talk on deconstruction and kenosis, I was told by a member of the audience, "You must be a Christian because only Christians would care to ask such questions." Further, in regard to a book manuscript I was working on concerning Evangelical Christianity and environmental ethics, I was advised (by a senior scholar in continental philosophy) to publish it under a pseudonym because just having the term "evangelical" anywhere on my vitae would exclude me from consideration at most universities.

53. I was once told by a faculty member at a Christian college, to which I had applied for a faculty position, that I could not be hired because my postmodern perspective was "dangerous to the students."

54. This is why I have chosen to identify myself as a Pentecostal rather than simply as a Christian. To many, Pentecostalism is often taken to be by definition a "fundamentalist" version of Christianity. That said, even though *some* Pentecostals are rightly considered "fundamentalists," I hope that my work will attest to the falsity of assuming the necessity of such a connection.

55. While analytic philosophy of religion is more likely to adhere to this suggestion regarding argumentative standards than is CPR, often what passes as "rigor" in analytic philosophy of religion serves more as a statement of philosophical style than as an attempt to be clear and lucid. Similarly, what is often presented in CPR as an attempt to convey what cannot be conveyed, to say the unsayable, and to express the paradoxical structure of "the impossible," is better understood as an expression of a different philosophical style (set against what is perceived to define analytic philosophy of religion) than as a rejection of clarity, lucidity, and rigor. Simply put, what passes as "rigor" within a community is always reflective of the norms of the community itself. Hopefully, the present book demonstrates how CPR can be expressed and considered in terms that are recognizable and intelligible to those working in analytic philosophy of religion. Alternatively, I hope that it demonstrates that the concerns of analytic philosophy of religion are not entirely absent from CPR (and vice versa).

56. Caputo's claim is: "All over Anglo-America, logicians and epistemologists, from the Dutch Reformed to the Roman Catholic confessions, hasten to stretch a net of argumentation under faith in the divine being, lest the leap of faith end up falling to the floor in a great crash" ("Who Comes after the God of Metaphysics," in *The Religious,* ed. John D. Caputo (Oxford: Blackwell, 2002), 1–19, 2).

57. Elsewhere I defend the notion of a deconstructive foundationalism; see *God and the Other: Ethics and Politics after the Theological Turn* (Bloomington: Indiana University Press, 2011), chapter 11.

58. Several of Caputo's own works can be read as positive examples of Christian apologetics in this sense of calling Christians to reevaluate their own account of Christianity. In *Philosophy and Theology, On Religion,* and *What Would Jesus Deconstruct?* Caputo operates in the same line as Kierkegaard's attempt to "bring Christianity to Christendom." In these texts, Caputo speaks to a popular, generally religious, audience and appears to be willing to locate himself more firmly in the Christian tradition and in relation to the claims by which that tradition has historically been defined.

59. David K. Clark, *Dialogical Apologetics: A Person-Centered Approach to Christian Defense* (Grand Rapids, MI: Baker Books, 1993), 114.

60. Stackhouse, *Humble Apologetics,* xvi.

61. Ibid., 34.

62. William C. Placher, *Unapologetic Theology: A Christian Voice in a Pluralistic Conversation* (Louisville, KY: Westminster/John Knox Pres, 1989), 11.

63. Clark will also term this "audience-sensitive" apologetics (*Dialogical Apologetics,* 109).

64. Ibid., 102.

65. Stackhouse, *Humble Apologetics,* 141.

66. Ibid., 109–10.

67. Clark, *Dialogical Apologetics,* 110.

68. For a good example of what such a cumulative case account might entail, see C. Stephen Evans, *The Quest for Faith: Reason and Mystery as Pointers to God* (Downers Grove, IL: InterVarsity Press, 1986).

69. Stackhouse, *Humble Apologetics,* xi; see also 36.

70. Goodchild, introduction to *Difference in Philosophy of Religion* (Aldershot, UK: Ashgate, 2003), 2.

71. Stackhouse, *Humble Apologetics,* 107. I make this point about postmodern epistemology more broadly elsewhere (e.g., see *God and the Other,* chapter 11.

72. Of course, epistemic certainty should not be confused with the religious confidence that might be said to be found within a relationship with God.

73. See Merold Westphal, "The Importance of Mystery for the Life of Faith," *Faith and Philosophy* 24, no. 4 (October 2007): 367–84. See also Evans, *The Quest for Faith.*

74. Stackhouse, *Humble Apologetics,* 111. As Cornel West writes, "Of course, the fundamental philosophical question remains whether the Christian gospel is ultimately true. And, as a Christian prophetic pragmatist whose focus is on coping with transient and provisional penultimate matters yet whose hope goes beyond them, I reply in the affirmative, bank my all on it, yet am willing to entertain the possibility in low moments that I may be deluded" (*The American Evasion of Philosophy: A Genealogy of Pragmatism* [Madison: University of Wisconsin Press, 1989], 233; cited in Stackhouse, *Humble Apologetics,* 111).

75. Here, I find the work of Chantal Mouffe (especially her defense of a "radical and plural" democracy that depends on "agonism" while striving to avoid "antagonism") to be of great value for rethinking religious discourse in a multicultural and postmodern world (see *The Democratic Paradox* [London: Verso, 2000]). See also Stephen Minister's chapter in this volume.

76. In an essay written to a more general audience, I consider the problems that can accompany the exclusivist tendencies of inclusivist language within religious communities ("We Are Still Them: Non-Denominationalism and the Hermeneutics of Silence," published online at www.theotherjournal.org/churchandpomo/2011/12/05/we-are-still-them-non-denominationalism-and-the-hermeneutics-of-silence/).

77. Wyschogrod, *Saints and Postmodernism: Revisioning Moral Philosophy* (Chicago: University of Chicago Press, 1990). In the final chapter of *God and the Other*, I provide a more thorough consideration of Wyschogrod's thought and its relevance to postmodern ethics and philosophy of religion.

78. This idea can also be found in the apologetic work of William Lane Craig (see *Reasonable Faith: Christian Truth and Apologetics*, rev. ed. [Wheaton, IL: Crossway Books, 1994], 299–302). Craig claims that "the ultimate apologetic is: your life" (302). Though I applaud the importance of testimony and personal transformation in Craig's account, his apologetic work is decidedly "classical" in ways that I find quite problematic.

79. I think that even Kierkegaard proposes such an apologetics of exemplars, though he does not express it in this way. For example, as Stephen Backhouse notes, "In [*Fear and Trembling*], the Knight [of Faith] was invisible to the wider world, and unable to express himself—even indirectly. In the non-pseudonymous *Discourses*...as the one who wills the good in truth, it is the suffering individual's chief task to break the 'silence,' even if this involves his life rather than his words" (*Kierkegaard's Critique of Christian Nationalism* [Oxford: Oxford University Press, 2011], 185).

80. This positive dimension of postmodern apologetics will likely be more plausible internal to some philosophical methodologies than to others. In particular, New Phenomenology, which Marion rightly claims is more about arguing for the possibility of religious phenomena than contending for the actuality of such phenomena, is likely to be somewhat suspicious of the move from negative to positive apologetics. This does not mean that new phenomenologists themselves would not be able to engage in such positive practice, but simply that they will likely go beyond a phenomenological methodology in order to do so. I address this issue elsewhere (see "On Shared Hopes for (Mashup) Philosophy of Religion: A Reply to Trakakis.").

81. Kierkegaard, *Journals and Papers*, vols. 1–7, ed. and trans. Howard V. Hong and Edna H. Hong (Bloomington: Indiana University Press, 1967–78). Citations to the *Journals* will be given first with the entry number of for the English translation (JP) and then for the Danish *Papirer*. JP 474; P IX A 2.

82. See, for example, JP, 187/P x2 A 119; JP 503/ P X1 A 467; JP 1144/P X4 A 422; JP 1915/ P X4 A 626; JP 3030/P IX A 253; JP 3842/P X4 A 279; JP 3862/P X4 A 280; JP 6708/P X3 A 663.

83. See Caputo, *What Would Jesus Deconstruct? The Good News of Postmodernism for the Church* (Grand Rapids, MI: Baker Academic, 2007). See also Bruce Ellis Benson's chapter in the present volume.

84. And, crucially, this is at least part of why the view of Kierkegaard as an irrational fideist is mistaken. No one has done more to demonstrate why the irrationalist charge does not stick to Kierkegaard than has C. Stephen Evans (see his *Kierkegaard's "Fragments" and "Postscript": The Religious Philosophy of Johannes Climacus* [Atlantic Highlands, NJ: Humanities Press, 1983] and *Passionate Reason: Making Sense of Kierkegaard's Philosophical Fragments* [Bloomington: Indiana University Press, 1992]).

85. See note 79 above. Clark also considers Kierkegaard a certain kind of apologist—an "existential apologist" (*Dialogical Apologetics*, 103–04). See also C. Stephen Evans, "Apologetic Arguments in Kierkegaard's Philosophical Fragments," in *International Kierkegaard Commentary: Philosophical Fragments and Johannes Climacus*, ed. Robert L. Perkins (Macon, GA: Mercer University Press, 1994), 63–84. Further, Julia Watkin suggests that Kierkegaard offers something like a defense of Christianity in her "Fighting for Narnia: Søren Kierkegaard and C. S. Lewis," in *Kierkegaard on Art and Communication*, ed. George Pattison (New York: St. Martin's Press, 1992), 137–49.

86. Levinas, *Otherwise than Being*, xlviii.

NOTES TO CHAPTER 1 REPLY 1 / BENSON

1. Friedrich Nietzsche, *Beyond Good and Evil*, trans. Judith Norman (Cambridge: Cambridge University Press, 2002), § 34.

2. Derrida, "Circumfession: Fifty-Nine Periods and Periphrases," in Geoffrey Bennington and Jacques Derrida, *Jacques Derrida* (Chicago: University of Chicago Press, 1993), 155.

3. Derrida, *The Gift of Death*, trans. David Wills (Chicago: University of Chicago Press, 1995), 108; and John D. Caputo, "Spectral Hermeneutics: On the Weakness of God and the Theology of the Event," in John D. Caputo and Giannia Vattimo, *After the Death of God*, ed. Jeffrey W. Robbins (New York: Columbia University Press, 2007), 53.

4. Perhaps analytic philosophers of religion are more guilty of ontotheology than their continental counterparts, but that assertion is far from self-evident and so would need some serious argumentation to sustain it.

5. John Calvin, *Institutes of the Christian Religion*, ed. John T. McNeill, trans. Ford Lewis Battles (Philadelphia: Westminster Press, 1960), vol. 1, 121.

6. Augustine, *Confessions*, trans. Henry Chadwick (Oxford: Oxford University Press, 1998), 10:6, 8.

7. This response to Simmons—in which I defend traditional articulations of Christianity—should be read as a companion piece to my more deconstructive chapter in this volume. As should be clear, I do not see deconstruction and definite Christian beliefs as being at odds with each other; rather, they should be

seen as complementary in the sense that one both affirms traditional Christian beliefs and also holds them up to the light of deconstruction.

8. Emmanuel Levinas, *Basic Philosophical Writings*, ed. Adriaan T. Peperzak, et al. (Bloomington: Indiana University Press, 1996), 141.

9. Martin Heidegger, "The Onto-theological Constitution of Metaphysics," in *Identity and Difference*, trans. Joan Stambaugh (New York: Harper & Row, 1969), 72.

10. Derrida writes: "There is not narcissism and non-narcissism; there are narcissisms that are more or less comprehensive, generous, open, extended" (*Points... Interviews, 1974–1994*, ed. Elisabeth Weber, trans. Peggy Kamuf et al. [Stanford: Stanford University Press, 1995], 199).

11. Bruce Ellis Benson, *Graven Ideologies: Nietzsche, Derrida, and Marion on Modern Idolatry* (Downers Grove, IL: InterVarsity Press 2002), 238–40.

NOTES TO CHAPTER 1 REPLY 2 / MINISTER

1. John D. Caputo, "Methodological Postmodernism: On Merold Westphal's '*Overcoming Onto-Theology*,'" *Faith and Philosophy* 22, no. 3 (July 2005): 294.

2. Merold Westphal, "Reply to Jack Caputo," *Faith and Philosophy* 22, no. 3 (July 2005): 297–300.

3. Caputo, *What Would Jesus Deconstruct?* (Grand Rapids, MI: Baker Academic, 2007), 40.

4. Westphal, "Reply to Jack Caputo," 299.

5. Søren Kierkegaard, *Philosophical Fragments* (Princeton, NJ: Princeton University Press, 1985), 37.

NOTES TO CHAPTER 2 / MINISTER

1. Caputo, *The Weakness of God: A Theology of the Event* (Bloomington: Indiana University Press, 2006), 1 and 7, respectively; hereafter cited as *WG*.

2. In an interview late in his life, Derrida said, "That is sometimes what I am charged with: saying nothing, not offering any content or any full proposition. I have never proposed anything, and that is perhaps the essential poverty of my work" ("Hospitality, Justice, and Responsibility: A Dialogue with Jacques Derrida," in *Questioning Ethics: Contemporary Debates in Philosophy*, ed. R. Kearney and M. Dooley [New York: Routledge, 1999], 74). In Caputo's recent work, he seems to move beyond Derridean deconstruction. See *The Weakness of God* and *What Would Jesus Deconstruct? The Good News of Postmodernism for the Church* (Grand Rapids, MI: Baker Academic, 2007); hereafter cited as *WWJD*. In these works, Caputo claims that he has supplemented deconstruction's critical strategies with "a theory of truth," the "truth of the event" (*WWJD* 30), which Caputo is happy to equate with the New Testament notion of the "kingdom of God" (*WG* 13). I think this is a good development, but one that does not go far

enough as he retains and extends Derrida's notion of "religion without religion" to theology and ethics.

3. Since my goal in this essay (and the goal of the other essays as well) is not to abandon the without, perhaps a better subtitle for the book would have been "Toward a Religion without Religion (with Religion)." I rather doubt though that any publisher would be happy with that. Moreover, this clumsy phrasing also indicates why I am content with dropping the qualifiers altogether: not because religion without religion was a bad idea, but because if it is really religion without religion (with religion), or theology without theology (with theology), or ethics without ethics (with ethics), then we might as well save some ink and acknowledge that what we are talking about is a religion with a theology and an ethics, even if it is a slightly different religion than the religions of the strong theologies.

4. *On Religion* (New York: Routledge, 2001), 93; hereafter cited as *OR*.

5. Moses Maimonides, *The Guide of the Perplexed*, trans. Shlomo Pines, vol. 1 (Chicago: University of Chicago Press, 1963), chapter 60, 145.

6. "On the Social Contract," in *Jean-Jacques Rousseau: The Basic Political Writings*, trans. Donald Cress (Indianapolis: Hackett, 1987), book 4, chapter 8, p. 226.

7. Ibid., 227.

8. Richard Rorty, *Objectivity, Relativism, and Truth* (Cambridge: Cambridge University Press, 1991), 33.

9. See Kierkegaard's *Philosophical Fragments: Johannes Climacus* (Princeton, NJ: Princeton University Press, 1985).

10. It should be noted that Caputo uses the term "fundamentalism" as a category defined by certain theological characteristics rather than simply as a descriptive term for a particular historical movement within Christianity and more recent movements within Islam. That said, Caputo clearly has these movements in mind as he suggests the true meaning of and motivations behind "fundamentalism." See *OR* 91–108.

11. A defender of Caputo might suggest that his commitment to determinate beliefs is no problem since Caputo himself recognizes the necessity of determinate religious traditions and his goal is not to get us to abandon determinate religious traditions for his deconstructive religion without religion, but instead to help us inhabit "the distance between them" (*OR* 36). However, this distance implies a qualitative separation between determinate religion and Caputo's religion without religion. It is this qualitative separation that I am questioning, as I think Caputo's religion without religion is best understood as another determinate interpretation of religion (and a very plausible one at that).

12. For Caputo's earlier writing on ethics, see *Against Ethics* (Bloomington: Indiana University Press, 1993).

13. See Jean-Paul Sartre's *Saint Genet: Actor and Martyr*, trans. Bernard Frechtman (New York: New American Library, 1963), 26ff.

14. See Bruce Ellis Benson's essay in this book for more on the difficulty of articulating a criterion for kingdom membership.

15. *The Prayers and Tears of Jacques Derrida: Religion without Religion* (Bloomington: Indiana University Press, 1997), 158; hereafter cited in the text as *PT*.

16. It is in defense of the autonomy of the other that Derrida famously endorses the classical emancipatory ideal in "Force of Law," in *Acts of Religion,* ed. Gil Anidjar (New York: Routledge, 2002), 258.

17. For Aristotle's account of *phronesis,* see his *Nicomachean Ethics,* trans. Terence Irwin (Indianapolis: Hackett, 1999), book 6.

18. Ibid., book 6; 5, 8.

19. Ibid., book 1; 3.

20. The only places where deconstructive techniques are employed are in the rejection of the nature/culture distinction that underlies the view that homosexuality is unnatural and the indication of the ambiguity of the Christian Scriptures with regard to the status of women. Of course, neither of these uses recommends a particular conclusion or policy position, but simply knocks down specific arguments for particular conclusions. Moreover, one could formulate, and other thinkers have formulated, these objections without any mention of deconstruction.

21. Emmanuel Levinas, *Otherwise than Being or Beyond Essence,* trans. Alphonso Lingis (Pittsburgh: Duquesne University Press, 1981), 162.

22. Alain Badiou, *Saint Paul: The Foundation of Universalism,* trans. Ray Brassier (Stanford: Stanford University Press, 2003), 4.

23. Alain Badiou, *Ethics: An Essay on the Understanding of Evil,* trans. Peter Hallward (New York: Verso, 2001), 1; my emphasis.

24. Ibid., 25.

25. Ibid., 13.

26. Ibid., 42.

27. Badiou, *Saint Paul,* 84.

28. Ibid., 108.

29. Ibid., 99.

30. Ibid., 97.

31. *Otherwise than Being,* 157; quoted from Isa. 57:19.

32. *Is It Righteous to Be? Interviews with Emmanuel Levinas,* ed. Jill Robbins (Stanford: Stanford University Press, 2001), 246; cf. 116.

33. Ibid., 115.

34. *Otherwise than Being,* 160.

35. Ibid., 216.

36. Chantal Mouffe, *On the Political* (New York: Routledge, 2005), 24–25.

37. Ibid., 11–16.

38. Ibid., 20, 52.

NOTES TO CHAPTER 2 REPLY 1 / HANSON

1. Jean-Luc Marion, *God without Being,* trans. Thomas A. Carlson (Chicago: University of Chicago Press, 1991), chapter 1.

2. See Slavoj Žižek, *Violence* (New York: Picador, 2008), 85–88; and Žižek *On Belief* (London: Routledge, 2001), 68–69.

3. For a history of this process in early modern Christendom, see Roland H. Bainton, *The Travail of Religious Liberty* (New York: Harper, 1958).

4. I am drawing here on some points made by John Milbank. For example, he writes, "To stress negativity, and 'exact' opposition, as with deconstruction, is therefore to remain within the same, and to exclude from view the infinite variety of possibly different readings, which are positively affirmed and 'added to' the text, rather than negatively implied by it." *Theology and Social Theory: Beyond Secular Reason* (Oxford: Blackwell, 1993), 310.

5. See Slavoj Žižek and Glyn Daly, *Conversations with Žižek* (Cambridge: Polity Press, 2004), 105–06.

6. This moment in the parable reminds any universalism that the kingdom arguably is not and ought not to be imposed upon those who are not interested in being a member of it.

7. I would argue it is in the same vein that we should read the declarations of "reward" that Jesus makes in the Sermon on the Mount. Such a reading would oppose Caputo's inadequate interpretation advanced in the "Edifying Divertissement" on deconstruction and the kingdom of God in his *The Prayers and Tears of Jacques Derrida: Religion without Religion* (Bloomington: Indiana University Press, 1997).

Notes to Chapter 2 Reply 2 / Simmons

1. John D. Caputo, *The Weakness of God: A Theology of the Event* (Bloomington: Indiana University Press, 2006), 9.

Notes to Chapter 3 / Hanson

1. The irony is probably intentional, but it was surely intended by Kierkegaard too. "Literature in Secret" appears in English translation only in the second edition of *The Gift of Death*, trans. David Wills (Chicago: University of Chicago Press, 2008), 123. All references are to this edition and are hereafter cited as *GD*. All references to *Fear and Trembling* are from the Howard V. and Edna H. Hong translation (Princeton, NJ: Princeton University Press, 1983) and are hereafter cited as *FT*.

2. Though I find few commentators who devote much attention to this thematic, which will be central to all that follows here, John Lippitt's close textual analysis in his *Routledge Philosophy Guidebook to Kierkegaard and "Fear and Trembling"* (London: Routledge, 2003) has a great deal to commend it, and many of my observations from the text are seconded by or dependent upon what he has written, though I think he too does not make enough of the importance of relationship and the transformation thereof by faith.

3. The assumption is generally made that the "man" of the Attunement is Silentio himself, but not much warrants the identification. In fact, it is my argument that Kierkegaard keeps this section anonymous in order to deliberately keep it abstract and focused on methodological concerns, such as how to speak about Abraham properly, rather than on the pseudobiography of Silentio. Whether Silentio is the "man" of the Attunement or not may matter less, though, than the question of whether he is the "poet" of the Eulogy on Abraham, an identification I find even more problematic.

4. So the careful reader will note that the four movements do not move our unnamed man to any greater understanding and that any number of similar ways fare no better. (Other variations can be found in Kierkegaard's journals, proving that he had considered alternative possibilities and selected only these four as representative.) Finally it should be noted that what attracts the "man" to the story of Abraham in the first place is not the "beautiful tapestry of imagination but the shudder of the idea" (*FT* 9). So while it may be right to call these movements "lyrical" it is not their lyricism that matters, and in fact this is the first of many covert assertions in *Fear and Trembling* that poetic, aesthetic, or lyrical approaches to the Abraham story are not the most constructive.

5. Similarly, in the vitally important introduction to *The Concept of Anxiety*, Vigilius Haufniensis describes ethics as never uplifting but always crushing with the demands of ideality. The ideality of ethics is peculiar to it, inasmuch as unlike the other "ideal" sciences, ethics tries to make its ideality actual and in so doing assumes that every individual has the capacity to meet its inflexible standards, expectations that cannot be disappointed or altered (*The Concept of Anxiety*, trans. Reidar Thomte [Princeton, NJ: Princeton University Press, 1981], 16–17). As Haufniensis says pithily, "The more ideal ethics is, the better" (17).

6. There is a connection here between *Fear and Trembling* and a rewarding footnote in the introduction to *The Concept of Anxiety* that refers explicitly to Johannes de Silentio's undertaking in *Fear and Trembling:* "In his work *Fear and Trembling* (Copenhagen: 1843) Johannes de Silentio makes several observations concerning this point. In this book, the author several times allows the desired ideality of esthetics to be shipwrecked on the required ideality of ethics, in order through these collisions to bring to light the religious ideality as the ideality that precisely is the ideality of actuality, and therefore just as desirable as that of esthetics and not as impossible as the ideality of ethics." *The Concept of Anxiety*, 17n. I will have more to say about this meeting of the desirability of the aesthetic ideal and the (im)possibility of the ethical ideal in the concluding section of this paper.

7. Silentio adapts the Danish folk tale to his own purpose. In his version the merman is intent on ravishing Agnes, whose perfect innocence and trust in him vanquishes his desire and forces a moment of decision for the merman. That he cannot go through with his plan is certain; but will he condemn himself to self-lacerating guilt or will he repent and be restored to full humanity?

8. On this possibility the merman could be like the typographical error that gains consciousness of itself in the example Anti-Climacus provides from *The Sickness unto Death:*

Demonic despair is the most intensive form of the despair: in despair to will to be oneself...in hatred toward existence, it wills to be itself, wills to be itself in accordance with its misery. Not even in defiance or defiantly does it will to be itself, but for spite; not even in defiance does it want to tear itself loose from the power that established it, but for spite wants to force itself upon it, to obtrude defiantly upon it, wants to adhere to it out of malice—and, of course, a spiteful denunciation must above all take care to adhere to what it denounces. Rebelling against all existence, it feels that it has obtained evidence against it, against its goodness. The person in despair believes that he himself is the evidence, and that is what he wants to be, and therefore he wants to be himself, himself in his torment, in order to protest against all existence with this torment.... Figuratively speaking, it is as if an error slipped into an author's writing and the error became conscious of itself as an error—perhaps it actually was not a mistake but in a much higher sense an essential part of the whole production—and now this error wants to mutiny against the author, out of hatred toward him, forbidding him to correct it and in maniacal defiance saying to him: "No, I refuse to be erased; I will stand as a witness against you, a witness that you are a second-rate author."

See *The Sickness unto Death,* trans. Howard V. and Edna H. Hong (Princeton, NJ: Princeton University Press, 1980), 73–74.

9. Alfred Hitchcock famously said, "Drama is life with the dull bits cut out," a sentiment that reminds me of the incapacity of aesthetics to actually capture "life," which as Kierkegaard reminds us has to be lived in full, including all the dull bits. Faith, I argue here, is what makes the "dull bits" as dramatic as the aesthetic highlights. Faith invests even the pedestrian with the sublime.

10. I regard this sense of analogy as different from the traditional broadly Neoplatonic view, about which I share the reservations of James K. A. Smith in his *Speech and Theology: Language and the Logic of Incarnation* (London: Routledge, 2002). See especially "The Specter of Platonism: Reconsidering Participation and Incarnation," 170–82.

11. Elaine Scarry speaks of this imaginative analogy when discussing Odysseus's encounter with the ineffable beauty of Nausicaa on the beach of Phaeacia. The encounter with the beautiful strikes the observer as unprecedented, but only as unprecedented as any other encounter with the shockingly beautiful. Odysseus hails Nausicaa as beautiful in a way he has never met with before, until he remembers that the palm tree he spotted once that was beautiful in a similar fashion. Hence an analogy is constructed, but a loose one based on the power of imagination, which may or may not lead to meditations on truth or justice. Scarry thinks it does, though I am not convinced of the mechanism that she proposes for how this takes place. And it does not matter much to the limited point I am trying to make here. See *On Beauty and Being Just* (Princeton, NJ: Princeton University Press, 2001), 21–33. As perceptive a commentator as Louis Mackey has also argued for an imaginative analogy at work in Kierkegaard, and his account in *Kierkegaard: A Kind of Poet* (Philadelphia: University of Pennsylvania Press,

1971) makes some commendable observations while failing sometimes I think to draw the correct conclusion from them. Remarking on the abundance of images in Kierkegaard's writings, even those that seem most academic, he says, "To my knowledge the apparent contradiction between Kierkegaard's negative theology and his habit of thinking in images, similes, and analogies has never been officially noticed. But unless it is reconciled, it opens a gap between theory and practice that undermines Kierkegaard's whole program.... I am convinced that the path to reconciliation lies not through a *univocal* conception of the *content* of Kierkegaard's statements, formed in accordance with some reader's notion of what a philosopher and Christian apologist ought to mean by the things he says. Reconciliation, however, may be accomplished if all of Kierkegaard's statements, taken as *formal* entities, are understood by reference to their situation within the organic wholes of the works in which they occur, and by reference to their location within the whole corpus" (258–59). I agree with Mackey's description of how the imaginative analogies deployed by Kierkegaard operate. (He, like Scarry, thinks the images suggest a connection to the real, that the world has to be structured exemplaristically for them to work. That is possible, but I do not know that either Kierkegaard is [or I am] necessarily committed to that position, and certainly not in a straightforwardly metaphysical schema.) I too reject the notion of a univocal reading of his texts, but my point is that the distinction he is drawing between form and content in Kierkegaard's thought as a whole is an artificial one. To the extent that faith has control of our perception, form is already content-rich, and content is already formally beautiful and intelligible. In that sense I am advocating a radicalization of Mackey's position. I am also rejecting Derrida's position. In one of the most vexing sentences to me in *The Gift of Death* he wrote, "the absolute uniqueness of Jahweh doesn't tolerate analogy" (*GD* 79). This seems to me patently untrue. Jehovah tolerates all manner of analogies, and if anyone does not tolerate analogy it is Derrida himself.

12. It is worth remembering the Scriptural background of speaking in tongues as this miracle is described in the paradigmatic account of the apostles' preaching after the Pentecost in the book of Acts. When the apostles speak in tongues at that event they do not speak glossolalia but in words intelligible to their listeners and equally intelligible to themselves, though the speakers and hearers do not understand a language in common. Pentecost is thus the reversal of the confusion of language inflicted upon prideful men by God at the tower of Babel. See Acts 2:4–8: "And they were all filled with the Holy Ghost, and began to speak with other tongues, as the Spirit gave them utterance. And there were dwelling at Jerusalem Jews, devout men, out of every nation under heaven. Now when this was noised abroad, the multitude came together, and were confounded, because that every man heard them speak in his own language. And they were all amazed and marveled, saying one to another, Behold, are not all these which speak Galilaeans? And how hear we every man in our own tongue, wherein we were born?"

13. Of course prattling nonsense is heard often enough in our day and in Kierkegaard's. The distinction between empty "chatter" as he would most certainly

call it and the authentic proclamation of faith is one that is (like the other distinctions limned in *Fear and Trembling*) difficult for an outsider to discern. To fully explore this issue one would have to devote considerable attention to the theme of chatter in Kierkegaard, but this quote from *Two Ages* is both representative and suggestive of the possibilities inherent in such a project and speaks to the questions I am pursuing here:

> What is it *to chatter?* It is the annulment of the passionate disjunction between being silent and speaking. Only the person who can remain essentially silent can speak essentially, can act essentially. Silence is inwardness. Chattering gets ahead of essential speaking, and giving utterance to reflection has a weakening effect on action by getting ahead of it. But the person who can speak essentially because he is able to keep silent will not have a profusion of things to speak about but one thing only, and he will find time to speak and to keep silent.... But chattering dreads the moment of silence, which would reveal the emptiness.

See *Two Ages,* trans. Howard V. and Edna H. Hong (Princeton, NJ: Princeton University Press, 1978), 97, 98. This point is touched on in *Fear and Trembling,* too, in regard to the tragic heroes, of whom Silentio writes, "If the meaning of his [the tragic hero's] life is in an external act, then he has nothing to say, then everything he says is essentially chatter, by which he only diminishes his impact" (*FT* 116).

14. Interestingly Silentio expresses his own lack of faith as a problem of shared language with God: "In the world of time God and I cannot talk with each other, we have no language in common" (*FT* 35).

15. This "negative" procedure is quite typical of Kierkegaard's general strategy. That it is at work in this section is convincingly demonstrated by Lippitt (21–29), among others.

16. The emphasis on the feminine foreshadows its return in Problema III. It is possible that Silentio in the end actually prefers in certain respects a stereotypically feminine narrative as an allegory of faith to the story of Abraham. This is demonstrated in his final demurral to the stories of Mary, Agnes, and Sarah (not Abraham's wife, but the bride of Tobias). Very little has been written on the weaning narratives; they are surely, besides Problema III and perhaps even including it, the least- known parts of the text. Other interpretations of note are provided by Edward Mooney in his *Knights of Faith and Resignation: Reading Kierkegaard's "Fear and Trembling"* (Albany: State University of New York Press, 1991); Linda Williams in her "Kierkegaard's Weanings," *Philosophy Today* 42, no. 3 (1998): 310–18; and George Pattison in chapter 8 of his *Kierkegaard's Upbuilding Discourses: Philosophy, Literature and Theology* (London: Routledge, 2002).

17. It is more than arguable that Abraham has taken matters into his own hands before, by sleeping with Hagar in order to force the fulfillment of the covenant promise made to him and Sarah.

18. I have to acknowledge the contribution made to my understanding of these passages by a former student, Alexander Kim of Boston College. He

pointed out to me that the scriptural account of the choice of weaning as an image cannot be accidental or unrelated to the Abraham tale, for it occurs in the chapter immediately preceding the one containing the test of Abraham:

> And the LORD visited Sarah as he had said, and the LORD did unto Sarah as he had spoken. For Sarah conceived, and bare Abraham a son in his old age, at the set time of which God had spoken to him. And Abraham called the name of his son that was born unto him, whom Sarah bare to him, Isaac. And Abraham circumcised his son Isaac being eight days old, as God had commanded him. And Abraham was an hundred years old, when his son Isaac was born unto him. And Sarah said, God hath made me to laugh, so that all that hear will laugh with me. And she said, Who would have said unto Abraham, that Sarah should have given children suck? for I have born him a son in his old age. And the child grew, and was weaned: and Abraham made a great feast the same day that Isaac was weaned. And Sarah saw the son of Hagar the Egyptian, which she had born unto Abraham, mocking. Wherefore she said unto Abraham, Cast out this bondwoman and her son: for the son of this bondwoman shall not be heir with my son, even with Isaac. And the thing was very grievous in Abraham's sight because of his son. And God said unto Abraham, Let it not be grievous in thy sight because of the lad, and because of thy bondwoman; in all that Sarah hath said unto thee, hearken unto her voice; for in Isaac shall thy seed be called. And also of the son of the bondwoman will I make a nation, because he is thy seed. (Gen. 21:1–13)

So each weaning narrative ends with a lamentation for a child who is separated definitively from a parent, and what suggests itself is that the separation between Ishmael and Abraham is being covertly referenced. I think it primarily the case that the weaning narratives continue to refer to the relationship of Abraham and Isaac as well as the relationship of Abraham and God as a heavenly parent, but a possible secondary reference to Ishmael is unavoidable, for it is precisely on the occasion of Isaac's weaning that the relationship of Ishmael to Abraham is broken, at the instigation of a distressed maternal figure, Sarah, whose name evokes her own laughter and the laughter of the blessed more generally but who herself apparently cannot abide being laughed at. The shadowy presence of Ishmael in these passages is further supported by one of only two references to Hagar in the entire published corpus (both in *Fear and Trembling*), occurring in the third movement of the Attunement. Is it possible that Ishmael makes sport of Isaac precisely because he has been weaned? Does he mock Isaac's distress at no longer being at his mother's breast?

19. Change in relationship is again what Kierkegaard takes as the aim of communication. It is brought about paradigmatically in faith and in Kierkegaard's favorite analogue thereof, marriage.

20. My friend and colleague Brian Gregor has pointed out that there is a parallel passage to this one in *The Sickness unto Death,* wherein Anti-Climacus discusses the case of despair over sin: "Such a person emphatically declares, perhaps in ever stronger terms, that this relapse plagues and torments him, brings

him to despair, and he says: 'I will never forgive myself.' This is supposed to show how much good there is in him, what a deep nature he has. It is a subterfuge.... No, his despair over the sin is a far cry from being a qualification of the good, is a more intensive qualification of sin, the intensity of which is absorption in sin—and it is this most of all when he is passionately repeating this phrase and thereby denouncing himself (the least of his considerations), when 'never will he forgive himself' for sinning like that (for this kind of talk is exactly the opposite of the brokenhearted contrition that prays God to forgive)" (*The Sickness unto Death*, 111).

21. In fact, Kierkegaard's purpose is not to meditate on responsibility per se, though *Fear and Trembling* has been read by Levinas and Derrida as if it is principally about responsibility, a word that rarely occurs in the text.

22. Like the knight of faith on his way home, convinced that his wife has a rich banquet of roast lamb's head and vegetables though he knows they cannot afford such a meal, the reward of faith cannot be just what we expect. The point of the knight of faith's conviction about a topic as mundane as his waiting supper is that whatever his wife puts on the table *is* roast head of lamb with vegetables, even if it is not. He is happy and secure in his love because whatever comes from the hand of the beloved is for him a banquet, regardless of how sumptuous (or not) it may seem.

23. Similarly, what is on the dinner table does not matter to the knight of faith. If his wife does not have ready the dish he expects, "curiously enough, he is just the same" (*FT* 40).

24. The importance of this dimension of Levinas's thought has been remarked upon extensively, but I single out for special attention Hilary Putnam's treatment in his *Jewish Philosophy as a Guide to Life: Rosenzweig, Buber, Levinas, Wittgenstein* (Bloomington: Indiana University Press, 2008). What I appreciate about Putnam's discussion is his effort to read the emptiness of the "hineni" behind and within each actual concrete response. The "hineni" is not for him an empty figure arbitrarily coupled with any actual concrete response but is its secret life. This seems to me a more promising direction that even Levinas himself is not always able to clearly pursue. Likely in reaction to Derrida's "Violence and Metaphysics" in *Writing and Difference*, trans. Alan Bass (Chicago: University of Chicago Press, 1978), Levinas emphasized in *Otherwise than Being* the degree to which the "saying" is "betrayed" by the "said" in an arguably more problematized formulation of his otherwise familiar dynamic from *Totality and Infinity*, trans. Alphonso Lingis (Pittsburgh: Duquesne University Press, 1969). By my lights, one of the most pronounced developments in *Otherwise than Being* might be a new and oftentimes polemical emphasis on the incapacity of the said to convey the saying without "betrayal." Sometimes Levinas is more ambiguous on this point, as when he writes, "For the saying is both an affirmation and a retraction of the said" (*Otherwise than Being or Beyond Essence*, trans. Alphonso Lingis [Pittsburgh: Duquesne University Press, 1998], 44). But on the very same page, his tone against the said sharpens: "The hither side, the preliminary, which the pre-originary saying animates, refuses the present and manifestation, or lends

itself to them only out of time. The unsayable saying lends itself to the said, to the ancillary indiscretion of the abusive language that divulges or profanes the unsayable." For my part I would point out that the scriptural usages of this language are never context-free. When God calls to his chosen and they respond "Here I am," they do so in response to a definite calling of God upon their lives; He calls Samuel and Abraham and others because he has for them a specific appointed task.

25. In like fashion, which girl will be the lad's princess does not in some sense matter, as I asserted above. In another sense, though, it matters vitally, because she will be irreplaceable.

26. The knight of faith expects a dinner from the one he loves and who loves him in return, but even if it is not the dinner he imagines, he still expects *something* resembling dinner. For he knows the one he loves and knows as well as any man can that he is loved in return. One thinks of the Gospel passage from Matthew 7:9: "Or what man is there of you, whom if his son ask bread, will he give him a stone?"

27. Emmanuel Levinas, "Kierkegaard: Existence and Ethics," in *Proper Names,* trans. Michael B. Smith (London: Athlone, 1996), 74.

28. Hence Abraham's faith *for this life.* It is in the light of faith that the child is a child of promise, that the events of his life take on meaning.

29. As Merold Westphal observes, "It is important to remember that *Fear and Trembling* does not stage a confrontation between the right as such and the holy. Outside the text of *Fear and Trembling* I know of no evidence to suggest that Kierkegaard thought there was or might be a conflict between them; and inside the text of *Fear and Trembling,* no such confrontation takes place (though much of the literature renders itself irrelevant to the text by failing to notice this crucial fact)" ("Johannes and Johannes: Kierkegaard and Difference," in *International Kierkegaard Commentary: "Philosophical Framents" and "Johannes Climacus,"* ed. Robert L. Perkins [Macon, GA: Mercer University Press, 1994], 18).

30. See my "At the Limits of Religion without Religion: A Problem That Cannot Be Resolved," *Philosophy Today* 53, no. 2 (Summer 2009).

31. Levinas in his own way, too, holds apart the empty formalism of the Other, whose communication to me is nothing but the prohibition against murder and who prior to all intentionality and all thematization *is* a sign of nothing other than itself. Levinas's theory of the privileged form of truth that belongs to the relation with the Other involves a formal determination that differs heterogeneously from ordinary modes of truth and in the unique case of which has for its content only its formal mode of presentation.

Michel Henry also separates a privileged mode of truth as Life or phenomenality, the condition of all intramundane truth or phenomena. Once again the former is designated as absolute in the fullest sense of the word, standing in an untouchable realm of lived experience and sheer immanence, wholly foreign to the world of transcendent experience. Despite apparent differences, Levinas's and Henry's approaches (and clearly I am adding in Derrida's as well) very nearly coincide on a central issue, namely, the form of truth that each privileges as distinct from and in some way superior to the truth that belongs to ordinary intramundane experience. For Levinas this privileged kind of truth is that of the Other in her radical transcendence and alterity. For Henry, the privileged mode of truth is that of Life, which is felt only immanently and has no relationship with the world. Both, though, characterize their respective preferred modes of the true as a kind of experience in which there is no discernible difference between the form and the content of that experience. For both, experience par excellence is experience wherein form *is* content.

32. With many other commentators I reject the reading of Kierkegaard as a divine voluntarist, or someone who holds that whatever God declares good is automatically made good. I think the point of the story is that we learn to appreciate or reappreciate the Good thanks to what God has specifically revealed about it. The culmination of the events on Moriah shows that God does not desire human sacrifice, something he is pleased to remind his followers of on this occasion. In this respect my reading bears some similarity to that of Stephen Mulhall in the final portion of his *Inheritance and Originality: Wittgenstein, Heidegger, Kierkegaard* (Oxford: Oxford University Press, 2001) and to Lippitt 161–71.

33. The reference of course is to Tarquinius's relationship to his son, yet another father-son relationship. Tarquinius was the last king of Rome before the republican period. His son was in exile in a foreign city and had gained a position of trust by deceiving the locals that he was in flight from his father and seeking their protection. This is a ruse to gain their trust and to undermine Rome's enemy from within. Given that ruse, Tarquinius's son sends a messenger back to Rome to ask his father for instruction. Not knowing whether the messenger could be trusted or not, Tarquinius tells the messenger nothing. Instead he goes into the garden and strikes off the tops of the tallest poppies with his cane. The messenger returns to Tarquinius's son and reports to him that his father bears him no message at all. "Your father said nothing. All he did was strike the heads off the tallest poppies in his garden." The son though understands that this *is* the message. The message from Tarquinius is that his son should execute the leading men (the tallest poppies) of the enemy city in order to seize power himself and make the city vulnerable to conquest by the Roman army.

34. I want to thank my friends Brian Harding and Adam Rutledge and my friend and colleague Michael R. Kelly for reading this text and providing a number of helpful suggestions. Thanks also go to Fr. Patrick Gray of the Church of the Advent in Boston, who allowed me to present a series of lectures on this material in the spring of 2009, and to everyone who attended my lecture series and asked stimulating questions.

Notes to Chapter 3 Reply 2 / Minister

1. *Fear and Trembling,* trans. Howard V. and Edna H. Hong (Princeton, NJ: Princeton University Press, 1983), 9; hereafter abbreviated as *FT.*

2. While this is also undoubtedly true for Derrida, with whom Hanson's essay is more directly engaged, my brief comments herein will focus on Levinas

since, as I have argued elsewhere, Levinas has more to offer in the way of a positive account of religion. See my "Derrida's Inhospitable Desert of the Messianic," *Heythrop Journal* 48, no.2 (March 2007): 227–42.

3. Emmanuel Levinas, *Collected Philosophical Papers,* trans. Alphonso Lingis (Pittsburgh: Duquesne University Press, 1998), 59, 107.

4. For more on Levinas's reading of Kierkegaard, see Merold Westphal, "The Many Faces of Levinas as a Reader of Kierkegaard," and J. Aaron Simmons, "Existential Appropriations: The Influence of Jean Wahl on Levinas's Reading of Kierkegaard," both in *Kierkegaard and Levinas: Ethics, Politics, and Religion,* ed. J. Aaron Simmons and David Wood (Bloomington: Indiana University Press, 2008).

5. Levinas, *Proper Names,* trans. Michael B. Smith (Stanford: Stanford University Press, 1996), 76.

6. Ibid., 77.

7. Ibid., 77.

8. Levinas, *Entre Nous,* trans. Michael B. Smith and Barbara Harshav (New York: Columbia University Press, 1998), 97.

9. Claire Katz, "Raising Cain: The Problem of Evil and the Question of Responsibility," *Cross Currents* 55, no. 2 (2005): 216.

10. Søren Kierkegaard, *Sickness unto Death,* trans. Howard V. Hong and Edna H. Hong (Princeton, NJ: Princeton University Press, 1980), 40.

Notes to Chapter 4 / Dalton

1. Anders Nygren, *Agape and Eros,* trans. Philip S. Watson (Philadelphia: Westminster Press, 1953), 34.

2. Ibid., 41.

3. Ibid., 48. See also Augustine, *Enchiridion on Faith, Hope, and Love,* trans. J. B. Shaw (Washington, DC: Regnery, 1961), 5.

4. Clement of Alexandria, *Exhortation to the Greeks, The Rich Man's Salvation, To the Newly Baptized,* trans. G. W. Butterworth, Loeb Classical Library (Cambridge, MA: Harvard University Press, 1919); Origen, *On First Principles,* trans. G. W. Butterworth (Gloucester, MA: Peter Smith, 1973); Augustine, *Enchiridion;* Barth, *Church Dogmatics: A Selection,* trans. and ed. G. W. Bromiley (New York: Harper, 1961); Lewis, *The Four Loves* (New York: Harcourt, 1988); Pieper, *Faith, Hope, Love* (San Francisco: Ignatius Press, 1997); Scheler, *Ressentiment,* trans. Lewis B. Coser and William W. Holdheim (Milwaukee, WI: Marquette University Press, 2007).

5. Augustine, *Enchiridion,* 139, 140, 136.

6. Pope Benedict XVI, *God Is Love: Deus caritas est* (San Francisco: Ignatius Press, 2006), 27, 24.

7. Ibid., 16.

8. Plato, "Phaedrus," in *Euthyphro, Apology, Crito, Phaedo, Phaedrus,* trans. W. R. H. Lamb, Loeb Classical Library (Cambridge, MA: Harvard University Press, 1914), 242c; hereafter cited in the text.

9. *Liddell and Scott's Greek-English Lexicon* (Oxford: Clarendon Press, 1984).

10. Cf. Plato, "Symposium," in *Lysis, Symposium, Gorgias*, trans. W. R. H. Lamb, Loeb Classical Library (Cambridge, MA: Harvard University Press, 1925), 191b.

11. Cf. Plato, *The Republic of Plato*, trans. Francis MacDonald Cornford (Oxford: Oxford University Press, 1941), book 4, 437c.

12. Hyland, "῎Ερως, ᾽Επιθυμία, and Φιλία in Plato," *Phronesis* 13 (1968): 32, 40.

13. Cf. Plato, "Phaedrus," 251c–e.

14. Nygren, *Agape and Eros*, 31; hereafter cited by page number in the text.

15. Barth, *Church Dogmatics*, 177, 180, 186.

16. Ibid., 188, 189, 190.

17. One must remember that in Greek Πόρος, resource, has two different meanings. It not only expresses resource in terms of abundance, but also in terms of "ways and means." As such, Πόρος can also be used to express a kind of passage or "way across," hence its antonym is *aporia* (ἀπορία), meaning stuck, blocked, or finding no way out (cf. "Πόρος," in *Liddell and Scott's Greek-English Lexicon*).

18. Plato, "Symposium," 203c–e.

19. Understanding the way in which *Eros* is the movement between absence and presence that unites the two in its being is a significant key to understanding how Plato accounts for *erotic* mania. We shall return to this idea in greater detail later in the chapter.

20. Mitchell, *The Hymn to Eros: A Reading of Plato's Symposium* (Lanham, MD: University Press of America, 1993), 129.

21. We must of course be careful when using the explorations pursued in the *Cratylus* to present a purely Platonic view, since everything Socrates investigates therein he does under the adopted assumption that beings are in motion, and thus that being itself is motion, which is an assumption which he denies near the end of the dialogue. Nevertheless, his analyses of desire, when taken to establish a kind of taxonomy, are not affected by this later denial. Thus, it is not his definitions of them that are questionable in light of this denial, but the way in which these definitions are employed in the attempt to say something about the nature of being.

22. Plato, "Cratylus," in *Cratylus, Parmenides, Greater Hippias, Lesser Hippias*, trans. H. N. Fowler, Loeb Classical Library (Cambridge, MA: Harvard University Press, 1926), 398c–d.

23. It is interesting to note here that the next major section of the *Phaedrus* concerns itself with both the notion of infection and disease and with the concept of cure, or *pharmakon*, present in the act of writing, as is rigorously explored by Jacques Derrida in "Plato's Pharmacy," *Dissemination*, trans. Barbara Johnson (Chicago: University of Chicago Press, 1982). Perhaps the act of writing could be read as a possible *pharmakon* suitable to treating the kind of infection manifest in erotic transcendence. This is a relation that cannot be explored suitably in this investigation but nevertheless warrants further study.

24. Plato, "Cratylus," 420b–c.

25. Plato, "Theaetetus," in *Theaetetus, Sophist,* trans. Harold North Fowler, Loeb Classical Library (Cambridge, MA: Harvard University Press, 1921), 148e.

26. "Theaetetus," 148e. It is interesting to note that the word Plato uses here to describe the pains of labour, ὠδίνουσι, is the same word that he uses in the *Phaedrus* to describe the pain the soul feels when its wings are inspired to grow by erotic striving after the beyond ("Phaedrus," 251d). We will return to this relation in more detail later.

27. We must remember that Theaetetus has not been made "pregnant" by Socrates' questioning. Socrates is not the philosophic father of Theaetetus's intellectual pregnancy. Instead, he figures himself merely as a philosophical midwife helping Theaetetus to deliver a healthy baby—a child he had growing within him long before he met with Socrates. Socrates' only "children," then, are those he helped into the world, not those he fathered himself.

28. Plato also references the subject's passivity in regard to his or her inception upon the philosophic path where Parmenides mentions to the young Socrates that his troubles with the subject matter are a result of the fact that "philosophy has not yet taken hold upon you" (Plato, "Parmenides," in Fowler, *Cratylus, Parmenides,* 130e). Philosophy, it seems for Plato, is not an endeavor initiated by the subject, but one that *takes hold* of the subject—moves in and through a subject from outside.

29. Plato, "Symposium," 178d, 179b–180b.

30. Levinas's works are cited hereinafter in the body of this essay as follows: *BPW,* for *Basic Philosophical Writings,* ed. Adriaan T. Peperzak, Simon Critchley, and Robert Bernasconi (Bloomington: Indiana University Press, 1996); *CPP,* for *Collected Philosophical Papers,* ed. and trans. Alphonso Lingis (Dordrecht, The Netherlands: Martinus Nijhoff, 1987); *OB,* for *Otherwise than Being or Beyond Essence,* trans. Alphonso Lingis (Pittsburgh: Duquesne University Press, 1998); *TI,* for *Totality and Infinity,* trans. Alphonso Lingis (Pittsburgh: Duquesne University Press, 1969); and *TO,* for *Time and the Other,* trans. Richard A. Cohen (Pittsburgh: Duquesne University Press, 1987).

31. It is important to note here that Levinas spent a significant portion of *Totality and Infinity* treating what could be termed the ambiguity of the erotic phenomenon. On the one hand, he seems to suggest that *eros,* in its movement toward the other, follows the trajectory of metaphysical desire. Indeed, he suggests at times that in erotic love and its result, fecundity, one finds a satisfaction for metaphysical desire without finally being satisfied. On the other hand, he criticizes the erotic tendency to grasp the other as an object of pleasure and thereby return its trajectory to the orbit of the self. For more reading on Levinas, see the sections on *eros* in *Totality and Infinity;* see also Jean-Luc Thayse's excellent book, *Eros et Fécondité chez le jeune Lévinas* (Paris: L'Harmattan, 1998).

32. Plato, *The Republic,* book 7, 516b.

33. This "way out" should remind the reader of the Πόρος provided in *Eros.* The Other's appearance and solicitation through metaphysical desire offers a

"way out" of the enslavement to being, just as *Eros* provides a "way out" of the limitations of temporal beauty and into the stability of divine beauty.

34. We should note here Levinas's ambivalence toward the word *possession*. "Possession" seems to have for him both a positive and a negative ethical value. It is positive as used here, inasmuch as it indicates the entrance of the Other and the freedom from one's attachment to oneself introduced therein—that is, inasmuch as it signifies the subject's having been made the possession of the Good. But Levinas disdains possession to the point of condemnation where it expresses the subject's domination of the world through reason, *possessing* what is other and reducing that otherness to him or herself (*BPW* 9; *TI* 46, 158), or inasmuch as possession expresses the loss of independence, which Levinas associates with pagan ritual, in *Difficult Freedom: Essays on Judaism*, trans. Sean Hand (Baltimore: The Johns Hopkins University Press, 1990).

35. By claiming that the idea of infinity is "within me," Levinas is not trying to invoke the mysteries of Zeno's paradox (the possibility of reasoning an infinite contained within a finite). This would require reading the word *in* as a containment, and it is precisely this idea that Levinas is set against. The idea of the infinite is not "contained" inside of the finite, but overflows the finite—explodes the borders of the finite in such a way that it becomes irrevocably opened to the radically exterior (cf. *BPW* 136–38).

36. John Davenport was perhaps the first person to identify and trace out this connection in his 2000 article, "Levinas's Agapeistic Metaphysics of Morals: Absolute Passivity and the Other as Eschatological Hierophany," *Journal of Religious Ethics* 26, no. 2 (Fall 1998): 331–66. Though it was Davenport's goal there to critique Levinas and offer an alternative account of the demands of agapic love in the Christian tradition, he nevertheless recognizes within Levinas's accounts something akin to the Christian agapic love.

37. Max Scheler, for one, was adamant about the fundamental difference between such "charitable actions" and agape (see, for example, *Ressentiment*, 87).

NOTES TO CHAPTER 4 REPLY 1 / HANSON

1. Merold Westphal, *Levinas and Kierkegaard in Dialogue* (Bloomington: Indiana University Press, 2008), 5.

2. Søren Kierkegaard, *Works of Love*, ed. and trans. Howard V. and Edna H. Hong (Princeton, NJ: Princeton University Press, 1995), 106–07.

3. "It naturally follows that the person who has only a worldly or a merely human conception of what love is must come to regard as self-love and lovelessness precisely that which is love in the Christian sense" (Kierkegaard, *Works of Love*, 113).

4. See most notably his essays "Kierkegaard: Existence and Ethics" and "A Propos of 'Kierkegaard Vivant,'" in *Proper Names*, trans. Michael B. Smith (Stanford, CA: Stanford University Press, 1996). For detailed commentary on the relationship between Levinas and Kierkegaard, see my "Emmanuel Levinas: An Ambivalent but Decisive Reception," in *Kierkegaard Research: Sources, Reception,*

and Resources, vol. 11, *Kierkegaard's Influence on Philosophy;* tome 2, *Francophone Philosophy,* ed. Jon Stewart, Søren Kierkegaard Research Centre, University of Copenhagen (Farnham: Ashgate, 2012), 173–206. See also Merold Westphal, "The Many Faces of Levinas as a Reader of Kierkegaard," and J. Aaron Simmons, "Existential Appropriations: The Influence of Jean Wahl on Levinas's Reading of Kierkegaard," both in *Kierkegaard and Levinas: Ethics, Politics, and Religion,* ed. J. Aaron Simmons and David Wood (Bloomington: Indiana University Press, 2008).

   5. *Søren Kierkegaard's Journals and Papers,* ed. and trans. Howard V. and Edna H. Hong (Bloomington: Indiana University Press, 1975), 4447 (Pap. VIII B 71:6).

   6. Kierkegaard, *Philosophical Fragments; Johannes Climacus,* ed. and trans. Howard V. and Edna H. Hong (Princeton, NJ: Princeton University Press, 1985), 47.

   7. Kierkegaard, as usual, distinguishes these terms in the Danish: *Elskov* for erotic love and *Kjærlighed* for Christian agape or charity.

   8. Kierkegaard, *Works of Love,* 266–67.

NOTES TO CHAPTER 4 REPLY 2 / BENSON

   1. That a Google search of "philosophy" led me (after the Wikipedia article) to a line of skin care products only underscores this strange way in which commodities take on these sacred or almost sacred names.

   2. Slavoj Žižek, *The Puppet and the Dwarf: The Perverse Core of Christianity* (Cambridge, MA: MIT Press, 2003), 96. This is merely one instance of this point: Žižek has used it in various texts and interviews.

   3. Jacques Derrida, *The Gift of Death,* trans. David Wills (Chicago: University of Chicago Press, 1996), 49.

   4. *Oxford English Dictionary,* 2nd ed., s.v. "dogma."

   5. Jacques Derrida, "The Villanova Roundtable: A Conversation with Jacques Derrida," in *Deconstruction in a Nutshell,* ed. and with a commentary by John D. Caputo (New York: Fordham University Press, 1997), 21.

   6. Richard Chenevix Trench, *Synonyms of the New Testament,* ed. Robert G. Hoerber (Grand Rapids, MI: Baker, 1989), 188.

   7. As I have demonstrated in my chapter in this book, I think it is quite clear that Jesus was not primarily about inculcating a set of beliefs or doctrines, even if I hardly wish to deny that such doctrines are part of the Christian faith. But it is living out the Gospel that truly makes one a "Christian."

   8. Joseph Ratzinger, "Homily for Msgr. Luigi Giussani," *Communio: International Catholic Review* 31 (2004): 685.

   9. In *The Gift of Death* (100), Derrida plays with the ambivalence of the phrase *"plus de secret."* If we leave the "s" unpronounced, *plus de secret* means "no more secrets" or "no more secrecy." Yet, if the "s" is pronounced, the phrase means "more secrets" or "more secrecy." For more on Derrida's notion of secrecy and its relation to religious faith, see Jeffrey Hanson's chapter in the present volume.

NOTES TO CHAPTER 5 / BENSON

1. Adela Yarbro Collins notes that this remark falls within the category of "litotes" [λιτότς], an understatement that affirms by negating the contrary. With that in mind, Collins says: "The understated emphasis is on the scribe's nearness to the kingdom, not the fact that he does not yet belong to the kingdom." While that may be true, Jesus still does not say that the scribe has arrived—and that point is quite important. See Collins, *Mark: A Commentary* (Minneapolis: Fortress, 2007), 577.

2. Some commentators find this sudden reluctance to question Jesus quite surprising. In my interpretation, however, it makes perfect sense.

3. As Augustine notes, the Scriptures are "a text lowly to the beginner but, on further reading, of mountainous difficulty and enveloped in mysteries"; see Augustine, *Confessions*, trans. Henry Chadwick (Oxford: Oxford University Press, 1998), 3.5.9.

4. It is *not* incidental that the sermons given in many conservative churches focus far more on the epistles than the Gospels.

5. Of course, I am well aware that simply choosing to comment on what Jesus says in the four Gospels that have made it into the canon is *already* to make a kind of statement about the history of Christianity, given the various Gospels that did *not* make it into the canon.

6. It should at least be mentioned that historical violence done in the name of Christianity (and probably other religions) is sometimes quite exaggerated. That is not to say that it is not real or serious.

7. Jacques Derrida, "The Villanova Roundtable: A Conversation with Jacques Derrida," in *Deconstruction in a Nutshell: A Conversation with Jacques Derrida*, ed. and with a commentary by John D. Caputo (New York: Fordham University Press, 1997), 21. "Totally new"—what could that *possibly* mean? The rhetorical point is clear enough. Yet the statement is quite easily dismissed as hyperbolic.

8. The quotation in the heading is the famous question that the jailer asks of Paul and Silas in Acts 16:30. I am assuming that "being saved" is considerably more substantial than "getting to heaven," but I will not be discussing this point at length here.

9. I should point out that this latter way of describing salvation (accepting Jesus as savior) is not merely some "fundamentalist" formulation. It is clearly found in the Baptismal Covenant in *The Book of Common Prayer* used by the Episcopal Church in the United States of America (ECUSA). Baptismal candidates are asked a series of questions. One question is: "Do you turn to Jesus Christ and accept him as your Savior?" The response is: "I do." More conservative Christians are sometimes surprised to discover that this particular formulation is used by such a "liberal" mainline denomination. On the other side, I suspect that most Episcopalians fail to note this commonality with their more conservative counterparts.

10. Augustine, *Confessions* 11.14.

11. It is bequeathed to us from the King James Version and appears in such modern versions as the NIV and ESV—both translated by particularly conservative scholars.

12. Commentators vary quite considerably as to how they translate and then construe "*gennâthâ anôthen.*" Note that Nicodemus himself interprets it as "anew" or "again" and Jesus does not correct him.

13. How the Gospel writer knows of this private exchange is a question that I simply leave aside.

14. D. A. Carson, *The Gospel according to John* (Grand Rapids, MI: Eerdmans, 1991), 197.

15. This addition can be found in Matthew's Gospel but not in Mark's.

16. Norval Geldenhuys, *The Gospel of Luke* (Grand Rapids, MI: Eerdmans, 1950), 359.

17. Exactly what resisting the evildoer might be is not fully clear. Some commentators maintain that Jesus is simply saying that one should not retaliate. But even that interpretation is already disruptive.

18. Friedrich Nietzsche, *The Antichrist*, trans. R. J. Hollingdale (Harmondsworth: Penguin, 1968), §55.

NOTES TO CHAPTER 5 REPLY 2 / SIMMONS

1. Friedrich Nietzsche, *Beyond Good and Evil: Prelude to a Philosophy of the Future*, ed. Rolf-Peter Horstmann and Judith Norman, trans. Judith Norman (Cambridge: Cambridge University Press, 2002), 3.

2. For more on the call for "constructive postmodernism," see David Ray Griffin, *Whitehead's Radically Different Postmodern Philosophy: An Argument for Its Contemporary Relevance* (Albany: State University of New York Press, 2007).

3. Diane Perpich convincingly argues this point in *The Ethics of Emmanuel Levinas* (Stanford, CA: Stanford University Press, 2008).

4. I argue for this idea in more depth elsewhere; see "A Faith without Triumph: Emmanuel Levinas and Prophetic Pragmatism," *MonoKL International: Reflections on Levinas* 4, no. 8–9 (Fall 2010): 467–84.

5. See John D. Caputo, *What Would Jesus Deconstruct? The Good News of Postmodernism for the Church* (Grand Rapids, MI: Baker Academic, 2007).

6. Of course, I recognize that this term does not quite work here, but I know of no other term that would be much better—all are either too ontologically determinate or theologically vacuous.

7. Caputo, *What Would Jesus Deconstruct?* 33.

8. Although I cannot work out the details here, I think that Gianni Vattimo's notion of believing that he believes in God reflects existential confidence, but certainly not epistemic certainty. See Vattimo, *Belief,* trans. Luca D'Isanto and David Webb (Stanford, CA: Stanford University Press, 1999). Similarly, James K. A. Smith's conception of Pentecostal epistemology, which operates according to what he terms an "I know that I know that I know" hermeneutic also dis-

plays confidence without certainty. See Smith, *Thinking in Tongues: Pentecostal Contributions to Christian Philosophy* (Grand Rapids: Eerdmans, 2010), especially chapter 3.

9. See Cornel West, *The American Evasion of Philosophy: A Genealogy of Pragmatism* (Madison: University of Wisconsin Press, 1989); Merold Westphal, "Prolegomena to Any Future Philosophy of Religion Which Will Be Able to Come Forth as Prophecy," *International Journal for Philosophy of Religion* 4, no. 3 (Fall 1973): 129–50.

10. Caputo, *What Would Jesus Deconstruct?* 87.

11. Jacques Derrida, *Rogues: Two Essays on Reason*, trans. Pascale-Anne Brault and Michael Naas (Stanford, CA: Stanford University Press, 2005), 41.

12. An important area for future work in religion with religion is the possible resources of deconstruction for contemporary religious environmental activism, and vice versa.

NOTES TO CHAPTER 6 / WESTPHAL

1. Peter Berger gives a sociological reading of the theological claim, *extra excclesiam nulla salus* (outside the church there is no salvation). This means that religion is inherently "organized" and "institutional" and that religion without these structures is derivative from and dependent on them. See *The Sacred Canopy: Elements of a Sociological Theory of Religion* (Garden City, NY: Doubleday, 1967), 46.

2. Hegel, *Phenomenology of Spirit*, trans. A. V. Miller (Oxford: Oxford University Press, 1977), 47.

3. Ludwig Feuerbach, *The Essence of Christianity*, trans. George Eliot (New York: Harper, 1957), 14–15. Emphasis added.

4. See John D. Caputo, *Radical Hermeneutics: Repetition, Deconstruction, and the Hermeneutic Project* (Bloomington: Indiana University Press, 1987); Merold Westphal, *Overcoming Onto-Theology: Toward a Postmodern Christian Faith* (New York: Fordham University Press, 2001); Caputo's response to the previous text, "Methodological Postmodernism: On Merold Westphal's *Overcoming Onto-Theology*," along with my "Reply to Jack Caputo" in *Faith and Philosophy* 22, no. 3 (July 2005): 284–300.

5. *Sickness unto Death*, ed. and trans. Howard V. Hong and Edna H. Hong (Princeton, NJ: Princeton University Press, 1980), 87. Cf. The motto for Kierkegaard's *Philosophical Fragments*, "Better well hanged than well wed."

6. One could add the request that Simmons tell us what a "lucid argument" could be in a postmodern context. I am not suggesting, as some would, that we abandon talk of reason, truth, and argument, but only that we be very clear what we mean by these terms and how, if we locate ourselves in postmodern horizons, our accounts square with postmodern critique of modern accounts.

7. John Rawls, *Political Liberalism*, expanded ed. (New York: Columbia University Press, 2005), describes a comprehensive doctrine as rational just as

long as it does not seek to impose itself with violence. I assume that Simmons means something stronger than this. But what?

8. "An Occasional Discourse," in *Upbuilding Discourses in Various Spirits,* trans. Howard V. Hong and Edna H. Hong (Princeton, NJ: Princeton University Press, 1993), 3–154.

9. That religion can be a work of the flesh is central to my argument in *Suspicion and Faith: The Religious Uses of Modern Atheism* (New York: Fordham University Press, 1998).

10. Harry G. Frankfurt, *The Importance of What We Care About* (New York: Cambridge University Press, 1998).

11. For Jean-Luc Marion's list, which only goes up to Aquinas, see "In the Name," in *God, the Gift, and Postmodernism,* ed. John D. Caputo and Michael J. Scanlon (Bloomington: Indiana University Press, 1999), 34–35. Cf. 21 and 40.

12. In *Pseudo-Dionysius: The Complete Works,* trans. Colm Luibheid (Mahwah, NJ: Paulist Press, 1987).

13. There is an important hermeneutical circle here. The doctrine of analogy presupposes a doctrine of creation and participation and thus a determinate theism that is hard to find in most theologies that call themselves deconstructive or postmodern.

14. See Fran O'Rourke, *Pseudo-Dionysius and the Metaphysics of Aquinas* (Notre Dame, IN: University of Notre Dame Press, 1992).

15. While it may not be true of Maimonides, all of the apophaticist theologians in my list have theologies that would have to be described as very thick. Hegel and Feuerbach can help us to see why it is no easier to justify a thin theology than a thick one.

16. See Jean-Luc Marion's treatment of *conceptual* idolatry in the first two chapters of *God without Being,* trans. Thomas Carlson (Chicago: University of Chicago Press, 1991).

17. Karl Barth's distinction between revelation (as God-given) and religion (as human response and interpretation) is relevant here. See "The Revelation of God as the Abolition of Religion" in *Church Dogmatics,* vol. 1, part 2, *The Doctrine of the Word of God,* trans. G. T. Thomson and Harold Knight (Edinburgh: T & T Clark, 1956), 280–361. In his retranslation of this section, Garrett Green calls attention to the unfortunate translation of *Aufhebung* as abolition, suggesting sublimation instead. We could also speak of the teleological suspension of religion in revelation. See *On Religion: The Revelation of God as the Sublimation of Religion* (New York: T&T Clark, 2006).

18. Hence the Lutheran slogan, "Word and Spirit," signifying that it is only when the Holy Spirit becomes the teacher who gives the learner what Johannes Climacus calls the Condition, the ability to recognize the speech as the voice of God, that the spoken word becomes the living word and we are addressed by God.

19. This is why I do not see as helpful Minister's suggestion that we say that Sarah and the others might have known and understood *to some degree* but not fully.

20. People do not accuse Derrida of playing (arbitrarily) with texts as often as they used to. Perhaps they have begun to notice the detailed care he gives to what is there in the text and now "close" his readings are. I give Hanson high marks for following his lead in this regard.

21. In *Fear and Trembling* the universal is always social and historically particular. It is not some principle of pure reason a la Plato or Kant.

22. The speaker may "see" things that the listener cannot see, and vice versa, since they occupy different horizons. But any horizon is a limited field of vision beyond which stands what cannot be seen (from there). Structural silence puts this point in terms of speech instead of vision, which is appropriate for a philosophy that has so decisively taken the linguistic turn. This finitude of discourse may be seen as the basis for Caputo's apt description of deconstruction as a "generalized apophatics" in *The Prayers and Tears of Jacques Derrida: Religion without Religion* (Bloomington: Indiana University Press, 1997), 41. No discourse can be adequate to its intended referent.

23. Jacques Derrida, *The Gift of Death*, trans. David Wills (Chicago: University of Chicago Press, 1995), 68, 77–78, 82.

24. Since Hanson's Derrida does not make this distinction, Dalton's suggestion that this Derrida remains in the sphere of resignation makes a lot of sense. But in the text Derrida's emphasis is precisely on responsibility and thus relation and not on a possibly solipsistic resignation.

25. This does not mean that we do not try to construe the inscrutable. Thus, for Derrida we try to say justice in the form of law and for Barth, in a Kierkegaardian spirit, we try to say revelation in the form of theology. For Derrida, see "Force of Law: The 'Mystical Foundation of Authority,' " in *Acts of Religion*, ed. Gil Anidjar (New York: Routledge, 2002), 228–98. See Barth, *Church Dogmatics*, 280–361. But in each case, the said is surpassed by the unsaid.

26. "Transmoral" obviously does not mean indifference to the right and the good. It means the teleological suspension of the ethical, the claim that there is a higher criterion of the right and the good than the present age, its social institutions, and its cultural values (*Sittlichkeit*).

27. Remember that Hanson has described these narratives as examples of how *not* to tell the Abraham story.

28. *Works of Love*, trans. Howard V. Hong and Edna H. Hong (Princeton, NJ: Princeton University Press, 1995), 154–74.

29. See *Christ and Time: The Primitive Christian Conception of Time and History*, trans. Floyd V. Filson (London: SCM Press, 1951).

30. *The Concept of Irony; Schelling Lecture Notes*, trans. Howard V. Hong and Edna H. Hong (Princeton, NJ: Princeton University Press, 1989), 319.

31. That the self and consciousness are always "contaminated" in this way and never "pure" I argue in "The Prereflective Cogito as Contaminated Opacity," in "Spindel: The First-Person Perspective in Philosophical Inquiry," supplement, *Southern Journal of Philosophy* 45, no. S1 (2007): S152–77. Those on both sides of the "religion with or without religion" debate tend to agree on this point.

32. Ibid., S152–77.

33. For a vigorous defense of the harmony of the Augustinian account of Christian love in response to Nygren, see John Burnaby, *Amor Dei: A Study of the Religion of St. Augustine* (London: Hodder & Stoughton, 1938). See also Eric Gregory, *Politics and the Order of Love: An Augustinian Ethic of Democratic Citizenship* (Chicago: University of Chicago Press, 2008).

34. It is worth noticing that in his early writings Levinas speaks of justice and is reluctant to speak of love. In his later writings, especially *Entre Nous*, he speaks freely of love, but to distinguish it from the eros that is *epithumia*, he calls it "love without concupiscence." So including his work as a phenomenology of agape is appropriate.

35. Even God seems to be the depth dimension of the human other by virtue of which I experience unconditional and infinite obligation. I have argued that Levinas's philosophical writings, taken as a whole, represent more nearly an atheism like Feuerbach's than an Abrahamic monotheism. See *Levinas and Kierkegaard in Dialogue* (Bloomington: Indiana University Press, 2008), especially chapters 3–4.

36. Remember that deconstructive apophaticism for Derrida and Caputo is without religion, while the apophatic strands of the Christian tradition are with religion. Derrida himself acknowledges this when he points out that unlike Pseudo-Dionysius, he does not begin his negative theology with a prayer to the Trinity. "How to Avoid Speaking: Denials," trans. Ken Frieden, in *Derrida and Negative Theology*, ed. Harold Coward and Toby Foshay (Albany: SUNY Press, 1992).

37. See John D. Caputo, *What Would Jesus Deconstruct: The Good News of Postmodernism for the Church* (Grand Rapids: Baker Academic, 2007).

38. Jacques Derrida, *Of Grammatology*, trans. Gayatri Chakravorty Spivak (Baltimore, MD: Johns Hopkins University Press, 1974), 158.

39. *Truth and Method*, 2nd ed., rev. trans. Joel Weinsheimer and Donald G. Marshall (New York: Crossroad, 1991), 296.

40. For a comprehensive setting of Jesus in his Jewish context, see N. T. Wright, *Jesus and the Victory of God* (Minneapolis: Fortress Press, 1996).

41. Westphal, *Suspicion and Faith*.

NOTES TO CHAPTER 7 / CAPUTO

1. By "exclusive truth," I do not merely mean the law of the excluded middle, that an assertion cannot be both true and false. I make numerous propositional claims that I hold are true so that the cost of denying them is to hold something not true. I mean privileged access, that something has been made accessible to a certain number of people but not to everybody and that if you do not believe it you are at worst wrong or at best merely in the dark. A statement like "Jesus is uniquely God incarnate" is treated as representationally true or false, representing a supernatural state of affairs unknowable unless it is revealed, something that has been revealed to Christians, who are defined by this privilege. Christians accept its truth, and anyone who denies it is wrong, anyone who has never heard

of it is at a disadvantage through no fault of their own, and those who have heard it and ignore or reject have put themselves at a disadvantage. The latter problem beset Saint Paul, who was worried about his own people, the Jews, who rejected Christ. Paul had the advantage of privileged access, in that he was given the special privilege of being visited by the risen Christ, authorizing him to assure those who were lucky enough to be in the right place at the right time to hear him preach that he was right about this proposition. It is really not much consolation to other traditions, which know or care little or nothing about Christianity, to learn that in this charitable exclusivism not everything they think is "*entirely incorrect*" (Simmons). From such "charity" may the Lord protect us. Such claims would be more credible if they came accompanied by the belief that the *others* are the ones who got privileged access and *we were left out*. Would that not be even more charitable? We do not need charity here; we need justice, doing justice to others, justly recognizing that nobody has any privileged access in matters like this, which is the advantage of seeing that we have to do here with theopoetic differences and not competing representational assertions. Little or nothing is gained when the proponents of privileged access admit that their knowledge is incomplete, that much remains mysterious, that they who have been given privileged access are but finite beings.

2. *Concluding Unscientific Postscript to "Philosophical Fragments,"* Kierkegaard's Writings, vol. 12, part 1, trans. and ed. Howard V. and Edna H. Hong (Princeton, NJ: Princeton University Press, 1992), 118.

3. Quentin Meillassoux, *After Finitude: An Essay on the Necessity of Contingency*, trans. Ray Brassier (London: Continuum, 2008), 28–49.

4. All references to essays within this book will be given parenthetically as the first letter of the author's last name, for example, S (Simmons), M (Minister), B (Benson), and so on.

5. Minister makes the same mistake by saying that Derrida holds no positions, a statement he makes in almost perfect innocence of Derrida's distinction between positions and affirmations.

6. I was prepared in mathematical logic under Hugues Leblanc, who was a student of Quine at Harvard, and I had a special interest in the method of "natural deduction" developed by Gerhard Gentzen (1909–45), a brilliant young German logician who died tragically at the end of World War II. The earliest graduate courses I taught were in mathematical logic, and I had begun to use it in an early publication on Kant's critique of the ontological argument.

7. Martin Heidegger, *Of Time and Being*, trans. Joan Stambaugh (New York: Harper & Row, 1972), 2, 25.

8. John Milbank makes a "complete *concession*" to the idea that Christian theology is "contingent historical construct"; see *Theology and Social Theory: Beyond Secular Reason* (Oxford, UK: Blackwell, 1993), 2. For some good criticisms of this movement, see *Deconstructing Radical Orthodoxy: Postmodern Theology, Rhetoric, and Truth,* ed. Wayne J. Hankey and Douglas Hedley (Aldershot: Ashgate, 2005).

9. I will use the following abbreviations internally: *AE* for *Against Ethics: Contributions to a Poetics of Obligation with Constant Reference to Deconstruction* (Bloomington: Indiana University Press, 1993); *DN* for *Deconstruction in a Nutshell: A Conversation with Jacques Derrida*, edited with a commentary (New York: Fordham University Press, 1997); *OR* for On Religion (London: Routledge, 2001); *P&T* for *The Prayers and Tears of Jacques Derrida: Religion without Religion* (Bloomington: Indiana University Press, 1997); *PT* for *Philosophy and Theology* (Nashville: Abingdon Press, 2006); *WG* for *The Weakness of God: A Theology of the Event* (Bloomington: Indiana University Press, 2006); *RH* for *Radical Hermeneutics: Repetition, Deconstruction and the Hermeneutic Project* (Bloomington: Indiana University Press, 1987); *WWJD* for *What Would Jesus Deconstruct?: The Good News of Postmodernity for the Church* (Grand Rapids: Baker, 2007).

10. I spent my professional career at Villanova, a Catholic university, where I was known for promoting the Catholic mission of the university. After I retired from Villanova, I took on a seven-year appointment at Syracuse University, in a secular religion department, where my job was to conduct a conversation about the events that are going on in theological and religious traditions. With + Without = With/out. See my concluding paragraphs.

11. Martin Hägglund, *Radical Atheism: Derrida and the Time of Life* (Stanford, CA: Stanford University Press, 2008). See my response to Hägglund in "The Return of Anti-Religion: From Radical Atheism to Radical Theology," *Journal for Cultural and Religious Theory* 11, no. 2 (Spring 2011): 32–125.

12. Gilles Deleuze, *The Logic of Sense*, trans. Mark Lester with Charles Stivale, ed. Constantin V. Boundas (New York: Columbia University Press, 1969), 149.

13. For a constructive account of the relationship between continental and analytic philosophy of religion, see Nick Trakakis, *The End of Philosophy of Religion* (London: Continuum, 2008).

14. Jacques Derrida, *Rogues: Two Essays on Reason*, trans. Pascale-Anne Brault and Michael Naas (Stanford, CA: Stanford University Press, 2005), 110.

15. I hasten to add that many of the present contributors lack tenured positions and to their credit are testing other borders—between continental and analytic philosophy, even as their interest in religion could make secular philosophers (and hiring committees) uncomfortable.

16. See the exchange between Jeffrey Robbins, Clayton Crockett, Victor Taylor, and me, on the one hand, and Donald Wiebe, on the other hand, in *Bulletin of the Council of Societies for the Study of Religion* 37, no. 2 (April 2008): 31–48 and 37, no. 3 (September 2008): 77–86.

17. "The Perversity of the Absolute, the Perverse Core of Hegel, and the Possibility of Radical Theology," in *Hegel and the Infinite: Religion, Politics, and the Dialectic*, ed. Clayton Crockett, Creston Davis, and Slavoj Žižek (New York: Columbia University Press, 2011).

18. *Hegel: Lectures on the Philosophy of Religion; One-Volume Edition: The Lectures of 1827*, trans. and ed. Peter C. Hodgson (Berkeley: University of California Press, 1988), 80–85.

19. Catherine Keller, *The Face of the Deep: A Theology of Becoming* (London: Routledge, 2003).

20. Of course, as Hegel himself points out, there are concepts *in* theology—the conceptual apparatus of dogmatic theology—but they are constructions that remain within the imaginative framework of the *Vorstellung*. One might distinguish concepts *in* theology from concepts *of* theology.

21. This point, that my "without" implies a certain phenomenological reduction, or as I would say radicalization, one that is profoundly different from Marion's neophenomenology, was singled out by Kevin Hart in an essay titled "Without," to which I have responded. Jean-Luc Marion and I (and Derrida) have very different, even opposite ideas of "without." Hart was the first one to make an argument against me on behalf of the "with," but showing considerably more sensitivity to how the "without" works in the work of Jacques Derrida than do my present critics. See Hart's essay in *Cross and Khôra: Deconstruction and Christianity in the Work of John D. Caputo*, ed. Neal Deroo and Marko Zlomislić (Eugene, OR: Wipf and Stock, 2010), 80–108, and my response in the same volume, "Only as Hauntology Is Religion without Religion Possible," 109–17.

22. Slavoj Žižek and John Milbank, *The Monstrosity of Christ: Paradox or Dialectic*, ed. Creston Davis (Cambridge, MA: MIT Press, 2009), 254.

23. Mark Twain was good at exploring these accidents of birth. His memorable *The Tragedy of Pudd'inhead Wilson* explores the fate of two babies switched in the cradle, one the son of a slave who was quite white, the other the son of a wealthy man, and the utterly different people they became as a result. Imagine the same switch of infants between Christian and Islamic families or lands.

24. Graham Ward, *Cities of God* (London: Routledge, 2000), 259.

25. *Mother Teresa: Come Be My Light; The Private Writings of the Saint of Calcutta*, ed. Brian Kolodiejchuk, M.C. (New York: Doubleday, 2007).

26. Edmund Husserl, *Cartesian Meditations*, trans. Dorion Cairns (The Hague: Martinus Nijhoff, 1960), 116–17.

27. John L. Allen Jr. "Bishops' Staffer on Doctrine Rips Theologians as 'Curse,'" *National Catholic Reporter*, August 19, 2011, 6.

28. Caputo, *The Mystical Element in Heidegger's Thought* (Athens: Ohio University Press, 1978); 2nd rev. ed. with a new introduction (New York: Fordham University Press, 1986).

29. Martin Heidegger, *Being and Time*, trans. John Macquarrie and Edward Robinson (New York: Harper & Row, 1962), 354.

30. Of course, the time machine might prove evangelical fundamentalism right. I just think that the "good reasons" are against this possibility and that apologists who argue along these lines are content with a draw, which allows them to withdraw into the safety of faith.

31. Jacques Derrida, *The Other Heading: Reflections on Today's Europe*, trans. Pascale-Anne Brault and Michael Naas (Bloomington: Indiana University Press, 1992), 9–10.

32. I am glad to hear that, according to William Wood, "On the New Analytic Theology; or, The Road Less Traveled," *Journal of the American Academy of*

Religion 77, no. 4 (December 2009): 941–60, there is now a more robustly theological version of analytic philosophy of religion, but the strictly formal mode of argumentation remains a handicap in these matters.

33. See Richard Kearney, *Anatheism: Returning to God after God* (New York: Columbia University Press, 2010).

34. *Heidegger and Aquinas: An Essay on Overcoming Metaphysics* (New York: Fordham University Press, 1982).

35. In *Theology and Social Theory: Beyond Secular Reason* (Oxford: Basil Blackwell, 1990), 2.

36. See Derrida's *Of Spirit: Heidegger and the Question,* trans. Geoffrey Bennington and Rachel Bowlby (Chicago: University of Chicago Press, 1989), 109–13.

37. In *The Gift of Death,* trans. David Wills (Chicago: University of Chicago Press, 1995), 49.

38. John D. Caputo, *The Mystical Element in Heidegger's Thought* (New York: Fordham University Press, 1982).

39. See Žižek and Milbank, *Monstrosity of Christ,* 172.

40. See John D. Caputo, "The Hyperbolization of Phenomenology: Two Possibilities for Religion in Recent Continental Philosophy," in *Counter-Experiences: Reading Jean-Luc Marion,* ed. Kevin Hart (Notre Dame, IN: University of Notre Dame Press, 2007), 66–93.

41. "What Is Merold Westphal's Critique of Ontotheology Criticizing?" in *Gazing through a Prism Darkly: Reflections on Merold Westphal's Hermeneutical Epistemology,* ed. B. Keith Putt (New York: Fordham University Press, 2009), 100–15; and "Methodological Postmodernism: On Merold Westphal's *"Overcoming Onto-Theology,"* *Faith and Philosophy* 22, no. 3 (July 2005): 284–96.

42. I think the central issue between orthodoxy and deconstruction is this: Orthodoxy treats the Scriptures, and hence theology insofar as it is true to the Scriptures, as God's word about God, so that God enjoys the status of a transcendental signified, and deconstruction thinks that "God" is a provisional unity of meaning that is an effect of the play of traces. This does not mean "God" has no reference, but it does mean that "God" is not a transcendental signifier and that God is not a transcendental signified. *Il n'y a pas de hors-texte.*

43. "Epoche and Faith: An Interview with Jacques Derrida," in *Derrida and Religion: Other Testaments,* ed. Yvonne Sherwood and Kevin Hart (New York: Routledge, 2005), 39.

44. Derrida was quite pleased with the theological unfoldings of deconstruction. See "The Becoming Possible of the Impossible: An Interview with Jacques Derrida," in *A Passion for the Impossible: John D. Caputo in Focus,* ed. Mark Dooley (Albany: SUNY Press, 2003), 21–33.

45. The arguments made in this paragraph have long preexisted deconstruction. I am adding that the play of traces accounted for in deconstruction gives us the wherewithal to redescribe religious experience in terms of the event and hence provides an alternate account of Christianity that is superior to the tradi-

tional orthodox view, which is constantly trying to explain why it is and is not saying *extra ecclesiam nulla salus est.*

46. I take this expression from Jacques Derrida, "Scribble (Writing-Power)," *Yale French Studies* 58 (1979): 116–47.

47. Eckhart's "Defense" against the Inquisition can be found in *Meister Eckhart: The Essential Sermons, Commentaries, Treatises and Defense,* ed. Edmund Colledge and Bernard McGinn (New York: Paulist Press, 1981).

48. John van Buren, *The Young Heidegger: Rumor of the Hidden King* (Bloomington: Indiana University Press, 1994), 167.

49. See the interesting point made by Jacques Rolland in Emmanuel Levinas, *On Escape,* introduced and annotated by Rolland, trans. Bettina Bergo (Stanford, CA: Stanford University Press, 2003), 89–90.

50. The implicit atheism of Derrida that Merold Westphal refers to is the personal belief of Jackie Derrida. Deconstruction itself, if there is such a thing, is not an argument against the existence of God as Simmons claims.

51. For a superb inventory of Derrida's evolving references to God, see Steven Shakespeare, *Derrida and Theology* (London: T & T Clark, 2009).

52. See Hélène Cixous, *Le Prénom de Dieu* (Paris: Grasset, 1967), and "Promised Belief," in *Feminism, Sexuality, Gender, and the Return of Religion,* ed. Linda Martín Alcoff and John D. Caputo (Bloomington: Indiana University Press, 2011).

53. Jacques Derrida, "Circumfession: Fifty-Nine Periods and Periphrases" in Geoffrey Bennington and Jacques Derrida, *Jacques Derrida* (Chicago: University of Chicago Press, 1993), 154–55; "Epoche and Faith," 46–47.

54. Michael Novak, *The Experience of Nothingness* (New York: Harper Torchbooks, 1978).

55. "It is possible to see deconstruction as being produced in a space where the prophets are not far away...I am in fact still looking for something...[in a] search without hope for hope.... Perhaps my search is a twentieth century brand of prophecy? But it is difficult for me to believe it." Interview with Richard Kearney in *Dialogues with Contemporary Continental Thinkers: The Phenomenological Heritage; Paul Ricoeur, Emmanuel Levinas, Herbert Marcuse, Stanislas Breton, Jacques Derrida,* ed. Richard Kearney (Manchester, UK: Manchester University Press, 1984), 119.

56. Derrida, *Rogues,* xiv, 157–58. In "The University without Condition," in Jacques Derrida, *Without Alibi,* ed. and trans. Peggy Kamuf (Stanford, CA: Stanford University Press, 2002), 202–37, the university means the unconditional right to ask any question, which is a weak force (no army) of resistance and dissidence to the "sovereignty" of the state and the church, of the media and popular culture, etc That means the university might be found off campus (*without* a university); see also "Epoche and Faith," 41–43.

57. Viewed in these terms, the only thing that exists is one concrete messianism or another. That certainly goes for Jacques Derrida himself, who is easily "identifiable" as a leftist twentieth century figure, a multicultural intellectual of

Franco-Algerian Jewish birth (and American stardom), an outspoken advocate on behalf of the exile, the immigrant, the displaced; a critic of the hegemony of the Western and especially Anglophone democracies in world politics; a critic of racism, censorship, capitalism, capital punishment, and the media; a radical philosopher; and so forth—all the stuff that makes up the obituary of a famous man who lived and died in a specific place and time. The concrete work and writings of Jacques Derrida have an identifiable pedigree, an historically documentable lineage. Who would have imagined otherwise? That certainly goes too for "Caputo," this spook who haunts the present volume, who has chosen to venture with deconstruction deeper into the dark woods of theology than Derrida himself dared go. It hardly bears repeating (but for the present volume!) that Derrida had views, and that those who philosophize in the wake of Derrida make claims, propose arguments, defend positions that they think are right, rightly passing for this or that, just as Derrida himself took very clear stands about numerous controversies in literary theory, the history of philosophy, and global politics. It is not a performative contradiction, as my fellow contributors to the present volume seem to think.

58. Kierkegaard, *Fear and Trembling* and *Repetition,* Kierkegaard's Writings, trans. and ed. Howard and Edna Hong, vol. 6 (Princeton, NJ: Princeton University Press, 1983).

59. Ibid.

60. See the debate I had with James L. Marsh, where Merold Westphal was the slash between us, in *Modernity and Its Discontents* (New York: Fordham University Press, 1992).

61. That is why one reviewer of Hägglund's book said I was an "easy target"—because I am an "infamous" "evangelical advocate" of a "religious" Derrida. Danielle Sands, "Review Article: Hägglund, *Radical Atheism: Derrida and the Time of Life,*" *Parrhesia* 6 (2009): 75.

62. Dale Martin, "The Promise of Teleology, the Constraints of Epistemology, and Universal Vision in Paul," in *St. Paul among the Philosophers,* ed. John D. Caputo and Linda Martín Alcoff (Bloomington: Indiana University Press, 2009), 98.

63. Paula Fredriksen, "Historical Integrity, Interpretive Freedom: The Philosopher's Paul and the Problem of Anachronism," in Caputo and Alcoff, *St. Paul among the Philosophers,* 177.

64. Martin, "Promise of Teleology," 101.

65. Levinas states his project starkly in *On Escape,* a youthful work, that being fills us with nausea and, therefore, the question of philosophy is how to get out.

66. Slavoj Žižek, *The Parallax View* (Cambridge, MA: MIT Press, 2006), 380–85.

67. Žižek and Milbank, *Monstrosity of Christ,* 302.

68. After *Radical Hermeneutics* appeared, the similarity of my argument to Berlin's, which I was delighted to learn, was pointed out by Ronald H. McKinney, "Towards a Postmodern Ethics: Sir Isaiah Berlin and John Caputo" *Journal of Value Inquiry* 26 (October 1992): 395–407. See my reply, "The Difficulty of

Life: A Response to Ronald McKinney," *Journal of Value Inquiry* 26 (1992): 561–64.

69. *Religion with/out Religion: The Prayers and Tears of John D. Caputo*, ed. James H. Olthuis (London: Routledge, 2001). See my "Hoping in Hope, Hoping against Hope: A Response," in the same volume (120–49), in which I am very much taken up with the question of the "with/out," which my critics are raising.

Bruce Ellis Benson is professor of philosophy at Wheaton College in Illinois. Benson is the coeditor of five books, including *Words of Life: New Theological Turns in French Phenomenology* and *Transforming Philosophy and Religion: Love's Wisdom*, and is the author of *Pious Nietzsche: Decadence and Dionysian Faith; The Improvisation of Musical Dialogue: A Phenomenology of Music;* and *Graven Ideologies: Nietzsche, Derrida, and Marion on Modern Idolatry*. He is currently writing a book with J. Aaron Simmons titled *New Phenomenology: A Philosophical Introduction*.

John D. Caputo is the Thomas J. Watson Professor of Religion Emeritus at Syracuse University and the David R. Cook Professor of Philosophy Emeritus at Villanova University. His major works are *Radical Hermeneutics: Repetition, Deconstruction, and the Hermeneutic Project; The Prayers and Tears of Jacques Derrida: Religion without Religion;* and *The Weakness of God: A Theology of the Event*. He has also addressed a wider audience in *On Religion* and *What Would Jesus Deconstruct? The Good News of Postmodernism for the Church*. He has an interest in interacting with church and community activists such as the emergent church. He is currently finishing a book titled *The Insistence of God: A Theology of "Perhaps,"* which is a sequel to *The Weakness of God*.

Drew M. Dalton is assistant professor of philosophy at Florida Southern College. His research and teaching interests are in phenomenology, German idealism, and psychoanalysis. His latest book, *Longing for the Other: Levinas and Metaphysical Desire*, explores Levinas's account of metaphysical desire and the possible relation between human longing and ethical phenomena such as reckless consumerism, global war, and religious extremism. He is currently working on a book exploring the ethics of resistance and is writing a textbook on ethics in the social service sector.

Jeffrey Hanson is a research fellow and lecturer at Australian Catholic University. Hanson's research focuses primarily on the work of Søren Kierkegaard and the French phenomenological tradition. He is coeditor of *Michel Henry: The Affects of Thought* and editor of *Kierkegaard as Phenomenologist: An Experiment.*

Stephen Minister is assistant professor of philosophy at Augustana College in South Dakota. His research engages the continental tradition, especially the writings of Emmanuel Levinas, and focuses on the relationship between reason and responsibility, the role of commitment in ethics and religion, and practical issues such as human rights and global poverty. He has published numerous articles and book chapters, including essays in the *Journal of the British Society for Phenomenology, Symposium: Canadian Journal of Continental Philosophy, Heythrop Journal, Philosophy Today,* and *Philosophy Compass.* He is currently working on a monograph addressing the practical implications of Levinas's work titled *De-facing the Other: Reason, Ethics, and Politics after Difference.*

J. Aaron Simmons is assistant professor of philosophy at Furman University. He is the author of *God and the Other: Ethics and Politics after the Theological Turn* and coeditor of *Kierkegaard and Levinas: Ethics, Politics, and Religion.* He is currently writing a book with Bruce Ellis Benson titled *The New Phenomenology: A Philosophical Introduction.*

Merold Westphal is Distinguished Professor of Philosophy Emeritus at Fordham University. In addition to two books each on Hegel and Kierkegaard, Westphal is the author of *Levinas and Kierkegaard in Dialogue; Overcoming Onto-theology; Suspicion and Faith: The Religious Uses of Modern Atheism; Transcendence and Self-Transcendence: On God and the Soul;* and *Whose Community? Which Interpretation? Philosophical Hermeneutics for the Church.*